Profit and Passion

7

Profit and Passion

Transactional Sex in Colonial Mexico

———

Nicole von Germeten

UNIVERSITY OF CALIFORNIA PRESS

University of California Press, one of the most distinguished university presses in the United States, enriches lives around the world by advancing scholarship in the humanities, social sciences, and natural sciences. Its activities are supported by the UC Press Foundation and by philanthropic contributions from individuals and institutions. For more information, visit www.ucpress.edu.

University of California Press
Oakland, California

Library of Congress Cataloging-in-Publication Data

Names: Germeten, Nicole von, author.
Title: Profit and passion : transactional sex in colonial Mexico / Nicole von Germeten.
Description: Oakland, California : University of California Press, [2018] | Includes bibliographical references and index. |
Identifiers: LCCN 2017045678 (print) | LCCN 2017046755 (ebook) | ISBN 9780520969704 (ebook) | ISBN 9780520297296 (cloth : alk. paper) | ISBN 9780520297319 (pbk. : alk. paper)
Subjects: LCSH: Prostitutes—Mexico—History.
Classification: LCC HQ151.A5 (ebook) | LCC HQ151.A5 G47 2018 (print) | DDC 306.740972—dc23
LC record available at https://lccn.loc.gov/2017045678

Manufactured in the United States of America

27 26 25 24 23 22 21 20 19 18
10 9 8 7 6 5 4 3 2 1

Dedicated to my parents, Joan and Jim von Germeten

CONTENTS

ACKNOWLEDGMENTS

In this short acknowledgment, I can list only a few of the many individuals who influenced this project. First, I am very grateful for the kindness of my students and colleagues at the School of History, Philosophy, and Religion at Oregon State University. This especially includes members of the writing group organized by Marisa Chappell and Kara Ritzheimer, who read and edited several chapters with their typical energy and intelligence. Robert Nye continued to give his very useful feedback and dependable editing, and I am so lucky to benefit from the friendship and hospitality of both Bob and Mary Jo Nye. Trina Hogg offered very helpful theoretical suggestions in the final revisions phase. Ben Mutschler and Dwanee Howard facilitated funding for research travel. The OSU Center for the Humanities, under the direction of David Robinson, awarded me a term off teaching to begin the writing process and opportunities to present my work. Joseph Orosco hosted an enlightening conversation with his session on sex work today. Undergraduate students in my History of Sexuality and Latin American History classes helped me by reading and discussing drafts of these chapters. I had the great fortune to enjoy the humor, intelligence, and impressive discipline of graduate students Aimee Hisey and Abby Perkins. They both helped and supported me at a moment's notice and made me laugh for years while I worked on this book. Aimee especially deserves thanks for her work on the bibliography, footnotes, and chapter 1. She, nor anyone else acknowledged here, bears no responsibility for any errors in this text.

Outside of Oregon, I enjoyed insightful editing and content suggestions from Marie Kelleher, Kristen Block, Martin Nesvig, and Ken Mills. Marie also kindly invited me to present at Cal State Long Beach, as did John Hunt at Utah State

University. Linda Arnold and Karen Melvin provided valuable references for archival material that I would not have found without their guidance.

At University of California Press, I am grateful for the enthusiasm and support of Bradley Depew and Kate Marshall, as well as Margaret Chowning. I humbly thank Pete Sigal and Zeb Tortorici for reading the manuscript draft that they received and offering suggestions that greatly improved the book.

I appreciate my ongoing conversations with Michael Lopez about chapter 5 and his perspective on the topic of the book, as well as many other things. Thank you to Inez for your exceptional kindness and humor and your thoughtful insistence on my dedicating this book to my parents.

Introduction

There are passionate whores and polished whores, painted whores and illus-
trious whores, whores of reputation and those who have been condemned. . . .
There are some who work at night, others who work by day. . . . There are
eastern whores, western whores, northern whores, whores who wear dis-
guises, drunk whores, reserved whores, whores that range in age from very
young to very old. There are rising whores and falling whores, whores with
hymens and whores without, Sunday whores, and whores who wait until
Saturday to wash. . . . There are perfect whores, secret and public whores,
devout whores, hypocritical whores, whores young and old, whores whose
pockets jingle when they walk. There are pandering whores and modern
whores, mature whores and celestial whores, and those who try to live a good
life in shut up houses, as well as honest women who try the trade according
to their need.[1]

In a picaresque tale set in early-sixteenth-century Rome, a scene opens with La
Lozana Andaluza (her name, loosely translated, means "the lusty Andalusian
woman") relaxing in bed with a client. As a single woman and émigrée from Spain,
La Lozana wants to learn from her satiated lover about the "life that concubines
lead in this province." After hearing his response, the litany quoted above, La
Lozana expresses fatigue with this list of the seemingly countless *putas* "whores")
on the Roman streets, "as thick as bees in a beehive."[2] This 1528 account describes
the early-modern world (specifically, regions under Spanish influence) as an era
when whores proliferated, offering their clients almost endless options in terms of
age, looks, experience, methods, and attitudes. Seduced by this fictional pillow
talk, this book tells the history of women labeled public women, whores, and prostitutes in New Spain's archival records, embracing the complexity of "all the characters who populate the prostitute imaginary," as well as the ambiguities and limitations of documenting the history of sexuality via written sources.[3]

This book takes for granted that Spanish and Spanish American literary and
legal understandings of gender and sexuality have vital importance in the context
of the rise of global imperialism. Spain's New World viceroyalties, especially the
geographic region that is now Mexico (a section of the Viceroyalty of New Spain),

1

dominated in terms of population and wealth across four centuries of American history. The Spanish viceroyalties and the nations that emerged from their legacy in the nineteenth century have been envisioned for too long as marginalized, "borderland," violent, bloody, dystopic, tragic, and, in a word, failed. Jorge Cañizares Esguerra and James E. Sanders eloquently argue for decentering this patriotic tale and remembering the Spanish Empire as the prevailing and foremost power in the Atlantic World from the sixteenth to the nineteenth centuries.[4] The Spanish American historic trajectory is normative, not a curious marginal note about a "minority" population. By tracing the textual history of transactional sex in New Spain, this book builds a bridge between medieval sexuality and the twenty-first–century surveillance and bureaucratization of private lives, from the perspective that sexuality is "at the center of the colonial archive, rather than at its margins."[5]

To return to La Lozana Andaluza, this woman represents more than an item available in the bountiful street catalogue described in the opening quote. On the contrary, her fictional personality brings up the question of sexual agency for women in the past. The tale of her life revolves around her shaping her own destiny by traveling from Spain to Italy. "What I want," she declares, "is for [men] to need me, not for me to need them. I want to live by my own labor. . . . I only want to live by my profession." To that end, La Lozana puts a green branch behind her ear to indicate that she is a *ramera* ("whore," from the Spanish word *ramo* or "branch") and displays herself at a lattice window, but she shows only her hands. She manages to make a living off her lovers, in the form of fine meals, gifts, and cash. She also helps other couples come together in the classic medieval occupation of bawdry *(alcahuetería)*, prospering financially even though, with a shocking lack of conventional femininity, she claims that she has forgotten how to spin.[6] Male characters observe that "[La] Lozana wants something better" than any other woman in Rome, "to be independent." She succeeds in these ambitions because she knows "how to use her wiles" and is "always spoken to with respect." The women she meets on her journeys describe her as beautiful, "bold and loquacious." Knowing her own needs and maintaining her standards, she "insists on getting her share" and "nothing but the best for her."[7]

Inspired by these quotes, this book could celebrate the personal agency of La Lozana and her Mexican peers, seducing readers with their tenacious survival skills and courageous resistance to oppressive viceregal gender hierarchies. But Ann Laura Stoler warns historians against "charmed accounts" that "seduce and comfort." She instead suggests a "rough and charmless colonial history track . . . [that] might dispense with heroes—subaltern or otherwise." She proposes good and evil as "*historical* rather than *transcendent* categories."[8] Along these same lines, Walter Johnson cautions scholars to avoid a simplistic, self-congratulatory tone derived from unfounded pride in their own understanding of historic individuals as conscious actors in their own lives.[9] The process of writing archives itself complicates agency. My use of the term *scribal* underscores the notaries—*escribanos*—who physically created all of the cases, with their act of writing testimonies. We do not actually know whose "voice" emerges from these written texts, who is the "I," other than the penman himself, a kind of shadowy ventriloquist, "someone who could give other people an official voice." Spanish aphorisms linked escribanos to putas, in that both occupations worked off of verbal cons.[10] Hearing and sharing these projected voices, making "ink on parchment *speak*," may represent nothing more than a social historian's fantasy.[11]

The various written words used in this book inscribe labels of immorality, difference, and disease on women's bodies. It is open to question if these differences are "biological or universal," but they do require "cultural marking" within a specific historical and social context. In her work on inscribing and reading inscriptions on bodies, Elizabeth Grosz argues that the "real material body" does not exist but that "representations and cultural inscriptions quite literally constitute bodies." The body and writing intersect, creating objects that read as various past and present "systems of social coercion, legal inscription, and sexual and economic exchange."[12] Textualizing the body involves several people who contributed to the writing of every paper file: the women under discussion, other deponents, the scribe and court officials present, and, of course, the historian herself. However, what remains for the historian to read and re-narrate is the paper where these individuals inscribed their own and others' bodies, not the inscribed body itself.

But archives may not represent as clear an assertion of state power and ways of knowing as some theorists once thought. They instead contain "mad fragmentations ... that just ended up there" and piecemeal "records of uncertainty and doubt," as anxious officials tried to catch their paper trails up with colonial situations that had exceeded their comprehension and control.[13] Even as they appear efficient and organized due to their repetitiveness or controlled structure, criminal archives record disorder because "out of the darkness [the archive] snatches breathless, disjointed beings, summoned to explain themselves before the court ... mixing lies and the truth, hatred and cunning."[14] Zeb Tortorici notes that scholars write the history of sexuality based on the most illegible tracings, which historians seduce into our own "affective engagements" to produce our historiographical narratives. Scribes wrote testimonies according to their own "submerged" but "specific scripts" that preserved illegibilities in the archives of transactional sex.[15] But similar to when we first fall in love, we seek in archival documents a scribal mirror of ourselves, which gives us pleasure by reflecting back our desires, our dreams, and our "sense of self," but we actually are reading vestiges not intended for us, "fragmented written traces of *something else*."[16]

Spain's and Mexico's archives inscribe certain early modern women as "whores [*putas, rameras*]" or "public women [*mujeres públicas*]," much later writing them as "prostitutes," as well as male and female panderers (*rufianes* and *alcahuetas*).

These references exist in files that are not consistent over time and, in terms of details provided, vary in both quality and quantity. Sources for the sixteenth and seventeenth centuries include prescriptive royal decrees, law codes, and short court cases. Much of the history of Mexican commercial sex was "unwritten" in this era, either due to its commonness, "because it could not yet be articulated," because "it could not be said," or because a choice was made to ignore it or remain inattentive to it.[17] In the eighteenth century, some of the cases grew longer and more detailed, allowing for more complicated characters to emerge from the accounts that women gave of their lives. The late viceregal state also created shorter and much more plentiful records with a modern statistical bent.[18] The archive consists of a growing quantity of documentation over the centuries. The changing terminology for prosecuted women, voiced by kings, jurists, magistrates, inquisitors, and bishops, as well as disgruntled husbands and neighbors, foreshadowed the increasing regulation, criminalization, and polarizing politics of modern global transactional sex.[19]

Language within the documents outlines a story of how the judicial identity of women changed over time. In the sixteenth century, prosecuted women in the Americas began to testify in court by asserting their good reputations because their accusers framed them as sinful, not criminal. In 1623, King Phillip IV mandated the closure of legal brothels in his empire, reinforcing a broad European trend toward enclosing women perceived as lacking effective male guardians who could monitor and confine their sexuality. Despite the growing criminalization of selling sex, women continued to respond to accusations with denials and assertions of dignity. The more extensive case records of the eighteenth century prove the ineffectiveness of the previous century's royal pronouncements, as well as the increasing efforts to police plebeian sexuality. By the nineteenth century, magistrates focused on young women whom they now called "prostitutes [prostitutas]," and viewed them as childlike victims of rapacious procuresses and panderers, innocents who needed rescuing, often from their own parents and siblings. Officials allowed themselves these sentimental leanings—the archival record contains certain prescribed feelings and represents more than just a pose of rationality and control.[20] It was not until the closing years of the viceregal era that some women finally referred to themselves as prostitutes in an effort to fit into this victim-versus-criminal dichotomy. The nineteenth century also saw the definitive return of regulated brothels and government-controlled prostitution in Europe, its colonies, and the Americas.

Literary portraits of whores and bawds such as La Lozana Andaluza, The Book of Good Love, Santa, and the Tragicomedy of Calisto and Melibea add more imaginary detail to the elusive, ambiguous documentary records.[21] Written records of all kinds relating to this topic contain familiar fictional plots, including those written on the pages of viceregal court cases. Inside these files, officials and deponents create stories that fit accepted narratives. To highlight how trial narratives intertwine with fictional imaginings, each chapter in this book introduces its topics via a work of literature in Spanish but follows through on the chapter's themes with analysis of legal codes, government decrees, and records from a variety of juridical settings, including criminal and ecclesiastical courts and the Holy Office of the Spanish Inquisition. Over the course of the book, these introductory passages shift to actual trial discourse, to suggest the blending of fictional and archival texts.[22]

Thinking about how artistic creations imagine sex work highlights the built-in dichotomies of literary narrations. Since ancient times, literature and, more recently, films about sex work almost always follow either a libertine or sentimental narrative. In other words, women written as whores end the story prosperous and free or punished (usually by a painful death) for their behavior.[23] Sentimental stories have unwilling heroines forced into selling sex by villains or poverty, while libertine tales focus on success, personal agency, and empowerment. In the Spanish tradition, *La Lozana* falls into the libertine style because the heroine achieves wealth, redemption, and stability, while in contrast the more emotionally charged *Tragicomedia de Calisto y Melibea (La Celestina)* ends in suicide, murder, and tragedy. Both narratives fall into conventional Christian morality in their portrayals of redeemable, penitent whores who live and prosper, brave women who use their agency to remove themselves from a bad situation due to their utter innocence and the duping of an evil man, or immoral unrepentant sinners who die off at the end.[24] In all of these scenarios, the overly dramatic, simplified fictional (but also highly erotic) versions of "fallen" women's lives hide a variety of more complicated on-the-ground understandings of socially appropriate sexual behavior, especially those that operate outside the bonds of monogamous heterosexual matrimony.[25]

Case files including women litigants and defendants in the Spanish viceroyalties sometimes offer more ambiguity than the opposing poles common in literature: female passive victimization versus criminal deviance.[26] But deponents also did borrow from literature to tell their autobiographies to fit these "enforced narrations."[27] So how can a historian narrate the archival traces of women labeled "whores," "public women," and "prostitutes" in Mexican archives without either glorifying their sexual agency or representing them as nothing more than pitiful victims of gendered injustice?[28] Does life itself have narratives, or are they only a result of judicial and archival structures, which we reinforce in our scholarly historiography? Stoler and Kathryn Burns, drawing from the massive literature of the "archival turn," encourage historians of colonialism to attempt an ethnography of the archive itself, resisting organizing its incoherencies, ambivalences, and ambiguities into familiar stories.[29]

Sex-worker activism also provides a number of key theoretical structures that help avoid narrative simplicity. First, as an overarching goal, sex-worker activists emphasize inclusivity and intersectionality within the occupation in terms of race, gender, and sexuality and stress the complexity of the sex-work experience. Following this fundamental dictate, this book encompasses rich and poor women of European, African, and indigenous ancestry.[30] Sex workers' writings instruct readers that the sex act is not the essence of the lives of those in the sex industry but obsesses only those moralizers and reformers who seek to control or criminalize selling sex.[31] Most viceregal court documentation does not refer to explicit sex acts but, instead, reveals very familiar contemporary concerns about honor, family, racial difference, material wealth, violence, and the negotiation of the authorities' involvement in private life.[32] Lastly, writings from twentieth- and twenty-first–century sex workers emphasize the performative and practical nature of their occupations, stressing that they work within the social, racial, economic, and cultural realities of today's world. To take a stand as an ally against the mislabeling, criminalizing, stigmatizing, and daily violence against sex workers that continues to the present day, the writings of recent and current sex-industry workers frame my understandings of what is at stake in my own contribution to the history of transactional sex.

THE TEMPTATIONS OF TERMINOLOGY

Throughout this book, I translate Spanish terms into English following bilingual dictionaries dating from the centuries under discussion, tracing the change over time in the judicial and popular use of these terms from the medieval era to the nineteenth century. Sometimes this means using unfamiliar words in English, such as *bawd* (explored in depth in chapter 1) and words that still raise our hackles, such as *whore*. As strange or offensive as these words sound to our ears, they do capture the uses during the eras presented in this book. But defendants inscribed in this way almost always used the judicial process to erase the writing on their bodies. This very purposeful denial obfuscates all evidence of viceregal transactional sex. To seek solid data confirming a definitive vision of women who took part in transactional sex would change my role from that of a curious historian enticed by scribal seductions, to that of a simulacrum of a viceregal bureaucrat who believed that categorization meant control over the uncontrollable, an ideology that "sustain[s] the fantasy of the colonial panopticon."[33]

To explain why the word *whore* has such a longstanding negative connotation, we must look back to the origins of Christian sexual moral ideologies and even to the pre-Christian era. Kyle Harper argues that ancient pagan Romans depended on a ubiquitous sex trade to distinguish and protect the boundaries between "good" and "bad" women, labels that derived from marital status and social reputation (public honor). Early Christians took a stand against pagan sexuality and based their own distinct group identity around a much more restricted notion of sexual activity. For Christians in the early centuries, virginity represented the ultimate exercise in free choice, an ideal behavior available to only the most moral, spiritual humans. Christians transformed sex that happened outside of heterosexual procreation and monogamous marriage into private sin, a sign of an individual's personal choice to succumb to the temptations of the flesh and the devil, together with a lingering taint of public dishonor. Added to these ideas from early Christianity, moralizers point to a lust for luxuries as a critical factor in moral, social, and sexual "falls." The label of "whore" and its equivalents in other European languages denigrated a woman's greed for luxuries and her reputation for nonmonogamy, much as it does today, but did not necessarily refer to a specific occupation subject to legal sanctions.[34] Over time, the concept of whore has functioned as an insult to both a woman's public honor and her private sins.

While *whore* was and remains a broad insult to morality, *prostitute* usually designates a somewhat more specific behavior or occupation. Spanish-speakers did not use the term *prostitution* as we currently understand it, the unlawful selling of sex acts or "the in-person physical exchange of sexual services for money or goods," before the eighteenth century.[35] By 1800, law codes in Spain and the Americas had not specifically criminalized prostitution, but the term came into general use in court records. Part of the imperial power of the term *prostitution* resides in its vagueness, its availability for application to any suspect woman. Even in the early twentieth century, British imperialists still did not have a clear definition in mind when writing laws against prostitution or arresting women for the crime. Unlike the present, when law enforcement sets up hotel and street "stings" to entrap sex workers, late-nineteenth-century authorities noted that, in terms of catching someone in the act of prostitution, "direct proof is for obvious reasons unattainable."[36] Therefore, both the *whore* and *prostitute* labels function very well within the context of obfuscating texts with confusing uses of evidence.

The origins of a broad understanding of the term *prostitute* go back at least as far in history to a sixteenth-century Latin-English dictionary. Sir Thomas Elyot translates *prostituere pudiciriam* in a way similar to the common Spanish phrase *mujer publica* (public woman), without implying any illegal status: "to be a commune harlot . . . to be commune to al men or women in the acte of lechery."[37] In the seventeenth and eighteenth centuries, "prostituting" oneself referred to corrupting one's own endeavors (broadly conceived, not just sexually) for monetary gain. My cases do not use the terms *prostituta* or *prostitución* until the eighteenth century, so I do not use this term either, and when I do, only as a direct quote from my sources. Although the early twenty-first century remains caught in the regulatory and criminalizing era that began in the nineteenth century, historians should not project this criminalization back to centuries when it did not exist.[38]

While much more historically accurate than *prostitute* for the centuries before 1800, the word *whore* still sparks controversy, although I use it throughout this book as a translation of the Spanish words *ramera* and *puta*. Within the sex industry, the debate continues about whether or not to reclaim it in a parallel gesture to the reap-propriation of *queer*.[39] *Whore* "may be the original intersectional insult" because calling someone a whore implies an array of personal traits that our society deplores, including: poverty, of a nonwhite race, unmarried, nonmonogamous, victimized by violence, drug-addicted, uneducated, of a lower class, diseased, homeless, emotion-ally duplicitous, and sexually deviant. Any "stigmatized woman or feminized man" can suffer the label *whore*, as long as it remains a shameful word, tied to the negative traits listed above. "Whore solidarity" in part means working toward a time when women, upon hearing this word said in their vicinity, will not react with fear or shame or quickly correct the speaker for their mislabeling. A defiant reclaiming of *whore* and the complex history of whores presents an opportunity to analyze and reshape the negative, shaming implication of this word, without falling into discur-sive traps such as using *prostitute* instead.[40]

Obviously, the phrase *sex work* lacks the primeval shaming intention of *whore*. A critical goal of sex-work activism since the 1970s has been to recognize that sell-ing sex is a job, not a criminal fulltime occupation (prostitution) or a permanent immoral status (whore). While sometimes a broad term is required while discuss-ing this topic, I avoid using *sex work* extensively while discussing my case studies because it has a modern connotation of labor rights and does not effectively convey the subtler and changing terms in common use when Spain reigned in the Ameri-cas. However, in line with its use by activists and allies, it is preferable to say and write "sex work" instead of "prostitution," when an overarching term is necessary, even for eras before the twentieth century, because *sex work* lacks *prostitution's* anachronistic implication of social and familial marginalization and illegality. Recent writings by sex workers confirm that the word *prostitution* is used only by "anti-prostitution" groups.[41] Of course, in daily life, sex workers call themselves providers, girls, ladies, entertainers, escorts, or any number of other specific labels pointing to their areas of specialization, but never self-refer as prostitutes. Over the centuries, stigmatization has necessitated creating several identities, while the per-formative nature of sex work transforms necessity into a creative challenge.

Vaguer, condescending terms for sex work imply moral condemnation and obscure what exactly goes on when sexual acts or other kinds of intimacy are exchanged for gifts, cash, or protection. When one speaks of women "selling them-selves" or "selling their bodies" or uses such phrases as "they served with their own bodies," what do "themselves" or "their bodies" really mean in these comments, if not a woman's genitals?[42] Using kitschy, evasive phrases such as "selling one's charms" does not water down this grotesque implication.[43] These terms equate an act of potential contact with a woman's genitals as a purchase of her whole self, her entire body, even her soul. Those who use these synecdoches are not offering humor, pity, or protectiveness but instead exhibit an extreme form of misogyny that sees women as nothing more than genitalia for men to buy. Their phrasing is not even accurate. In a paid sexual transaction of any kind, sellers never exchange or trade on "their selves" or their bodies. Sex workers over the course of many eras and on a range of continents may have avoided physical contact between bodies; instead, they may have just talked to, eaten with, performed domestic tasks for, entertained, played music for, danced with, or attended events with their clientele. Whatever bodily contact they allowed formed part of a larger performance that may have involved sex acts or may have focused more on other kinds of intimacy, companionship, and communication. What sex workers sell now and throughout history is a performance that *may* include such elements as the sellers' disguised or costumed physical appearance, a range of personalities and roles, intimacy, and perhaps sexual release.[44]

I identified the records in this book by searching for terms that I knew were used before 1825, including specific words (and all of their possible derivations) such as *mujer pública, casa publica, ramera, alcahueta, puta,* and *prostituta,* but also very vague concepts such as *escandalosa* or even simply *mujer mala.* This book does not deal with other transactional situations such as long-term concubinage but purposefully concentrates on women labeled as engaged in public, commercialized sexual exchange.[45] The archival inscription of these labels. of course, does not prove that women fit their definitions. Assuming that they did accepts that the authorities applied correct labels to them and reuses "colonial categories" as "analytical vocabulary," as opposed to "transient, provisional objects of historical inquiry."[46] Due to their evasiveness and the ambiguity in the paperwork of the time, we cannot assume penetrative sex took place unless witnesses in the documents specifically state it, and even in that case they might have lied in their sworn statements. If eyewitnesses admitted to seeing or participating in a sex act, the scribes recorded it in generalized, euphemistic terms. Creating either a libertine or sentimental narrative from these fragments hides the incoherencies of the files themselves.

THE HISTORIOGRAPHY OF TRANSACTIONAL SEX IN NEW SPAIN: HIDDEN IN PLAIN SIGHT?

In his study of the early Christian debate over sex for sale, Harper argues that "prostitution is important, even central, to the history of sex." This generalization applies well to the Spanish-speaking world, as Eukene Lacarra Lanz observes that "prostitution" was not "marginal in Iberian society, considering the cultural, economic, political, and social import it reached in medieval and early modern Spain."[47] Historians of Spain prove Lanz's point in their prolific scholarly investigations into the history of brothels, bawdry, courtesans, and streetwalkers from the sixteenth to the nineteenth centuries and beyond.

In contrast, historians of the viceroyalties have not taken intensive interest in this topic but have given it only sidelong glances. It could even be argued that they have contributed to its erasure by either ignoring it or exaggerating its suppression. Many popular and highly regarded monographs explore government regulation and attitudes toward sex work in late-nineteenth– and early-twentieth–century Spanish America. But for the viceregal era (1492–1824), when historians discuss what they usually call "prostitution," they often emphasize misogynistic rhetoric against women and repressive control, despite the widely acknowledged evidence of Iberian and American women's effective use of their economic and legal rights in all other settings.[48] The loud, commanding voices of prescriptive sources drown out the evasive language and denying stance of female defendants. Our valid appreciation of the struggles of Spain's female colonial subjects against the repressive patriarchy of their era has resulted in avoiding the morally complex and controversial story of their voluntary participation in selling sex for money or gifts or brokering relationships for less prosperous, younger women.[49] The only full-length monograph in Spanish or English is by Ana María Atondo Rodríguez, entitled *El Amor Venal y la Condición Femenina en el México Colonial*, published in 1992. This topic remains "peripheral to the colonial stories [historians] have chosen to tell" and is one of the "histories suspended from received historiographies."[50]

However, many histories document an explicit, core assumption of sex as a form of exchange in this culture.[51] In the act of sacramental marriage, young women in the viceroyalties converted their sexual capital into economic and social capital, generally within the context of their parents' or guardians' machinations. If they eloped with their own choice of husband, they risked losing all or part of their inheritance.[52] Among the elite, women who were ensconced within a family support network brought dowries with them into marriage and received *arras,* or a significant gift of money from their grooms, to further bolster their financial stability. Lucky orphan girls who lacked the financial padding of a natal family received charitable donations to fund their dowries, making them more attractive potential wives.[53] Unmarried Spanish American women could more directly convert sexual or erotic capital into currency by suing their lovers for defloration.[54] Winning a defloration or breach-of-promise case rewarded women with money that they could use for child support or a dowry to marry another man. Often these women enjoyed family support and advocacy as they litigated their defloration compensation suits. And far along this spectrum, women labeled as "public," or courtesans, whores, and prostitutes, most of whom worked in the company of their mothers, sisters, or husbands, commodified their sex acts by insisting on direct compensation (cash or gifts) before proceeding with an intimate relationship. These women did not require or demand a religious benediction before they had sex, although they generally did work within a conventional domestic setting, not unlike respectably married daughters.[55]

Day-to-day sexual norms in the New World did not conform to the gender ideals mandated by the Council of Trent (1545–1563).[56] As a result, this book focuses on the textual tensions and evasions of political leaders, clerics, and moralizers who censured sexually entrepreneurial women while simultaneously tolerating them and only sporadically persecuting them. To introduce these cultural and juridical contradictions, chapter 1 details early-modern legal, literary, and popular understandings of the commonly used terms *ramera* and *alcahueta,* using fictional examples as well as court cases set in sixteenth-century Mexico City. Spanish law codes shaped the American experience of transactional sex to a degree, but lacking a documentary record, it is difficult to know if the important Spanish institution of the legal brothel became popular in the New World. Instead, the scant surviving texts testify to exchanges of money and gifts for sex and intimacy that took place within family homes. Chapter 1 explores several other distinctly New World interpretations of transactional sex, such as how, from the first decades of Spanish rule in Mexico, women of African and indigenous descent shaped Spanish American understandings of how to negotiate and carry out illicit relationships, especially in the familiar, popular, and sometimes lucrative occupation of bawdry.[57]

Chapter 2 examines the crown's motivations for closing regulated brothels and investigates the negotiation of increasingly illegal sexual transactions in the seventeenth century. American tribunals of the Holy Office of the Spanish Inquisition targeted the erotic magic that often accompanied selling sex in this era. Bawds and sorceresses (including women of African and indigenous descent) merged as a conjoined threat. Although brothel manageresses still enjoyed an elite clientele, simultaneously they faced suppression due to royal mandates to close their houses. Despite the patronage of viceregal officials, these women endured increasing stigmatization after this first step in criminalization. Even with their growing illegality and vilification, in seventeenth-century cities women offered a multilayered range of sex for sale, racially and socially diverse, in a variety of settings. However, archival evidence remains sparse until the eighteenth century, when, under the reforms of the Bourbon dynasty, documented prosecutions picked up significantly as more modern mechanisms for urban policing developed.[58]

The first two chapters provide the early-modern historical and juridical background required to understand the new categorization of women as "prostitutes" in the 1700s, the topic of chapters 3, 4, and 5. In the eighteenth century, a substantial paper trail records how streetwalkers, middle-class mistresses, and elite courtesans endured more frequent judicial encounters than in previous centuries.[59] But in a typically viceregal paradox, increasing surveillance tended toward a benign paternalism for certain kinds of women, especially kept women (chapter 3) and elite courtesans (chapter 4). These chapters narrate the lives of several women who lived in comfort and respectability with their families, or were supported by their lovers, but who withstood neighborly gossip or official campaigns against them due to their suspicious wealth and noisy social lives.

Chapter 4 examines the pinnacles of the Spanish American demimonde, where transactional sex and professional theater and dance intersected.[60] These women wrote themselves into the archives due to their self-promotion and their own materialism, libertinism, and social ambition. Starting in the seventeenth century, these courtesans drew attention to themselves as they flaunted sumptuary laws in their triumphantly opulent clothes, housing, and lifestyle, underwritten by rich and courtly lovers. Courtesans could call on powerful men to sprint to their aid at a moment's notice, but despite their personal power, their benefactors cherished them as delicate creatures needing their protection. These legendary symbols of viceregal decadence continue to fascinate us to the present through their portrayals in popular culture.

At the other end of the spectrum, chapter 5 turns to poor women recorded into the nightly logs because late-colonial reformers made a concerted effort to clear the streets of drunks, street solicitors, and vagrants. The police dockets for the 1790s preserve traces of the interactions between patrolmen and women working on the street.[61] This extensive documentation allows for statistical analysis of women arrested for solicitation or public lewd acts. The authorities reacted by attempting to force these women back into their family homes or jobs as servants, the very situations that compelled them to sell sex in the first place. Although hundreds of women appear in the police notations, still their actual crimes often remain very vague.

Chapter 6, set in the early nineteenth century, remains in this plebeian milieu but concentrates on two women's complex efforts to self-fashion themselves as respectable ladies. In the context of an increasingly "modern" idea of regulating prostitutes and brothels, these two women consistently denied accusations made by nosy neighbors as well as ineffective street policing by the weakening imperial state. With trial-based performances, they rejected efforts made by men, their families, and even law enforcement to confine them inside of more traditional partnered arrangements. The woman known as La Sargenta ("Sergeant Lady" or "the Sergeant's Woman") assumed the character of a quiet servant, even while her accusers portrayed her as a drunken streetwalker. Around the same time, a brothel manager and clothes dealer also carried out an elaborate manipulation of multiple identities in her trial.

Perhaps because eighteenth-century courtesans often worked as dancers or actresses, their statements take on a dramatic tone, an exaggeration of the normal role-playing common to all juridical case files. Even beyond the idea of the accused women's consciously and simultaneously performing their sexuality and respectability, the connection between theater and public sexuality helps explain a new judicial attitude and rhetoric that emerges in the final decades of the Spanish American viceroyalties. Chapter 7 explores late-viceregal cases involving mothers accused of trying to convince men to pay for nonmarital sex with their daughters, as well as brothels organized inside of family homes, managed by young women's parents or sisters. The official language and attitudes in these files echoes early-eighteenth-century popular "she-tragedies," in which the heroine's sexual desirability led to her own "fatal suffering." Through no moral fault of her own, the leading character suffers "a sexual crime in which she participates unwittingly or even unwillingly," creating an idea of women as passive objects of desire. These performances of violation link sexual voyeurism to pain and violence.[62] The cases discussed in chapter 7 follow this theatrical plotline. When judicial officials dwelled on extensive verbiage describing the physical and emotional torment of women they viewed as victimized by late-eighteenth– and early-nineteenth–century panderers (including their older sisters and parents), they reified misogyny and paternalism through their understanding of women as weak and sexually passive. In contrast to chapter 5, here they "rescued" these young women from their own families, only to place them in what they viewed as appropriate marriages.[63]

The conclusion of this book looks ahead to international efforts to regulate brothels and prostitution in the mid- to late nineteenth century. After 1800, these regulations transformed prostitutes from "victim[s] to villainess[es]," and from "sentimental" objects of pity to vectors of "contagion."[64] We continue to struggle with these dichotomies on a global scale. Increasing state intervention and popular stigmatization typify the ongoing political nature of sexuality in the twenty-first century.[65]

Despite their denials and efforts to evade textual traces, over the centuries of viceregal history, women sold sex on the street, or independently solicited men on the street or in taverns to take back to their humble accommodations, or worked in taverns for a male or female panderer. Some women lived discreetly as servants or mistresses in long-term compensated sexual relationships. In New Spain, patrolmen on the city streets, the local justices, and even the Catholic Church chose to leave most of these exchanges and relationships alone, probably because they were enmeshed in commercial sex themselves, saw its value, or agreed with the general population that tolerated it. Usually they followed a policy of avoiding unnecessary disruption of the status quo and "ignor[ed] all but the most scandalous and public of sexual activities," such as when a woman's "behavior caused problems in the wider community," "drew attention" to law breaking, or caused public disorder.[66] The authorities preferred to let all concerned go about their business as usual, without leaving much of a paper trail. Any intervention that took place probably served its purpose in convincing those involved to moderate their public activities, at least temporarily.

Although La Lozana's lover saw whores everywhere, the women under investigation in this book, seeking to keep their sex lives private to the degree possible, evasively prevented the creation of written documentation of their status as "public women." Today, our laws allow for the prosecution of women for a verifiable (even recorded) act of offering or exchanging money for sex, but in the past, church and state targeted women more broadly for their immoral reputations, using labels such as *whore* to juridically besmirch their status as good women. It follows that viceregal judicial conventions demanded that those subject to these labels always pleaded innocent. A woman would never openly admit her moral stigma in court, even though she might say that she made a few unfortunate mistakes due to her "fragility," or that men or procuresses had victimized her.[67] Not wishing to inscribe her alleged disrespectability, the defendant always made an effort to find witnesses to back up the fact that she had a good reputation.[68] During this process, women performed a gendered manipulation of emotions, honor, public reputation, morality, and victimization in their testimonies. This "performance . . . mitigate[d] the whore stigma, offering some prostitutes ways to distance themselves from traditional [oppression]."[69] But when the idea of a victimized prostitute began to take hold, prosecuted women had an identity that they could sustain while still holding onto respectability and even desirability as an honorable wife.

The women in this book prove that, whenever and wherever the words *whore* and *prostitute* are considered insults, women have to constantly defend their reputation and verbally dissimulate to avoid the dangers and shame of negative categorizations or to fit into a dehumanized, pity-provoking role. Meanwhile, the very existence of women labeled "whores" or "prostitutes" allows other "good" women to enjoy the social benefits of sexual respectability.[70] There remain so many reasons for these scribal seductions.

1

Bawds and Brothels

Now as for the go-between, this should be some woman who is kin to you and who will be loyal to you. . . . Make sure that your go-between is skilled and subtle in her speech; she must be able to lie with ease and to understand the lady's reactions. . . . If you have no such relative, find one of those old crones that frequent the churches and know all the back alleys—the ones with the huge rosaries dangling from their necks.

"Archpriest," she said, "one makes the old woman trot if he needs her, and you must do the same because you have no other. You must treat this old woman well, for she can help you. . . . Never call me vile or ugly names. Call me 'Good Love' and I will be loyal; people are pleased by pleasing names, and good names cost no more than bad ones."

For the old woman's sake and to speak the truth, I have called my book Good Love, *and so do I call her always. Because I treated her well, she was a real asset to me.*

Again being alone, without a sweetheart, I sent for my old woman and she said, "What now?" Then she laughed, saying: "Greetings, my good sir. Here comes good love, as good as a trusted friend could hope to find."[1]

Juan Ruiz, known as the Archpriest of Hita, wrote his humorous and devout *Book of Good Love* around 1320 and endowed his character Trotaconventos with great verbal skill and flexibility in dealing with her clientele. Ruiz depicts her as a crafty old woman but also names her "good love," in honor of what she provides him through her talent with words. The narrator both fears and trusts Trotaconventos with all his emotional and sexual happiness.[2] Women labeled whores and bawds produced an enormous textual record in Spain, in the form of legal, political, and literary sources that document the complexities and nuances of working in this trade. However, in New Spain, more subtle scribal seductions took place. Clients, officials, and male and female purveyors purposefully obscured the sexual marketplace. As observed by Josefina Muriel, "prostitution *[sic]* had a perfectly clear place and was peacefully tolerated by the authorities."[3] Especially for the sixteenth and seventeenth centuries, highly legible peninsular literature, law codes, and the history of increasing regulation and eventually suppression underscore transactional sex's textual erasure and its hidden prevalence in New Spain.

Three kinds of written expressions of Iberian commercial sex prefaced the elusiveness of American interpretations. First, in Spain, jurists, poets, dramatists, and moral/religious commentators recorded a wide range of understandings of disreputable women that did not clearly define what constitutes a woman who sells sex acts, versus a promiscuous woman who makes no money off her behavior, versus a woman simply known as having an immoral reputation.[4] A second aspect highlighted in written documentation was the crafty and sly male or female bawd—rufianes and alcahuetas (or masculine, *alcahuetes*) like Trotaconventos—who caused the most official worry from the medieval era until well into the seventeenth century.[5] Lastly, from the 1200s to the 1600s, increasing crown and municipal control of legal brothels *(mancebías)*[6] dominated the Iberian legal discourse, leading to a large body of regulations that the viceregal authorities did not leave a record of enforcing. Sixteenth-century Spaniards brought these late-medieval laws and customs to the New World, where participants apparently veered away into a more informal street- and home-based practice that left only the slightest traces of its existence.

The first half of this chapter mines the prolific files of Iberian brothels and pandering. The second half of the chapter draws from a much smaller transactional-sex archive for sixteenth-century Mexico City. In the new viceregal capital, the crown-regulated brothels could not displace the older tradition of male and female go-betweens who masterminded sexual relationships, often in a hospitable setting.[7] This more domestic milieu for engaging in sex for gifts or money did not limit its entrepreneurial nature but obscured it from surviving scribal annotations. Both procurers and their clientele used their time before the courts to disguise their reputations, tactics that further obfuscate how women in Mexico transacted in sex. Sex for sale in the sixteenth-century viceroyalties operated on the fringes of legality and surveillance. In an effort to clarify some of the subtleties of writing transactional sex, throughout this section of the chapter I will point out the terminology that led me to a particular case—that is, how the case was verbally catalogued within Mexico's national archive.

LEGAL DEFINITIONS

To begin with the legal context, sex for sale existed in various forms in Roman and Visigothic Spain, as well as when Muslim rule dominated the peninsula, because from ancient times, gendered social hierarchies created an idea that men needed an easily accessible sexual outlet to protect women born to elite, protected status.[8] The laws that most affected the American viceroyalties emerged out of medieval monarchs' efforts to consolidate their authority through promulgating legal codes.[9]

In the second half of the thirteenth century, the *Siete Partidas* or "Seven Sections" of the Castilian King Alfonso X (known as "the Wise") put in place the judicial understanding of selling sex, drawing from Roman jurisprudence, canon law, and the *fueros*, or customary Iberian laws.[10] However, the naming or categorization of an act or status within the Siete Partidas did not necessarily assign a punitive function to the given act or status. Legal texts could define nonmarital or nonmonogamous sexual statuses without criminalizing them.[11]

For example, the Siete Partidas did not elaborate regulations against women who made an income off their own sex acts, although Alfonso X and his compilers/jurists did use the word *putería* ("whoring"). Putería comes up in the fourth Partida, which discusses family relationships broadly, including those between servants and vassals and their masters. This official acknowledgment of the institution's legal existence without specifying judicial repercussions for working in the brothel served to grant these women a legal identity or status.[12] While not criminalizing women who sold sex with a specific judicial sentence, the Siete Partidas burdened their children with a heavy load of moral condemnation due to their maternal lineage. Of course, the Partidas, with the purpose of strengthening crown justice, operated from a hierarchical, patriarchal frame of reference, valorizing male-led families and states. This was the emphasis in this law code's legal use of *putería*.[13]

Marriage and children occupy much of the content of Partida Four, including Title Fifteen, Law One, which discusses illegitimate children. This section comprises just one of the many legal categories for the various permutations of children born out of wedlock. Iberian law codes had to deal with a wide variety of birth patterns for heirs due to the essentially polygamous practices of the high nobility and others in medieval and early-modern Spain.[14] An obsession with lineage and property inheritance overcame any regard for adhering to monogamy within the relatively new institution of sacramental Christian marriage—marriage having become a sacrament only at the Fourth Lateran council in 1215.[15] According to the Siete Partidas, children born of women who "*estan en la putería* [are involved in whoring]" should be known as *mánceres*, a reference to their sinful birth and to the fact that, according to Alfonso X and his jurists, these children could not know who to claim as their father, due to the assumption of multiple sex partners on the part of their mothers.[16] This statement served to protect men from women who might claim that their children had inheritance rights. If the man could paint the woman as a whore, he could easily reject her claims, based on this section. The law further adds that these children were engendered in evil and born to vile status.

In contrast, other titles (especially Title Fourteen) in the Fourth Partida discuss *barraganas*, or legal, recognized concubines, with much less disdain. These concubines' status as protected by one man probably made them a more palatable option for the Partidas's compilers. Barraganas could legally draw up contracts with their male partners, in a similar fashion to the way a tradesman's apprentice or a domestic servant negotiated their employment.[17] This suggests that women who operated outside male control most intimidated the medieval lawmakers, as they represented a threat to patriarchal moral codes.[18]

The Seventh Partida deals with acts considered evil and deserving of punishment—what we would call criminal law, as opposed to the family law discussed above. Title Six, Law Four discusses *"los infamados"* or reprobates known as *"lenones"* or "alcahuetes" (elsewhere called ruffians),[19] starting with a definition from the Roman context: "'Leno' in Latin means the same as *alcahuete;* a man such as this has his female servants or other free women in his house, commanding them to do evil with their bodies for money . . . he is reprobate for this."[20] Despite the very strong literary and grassroots tradition of female procuresses (alcahuetas), further explored below, here the Siete Partidas defines them as men only.[21]

Male and female panderers took a variety of forms. Ruffians in early-modern Spain offered protection from violence and helped when women faced law enforcement. They collected a certain amount of money from women who sold sex, sometimes also interacting with them in the role of a boyfriend. In contrast, male and female procurers (alcahuetas and alcahuetes) received money directly from male clients in exchange for setting up meetings and arranging safe locations for these encounters. This second category seems to fit best with common early-modern use of the word *alcahueta*. In terms of working as sexual intermediaries, the word *tercera* (third) also covers this kind of activity. Lawmakers and moralizers hated procurers because they allegedly drew men and women into sexual commerce through their legendary clever and subtle verbal ploys.[22]

Title Twenty of the Siete Partidas contains two laws that deal with alcahuetes/as in more detail. Here, the first lines of the title seem to treat what would more commonly be called ruffians—violent panderers—as opposed to the more sophisticated female intermediaries (alcahuetas). This title breaks alcahuetes (loosely interpreted) down into five categories:

> *evil rogues who guard whores that are publically in* putería, *taking part of what they earn; secondly those that go about as panderers for those seeking them; thirdly, when men raise in their houses captives or other servants knowing that they do evil with their bodies; the fourth is a man so vile that he panders his own wife; the fifth is if someone consents that a married or other well-placed woman fornicates in his house, for something that she gives to him, although he does not go about procuring for them.*[23]

Only the last two categories discuss the intermediary tradition. The Siete Partidas go on to say that alcahuetes/as do great evil by convincing good women to do evil and by pushing those who are just starting to commit errors into becoming much worse. These men cause women dishonor by the evil done with their bodies. In punishment, the Siete Partidas say that alcahuetes should be brought before judges, and if they are proven to be rogues, they should be ejected from the town along with their whores (putas). Those procurers who rent rooms to "evil women" involved in putería should lose their houses and pay ten pounds of gold. Any slave woman having sex for money and giving some of it to her master should be freed, and if she is a free woman, she should receive money for her dowry. Men who pander their own wives, other married women, virgins, nuns, or widows with a good reputation deserve the death penalty. This title ends with the note that all of these laws also apply to women: procuresses or alcahuetas. The next title moves on to sorcerers and diviners, crimes closely connected to alcahuetería (see chapter 2).

As these complex medieval legal definitions show, procuring encompassed a broad range of activities. The Siete Partidas blended together what archival court cases show to be the very different functions of male and female procurers. Across Europe, grammarians used Latin terms to define alcahuetería and demonstrated confusion about gender roles within this profession. In a Castilian dictionary dating from 1516, alcahuete is simply defined as *lenocino*. In 1570, alcahuetería is equated with *rufianismo* in Italian. A Spanish-English dictionary from 1591 translates alcahueta as a bawd or *lena*.[24] In their interactions with litigators, courts viewed procurers as criminals.

In contrast to procurers, the Siete Partidas do not provide a simple definition for the women who made their income from sexual commerce. While they are written and, therefore, acknowledged as a category, their legal status is ambiguous and obscured, even in this most basic, fundamental Spanish law code. While making them indecipherable as actual criminals, this semi-erasure also suggests the importance of a grassroots social or moral understanding of these women's acts and reputations, which may or may not show up in the surviving documentation. Specific case studies underscore their illegible textual identity.

Even the terminology used in legal codes, royal decrees, court cases, and witness statements varies widely and often contradicts itself. Castilian King Enrique III in the 1398 Cortes de Toro made a distinction between "putas públicas [public whores]," clarifying that rameras were on the other hand "encubiertas [secret whores]."[25] As private concubines, rameras had to pay a larger tax because they were thought to make more money working with a select clientele outside the public brothel.[26] The first time this word appears in a Spanish dictionary was in Antonio de Nebrija's 1495 vocabulary of Spanish and Latin words, where interestingly Nebrija defines ramera as a "puta onesta [honest whore]" or, in Latin, *meretrix*. The same definition continued in the 1505 and 1516 dictionaries, where the entries for puta continue to equate this word with ramera or meretrix.[27] Therefore, if a public whore equates to an honest whore, the definitions of ramera had changed from the late fourteenth century to the sixteenth century. Despite the unstable terminology, a classification emerges: public women and brothel workers (implying sexual accessibility to all men) contrasted with secret or semimonogamous concubines. Of course, this distinction matters only when everyone could publicly acknowledge the existence and functioning of the legal brothel. In the more ambiguous American context, Spanish officials in the New World frequently applied the term *mujeres públicas* to a wide variety of women.

While panderers had a clear punitive threat applied to their actions, public women and concubines did not—their crimes faced moral not criminal sanction. The authorities attempted to legislate over women's clothes, hair, jewelry, and other markers to make a clear public distinction between sexually controlled women and women perceived as promiscuous.[28] For example, in this society only young virgin girls traditionally wore their hair uncovered and displayed its beauty. A covered head signified a sexually active adult woman. But women labeled whores also took pride in showing off their beautiful loose hair, rejecting the standard expectations for a secluded married woman's appearance.[29] The crown often failed in enforcing sumptuary laws or policing fashion. The fact that early-modern women with virtuous reputations imitated the official dress designated for whores has confounded historians since the nineteenth century. Historians, assuming that all women in the past also bought into the official condemnations of non–sexually conforming women, could not grasp why some honorable women actually wanted to emulate scandalous women's appearance and dress.[30] In fact, literary sources such as *La Lozana Andaluza* (introduction) and *La Celestina* (chapter 2) portray sixteenth-century courtesans as the cosmetologists of their day, helping women in the arts of hair dye, makeup, facial hair removal, care of their hands, and even dental health.

One fascinating medieval definition does a better job than the sumptuary laws in defining these women, even if it probably misunderstands their lives completely: rameras were "women who don't spin," a definition perhaps inspired by La Lozana's rejection of this feminine task.[31] In other words, whores, unlike all other women, neither made their living nor just passed their time by doing needlework. They rejected the essential task of a genteel or hardworking woman.

BROTHELS IN SPAIN

The Siete Partidas's harsh condemnation of panderers and procuresses may derive from royal patronage of legal brothels, even in this early era of Spanish history. Independent mediators competed with the municipal, crown, and even church ambitions to capitalize on sex for sale.[32] Preceding the opening of legal brothels, licensed sex workers operated in Seville and Cordoba and paid taxes to the Islamic rulers.[33] Under Christian rule, crown or municipalities or even religious institutions tended toward owning brothels instead of taxing independent women. From approximately

1300 until the late sixteenth century, regulated legal brothels flourished throughout the re-Christianized Iberian Peninsula. Valencia and Barcelona had documented brothels from the early fourteenth century, while Castilian monarchs regulated this institution at least from the mid-fifteenth century.[34] They viewed legal brothels as an opportunity to enclose male violence and competitiveness into a bounded area.[35] Street-level commercial sex led medieval urban dwellers to make legal complaints mainly because it caused neighborhood violence.[36] Brothel regulations stipulated that men had to surrender their weapons upon entering, and thus this separated space served as a possible deterrent to street battles.

Politically, the grant of a brothel license helped unstable or contestable monarchs (including Ferdinand and Isabella) reward those subjects who served them loyally. Those who received monopolistic access to the bounteous brothel revenue could hand down this privilege to their heirs, and thus the recipients of these privileges jealously defended the institution.[37] Access to prized crown brothel monopolies actually predated the Christian reconquest. For example, the great "whoremonger" Alonso Yáñez Fajardo received enormous benefits from a royal grant to the brothel monopoly for numerous cities, including all of Granada, six years before its official conquest by the Catholic monarchs.[38]

Financially, regulating sex work by legalizing only one official brothel in each town or city created many opportunities for the judiciary to collect a huge income in fines, even beyond the steady taxed income brothels generated as successful businesses.[39] Iberian brothels made their large profits not for their residents but for their managers, the monarchs, and the municipalities that later received their revenue.[40] Collecting fines on all possible minor infractions against the strict brothel regulations generated enough income to fund public offices. Overall, regulated sex work allowed late-medieval and early-modern Iberian authorities to attain the perfect balance between an apparently benign paternalistic tolerance and the possibility of harsher but lucrative enforcement of laws at any whim.[41] Legal brothels extended the reach of both Iberian monarchs and town governments and helped consolidate their authority in this era of growth in crown legal institutions. Looking ahead to the second half of this chapter, apparently the Spanish crown either could not or did not want to extend this reach effectively to the Americas.

Despite the tradition of philosophical and theological writings that encouraged humans to control their baser passions, and the view of sexuality as an opposing force to spirituality, in medieval and early-modern Iberia and across Europe, the general population, church, and state voiced a discourse of brothels as a public good, especially from the mid-fourteenth century to the early sixteenth century.[42] As a result, clients who visited legal state or municipal brothels received sexual services at a reasonable cost. This society viewed nonmonogamous, transactional sex as a right that all men should have and as a benefit for everyone, not a luxury for the privileged. For centuries, many Spaniards rejected the concept that simple fornication between two consenting unmarried adults was a moral wrong, despite Christian and later Catholic attempts to enforce chastity more and more through campaigns celebrating the Immaculate Conception.[43] The common man logically questioned why the king would license brothels if there were something wrong with enjoying "no strings attached" sex.[44] Even some women whose husbands frequented brothels seemed open minded about this activity, although many others argued that visiting whores justified financial reparations for the wife. Apparently, one late-medieval wife described her husband with great love and affection, noting that other than the fact that "*era putanero mucho de mujeres* [loosely translated: he was a real whorehound]," he was as good and pious as Saint Francis, and she would lay beside him for eternity in adjoining coffins.[45]

What was it like for a man to visit a legal brothel in medieval or early-modern Iberia? Different descriptions survive from male visitors, especially for the highly successful Valencian *mancebía,* giving the twenty-first–century reader the impression of a pleasurable outing, and the promise of an illusion or fantasy world of illicit sexual excitement operating under fully legal conditions with very strict rules.[46] Most municipal brothels, including Valencia's, operated on the edge or just outside of the central city. In Valencia, the brothel was a small walled quarter containing two to three hundred women, working out of rooms organized along three or four streets. Men entered the brothel via one entrance only, interacting with a guard. The guard would ask men to surrender their weapons and even promise to safely watch over their cash. Once inside the brothel, men observed and admired beautifully dressed, elegant women sitting under bright lanterns in front of their rooms, or they could enter taverns and inns. Spending time with the female residents had a fixed, standard cost.[47] In Seville, by contrast, municipal officials rented out simple huts by the Guadalquivir River, and these clustered dwellings functioned as the brothel. The town took care to repair and maintain the buildings.[48] Brothels forbade the entrance of non-Christians, so Islamic or Jewish men who snuck in with assumed false identities risked severe judicial consequences.[49]

How did women experience life in the legal brothels? We know very few specific details from the female point of view, beyond the regulations. Women who worked in brothels were supposed to be officially registered by giving their names, ages, parents, and places of origin to municipal authorities. Every brothel worker had an alias that she also provided in the registration process.[50] The women had to be nonlocals and nonnoblewomen over the age of twenty. They paid fees to the brothel managers but received linens, clothing, and housing in return. Some historians view brothel work as a desperate recourse for poor women victimized by the countless natural and manmade disasters of their male-dominated era. However, in 1553, King Phillip II noted in frustration that many brothel women illegally left their places of work in the evenings to live in their "palaces," where they met with male clients. Even worse, in Phillip's view, they acted like honorable women.[51]

Through legalizing and regulating brothels, Iberian monarchs and municipal governments hoped to impose centralized control over the endemic violence in their society, an era of internal conflicts, independent warlords, and busy ports full of transient men. Monarchs such as Ferdinand and Isabella, along with their predecessors earlier in the fifteenth century, spent decades trying to tamp down the power of powerful grandees who dominated both cities and the countryside. These nobles gathered delinquents, ruffians, and rogues around them as their own personal bodyguards or entourages and encouraged them to foment urban disorder. The aristocratic strongmen, objecting to the monarchs' efforts to centralize power and authority, also willingly protected these "evil doers" from nascent crown justice.[52] Ruffians roamed the streets, provoking brawls with little fear of judicial retribution because "those in charge of prosecuting them were often the ones who gave protection to law breakers."[53] Monarchs and some royal justices viewed these men as vagabonds and "men who lived by evil arts" and equated them with ruffians, often banishing them from residing inside any given town.[54] Ruffians faced severe penalties for managing women, according to a decree issued by Enrique IV in 1469, in continuation of the antipandering tone of the Siete Partidas.[55] The crown and municipal authorities hoped that regulated brothels would decrease street fighting and even the grandees' ability to foment general societal violence. For the purposes of controlling street-level violence, criminal vagabonds, and overweening aristocrats, one might assume that the crown also would want legal brothels in their American viceroyalties, but in fact this invasive, regulatory approach did not come to fruition in the New World.

TRANSACTIONAL SEX OUTSIDE THE BROTHEL— CLANDESTINAS AND ALCAHUETAS

The opportunities for nonbrothel paid sex unfolded in the Spanish viceroyalties following centuries' old peninsular patterns for *clandestinas* who sold sex outside of the licensed brothels. Back in Iberia, ruffians found many female collaborators despite regulated, legal brothels and the serious punishments for selling sex outside these approved institutions. These sexual entrepreneurs took advantage of location and opportunity. In and around brothels, taverns and inns prospered. These places employed female servants, jobs taken on by both brothel workers and clandestinas. Men, including the innkeepers themselves, illegally procured one or several female servants who might host clients in rooms for entire nights. A lesser number had female managers or worked for their own husbands. Since non-Christian men who entered the legal brothels risked extreme punishments, Jewish and Islamic or Morisco men offered clandestinas a booming business. Criminal records prove that clandestinas flourished alongside the brothel. In late-medieval Valencia, on average around 115 clandestinas faced prosecution annually, representing almost one-third of all local criminal trials. Street ruffians still caused public violence, but they also helped towns make a great deal of money in punitive fines.[56] In some cases, cruel slurs captured in documents suggest that clandestinas were too old, dirty, sick, ugly, or all of the above, for working in the public brothel. Women perceived as too scandalous or loud had to leave the public brothel, which suggests that clandestinas lacked some of the characteristics perceived as sexually attractive to men.[57] In fact, some clandestinas offered their potential clients the opposite end of the spectrum: discretion, secrecy, exclusivity, wealth, social prominence, and sophistication, outside of the common "sewer" of the brothel.[58]

Some clandestinas in Spain and the viceroyalties relied on bawds to arrange their liaisons. The literary figure of the alcahueta has a much more complex and even sympathetic history than the universally disrespected male ruffian. Law codes including the Siete Partidas codified harsh punishments for bawds, but many classics of Castilian literature humanized this figure. The title of their occupation derives from the Hispanic Arabic term *alqawwád*.[59] From before the Christian reconquest of Spain, Islamic literary treatises acknowledged the essential role of the bawd in setting up illicit liaisons. This genre of literature explored the phenomenon of nonmarital affairs that required a mediator. In these tales, sexual encounters were in a sense love triangles or even squares. The fact that women socialized separately from men did not stand in the way, but affairs required a subtle mediator, a witty verbal interlocutor to bridge gender communication gaps. Stories depicted how both the bawd and the female lover cooperated to entrap a man and dupe a husband, showing off their intelligence and sophistication. To have the skills to move in men's and women's worlds, the bawd had to possess the wisdom of age. Some of these portrayals even imply that she redirected her own desires into organizing other people's trysts.[60] In the fourteenth century, Ruiz immortalized this Islamic literary tradition for Christian readers with the enduring bawdy character of Trotaconventos, a sly old woman who added more complexity to the non-Christian portrayals from early eras. In other medieval Christian writings, the bawd figure assumes a very maternal role, sometimes actually procuring her own daughters' lovers. This terminology and personality characterization perhaps connects to the fact that brothel manageresses in medieval and early-modern Spain carried the official occupational title of "mother."[61] Sixteenth-century poetry also represents the bawd as an essential guide for the novice courtesan.[62] Although Trotaconventos, Lozana, and Celestina (chapter 2) are fictional creations, their literary portrayals flesh out the ephemeral traces of nonfictional bawds found in archival documentation.

SELLING SEX IN THE NEW WORLD

Beginning in the 1520s, the Spanish crown initially extended the policy of licensing brothels from Spain to its American viceroyalties. In 1526, Bartolome Conejo received a license to found a royal brothel, or "casa de mujeres públicas," in San Juan, Puerto Rico.[63] The license stated that this foundation was "necessary" to avoid "inconveniences." A similar arrangement was made the same year with Juan Sanchez Sarmiento, in the city of Santo Domingo.[64] By 1538, Queen Isabel of Portugal had approved the foundation of a whorehouse in Mexico City, although in this case a specific individual did not make the request.[65] The Mexico City *cabildo* chose a location for it behind the Hospital de Jesus Nazareno on the Calle de Mesones (known as "whores' street" or *"la calle de Las Gayas"*). Cartagena also had a brothel in the late sixteenth century, according to a Holy Office sorcery investigation.[66]

These Spanish American legal brothels did not leave a great deal of evidence of their existence, in contrast to the extensive paper trail in Spain, which records many petty infractions. We can speculate that perhaps the viceroyalties lacked officials with the time or interest to enforce the ever increasing rules, even if it meant a good income in fines. Without a lucrative brothel monopoly in place, American judicial authorities had no motivation to prosecute clandestinas, so these women, as well as their ruffians and bawds, completely took over the trade in sex.[67] Viceregal sexual commerce moved permanently to street solicitation, or private houses where bawds managed their servants and family members or rented out their rooms and procured clients for women. Spanish, Indian, and *casta* women worked out of unofficial brothels as well as in taverns, *pulquerías,* gaming houses, public baths, *temescales,* and luxurious rooms.[68]

Crown regulation picked up from the 1560s to the 1580s, foreshadowing suppression in the seventeenth century (chapter 2). Phillip II imposed new and more serious penalties on ruffians in a 1566 decree, an extension of his father's policies noted above. The king also commanded that husbands who consented to their wives' "doing evil with their bodies" for money should receive the same harsh punishments as did any other ruffian: public shaming on the first offense, along with ten years of rowing in the galleys, and one hundred lashes (individual strokes with a whip of a varying degree of intensity) and a perpetual sentence of galley slavery for the second offense. One surviving document indicates that the sentence of galley slavery might actually bring ruffians to the Caribbean, where they possibly could restart their occupation in a new locale.[69] The crown also began issuing a long series of recurring decrees against *"pecados publicos"* (public sins including adultery, concubinage, and pandering) in this era. For example, a 1570 royal *cedula* promulgated by the viceroy of Peru demanded that the viceroy of New Spain and the high courts of all Spanish American territories punish public sins as a gesture of mourning for the death of Phillip II's wife, Ana of Austria.[70] A similar decree came out of Madrid in 1583, due to the death of the *infante* Diego, heir to the throne.[71] Spanish monarchs repetitively propagated these decrees into the next century.[72]

This general trend of increasing strictness against ruffians and bawds produced more written records of the offense. In Mexico City, the national archive preserves clerical cases against two men, four women, and one couple for the crime of procuring, dating from 1555 to 1585. Given the way that Phillip II had begun to repeatedly proclaim his moralizing bent, other prosecutions may have taken place, but the archival traces have not survived. These seven cases represent all the court cases that I could find dealing with sixteenth-century commercial sex in the viceregal capital. I was able to locate these files because the case descriptions used the term *alcahueta,* as well as *consentidor* (procuress) and *tercera.*[73] In terms of racial designations, they involve a broad spectrum of Mexico City's residents, bringing in individuals of African, indigenous, and Spanish descent to testify before the ecclesiastical and inquisitorial courts. All of the accused had plebeian status, even the Spaniards. Although the evidence gives a brief glimpse into how procurers worked on the street level or in taverns, paid sex generally took place within family homes.

In the oldest case, dating from 1555, Francisco Saavedra, an *alguacil* for the archbishop of Mexico City, accused a forty-year-old indigenous women, addressed as both Ana and María Tepe, of making money as an "alcahueta" for "Indians, Spaniards, Blacks, and mestizos."[74] The accused denied all of the accusations, claiming that she made her income by selling her tortillas. The eight male Spanish witnesses for the prosecution backed up Saavedra, although their statements refined the racial parameters of Tepe's business model. In a canny exploitation of postconquest sexual opportunities, this woman, who may have remembered the early years of the Spanish invasion of Mexico, allegedly made money by carrying messages between *india* and mestiza women and Spaniards, leading to carnal access. Seeing an opportunity for profit based on her customers' expectations, Tepe seems to have quickly learned and adapted herself to the Spanish alcahueta tradition. In line with the Siete Partidas's traditional penalties (ejecting bawds from their towns of residence), Tepe received a sentence of two years' banishment two leagues outside the archdiocese of Mexico. If she violated these terms, she risked two hundred lashings and four years' banishment.

Two of the alcahuetas accused in the 1560s and 1570s allegedly arranged for their own daughters to have sex for their mothers' (or, more broadly, their entire households') monetary gain. In 1567, Mexico City archdiocesan officials accused a married Afro-descended woman (labeled a *negra* but without reference to enslaved status) named Luisa de Espinosa of procuring in her house for her own daughter as well as two indigenous women and possibly one Spanish woman.[75] We can speculate that Espinosa's year of birth was approximately 1530, and that she perhaps came from Spain or the Caribbean because she apparently lived as an acculturated Afro-Spaniard. Bawdry featured among the Spanish traditions she personally helped propagate in Mexico City. Six witnesses (five men and one mestiza) testified that Espinosa allowed men to have carnal access with her daughter (a *mulata* named María Pérez) and two indias who lived in their house, in return for money or other gifts. All of the witnesses lived nearby and had known Espinosa over a period of years. They claimed that they saw mulatto and mestizo men entering the house frequently for sexual purposes. Some of the witnesses testified that Luisa had approached them as potential clients. All of these testimonies suggest a home brothel. This case ends with a demand for Espinosa's imprisonment and does not include her reaction to the accusations.

In 1577, the *fiscal* of the archdiocese of Mexico accused María de Ávila of allowing men to fornicate with both of her daughters for personal gain or *intereses,* causing scandal and whispering among her neighbors.[76] He warned her that she should live in Christian seclusion, protecting her daughters. In this case, no further information exists other than a call for witnesses. This scanty documentation sounds like the start of a case against Ávila for brothel keeping, not an example of matchmaking that did not quite lead to marriage, which seems to be the situation in the next family investigation.

In 1582, although the archbishop's court used the term *alcahueta* in an accusation against the parents of sixteen-year-old Ana de Alameda, the details suggest not sex for pay but long-term concubinage or *amancebamiento.*[77] Perhaps the court categorizing this situation as bawdry implied greater official moral outrage and a desire to crack down on common sexual practices in the family's plebeian setting. Neighbors' statements referred to the parents as *encubridores* (someone who hides something illegal) and *consentidores,* not alcahuetes. None of the litigants received any racial designations, suggesting that they all presented themselves to the court as Spaniards. However, the court labeled two of the witnesses as mestizas and another mulatto. The parents, thirty-six-year-old Juan Rollon, a *platero de oro,* and thirty-nine-year-old Isabel Martin, said they were both born in Mexico City, perhaps first-generation Creoles.[78]

Witnesses said that Alameda and her parents willingly shared their home with Martin de la Herrería over a period of months and received money in exchange for tolerating this sinful cohabitation. All four allegedly ate together, and all slept in the same room, in three separate beds. The married couple slept apart due to illness, but Alameda slept with Herrería, according to the witnesses. The prosecuted litigants, when asked about how their daughter "*comunicaba con mucha desenvoltura* [had a shameless interaction]" with her lover, explicitly denied any sexual relationship between Herrería and Alameda, although the girl had given birth recently.[79] They claimed that all of the hostile witnesses were living in sin themselves and, therefore, could not be trusted to testify honestly, in an effort to erase the criminal label applied to their profitable domestic arrangement.[80] These scanty textual records of domestic alcahuetería faintly record the familial setting for transactional sex in the first few decades of the viceroyalty, inscribing it in a barely visible fashion onto the poor and/or nonwhite bodies inhabiting the new viceregal court.

A RUFFIAN

Two trials in 1570s Mexico City involved men accused of *lenoncinio* or procuring their own wives for other men. The sixteenth-century term frequently used in these cases is *consentidor*, implying that the men consented to and benefited from their wives' affairs. These men apparently made a living by organizing or approving of their own wives' multiple sexual partners. In the course of the first case, a very morally suspect couple formally inscribed their shared honor through statements made by character witnesses. By writing the accused ruffian as a man who worried about his wife's honor, not as a panderer, the witnesses achieved the ultimate goal of sex-related trials: to assert, reformulate, or utterly transform a bad reputation into a respectable one.[81]

Antonio Temiño (age twenty-five) allegedly allowed his wife of four years, María de Guisas (age nineteen), to have sex with other men for gain, according to a 1571 investigation done by the archbishop's court.[82] Public scandal inspired the church authorities to question witnesses about this plebeian couple (they did not state a race label), probably in response to the 1570 decree against public sins. Testimonies create a character for Temiño that fits every medieval and early-modern negative assumption about ruffians. This man's character clarifies why Phillip II voiced moral outrage against pandering husbands. According to witnesses, everyone in their neighborhood knew that Temiño regularly took Guisas to a tavern run by Melchior de los Reyes around midnight or 1:00 a.m. and that they often returned drunk. While there, as his gainful employment, Temiño arranged for her to have sex for pay with different men. A witness stated that the tavern keeper gave Temiño a *cuartilla* of wine during these negotiations, and he took it with him as he left the tavern. This venue for Guisas's trade in sex follows the Spanish model of clandestine sex in taverns outside the legal brothel.

Guisas's clientele included a mestizo tailor named Juan Mallorquin. This man supposedly had open access to the couple's house, and on a recent occasion he had injured Guisas's arm with his sword in a drunken argument. Witnesses spoke of at least four other men who had paid for carnal access with Guisas with the full knowledge and consent of her husband. A mulatto called Juan de Perillo (who was also imprisoned in the archbishop's jail) claimed that he had heard a revealing conversation between the husband and wife. Allegedly, Guisas, in a drunken rage, had called Temiño a "knave, a great scoundrel and cuckold because . . . you sent me to earn with my body so that you would have some money *[bellaco bien bellaco cornudo porque . . . me enviaba de ganar con mi cuerpo para que os tuviese dinero]*." Temiño responded in kind, saying María de Guisas "lied, like a knave *[bellaca]*.[83]

It appeared to both these witnesses and the *provisor* that Temiño made a living by hustling his wife, but when questioned, both spouses denied every accusation. Both claimed that they were honorable people, with Guisas adamantly asserting her monogamous wifely virtue. The couple used this opportunity in court to redeem their reputation by not letting a single aspect of the accusations pass without denouncing them as false. In addition, Temiño made several petitions asking why he was suffering such a long imprisonment (a month) and especially why he had to endure a thick chain and irons on his legs.[84] If we understand his denials as written rhetorical stances and trust the witnesses for the prosecution, as the court did, this harsh treatment makes sense in terms of traditional Spanish censorious attitudes toward ruffians, dating back at least to the Siete Partidas.

Despite the claims made by hostile witnesses, ten plebeian Spanish men (ranging in age from mid-twenties to over sixty) denied that Temiño "consented" to his wife's having sex with other men. The evidence that they offered highlights Temiño's violent and jealous character. During the course of his defense, the witnesses created a written record of his honorable character for him, even though outside the court he preferred to use violence to shape his reputation.

Statements about Temiño take both a formulaic and more individualistic shape, both as the expected responses of character witnesses and glimpses of the real Temiño. Beginning on a positive note, most of the witnesses spoke of Temiño and his wife as good Christians. One witness affirmed that Temiño would never allow his wife to associate with dishonorable people, a confirmation of his honor. But his possessiveness went too far, beyond the honor code's dictates regarding men's roles as protectors of the sexuality of dependent women. Several of the witnesses stated that it was unlikely that such a suspicious and jealous man would allow his wife to have sex with other men. But his character emerges as worse than jealous: Temiño frequently beat María de Guisas, according to six witnesses, so much so that she appeared with a bloody face and feared for her life. One man claimed that he had stepped in to break up their fights. The court testimonies wrote Guisas as a victim of domestic violence, not a dishonorable woman.[85] While the witnesses for the defense redirected the investigation away from Guisas's alleged sexual improprieties, they also erased the evidence that Temiño worked as her panderer.

Although the deponents expressed the opinion that making an income off procuring did not suit a jealous, violent husband like Temiño, in fact, the persona they created for him sounds like that of a typical ruffian. If nothing else, Temiño's character witnesses certainly did not convince the court that he was a good husband. Guisas apparently received no sentence and probably did not remain imprisoned for very long during the trial, given that, at this time, royal law did not define her as a criminal. If a legal whorehouse did not exist in 1571 Mexico City, in theory she did not disregard brothel regulations by operating as a clandestina. On the other hand, procuring certainly was punishable, especially when a husband pandered his wife. Even those who spoke in Temiño's favor suggested that he certainly deserved some form of penance. The ecclesiastical court agreed with them and sentenced him to march to a mass on foot, carrying a candle. He also received a sentence of banishment from the archdiocese of Mexico for two years and admonishment to treat his wife more

appropriately within the bonds of matrimony. Because his prosecutors were church-
men not secular judges, Temiño avoided the sentence of ten years' galley slavery, as
Phillip's laws decreed. Temiño's ecclesiastical prosecution differs from crown intent
regarding ruffians, but it carried out royal decrees against public sin.

A BAWD

If they wished to avoid ruffians like Temiño, potential illicit lovers in sixteenth-
century Mexico City could call on bawds to arrange their affairs. Following in the
medieval tradition, these slightly older women mediated between men and women
by carrying persuasive messages and sometimes providing accommodations for
compensation. A Spanish woman named Catalina García helped bring the previous centuries' mediator traditions to New Spain. In 1570, García came before the
archbishop's court for allegedly helping to organize her friend María de Rojas's
encounters with at least three men.[86]

García knew how to convince her clients with words; she was persistent and
aggressive, and she masterminded locations for lovers to meet. In return for
arranging the affairs, carrying messages, and hosting the encounters, she received
a few pesos in compensation and, in one case, some sugar. García, at age thirty-
eight, had twelve more years of life experience than Rojas. Born in Castile and
living in New Spain since 1557, García also enjoyed a slightly higher social status
than Rojas did, claiming a tradesman husband and the ability to write and sign her
name very confidently. She may have even written convincing petitions in her own
hand.[87] In contrast, the court labeled Rojas (of unknown origins) a *soltera* (sexually active single woman), and she could not sign her name. The official accusations branded García not only as an alcahueta "for fornicating men and women,"
but also an encubridora and a tercera, an accessory to fornication and a mediator.[88]
Rojas may have sought to clear her own name through the intervention of the
court, while García intoned the expected rhetoric, using the legal formulas to
inscribe her good reputation against the accusations.

According to Rojas and three of her clients, García solicited each of the men as
they innocently (as the four accusers portrayed it) strolled past her house at various hours of the night and day. García called to them from her window or stood in
the doorway, alone and on occasion with her friend Rojas in the door with her. The
targeted men, age twenty, twenty-six, and thirty, were also plebeians, one described
as a mestizo and another working as a tailor. In classic bawd style, allegedly García
ignored all of their hesitation over engaging in "carnal access" with Rojas and
aggressively "persuaded" the four potential fornicators to submit with her persistent verbiage. When Rojas at first refused to have sex with the men, García asked
her over and over again (*"tantas veces"* or "so many times"), promising that each
man would "do very well" for her.[89] García convinced the men, on some occasions

instantly or otherwise over a period of time, to meet Rojas either at their shared house or at the men's accommodations.[90]

While Rojas and her lovers risked compromising their reputations by making these detailed accusations, sex exchanged for money and simple fornication between unmarried adults carried no criminal penalty at this time, so García had the most to fear in terms of legal sanctions. The clerical court took seriously and disliked what they heard about García from hostile witnesses, so an official called for her arrest and incarceration in the archdiocesan jail. When questioned directly about accusations of pandering, García (already described as an effective verbal persuader) refuted everything other than the fact that Rojas had lived with her for a few months. She justified this as an act of charity to help a sick friend.[91]

García built her own case by asserting her superb reputation as an honest married woman while simultaneously tearing down the trustworthiness of the testimonies. According to García, Rojas's accusations had no value because she was a "public whore [ramera]" who slept with many men for money. García denied any responsibility for either pandering her friend or controlling her "evil living [mal vivir]." Rojas was over twenty-five, unmarried, and did not seem to have a father, uncle, brother, or other relative in the area who might fear that her reputation degraded their honor. García denied any responsibility for her friend's behavior, maintaining that Rojas was "a free woman and she can go out wherever she wants at night [mujer libre y pudiendo salir donde quiso de noche]."[92]

Usually the word ramera was used in Spain for a clandestina, while "public" as a descriptor implied that a woman worked in the brothel, and everyone in the community knew it. Rojas could work publicly without violating brothel regulations, as they did not exist, and she was not subject to penal retribution or fines. Her occupation weakened her trustworthiness as a good witness in court, but it was not illegal. Therefore, it behooved García to verbally fit Rojas to the patterns of a bad woman through her immorality, not her criminality, in order to prove that García herself was a good woman.

A group of young Spanish plebeian men who appeared to be García's close friends (often visiting her house) attested to her good character. These men also confirmed the bad reputations of Rojas and her lovers in contrast to the perfectly respectable García. The witnesses for the defense answered the following series of typically leading questions:

> [Was García] a good Christian who lived in seclusion in fear of god and her reputation, providing a good example everywhere she went? Was María de Rojas a public woman, a whore that earned her money publicly with her body, for any price that they give her, and for this should it be understood that the witnesses lied in saying that [she used] an alcahueta? Were Rojas and García enemies because Rojas said that García had a bad marriage?

Lastly, the witnesses had to provide their character judgments of Rojas's three lovers, by definition lascivious and vile men who had lived in sin with Rojas. These questions solidified García's reputation and established that her accusers were sinful people and not good witnesses.[93] The defense claimed that Rojas had sex with lewd, libidinous men who carried on illicit affairs. They were *apasionado*, men enflamed by their baser passions to commit acts of lust while neglecting to call on reason to control their instincts.[94]

Every witness for the defense agreed that García had a good reputation and Christian character, in contrast to María de Rojas's. In describing Rojas, the men inscribed her body with her sexual sins: her indiscriminate and evil exchange of money for sex. They denounced her because she openly monetized her body.[95] While García lived a discreet and secluded life as a woman of honor, Rojas walked the streets alone, "wrapped in a sheet" like a common woman. A witness called her a public woman and a puta. She received money "with her body" from anybody and everybody who would pay. Two men testified that Rojas, a public woman and a whore (ramera), "sold her body" in order to eat.[96] The witnesses interpreted her lack of selectivity to mean that Rojas did not require the services of a bawd. They opined that given her sexual proclivities, a mediator simply was not necessary. In other words, Rojas took the initiative in sexual aggressiveness, and she did not require persuading and the subtle communication arts of a bawd. This interpretation recalls the age-old Islamic and Spanish definition of alcahuetas as subtle, sophisticated go-betweens for discreet lovers, not crass high-volume ruffians of the kind that an alleged whore such as Rojas might use.

This case, because of how it recorded a fight between former friends, records the most extreme verbiage available to denounce a woman's character. The animosity of all involved created a boldly written documentation of transactional sex. However, even with all of its specificity, some ambiguity remains. The testimonies made in her favor described García as a woman who lived an exemplary, secluded life, but at the same time she received male visitors.[97] Despite the witnesses' assertions that García was a reputable Christian, their statements leave room to consider that a respectable woman like her, who often conversed with young men at her house, men very willing to stand up for her in court, would make an excellent procuress. The witnesses never explicitly denied that García might have this occupation. They only refuted that Rojas needed help organizing her paying clients. If these young men did use García as their mediator in sexual liaisons, they would certainly wish to speak well of her in court, in order to continue enjoying her bawdy talents.

DOMESTIC PROCURING

The above cases demonstrate that without a thriving brothel, sixteenth-century male residents of Mexico City had several options for partaking in transactional sex. They could seek out women who pandered their servants or their daughters in a domestic setting, in a sense visiting informal family brothels. They could go to taverns, looking for women who had ruffians who took money in exchange for sex with their women, sometimes even their wives. This option could result in violent encounters with ruffians such as Antonio Temiño. Lastly, while walking the streets, they could look out for women selling sex (allegedly, what María de Rojas did) or contact a bawd like Catalina García. All of the above options suggest a lack of exclusivity, a level of somewhat indiscriminating sex that compared roughly with the legal brothels in Spain, aimed at a plebeian clientele satisfied to meet with "public women."

Men who chose a more discreet path had another very appealing option that fits with the most common understandings of nonmarital sex in the viceroyalties: the servant/master relationship.[98] This popular arrangement raised few eyebrows, other than when a husband openly marketed his wife as her go-between, mediator, host, and all the other third-party matchmaking roles that church and state had sought to stamp out for centuries. The archbishop's court had to take a second look at a case labeled "*lenocinio* [pandering]" in 1577, when the married couple Martin de Vildosola and Juana Rodríguez openly ignored Vildosola's previous sentence of banishment, scandalously continuing their polyamorous affairs for money.[99] Nosy neighbors inscribed the tale of this couple through their testimonies. Through this written evidence, we learn both the appropriate terms for this transactional arrangement and what the neighborhood viewed as offenses worth memorializing in a file. Testimony says that Vildosola encouraged Rodríguez to entertain at least three different men in their house, serving them meals, washing their clothes, and having physical contact with them on a regular basis for extended periods.[100] Rodríguez and Vildosola cultivated extramarital relationships for her that might last for years. Rodríguez's lovers included a cleric named Miranda, a notary named Miguel de la Zaragoza, and a blacksmith by the name of Hernando de Orgaz, good earners who could afford to compensate the couple for Rodríguez's attentions. The first two men perhaps even exerted useful power and influence to help maintain the couple's good fortunes.

Witnesses claimed to see Vildosola asking the men for money, complaining that the couple was poor and did not have enough to eat, and observers saw him receiving it directly from the patrons' hands to his. The deponents stated that this income provided the couple with the simple luxuries of fresh meat and chicken for their meals, as well as for Indigenous labor to make improvements on their properties.[101] Despite noting the money exchanged, the neighbors did not name Rodríguez as a whore or use any other negative terms describing her sexuality. Instead, the testimonies focused on the details that showed an intimate connection between Juana Rodríguez and her clientele, and how her husband "consented to his wife's carnal access and communication" with different men.[102] The witnesses only spoke of her as *amancebada*, or the concubine of her visitors, using no other labels. Vildosola does not appear to have the characteristics of a ruffian, and the witnesses did not refer to him as such, nor did they use any forms of the word *leno*. Vildosola instead acted more like a genteel alcahuete, a sociable man out for profit but disinterested in honor or marital fidelity.

This case does not include the couple's statements—most likely, following the pattern of all other cases of this kind, they would take the form of complete denials and excuses for all of the accusations of intimacy. But onlookers claimed that they saw very suggestive scenes between Rodríguez and Orgaz. Their nosiness narrates a story of the couple's private activities. An open door allowed neighbors to peer inside, including two spies in the form of children, ages thirteen and fourteen.[103] These children and other observers knew that Rodríguez openly committed adultery with the consent of her husband, which they proved by reports of loving personal gestures instead of sex acts or lewd behavior. The neighbors claimed that Orgaz often stayed with Rodríguez alone in the evening, in various states of undress, almost always without his shoes on and sometimes even completely barefoot, a clear sign of informality and intimacy. Bystanders alleged that Orgaz would lay in one bed with Rodríguez, while her husband slept in another, even while their son was present. Reportedly, an Indian man hosted the married couple, Orgaz, and another woman on the feast day of San Juan. Apparently, the group ate together in the house while Orgaz and Rodríguez touched each other openly in front of her husband: Orgaz allegedly lying propped up and surrounded by her skirts while Rodríguez combed and cleaned the dandruff out of his hair. Another deponent claimed that once, while chatting with the husband in the couples' doorway at 3:00 p.m., he saw the notary Zaragoza enter their house, eating a walnut. When Rodríguez entered, the notary began embracing and hugging her, putting the walnut from his mouth to hers. The lovers then sat down together very intimately.[104] The notary was heard to brag that Rodríguez was his concubine and praised her for her "*buenas carnes* [loosely: attractive flesh]," a rare archival verbalization of a woman's private sexual appeal.[105]

The lover who seemed most attached to Rodríguez, the blacksmith Hernando Orgaz, showed some agitation in the face of the couples' disregard of the banishment conditions and their spying neighbors. Allegedly, Vildosola told Orgaz that he should not worry; even though "rogues" tried to disturb them, he should always "come to my house and enjoy yourself with me and with my woman." Although at times he flaunted his public displays of affection, at other moments Orgaz feared detection and punishment after Vildosola's initial but ignored sentence of banishment. Since he did not want to stop visiting Rodríguez, he allegedly snuck in and out of the couple's house under the cover of darkness many times, even going so far as to disguise himself by dressing in an *habito de indio*.[106]

While their neighbors spied on and reported on these nonmonogamous scenes in response to the investigation into Vildosola and Rodríguez's disregard of the banishment sentence, the couple seemed unconcerned about secular and religious authorities, monogamy within marriage, sin, and even the laws against pandering.[107] Of course, two of Rodríguez's lovers represented church and state through their occupations as a notary and a cleric. Not only did these men disregard the sacrament of marriage openly, as well as a husband's claim to his wife's sexual fidelity, but they supported the couple when they suffered from fears of official surveillance and during their imprisonment.[108] Perhaps the couple believed that their discerning clientele and the domesticity of their transactional relationships would protect them from any judicial repercussions. However, many people, even children, living in their vicinity embraced their roles as voyeurs and sought to become contributors to the developing viceregal archive of sexual transgressions. I could argue that the couple carelessly publicized their domestic sex work and thus wrote themselves into the surviving documentation, but I think instead that their neighbors wanted to report their offenses as decipherable and legible to the religious authorities. However, exercising some restraint, the surrounding residents and the scribes they spoke to chose to name this as multiple simultaneous concubinage arrangements, not whoring.

In contrast to the voluminous legal and literary records for transactional sex in early-modern Spain, only fragmentary evidence records sex for sale in the first century of the Spanish viceroyalties. The cases presented in the second half of this chapter stress its domestic, even familial, context. This faint paper trail contrasts with the documenting of intensive brothel inspections and the prosecution of ruffians and clandestinas that took place in some parts of late-medieval and early-modern Iberia, a much more concerted effort to put in writing sexual control and official supervision. In the early decades of the sixteenth century, settlers first followed the fifteenth-century Spanish trend of founding legal brothels, but this pattern soon died off in favor of even older, perhaps more familiar, traditions such as family brothels, independent street solicitation, and liaisons organized by bawds or complicit husbands, often in a domestic setting. Within this urban, plebeian milieu, indigenous and Afro-descended bawds played a role in how sex was sold. All of the individuals mentioned in this chapter named and documented certain specific kinds of exchanges, both creating a New World sexual culture and writing the paperwork that would affect the archives of transactional sex for centuries to come.

2

From Whores to Prostitutes

I conjure you, gloomy Pluto, lord of the depths of hell; emperor of the court of the damned. . . . I, Celestina, am the best known of those who summon you, I conjure you . . . through the powerful serpents' venom from which this oil was compounded, and with which I anoint this thread. Come in all haste to obey my will, wrap yourself within its loops. . . .

I have everything anyone might want. Because wherever my voice is heard, I want to be prepared to set out my bait and set things in motion on my first visit.

Put your arms around each other and kiss, for I have nothing left but to enjoy watching. As long as you are at table, everything from the waist up is allowed. When you move away from it, I will set no limits because the King sets none.[1]

Before royal decrees mandated brothel closures, the fictional Celestina did it all: consulting women on their beauty regimes, running a brothel where she entertained many couples, and weaving seductive spells into ensorcelled thread, leading lovers to their tragic ends. Her powers revolved around her constant and persuasive talk, her use of dark magical conjurations, and the fact that the crown had not yet made selling sex illegal. This chapter is about how words eventually destroyed alcahuetas such as Celestina, as well as the new terminology for (and thus status of) public women, sometimes known as whores. During the seventeenth century, a significant shift took place in the conceptual history of transactional sex in the Iberian world, a movement toward the creation of the diseased, criminalized, and/or victimized prostitute, who, by the early eighteenth century, began to fill the shoes of the still-working sinful and immoral whore. However, this wording and the new kinds scribal seductions that it generated did not end the exchange of sex for cash, as rich and powerful men (as well as their poorer fellow clients) continued to want it and willingly pay for it. In fact, transforming women from morally corrupt and sinning whores to pity-inducing prostitutes may have even increased their eroticism for their wealthy patrons and the scribes who described them (who may have been at times one and the same person).

Throughout the seventeenth century, the traditional vocabulary of procuring (alcahueta, consentidora) predominates in the available cases, although the word *puta* also appears both in marriage disputes and Holy Office investigations, especially when the scribes wrote the precise wording of insults exchanged between litigants.[2] When the authorities of this era assume a more elevated tone in their pronouncements, they used vaguer terminology such as "worldly women *[mujeres mundanas]*" or "women who lead evil lives."[3] A transition occurred when the term *prostitute*, after 1700, started to become a common label applied with disdain and censure or pity and objectification. The new use of this word explicitly signified trading money for services and put a greater emphasis on greed for rewards, or victimization by a panderer, while both the older and ongoing use of "whore" more vaguely referred (and refers) to a woman with a publicly sexual reputation, who may or may not make an income off her sex acts.[4]

Although bilingual Spanish dictionaries mentioned the word *prostituir* and its translations into French, Italian, German, and English, dating back to the early seventeenth century, the words *prostituta* and *prostitución* do not appear in a Spanish monolingual dictionary until the end of the eighteenth century. Before then, French/Spanish bilingual dictionaries translate prostitution simply as *abandonnement*. The English translation offered is "debauched, exposed to common life." In 1783, the Spanish definition takes on a more sexual tone: "abandoned to all types of lewdness and sensuality." In 1788, Esteban de Terreros y Pando defines it as "abandonment to licentious lewdness, infamy," hearkening back to the traditional understanding of a whore. His definition for *prostituta* includes references to medieval terms such as "ramera [whore]," as well as the general idea of a prostitute as a lost or public woman, but he also significantly brings greed into the picture, mentioning "intereses" or gain.[5] Terreros y Pando also explains *prostituir* as a metaphorical insult in reference to corrupt, bribable judges or authors.

Coinciding with the gradual increase in the use of the term *prostitution* was the slow decline in stature of the medieval bawd. While the fourteenth-century Ruiz presented Trotaconventos (aka "Good Love"—a name that also had a religious resonance in this work) as an appealing, helpful, and funny character (chapter 1), in contrast, Celestina's erotic black magic caused both murder and suicide in Fernando de Rojas's 1499 work entitled *Tragicomedia de Calisto y Melibea*.[6] Rojas may have interpreted such a loquacious woman who operated in the public sphere as a horrifying contrast to the moral female, who ideally closed herself off in both her sex and her speech.[7] Every character in the *Tragicomedy* understood Celestina as a slick talker who could trick innocent women into committing sinful acts. The fact that she talked for a living defined Celestina as a disgraced woman and a danger to others. With his tale of Celestina's negative influence on the lives of her clients, Rojas warns readers to avoid old women who profit from their immense experience in the sexual realm. While she communicated great confidence in her function, other characters viewed her as notorious and infamous, or worse, a greedy witch who deserved a brutal, violent death.

Although she causes multiple tragedies, this early-modern bawd still speaks at times as a very sympathetic character. Celestina's soliloquies and persuasive discussions with her clients reveal her understanding of the cruel nature of love and sexual desire in her historic context. Humans crave sex like beasts, according to Celestina, and without a mediator's help, they would have no way to verbalize and thus satisfy their needs. She organizes sexual encounters in a perilous setting where people lose their health to unrequited passions and speak their affections and emotions painfully, because no licit sexual communication or fulfillment exists. Despite her proud self-assertions, Celestina also plaintively explains that, without inherited wealth or land, plotting affairs and selling potions provide her with the only way that she can earn an income.[8]

In this chapter, investigations of three Mexico City *celestinas* document both their traditional association with sorcery and the highly domestic and distinctly African and indigenous culture of seventeenth-century transactional sex. Framed by these cases in Mexico City, here I also discuss King Phillip IV's two decrees that banned brothels in his territories, tracing the seventeenth-century transition from an open and widespread tolerance of bawds and brothels to the gradual criminalization of the occupation that became known, by the early eighteenth century, as "prostitution." In this era, the crown forbade brothels, but this mandate was an empty rhetorical gesture with no practical application within the Mexican criminal justice system. Although Phillip IV and his advisors inscribed brothels and public women as important and widespread moral concerns, their judicial functionaries in the New World did not carry through on the mandates with effective policing and suppression. Why would they, when many of them wanted to continue to patronize these women? In response to these hidden scribal seductions, the archives of transactional sex did not expand in the seventeenth century. If they did, they have since disappeared.

Arguably, crown regulations created a paradoxical juridical quagmire for vice-regal judicial officials. Sanctions against transactional sex led to sparser documentation, which did not increase until well into the eighteenth century, an era when crown reformers prized written reports and statistics. To acknowledge that sex for sale still existed, which would happen if anyone started a secular court case against a brothel manager, meant that local law enforcement had to admit that, up to that point, it had disregarded the king's decrees. Additionally, a case from 1621 demonstrates that high-ranking bureaucrats comprised the brothels' key clientele. Within the complicated legal setting of overlapping imperial jurisdictions, hypocrisy, and subjects' need to show their obedience to the crown, instead of more criminal cases against brothels, a new group of royal functionaries found their niche in the indirect prosecution of bawds for African- and indigenous-influenced sorcery, a goal that fit more comfortably within the imperial mindset than writing limitations on male sexual proclivities. The American Holy Office Tribunal of the Spanish Inquisition investigated the popular practice of love magic, fueled by a European perception of indigenous and African colonial subjects as allied with the devil, and as potential sexual corrupters of Spanish women. In an urban, plebeian context, the authorities also worried about how the practice of seventeenth-century erotic magic disregarded official viceregal racial identities by bringing women together to cooperate in their goals of finding well-paying male patrons.[9]

Rojas's multitalented literary creation anticipated two bawds prosecuted by the Mexican tribunal of the Holy Office: Isabel de San Miguel, a procuress, con artist, and love-magic practitioner investigated by the Mexico City Inquisition tribunal in 1617; and the early-eighteenth-century innkeeper Doña Nicolasa de Guzman, who is discussed at the end of this chapter. These cases demonstrate both continuities and change over time in the archives of transactional sex. Both bawds found themselves involved in a Holy Office case due to their erotic magic rituals. Because their jurisdiction concerned heretical religious practices as opposed to lesser moral "sin-crimes" such as adultery, the inquisitors did not take a great interest in the details of the affairs that these women promoted but focused instead on the words, rituals, and objects that they used to influence the sex lives of their clientele. The inquisitors demonstrated an almost anthropological curiosity in recording spells that suggested the presence of African or indigenous healing practices.[10] Due to this scrutiny of their presumed non-European enchantments, Guzman and San Miguel faced Holy Office prosecution for sorcery not bawdry, despite the continuing illegality of procuring and, in the later case, the crown's decrees prohibiting brothels and establishing the policing of public women. Popular erotic rituals refused to die out, even as the vocabulary for transactional sex began to transform into more familiar criminalizing terms. Although her magical practices represented a Mexican version of Celestina's late-medieval swindles and tricks, Doña Nicolasa de Guzman also managed a very modern scam, making money off of what the authorities of the era had just begun to label "prostitution." After the criminalization of brothels, which only added to the longstanding disdain for bawds, the eighteenth-century inquisitors had more sympathy for Guzman's employees, who assumed a stance as victims in the written records.

A 1617 Holy Office investigation made an explicit connection between sorcery and earning money off sex with men.[11] A constable denounced Isabel de San Miguel, also known as Isabel Guixarro, a mestiza, to the inquisitors as a bawd and a trickster or *embustera,* who used magic to drive men mad with irrational desire for certain women. Witnesses labeled San Miguel as a renowned alcahueta, although they did not refer to her business as a brothel. It certainly seemed like it had this function: men confessed that they gathered at her house to socialize and eat with a variety of women before outings to the theater.[12] As well as offering this congenial hospitality, San Miguel organized and helped maintain illicit sexual relationships. Once she made the male partners smitten through her sorcery, San Miguel would offer the couples food, drink, and a bed in her house, hiding their affairs.

San Miguel derived her income from the relationships that she masterminded. As a poor woman who did not live with her working-class husband, she had already suffered imprisonment, banishment, and lashings at the hands of secular justice.[13] All of this probably resulted from her lack of elite clientele—she had no one to effectively protect her from judicial repercussions. The Holy Office inquiry questioned two of her humble female employees: two slaves, the thirty-year-old black woman Gerónima de Mendoza and the thirty-three-year-old mulatta Francisca Negrete. These women did not live with the bawd but with their own respective masters. Allegedly, San Miguel commanded Negrete to seek out men at various houses in order to seduce them into "desiring her" and rewarding her. San Miguel also organized a relationship between Mendoza and her nephew, a blacksmith. Her matchmaking efforts took place after San Miguel complained to her nephew about her dire poverty.[14]

When the affair between the blacksmith and Mendoza broke up, the enslaved woman felt very melancholic and jealous of her ex-lover's new companion. After consulting with another sorceress who lived in the barrio of Santiago Tlatelolco, San Miguel tried to sell Mendoza a spell to seduce the blacksmith again. The spell involved using a *tecomate* or jug filled with clean water in Isabel's room. The two women made cuts in each corner of the room with a knife and extracted some dirt, which they placed in the tecomate. San Miguel took a small insect or reptile from her breast and mixed it with some dust or dried herbs and stirred the mixture inside the tecomate. She then raised the jug to her ceiling then down to her floor, and beat it with her hands. After carrying out this ritual, the bawd ordered Mendoza to bathe her genitals and underarms with the mixture. San Miguel also directed her to mix it into her lover's hot chocolate. The blacksmith nephew confirmed that his aunt commonly did this kind of spell as part of her work to bring lovers together in her house. The inquisitors ordered San Miguel to jail and questioned her, but the case record ends at this point, with the accused affirming her innocence. This case demonstrates the popularity of indigenous spells and the diverse sexual milieu where Afro-descended women worked for Spanish or possibly mestiza bawds to have affairs with plebeian men. At this moment, written documentation of transactional sex survives only due to its affiliation with non-European magic and the inquisitors' desire to record such practices.

Another case also highlights a multiracial milieu for transactional sex and the domestic, intimate tone that prevailed in the sixteenth century. Just two years before the royal decree that banned brothels, a Spanish woman ran a kind of early-modern love hotel or house of assignation in Mexico City. In this case, aided by her rich and powerful clientele, the bawd, matchmaker, and innkeeper Ana Bautista received quite a lenient judgment after an investigation by the archdiocesan court for the crimes of procuring and concubinage.[15] Like Catalina García in chapter 1, Bautista enjoyed the support of men who were very likely her clients and eager to defend her excellent character in court. This trial reveals that negotiated sexual philandering among both men and women extended far into the highest ranks of Spanish society, even involving viceregal courtiers, and that a respectable woman might have success as a bawd while retaining her good reputation, aided by elite male protection.

As the forty-five-year-old widow of a high court attorney *(procurador)*, Bautista enjoyed long-term social contact across viceregal race and class hierarchies. She owned two different entertainment/hospitality venues and reportedly had at least two lovers since becoming a widow. Despite her husband's elevated bureaucratic rank, she did not enjoy the honorific title *doña* and thus came from plebeian origins. Although labeled a Spaniard in the trial records, Bautista in the past had owned a lodging house/pulquería known as the *"meson de la negra,"* or the "black woman's inn," conveniently located adjacent to the house of female seclusion on the Calle de Jesus de la Penitencia.[16] The name of her business suggests that her nonwhite ancestry played a role in her inability to attain the status of doña. At the time of her arrest, Bautista operated a different inn/pulquería near Mexico City's slaughterhouse. At both locations, she convinced several women to have affairs with her guests and provided them with the food and lodgings that they needed to maintain their illicit relationships.[17] Bautista was clearly an excellent business-woman and knew how to manipulate her patrons' support to protect her social and legal status at a level far above the efforts of her sixteenth-century predecessor Cat-alina García. However, neither of these women appears to have suffered extreme poverty, and both worked hard to cushion themselves with wealth and prosperity.[18]

Bautista procured for a wide range of men and women, allegedly persuading them into illicit acts that they would not have committed without her efforts. Wit-nesses listed a total of thirteen women and seventeen men, including widows and married and single individuals, who formed relationships due to her machinations and found an oasis for their affairs in her hospitable establishments. The hostess and bawd frequently coordinated liaisons between both male and female guests in her lodgings, both for residents or as a way to bring in more income in room rent-als, food consumption, and, of course, *pulque*. When she suffered prosecution for her illegal sale of alcohol, one of her clients, an alguacil (a law enforcement func-tionary), protected her while continuing his affair with a married woman. If the couples argued or fought, Bautista counseled them to return to reunite peacefully and continue their liaisons. She received gifts, services, money, and protection for her bawdry and from her own lovers, one of whom confessed that he wasted a "great quantity of gold pesos" on her.[19]

During her trial process, the inquisitors confiscated and inventoried her belong-ings, which was standard procedure for the tribunal and was how this institution funded itself. Although Bautista did not possess a huge number of goods, her rooms in the *calle de la carnicería mayor* had quite a luxurious feel, as did her dress. This was appropriate for a woman who ran a successful "casa publica" or brothel hosting wealthy men, even if these royal officials and their servants claimed to live there only as legitimate boarders.[20] Brothel-managers usually decorated their businesses to cater to at least the material standards of their intended clientele, if not with greater opulence than these men enjoyed in their own homes, in order to create and maintain an environment of fantasy and pleasure.[21] Appropriate domestic comfort in this era required religious art, imports from Asia, and furniture or bedding that offered places for guests to sit or lie down. Bautista decorated her lodgings with numerous religious *retablos,* chairs, cushions (including nine made of "Chinese velvet"), and a gilded wooden bed with a canopy. All of her furnishings suggest the bawd's ability to host several seated or lounging guests in relaxing comfort, especially in this era when many did not own a bed. Her clothes were all of imported fabrics in shades of black and brown, and she wore an elaborate black and gold velvet mantilla. Bautista's accusers testified that her lovers gave her gifts of clothing as well as money.

Married men and women committing adultery had a safe meeting place in Bautista's comfortable rooms, and some, including the bawd herself, enjoyed long-term illicit relationships. Most of her clients were labeled Spaniards, but she also procured lovers for two mulatas (both of whom were her servants and had affairs with Spanish men, including a cleric), a mulatto man, and a mestizo man. Over a period of time, Bautista's male clients ranged from laborers to priests and royal bureaucrats.[22]

Her elite clientele mitigated Bautista's treatment during both her trial and sentencing. Instead of imprisonment during the trial, she endured only house arrest.[23] Despite the fact that Bautista herself had lovers, her defense formulated a case that solidified her reputation as an honest, secluded, and devoutly Christian innkeeper who made a small income by providing room and board for important, honorable men, even up to the level of an associate of the viceroy, the Marquis de Guadalcazar.[24] The fact that she had lodgers suggested that she could easily make money as a moral landlady, with no need to procure for her boarders. According to statements in defense of her character, including from an official affiliated with the local high court *(audiencia),* her accuser nursed a violent passion for her that led to attempts to seduce her, break into her house, shame her and her guests by calling Bautista a "whore [puta]" and her guests "*cornudos* [cuckolds]," and finally bring her up on charges.[25]

The bawd and her defense team reformulated her bad reputation into a respectable one and created a victim out of an alleged evildoer in order to gain paternalistic sympathy from the judges.[26] Bautista denied all sexual misdeeds, and several useful witnesses, including the high court official, a notary, and two friars, backed up her claims to innocence. As a result of this appropriate script with approved

characters for the judicial theater, the court absolved her of all accusations, requesting only that she sever all ties and contact with her alleged current lover.[27] This
lenient outcome symbolizes the general presuppression viceregal tolerance for
bawds and brothels. Closing brothels clearly clashed with viceregal popular practices, necessitating the erasure of bawds like Bautista from the surviving records
until the late eighteenth century.

CRIMINALIZING BROTHELS

In 1623, Phillip IV (1621–1665) issued a royal decree to shut all brothels in his entire
empire, from Spain to the Americas. This proclamation did little to curb sexual
commerce. In fact, brothel closure only encouraged more sex work in the streets,
taverns, or private homes, but with even less judicial control and regulation.[28]
After the 1623 decree and another crown mandate seeking to enclose "worldly
women" in 1661, the identities of so-called "public" women in Spanish America
took on an increasing duality, as did this society's approach to transactional sex
overall. Brothel closure meant that sex for sale became an ever more open secret, a
very common illicit act, but something that crown bureaucrats could not admit
happened as a regular part of daily life. Regardless of the royal decrees, most
unmarried women still needed male financial assistance to survive and prosper.
They continued to support themselves by exchanging sex acts and extended sexual
relationships for money and gifts from men. In the late seventeenth and eighteenth
centuries, regulation and illegality created opportunities for many women to pur-
sue "kept woman" relationship status, sometimes with the help of erotic magic.
Men, of course including various authorities, benefited from this illicit practice,
and thus it remained undocumented.

Until after the mid-sixteenth century, no one debated public brothels' legality or
suggested closing them. They generated a large income for municipalities in Spain,
and some of this profit funded charitable Catholic institutions.[29] Hints of future
repression emerge in the 1560s, when Phillip II began to mandate stricter sanctions
against bawds and ruffians, which led to their prosecution in New Spain, under the
jurisdiction of the archbishop of Mexico (chapter 1). However, enforcing laws
against independent procurers might have served not to suppress selling sex
in general but instead to protect the licit income of crown or municipal brothels.
The tide began to turn definitively against legal brothels when devastating syphilis
outbreaks inspired preachers and clerics to interpret this plague as a divine punishment for lechery. Iberians understood syphilis as a new sexually transmitted
disease in the late fifteenth century. It spread rampantly in the context of the Italian
wars (where men and women of various nations gathered for both battles and sex)
in the 1490s and continued to debilitate armies over the course of the sixteenth
century and beyond.[30]

Spanish brothels enjoyed their greatest prosperity in the mid-sixteenth century, but the ongoing incidence of syphilis led Phillip II to compose and enforce more intrusive regulations in 1570.[31] After this point, on some kind of regular basis, brothel workers endured periodic medical inspections and had to leave the brothel for treatment if doctors found any trace of the pox. These reforms also warned against clandestine whores as destructive disease vectors, but this condemnation did not limit their clientele. Instead, by the late sixteenth century, working outside the brothel allowed elite concubines to avoid crown-mandated venereal-disease inspections.[32] Despite increasing regulations, most men apparently did not understand how they might catch syphilis. And even if rudimentary condoms existed in this era, they would have been very expensive for many public women. Instead of fearing syphilis, as clerics suggested, clients took a blasé attitude toward the physical and mental devastation that this disease could cause.[33] A late-fifteenth-century doctor warned that men could safely "sleep with a sick woman" if she only had *bubas* (sores and rashes) in her mouth, as long as he did not kiss her. Some courtly, libertine men even bragged about their sores, rejecting any notion of shame for this alleged divine punishment for their sins. A humorous poem observed that all men, even friars, prelates, and the king, enjoyed membership in the "brotherhood of bubas."[34] In the 1520s, observers still spoke of La Lozana's beauty, and she continued to attract many paying lovers, despite the fact that "she couldn't wear glasses if she wanted to" because "the pox" had "eaten away part of her nose."[35]

Cognizant of syphilis's rampant spread, Spanish municipalities began founding hospitals to treat and quarantine syphilitics by the early sixteenth century. Mexico City had an institution that treated syphilitics by 1539, called the Hospital del Amor de Dios, although no archives record if the viceroyalties mandated health inspections among those marked as selling sex.[36] In Valencia, Spain, around one hundred people a year entered the syphilis hospital. Later, the annual total increased to several hundred men and women. By the end of the century, three or four individuals slept in every available bed.[37] The inmates were not all brothel workers, but only these women had to endure exams due to their occupation. Seville also converted a plague hospital to a "hospital de bubas" in 1586.[38]

As syphilis provoked fears of divine retribution, Jesuit preachers started to speak against the corruptive influences of brothels in Seville. First, the Jesuits demanded the closure of Granada's brothel, and then they turned their attention to Seville. They rejected the historic justification of legal brothels as a "lesser evil" that prevented widespread sodomy or adultery.[39] Jesuits began "invading" the Seville brothel after 1616, and their desire to preach sermons in these legal businesses greatly disrupted the trade. Enthusiasm increased for "reforming" women, and clerical moralizers heartily embraced a familiar discourse of female brothel workers as victims in desperate need of redemption. This rhetoric also led to the opening of homes for so-called "repentant" women. Seville's city government devoted a great deal of time and effort to Jesuit proposals to reform the brothels, but by 1619, with the proclamation of strict new regulations, the brothel had declined precipitously. Women chose to abandon it for clandestine work, in a conscious choice to avoid the proposed frequent medical exams, sermons, and forced religious holidays that prevented them from earning a living.[40] By 1620, only eighteen women lived in Seville's once prosperous and large brothel. The fate of Seville's brothel may have had an influence on the almost invisible American brothels, as most Spanish immigrants passed through or spent time in this port.

Philip IV's motivation for decreeing brothel closure derived from the overpowering influence of his favorite, the Count Duke of Olivares, the members of the Jesuit order, as well as writers who argued that legal whoring opened the door to the devil's influence and who held that earthly law must acknowledge divine law and not promote sin.[41] Some Spaniards expressed an understanding of the reign of his father, Philip III (1578–1621), as an era of moral laxity and felt that Spain would prosper if the land returned to a time that they perceived as more virtuous.[42] In response to these pressures, on February 10, 1623, the young king made the following ruling:

> Prohibition of brothels and public houses of women in all the towns of these kingdoms. We order and command, that from here forward, that in no villa, or settlement in these kingdoms, will be allowed or permitted, a brothel or public house, where women earn money with their bodies . . . we command that all be closed.[43]

The king charged his counselors and judicial officials to take particular care to carry out this order, with the threat of losing their offices and paying substantial fines. Many believed that in practice the criminalization of brothels increased social chaos. In 1631, Seville's municipal authorities observed that their city suffered from far more street violence and disorder since the 1623 decree. They begged the king to allow a legal brothel again.[44]

Mourned and mocked in songs and poems, including Francisco de Quevedo's "Feelings of a *jaque* on the closing of the brothel," this ruling did not slow down transactional sex. Instead, public women appeared ever more frequently on the streets, and some observers claimed that *several hundred* brothels remained open in Madrid.[45] These women provided ongoing inspiration for the poems, novellas, and plays composed by literary masters including Cervantes, Ruiz de Alarcon, and Lope de Vega, as well as anonymous songs. Travelers to Spain in the seventeenth century described a widespread disregard for marriage and monogamy and believed that Madrid hosted thirty thousand public women, more than any other city in the world.[46]

Late in life, Philip IV noticed that his mandates had not decreased the number of "lost women" in his kingdoms. In 1661, he discerned that whores proliferated in the streets, plazas, and even up to the doors of his own palace. Their numbers "grew every day."[47] The king still believed that the lack of morals in his kingdoms caused his own personal misfortunes as well as national disasters. Both national and family calamities peaked around this time, with the death of two male heirs to the throne and the defeat of the Spanish army at Dunkirk. In desperation, Philip ordered law enforcement to identify the sexually active single women living in their jurisdictions, to visit their lodgings, and if the authorities found that they had no licit occupation, to incarcerate them in the women's jail.[48] Although these reforms coincided with the fact that Queen Isabel had a son late in 1661, ultimately Carlos II's profound mental and physical deficiencies ended the Spanish Hapsburg dynasty with his death in 1700. As an indication of the ongoing ineffectiveness of these decrees in terms of suppressing public women, Louis XIV's grandson, Philip V of Spain (1700–1724), repeated a very similar command in 1704: that officials should round up the "worldly women" who caused scandal in the public thoroughfares.[49] Regardless of the utter failure of these royal decrees in ending street solicitation and more private indoor transactional sex, the reforming and moralizing tone that the crown adopted reinforced efforts in cities and towns across the Spanish Empire to enclose women perceived as dangerously licentious. For example, in 1692, a new house for female seclusion and punishment opened in Mexico City. Its name, Santa Maria Magdalena, indicated its goal of enclosing public women.[50]

Seventeenth-century fears of scandal, social upheaval caused by immoral materialism, and marital infidelity—concerns that led to brothel closures, attempts to incarcerate public women, and royal decrees against "worldly women"—extended to every corner of the empire, even the remote outpost of the diocese of Guadalajara, New Spain. In this large territory, from the 1660s to the early eighteenth century, religious and secular authorities struggled with the same compulsion to enclose and suppress women's sexual activities. Repeated official pronouncements in these decades indicate the ineffectiveness of their efforts and why selling sex continued to have an ambiguous place in written documentation.

A new campaign began in 1664, when the president of the Guadalajara high court proposed a new prison to "punish women of scandalous life."[51] King Philip IV, with only months to live, rejected the petition. However, for the next two decades, high court officials and the bishop left a record of exchanges regarding their worries about "public sins [pecados publicos]," an oblique way of referring to the general toleration of adultery, concubinage, and transactional sex. In 1679, the high court asked for the cooperation of lower-level law enforcement to carry out the bishop's "remedies" to "avoid" public sins, in line with royal pronouncements on the ongoing issue.[52] In a suggestion eerily similar to twenty-first–century rehabilitative programs, the bishop proposed inaugurating a wool- and cotton-weaving workshop or even sending the poor to work as day laborers in the countryside, to "remedy the needs" of the multitude of poverty-stricken men and women and prevent their exposure to "vice." On a tour of inspection, Bishop Juan de Santiago de León Garabito reported that the perceived problem of "public sins" extended as far north as Sonora and Zacatecas, but his observations had little effect. Decades later, the bishop of Durango begged permission to open a house of reclusion due to the "high number of women found in this city that go around lost and in scandalous and pitiful nudity."[53] As the official complaints and suggestions for workhouses continued, the high court tried with little success to suppress the "bad life" of four sisters known as "Las Zayuletas." Several times in the 1680s, the justices banished these women from the city and tried to force them back to their husbands, their mother, or any "honorable house," where they would live "honestly and secluded," but failed to prevent Las Zayuletas from promenading around Guadalajara at odd hours of the night with married men. The sisters ignored orders of banishment.[54] This attempted crackdown coincided with a similarly ineffective investigation of the lives of over two dozen courtesans in Mexico City, who also evaded banishment, through their lovers' protection and their successful appeal to the authorities' patronage (chapter 4). Of course, from the 1670s to the 1690s, elite men living in sin (including an important functionary of the Guadalajara high court itself) also avoided repercussions, much to the frustration of the judiciary and the bishop.[55]

Shortly after these attempts at reform in the peripheries of New Spain, a woman called Doña Nicolasa de Guzman continued the medieval tradition of employing sorcery to lure men into paying for sex, leading to a Mexico City Holy Office investigation in 1711 that labeled her an *"alcahueta supersticiosa* [superstitious bawd]."[56] Again, a court run by clerics investigated what the Siete Partidas viewed as a criminal offense, indicating the ongoing confusion of sin and secular justice. This transitional case mixes the older understanding of celestinas and their "simple superstitious" practices with hints of modern "prostitution," an early use of this word in Mexican archives.[57] However, the inquisitors did not represent Guzman's employees (the so-called prostitutes) as greedy or criminal but, instead, following medieval understandings of the root of the transgression, focused on defaming the procuress as nefarious, impious, lewd, and deceptive.[58]

Tipped off by a girl in her employ who complained to secular law enforcement, the inquisitors accused Guzman of tricking women into "the impious occupation of earning their living with the prostitution and sale of their bodies."[59] Doña Nicolasa de Guzman operated a sophisticated mediation organization, in which she managed and housed these women and girls, but she did not actually directly arrange or escort them to their sexual liaisons. Not surprisingly, this clever bawd did not testify in the surviving preliminary Holy Office investigation, but four women described her procuring methods in detail, and their statements reveal the accused's high status and organizational skills. Guzman cooperated in her schemes with two colleagues: another alleged Spaniard known as "Chomba," and a woman called "La India

Ángela," apparently Doña Nicolasa's mother.[60] Although one witness, a young mid-wife, testified that Doña Nicolasa had a good reputation and that her painter husband devoutly participated in the Third Order of Saint Augustine, other testimonies portray her as a bawd who targeted vulnerable teenage runaways.[61]

Statements made by a fifteen-year-old orphan named Bernarda de Lara and her relatives reveal that Doña Nicolasa de Guzman balanced her respectable marriage to a pious man and her reputation as a procuress, even to the extent that she ran a kind of premodern outcall business. Young women willingly came to Guzman's house to escape their homes. Bernarda and her young relative Gertrudis explained that Bernarda had come from the countryside to Mexico City and moved in with Gertrudis's mother after the death of her own mother when Bernarda was about ten years old. Suffering as a charity case in her relatives' house, the orphaned Bernarda ran away one night after receiving a physical punishment from Gertrudis's mother. Bernarda made the choice to run to Doña Nicolasa's house, perhaps with full knowledge of how Guzman made her income, rather than endure more bad treatment from her relatives. After a month, Doña Nicolasa sent her to live with Chomba, who carried out the plan for Bernarda's violent defloration by the governor of the palace guard, an exchange worth three hundred pesos. Guzman and Chomba negotiated the exchange and arranged for Bernarda (accompanied by Chomba) to meet a *forlón* (a closed carriage with four seats; a luxurious conveyance in this era) one afternoon just before siesta. This lavish vehicle transported her to her deflowerer's bedroom, where the afternoon sex act with Bernarda cost him the price of an orphan's dowry, an exchange that highlights the monetization of virginity and marriage that permeated this society. Bernarda then returned to Doña Nicolasa's house to live with other young women also sent out to "earn their income with their bodies," which they did every night and some days.[62]

Spanish law traditionally adjudicated severe punishments for inducing virgins or otherwise honest women into whoring (chapter 1), but the early-eighteenth-century Mexican inquisitors did not follow up on this secular crime, instead interrogating the witnesses to discuss Doña Nicolasa de Guzman's use of love magic. Their accounts record that Guzman called on her mother, La India Ángela, to give powders to young women so that "men would desire them," as well as to "stupefy" their husbands so that married women could have affairs. Guzman gave the girls who lived in her house a yellow powder to carry with them at all times, tucked into their stockings. She also had them use incense smoke on their hands and faces for the same purpose. Bernarda received a small bag that Guzman told her to hide in her stockings so she could enchant men to desire her. The inquisitors found it to contain a few roots of an unknown plant.[63] Bernarda declared that she did not believe in the power of the bag of roots to attract men because she sometimes forgot to wear the stockings that contained it on her assignations with men. Presumably, this had no effect on their sexual interest in her.

While indulging in these arcane practices, Doña Nicolasa de Guzman managed a lucrative, efficient business, housing young women who had brief sexual encounters with men, not the more longstanding relationships that the previously discussed bawds organized with their clients. In a typically entrepreneurial American fashion of combining Old and New World practices, she took on the role of the traditional Spanish go-between, mixing indigenous magic and a business sense for negotiating sexual transactions for the richest and most powerful bidders. No record exists for Guzman's reactions to the accusations or for her defense or sentencing. The inquisitors may very well have dropped both of the cases involving Mexican bawds who used erotic magic, after these brief initial investigations, because they did not view these practices as worthy of too much investigatory attention or punitive action. But apparently, they saw value in recording indigenous and African-influenced love-magic practices. The young women who chose to live and work with her suffered no penalties or written censure whatsoever. Instead, the clerical judges recorded them as pitiful, vulnerable victims of Guzman's cons. They labeled their occupation "prostitution," but they did not treat them as criminals, at least not yet.

3

Respectable Mistresses

After you've won by urgent plea
the right to tarnish her good name,
you still expect her to behave—
you, that coaxed her into shame.

You batter her resistance down
and then, all righteousness, proclaim
that feminine frivolity,
not your persistence, is to blame.

Or which is more to be blamed—
Though both will have cause for chagrin:
the woman who sins for money
or the man who pays money to sin?[1]

Sor Juana Inez de la Cruz's poem observes the insincerity of late-seventeenth-century criticisms of transactional sex. Scribes recorded this late-baroque duplicity in their files when investigating women who asserted their "good name[s]" as they faced accusations of "feminine frivolity." Sor Juana eloquently criticizes the hypocrisy of male moralizing. But other than her voice, we do not know if and how other women, the women she discusses as the victims of the *hombres necios*, wrote themselves into this sexually hypocritical milieu—until we read the stories of the elusive kept women of the eighteenth century.

The inscription of certain doñas into the archives began when observant neighbors complained to officials about them. In response, the authorities listened and took notes as the plaintiffs told elaborate tales of their innocence, with supporting evidence added by favorable witnesses. The accused fashioned themselves as modest and reputable workingwomen or even pitiable ladies, making a living in decent jobs as servants to elite men or living at home in seclusion with their families. But servitude or paltry inheritances could not support their spending habits, nor did working as cigarette rollers.[2] Instead, they took advantage of the petty favors available from soldiers or salaried men or even more elite patrons, if possible. Their alleged sexual transactions and longer-term relationships took place inside homes, with funding for their housing provided by their clients. They clung to a vestige of recogimiento and reacted to denunciations by seducing the scribes into exploring their delicately balanced lives in depth to counter the writing of oral gossip about their immorality and scandal.

These women are the most ambiguous of any discussed in this book because they subtly and effectively integrated themselves into the lives of their clientele and, thus, had the patronage necessary to make their transgressions and disreputable labels illegible or even invisible in the written records of transactional sex. Church and state bureaucrats, along with low-ranking military officers, all generally Spaniards, patronized certain women as potential or real sex partners. These doñas did not entertain plebeian men and thus operated more like medieval and early-modern Spanish clandestinas, as opposed to the whores in brothels or the surrounding taverns and inns. Reclusive mistresses did not solicit in public, but the fact that they have an archival presence at all proves that they roused local suspicions due to the heavy male traffic to their abodes or other circumstantial evidence.

Especially in the second half of the eighteenth century, the heavy caseload of busy Bourbon administrators lifted the veil that until this point obscured plebeian street-level sex, elite courtesans and concubines, and the women who worked in relative indoor comfort somewhere in the middle of those two extremes.[3] Each of these categories generated very different kinds of texts because women's actual experiences of transactional sex varied depending on whether they "had their own dwellings" or "lived under the control or protection of others."[4] This chapter and the next two show how sex for sale in the eighteenth century encompassed very broad levels of exchange, from streetwalkers to fashionable "kept mistresses . . . women of great style, wealth and influence, who could even prove to be a power in the land."[5] The women in this chapter fit in between these two extremes in terms of their paper trail: they generated less paperwork than loquacious, highly cultured courtesans, and more than illiterate plebeians whose words appear only briefly in the police dockets of the era.

Women of good reputation but without wealth or solid male protection took a social risk when they interacted with men other than the members of their families. They occupied an especially vulnerable position in terms of defending themselves against any threat to their precarious honor. Living for longer periods in their own houses or apartments, they endured more surveillance from nosy, jealous neighbors. They lacked the courtesans' ability to manipulate powerful patronage at the top of the viceregal hierarchy for judicial protection. They also could not afford the many months or even years of writing their own petitions to assert their good reputation in court. However, due to their class rank, these kept women could easily deny illicit activity and call on their overall respectable status when faced with accusations. Due to their very effective scribal seductions, they sometimes even escaped any judicial retribution whatsoever, despite their prying neighbors' censorious interventions.

CHANGES IN GENDERED INTERACTIONS IN THE EIGHTEENTH CENTURY AND THE TERMINOLOGY OF TRANSACTIONAL SEX

In the eighteenth century, "the idea of offending society [began] to replace the concept of offending God."[6] While sin, honor, and shame remained part of many juridical discussions of sex for sale, the values of social good became more and more important in the justification for why the courts needed to at least rhetorically control female sexuality. Christian discussions of the spread of sin still held sway, but the legal rhetoric more frequently invoked the theoretical entity of a state or body of citizens as the opposing mass that needed protection from the dangers of promiscuous women. Eighteenth-century legal reform sought to de-emphasize sin as the motivation for prosecuting nonmonogamous or nonmarital sex, opening up more opportunities for secular authorities to adjudicate over personal life. However, ecclesiastical courts and religious houses of seclusion continued to handle some cases. Some eighteenth-century cases dealing with sex work survive because their sexually focused adjudication confused church and state authorities who, at this point, had yet to clarify which judicial entity had jurisdiction over crimes that offended morality and were not viewed as crimes in traditional, crown legal traditions such as the Siete Partidas.[7]

The confused eighteenth-century reactions by church, state, and neighbors to sexually active women often derived from increased opportunities for permitted or at least tolerated socializing between the sexes. These new social spaces challenged official ideas of public order and permissible gender interaction. While previously, gender-mixed gatherings with music and drink roused suspicions of idolatry or even satanic Sabbaths, gradually plebeian and even some elite women openly attended fandangos, public dance schools, and other parties, including illegal gambling houses.[8] These new or expanding venues drew the attention of eighteenth-century reformers. Some bureaucrats hypocritically railed against all kinds of social settings where plebeian men and women might indiscriminately interact, even dance schools. While coed dance instruction had existed in the viceroyalties at least since Cortés's era, church and state made a clear distinction between the formal dance of courtly parties, the dances men and women performed on stage during plays or operas, and the scandalous—even heathen—dancing of the lower classes, especially Afro-descended subjects.[9] Parties called *jamaicas*, which included dancing, music, and drinking, became more of a concern for the Bourbon authorities, especially because by then it had become more common for private individuals to organize these events either at homes or businesses. They were no longer strictly held with the support and approval of church or state.[10] The Holy Office even went so far as to prohibit some plebeian dances.[11]

In the eighteenth century, a gender-mixed clientele attended *escuelas de danza* ("dance schools"; businesses that functioned along the lines of a modern dance club) nightly, raising the ire of those who viewed these venues as morally suspect. In 1779, three weeks before his death, Viceroy Antonio María Bucareli y Ursua issued a strict 10:00 p.m. curfew for men who visited dance schools.[12] Bucareli could not justify completely forbidding dances, as some operated in a completely licit fashion, but he believed that they needed some rules to govern the interactions between men and women in order to prevent scandal and disorder. The burden of enforcing this rule fell on the managers of the dance schools, who risked a penalty of four years in forced military service in a presidio if they ignored it. Even the musicians could serve six months in prison for disobeying the curfew. In a (pen) stroke of irony, the court notary who signed and recorded this document was none other than the most infamous paramour of the era, Joseph de Gorraez, a lover of Mexico City's most notorious courtesan and actress, Josepha Ordóñez (chapter 4).

As noted in the last chapter, changing terminology affected all public women in this era. Writing women as "prostitutes" textually differentiated them from domestic, private, moral woman.[13] In the New and Old Worlds, this use of the term *prostitute* coincided with the publication of guides that listed and classified women who claimed this occupation. These guides had both a literary and commercial function.[14] For example, a London headwaiter called Jack Harris composed and circulated *Harris's List of Covent Garden Ladies,* an up-to-date guide to local sex workers, detailing their rates, services, appearances, and attitudes. When men asked for "girls" in taverns or inns, the porter might supply them with the list for their perusal. Women paid for their entries/advertisements in *Harris's List* and possibly received some protection from Harris himself, who also worked as a panderer. Existing printed copies of the *List* date from 1788 to 1793, although it may have circulated from the 1740s. Parisians also had access to various guides of this kind, including alphabetical and geographically organized lists of public women. The French guides provided many anecdotes and titillating stories, placing them more in the genre of erotica, although the listings for bordellos took a more factual approach, specifying the categories of women that patrons might find at various brothels.[15]

In 1783, an anonymous author circulated a similar guide for Mexico City, entitled *Guía de Forasteros de México,* listing all of the "prostitute women of this city," a knowing mockery of the less salacious practical guides for visitors.[16] Most likely, this guide contained some of the same kinds of information found in Harris's guide. The author of the *Guía* might have purposefully imitated the London *List* or similar guides from other cities. The Mexico City version may have spread in an informal way for many years, as did *Harris's List*. But unlike London, Mexico City had a local tribunal of the Holy Office of the Spanish Inquisition, a court that took great interest in censoring literature in this era. Horrified by the obscenities contained within the guide and by the possible moral degradation it would cause among the young men of the city, the Holy Office frantically banned the *Guía* in hopes of confiscating all existing copies. Anyone in possession of or reading this book risked a fine of two hundred ducats and excommunication. The tribunal wiped out any copies of this book, so there is no way of knowing more about the women who appeared within its pages. Even without seeing a surviving exemplar, its existence indicates the proliferation of sex for sale in this era and the widespread interest men had in buying it, as well as a new print culture dedicated to promoting the libertine lifestyle. A select class of well-off men in Mexico City sought to imitate and recreate the continental libertinism fad so popular at this time.

Written publications about the demimonde may have familiarized eighteenth-century litigators with the vocabulary of transactional sex. Some parents even felt that they could blame their sons' crimes on the corrupting influence of "prostitutes," or vaguely referred to public women, as threatening family wealth and stability. In the Bourbon reforming context of greater state intervention in private life, these parents reached out to the authorities to protect their patrimonies. Even earlier, in 1713, a widowed mother came before the archbishop's court to accuse her son, a cleric in minor orders, of disappearing from the home for periods of time to waste family money on "women who live evil lives."[17] He stole money and important inheritance documents from her to pay for his libertine indulgences. The son's dissolute and irregular lifestyle led to violent fights with his mother. The young cleric deployed older terms to insult her, including calling her a whore. He disparaged her by using the words *ramera, puta,* and *amancebada.* In this case, vague references to illicit women simply provide the general context for the son's misbehavior, but in another example a mother tried to manipulate her own low regard for public women as an excuse for her son's misdeeds. In 1796, the widow María Guerrero begged for leniency for her imprisoned son, whom she claimed did nothing more than shout at and beat a "known worldly woman *[una mujer mundana conocida por tal]*" in front of several witnesses.[18] Guerrero did not believe that such acts deserved imprisonment and presented her son as quite respectable and as the source of financial stability in their family. The authorities objected, labeling him a drunk and vagrant gambler who deserved a sentence of forced labor.

Readily deploying these vague terms in litigation does not indicate necessarily an overall increase in sex work or even a greater popular disdain for it. Instead, the wider use of the word *prostitution* and its older synonyms suggests that litigators believed that judicial officials would pay attention to their claims if they verbally affiliated their adversaries with commercial sex. Derogatory terms entered the judicial records of personal disputes at all social levels, especially those raised in objection to proposed marriages or in the context of divorce cases. While the above petitions made by mothers used a vague, older vocabulary, a male petitioner labeled the potential wife of his adopted son a prostitute, in response to her efforts to carry out the young man's promises of marriage.[19] In this case, the father felt that the pregnant woman's defloration and breach-of-promise suit justified this label, probably due to her lowly indigenous status.

Husbands pronounced the word *prostitute* and its cognates, along with other classic misogynistic vocabulary, to portray their wives as incorrigible adulteresses before ecclesiastical judges in support of their petitions for divorce. Certain formulas dominate the records because mutual divorces could not happen in this era. One person had to accuse the other of serious infractions against the sacrament of marriage. The ecclesiastical courts would not agree to any kind of divorce if both partners had behaved badly.[20] Therefore, each petitioner for divorce, buffered by as many character witnesses as they could find, presented themselves as an innocent victim, while each defendant apparently luxuriated in a bath of pure immorality.

Across the viceroyalties, women filed the overwhelming majority of requests for divorce, but when the rare man decided to take this path, frequently he focused his evidence on his wife's sexual immorality.[21] Sometimes the plaintiffs used vague terms, but other times the petitioners felt that using the word *prostitute* would help their case. For example, in 1788, Alonso Gavidia accused his wife, Doña Ana María Sanchez (or Saenz) Revollo, of prostitution with "many friends," and she was placed in a house of seclusion. Doña Ana, allegedly a "daring" and "arrogant" woman, lived a scandalous and libertine way of life and refused to obey her husband or try to reconcile within the bonds of matrimony.[22] A representative of the archbishop of Michoacán objected to these accusations as nothing more than slander caused by their extreme marital discord.[23]

Depending on the kind of accusations made, in the eighteenth century, husbands' litigation dealing with the immoral lives of their wives came before either the secular or the ecclesiastical courts, and the result could be incarceration in a variety of different kinds of institutions.[24] Even when not specifically starting the divorce process, husbands who felt that they could not control their wives' sexual activity petitioned for their imprisonment in a house of reclusion or even jail. For example, the actions of Doña María Ignacia Zamora, who cohabitated openly with her lover, promenading on the street and in pulquerías, led to an order at her husband's request to send her to the Casa de la Misericordia.[25] In many cities, secular women's jails, maintained by municipal law enforcement, coexisted with religious institutions for incarcerating women. These two institutions blurred frequently—one woman in Cartagena ended up in the women's jail when she filed for divorce due to her husband's impotence.[26] Women accused of prostitution might also end up in a Magdalene house, with strict rules for their behavior and dress. The Jesuits ran one of these houses in Mexico City from 1730 to 1767.[27] These competing locations for incarceration show the confusion and conflict between church and state jurisdiction over female sexuality in the eighteenth century.[28]

WORDS AS WEAPONS AGAINST UPWARD MOBILITY

Described with the old-fashioned Latin word for whore (meretrix), a young woman named Ana "La Tafolla" faced the ire of several Queretaro clerics and other *hombres de bien* when Don Jacinto Rodríguez presumed to marry her.[29] In 1744, these men objected to the marriage, despite the fact that Rodríguez willingly entered it after a period of concubinage with La Tafolla, who had cared for him during his periods of illness. According to her detractors, La Tafolla, in her vaulting ambition for social climbing, attempted to leap over racial barriers.[30] This audacity provoked a vituperative denigration of her character. Due to words recorded in legal documentation, a respectable servant was transformed into a whore.

The initial objection that the witnesses had to La Tafolla was her racial lineage. Her mother, grandmother, and aunts all had the designation of mulatas and worked as servants in various houses. Only one witness mentioned La Tafolla's father, but that did not help her case because he was also a mulatto. At the very young age of nine months, her mother brought her to live and eventually work for a nun in the Santa Clara convent whose name was Madre Juana de Santo Domingo la Tafolla. During her several years as a servant to Madre Juana, everyone who knew Ana called her *"la morisca de la Tafolla."*[31] Simply granting a woman this kind of sobriquet signified her questionable moral status. In line with her disrespectful nickname, La Tafolla (along with the rest of her female relatives) dressed in *sayas* and headscarves, which the witnesses perceived as standard garb for mulata servants. La Tafolla allegedly walked around barefoot and took orders from Madre Juana. All of these observations confirmed that she occupied an inferior social and racial position to the Spaniard Rodríguez.

While it was socially problematic, none of the clerics implied that any moral stain followed La Tafolla through her racial lineage, as she allegedly was born legitimately and all of her relatives worked as trusted domestics.[32] Her own individual character inspired more verbal objections to her marriage with Rodríguez than did her racial designation. Witnesses portrayed her as an evil woman on account of her sexuality, although they also noted her greed and her disruption of gender hierarchies. Her corruption did not take place when she served the nun. As a teenager, her mother moved her to serve at a private house, where La Tafolla lost her virginity to a "certain subject," possibly the son of a vegetable seller. At this point, La Tafolla's biography became cloudier. She fled to Mexico City, and witnesses said that she notoriously "prostituted" herself from this point forward. The witnesses chose this up-to-date term to describe La Tafolla, but the case rhetoric also described her as a public woman and, as noted, a meretrix.[33] She may have returned to Queretaro not long after, living with her lover for a period. At some point later she came to live with Rodríguez as his public and acknowledged concubine, but allegedly she maintained several lovers simultaneously, whom "she would seduce to satiate her appetites."[34] Along the way she became pregnant and convinced Rodríguez that he was the father.

Prompted by leading questions, hostile witnesses agreed that La Tafolla had a boisterous, arrogant, dishonest, and daring character. To back up their otherwise unproven accusations of her sexual improprieties, the litigators depicted her with the classic character traits of a whore: "avarice, rapaciousness, vulgarity, volubility, and lewdness."[35] A known troublemaker, she disturbed the peace in Rodríguez's house, scandalizing everyone with her brazenness. In an especially disrespectful course of action, La Tafolla tried to reorganize the accepted statuses of various dependents within the household and on her lover's haciendas. She forced Rodríguez to sell a loyal, useful household slave to a sugar mill, which the witnesses viewed as a shameful and unjust act. An elderly mulatto man said that servants avoided her due to La Tafolla's "natural evil." One of the deponents even reported that everyone knew La Tafolla had dressed as a man, wearing a scarlet cape and carrying a walking stick.[36] This virulently imaginative narrative conjures up a threatening woman intent on emasculating Rodríguez. The petitioners and witnesses implied with their statements that marrying La Tafolla would disrupt the natural social order and accepted gender roles. To Rodríguez's peers, her public reputation for sexual promiscuity meant she was necessarily greedy, dishonest, and assertive.[37] Her undiminished sexual appetites, proven by suppositions that she still had lovers while living with Don Jacinto, negated his apparently charitable act of redeeming a prostitute, according to those who opposed the marriage.[38] However, with Rodríguez as her patron and protector, even the cruelest insults did not push La Tafolla out of her elevated status as the wife of an elite man. With a powerful man defending her, she successfully changed her status, despite the thousands of words written against her.

NEIGHBORLY CONFLICTS IN BOURBON MEXICO CITY

In the second half of the eighteenth century, viceregal justice selectively enforced the illegality of procuring, and of managing or working in brothels. Neighborhood or rivals' complaints sparked many inquiries, which ended up investigated by church or criminal courts. Morally suspect women often faced difficulties from prying neighbors when they lived in rooms rented in larger buildings hosting several families or in crowded streets packed with *accesorias*, or semitemporary living spaces. In eighteenth-century Cadiz, the term *mujer de accesoria* even became synonymous with public woman.[39] In Bourbon-era Quito, "often, publicly scandalous behaviors that had endured for years became of sudden interest to the city's magistracy," allowing neighbors to settle old, simmering feuds arguably due to a "new interest in sexualized bodies."[40] However, all of the accused women and their male visitors in the cases that follow vociferously denied their guilt, and they usually escaped any serious judicial repercussions. Due to their categorical denials, it is hard to determine if some accused women ran brothels or sold sex out of their rooms or not.

Neighbors might exaggerate their accusations in this era, labeling a mildly scandalous kept woman a prostitute, readily embracing this new term. Accusers also made accusations of procuring against the relatives of alleged whores, drawing from an older vocabulary with the use of terms such as *alcahuetas/es, consentidoras/es,* and *terceras/os.* These words caught the attention of the authorities because procuring remained a serious offense, especially for the Mexican church. The fate of the victims of the neighborly finger-pointing depended upon how they inscribed into the record their gendered vulnerability and social status, and the status of the witnesses whom they could organize to speak in their favor.

Two young Mexican unmarried women experienced two very different reactions from the courts in similar cases adjudicated in the last few decades of the century. In both cases, the young women converted accusations against them into an opportunity to effectively rewrite their reputations, even beyond clearing their names from their neighbors' gossip. The first young woman, a fifteen-year-old orphan and soltera (sexually active single woman) from Toluca called Juana del Castillo, described as a *guerita* (fair little girl) with a ragged (*"trapienta"*) appearance, lived in a crowded apartment house known as the *"casa del polvorista."*[41] The other tenants had several damning complaints about Castillo and her associates' activities in the building. Of course, the defendants denied everything and presented their lives as almost blameless, except for a few sins that they trivialized or claimed to deeply repent.

This story began when, at age thirteen, Castillo's mother died, so she went to work as a servant. According to her aunt Ana Lugarda de Cervantes, this grew tiresome to her, so Castillo moved to Mexico City to live with Ana and her husband, Joseph del Castillo, a shoemaker. Joseph, a forty-year-old *castizo,* had many male shoe purchasers coming and going from their lodgings. In describing Castillo's daily life, Cervantes, a *castiza,* claimed that the girl might sometimes pass the time by playing in the doorway of their building because she was still a *muchacha.* Castillo herself said that she spent most days in sewing at a table inside their room. On holidays, she went out to look for work as a servant.[42]

The family did not attempt to deny some of their morally suspect habits. A man named Agustín Ayala, age twenty-three, regularly visited for meals, so frequently that some neighbors thought he was Castillo's husband and Cervantes's son. It turned out that Cervantes had adopted Ayala when he was around seven years old. As an adult, the orphan Ayala worked at a *vinatería* but still liked to visit his adoptive parents. The family also did not deny that Cervantes and her husband, Joseph del Castillo, regularly drank heavily, especially on Mondays and Tuesdays.[43] In her initial audience with the authorities, Cervantes admitted that when they drank, the couple had shouting matches, but that they kept their fights discreet from the rest of the building by closing the door to their room.

It should come as no surprise that their neighbors took a very different view on this disruptive family. Because the building had an entranceway with rented rooms near it, and other rooms surrounding a patio, residents could observe the comings and goings of their fellow tenants and their visitors, as well as hear any loud conversations. A priest in the cathedral heard complaints that male visitors seemed to have suspicious dealings with the disreputable family, who often assaulted their neighbors' ears with scandalous words. Due to these complaints, the diocesan court sent out a notary to question the other tenants, all of whom called themselves Spaniards. Some used the titles *doña* and *don*, indicating social superiority to Castillo and her guardians.

The building's manager, a Spanish woman who lived near the doorway to the street, made the most damning accusations against the family after they had rented from her for less than two months. The *casera* testified that the *anciana* (forty-seven-year-old Cervantes, whose heavy drinking perhaps aged her) either stood in the doorway or went out with Castillo a few times during the day. Why did their landlady interpret these activities as actionable? Allegedly, a short time after their excursions, frequently men, even priests, would enter and visit Castillo privately with the door to their room shut. While Castillo interacted with the men alone, her "aunt" would stand outside, waiting for other men. This witness also heard shameless words exchanged, including that Cervantes called Castillo a "puta," but that Castillo hid this occupation from her "husband" Ayala because it was how she made her living.[44] According to this deponent, Cervantes's rude vocabulary proved that she acted as young Castillo's bawd. The other residents did not confess many details about Castillo and Cervantes's alleged solicitations. One witness admitted that Castillo stood in the doorway of the building all day long. The other testifiers either did not spend much time at home or had seen only one or two individuals enter the room after speaking with the accused women.[45]

Two of the witnesses made an unusual request after their statements. They asked that the court keep their testimonies secret due to their fear of the family's retribution against them. The deponents viewed the accused as shameless, violent people. They especially mentioned Cervantes as particularly threatening. These fears probably derived from Cervantes and her husband's frequent rowdy inebriation and Cervantes's loud objections against the neighbors' complaints to the archbishop.

Cervantes allegedly shouted outside of her room, for everyone to hear, that her neighbors were all a "bunch of whores," they did not know anything about Castillo and Ayala, and they could go to hell.[46] As the case continued, Cervantes still roamed free, hiding from the investigation and her accusers, so her former neighbors did not want to provoke her attention or possible revenge.

At first, the court seemed convinced that Cervantes transacted in her niece's sex acts in their own home. After a series of harsh interrogations of Castillo, Joseph del Castillo, and Ayala, a different story emerged. Cervantes apparently did nothing other than consent to an illicit relationship between her two wards. With many expressions of regret, Ayala finally admitted that he and Castillo had engaged in a sexual relationship for six months. Cervantes allegedly told him to hide their sexual activities from the court. Her advice to perjure themselves added significantly to her guilt as a mediator for their nonmarital sex. The couple assured the court that they had committed no other crimes. When questioned if Ayala paid her any money, Castillo denied it.[47] These confessions and pleas for mercy satisfied the court. In the opinion of their advocates and church justice, after a year in jail, all three deserved their freedom. Without much elaboration, Castillo's advocate noted that if she walked on the street with Cervantes as "meretrices," the young girl bore no blame for this offense. Joseph del Castillo also did not deserve further punishment because the relationship between the two young people had remained a secret. The court reprimanded him only for his drinking and shameless conversations with his wife.[48]

The family's activities remain very blurred and unreadable even after Castillo and Ayala admitted their relationship. First, why did Cervantes flee and hide so effectively if she were not guilty? Second, why did she and her husband lie, calling Castillo her niece when Ayala said that there were actually no blood ties between Castillo and her foster family? Castillo also called Joseph del Castillo her uncle throughout her statement. It is possible that the trio faked a family connection to hide a more shameful procuring arrangement. Third, Ayala mentioned that both male and female visitors to the family's rooms seemed very annoyed when he was there during their visits, so he usually left. Why would his presence disturb the visitors if they were just buying shoes? Last, what motivated the neighbors to complain and fear these tenants? Possibly they just disliked their drunk, noisy racket and wanted to get the unpleasant couple in trouble, but the claims of procuring seem very serious for such a minor conflict amongst neighbors. Their stated fear of the accused couple also stands out as very unusual and difficult to comprehend in light of the very mild resulting judgment against the accused. The truth behind Juana Castillo's case remains mysterious. Did she and her guardians commit any other crime than engaging in or consenting to nonmarital sex between two single young people? This case pits statements made by very talkative, spying neighbors and crudely garrulous defendants against childlike protests of innocence. Given the judiciary's habitual paternalism, it should come as no surprise that the little blond muchacha's story won this battle of words.

DOÑAS AND TRANSACTIONAL SEX

In 1792, a young lady named Doña María Guadalupe Rojas faced similar neighborly and official admonishments for her lucrative affairs with several men. Doña María's short life encompassed a dramatic spectrum ranging from convent boarding school to alleged prostitution with the collusion of her mother, Doña Teresa, before she reached the age of twenty.[49] Doña María entertained a series of from three to six patrons in her moderately successful career, and she also enjoyed the cultural and social events typical of her era. Despite her affairs, she benefited from a comfortable, well-educated lifestyle, surrounded by her family, safe and stable in her older brother's home, an accesoria located in the Callejón de los Dolores.

Most likely, neighbors' complaints first brought Doña María to the attention of the criminal authorities who incarcerated her and her mother for prostitution and consent to prostitution. The accusations against Doña Teresa were vague and never hardened into anything tangible over the course of the case, especially because accusers and the court did not use the term alcahueta. Witnesses referred to Doña Maria as a "mujer vagamunda," with her mother's knowledge and cooperation, implying that they both lived a disorganized, immoral life.[50] The official court statements used the term prostitute, in line with late-eighteenth-century understandings of sex for sale.

In a rare example of family members' inscribing one of their own as engaged in commercial sex, Doña María's relatives did not deny some of her patronage relationships. Nor could the mother and daughter deny that Doña María bore an illegitimate child. Doña María presented the affair that led to the birth of her daughter as a result of her own "fragility," without mentioning seduction or false promises of marriage. The father was a lieutenant in the regiment based in Mexico City who deserted her after she gave birth, moving on to Veracruz. Perhaps in an effort to lessen her guilt, both Doña María and her mother said that this affair had made Doña Teresa physically ill. Doña Teresa said that she herself forbade the infant's father to visit.[51] None of the witnesses, including the accused themselves, presented this pregnancy as the cause of Doña María's moral decline. They could not deny that this infant proved Doña María's sexual activity, but they testified in a way that suited their desires to look righteous and even morally delicate before the court.

A woman who called herself Dona María's great aunt narrated a different series of events and placed the blame for the young lady's immorality on her mother. The elderly aunt, a Franciscan tertiary, said that she had raised Doña María in the Convent of Our Lady of the Immaculate Conception until she was approximately twelve years old. Then the girl moved on to the College of the Vizcainos, where she fell under her mother's influence. The mother began to take her daughter to a variety of events, possibly in an effort to find a male patron. Doña María left the college and began to attend dances, *tertulias* (defined in 1788 as entertaining, educational, or political gatherings), and games of chance.[52] One day the aunt visited the two ladies and found the mother asleep in the living room, with her daughter sleeping in the bedroom with a man named Don Angel, a *"cobrador del coliseo."* Don Angel's work with the Nuevo Coliseo theater brought Doña María into the social sphere where young women customarily sought male patrons. A few days after witnessing this damning domestic moment, the aunt observed that Doña María was pregnant. The aunt also claimed that she saw a very "decent" looking man speak to Doña Teresa about her daughter. The mother directed him upstairs, and when he returned, he gave her six pesos. She testified that another man called Don Pedro Estrada had a longer-term relationship with Doña María, giving her two pesos a day over a period of two years. The aunt also spoke of another lover called Don Fernando.[53] Most of the prosecution's witnesses in this case fit within the classic stereotypes of gossiping neighbors: three Spanish widows over the age of thirty with the verbal power to affect the course of litigation. Motivated by their allegations, the criminal court tracked down two of Doña María's alleged lovers to make statements.[54]

When questioned, these two men admitted to some of the accusations and denied others. A Don Pedro, age thirty-nine, confessed that he pitied Doña María's poverty after the birth of her child, so when he visited her he gave her money. He started with two pesos a visit, then increased his donation to up to six pesos a week. Doña María herself described the motivation for his compensated visits as "just for charity, he gave her succor." Her mother said that Don Pedro bought Doña María's necessities, such as shoes when she was barefoot. Neither of the alleged lovers admitted that anything untoward happened during Don Pedro's visits. A free mulata servant said that they did nothing more than play games until the gentleman left at 9:00 p.m. Doña Maria's brother did not object to her visitors, men who caused these allegations of dishonor within the walls of his own home and in the presence of his wife. The brother knew that an unnamed merchant frequented the house, but the visits took place when he was out of the house, so he did not presume to know more about them. His statement ended on that vague admission.[55] Doña María's sister-in-law, who lived in the same apartment, implied that the guests enjoyed more than games. She claimed that Doña María rejected Don Pedro's offers of marriage because he was too poor. As other witnesses mentioned, they officially broke off their relationship after two years. Doña María's mother said the girl herself rejected Don Pedro and told him to stop visiting, but the lover denied ever wanting to marry Doña María.[56]

The second alleged lover, Don Angel, age twenty-six, admitted to boarding in Doña María's home for three months and compensating her six *reales* a day for his food. He viewed this arrangement as a good option because he knew Doña Teresa's husband, and he needed inexpensive housing on his limited resources. Don Angel said that he contemplated asking Doña María to marry him, but he never gave her his promise because "he feared she was not a *doncella*."[57] Although not directly stating their affair as a fact, this judgmental narration stops just short of admitting it. Doña Teresa claimed that Don Angel lived with them only at the invitation of her son and that Doña María had rejected the proposal of marriage. The two assertions by relatives that Doña María rejected marriage offers from both Don Pedro and Don Angel, even if completely false, suggest that the young lady wanted to maintain her high sexual capital. Having two older relatives brag about her desirability as a wife for men of wealth and status in court may even have functioned as a kind of marketing strategy. Doña María and her relatives may have wanted to promote the fact that she would agree to marriage only with a wealthy man.

In this new era of gender-mixed socializing and new cultural opportunities, Doña María had many options well within the realm of respectability, other than for the most prudish, old-fashioned observer such as her aunt. Accompanied by her mother, Doña María attended dances without provoking any scandal, according to their own statements and that of three other witnesses. She danced, but deponents suggested that this in itself did not prove that she had committed sexual improprieties. A young Spanish man testified that Doña María "promenaded" on occasion with her mother, an act that an older Spanish widow interpreted as "libertinism" with a lover. The mother and daughter also spent time at the "Tertulia del Chino," a nearby establishment, possibly a kind of salon where they might have discussed literature and politics.[58] Their servant said that the ladies went out to houses only to "converse," implying no immoralities connected to this act.

Evidently, doñas of their social and educational status could engage in these activities, as well as have illegitimate babies and paying lovers, without serious judicial repercussions.[59] Ultimately, the criminal court released Doña María and her mother with no punishment, other than suggesting that they find another house where the young lady would not succumb again to the temptation of concubinage. The two women said that they had nowhere else to live, other than with Doña María's brother, but eventually Doña María went to live with her grandmother. The authorities justified this lax reaction to the case with the opinion that Doña María did not operate as a public or scandalous prostitute and that her mother did not procure her or engage in lenocinio (pandering). Instead, Doña Maria "had been maintained in illicit affairs with several individuals"; in other words, they readily admitted that she had sustained herself (and her mother) with a career as a kept woman.[60] The court's disinterest indicates that they did not view concubinage as a serious offense for a woman like Doña María.

THE LADIES OF THE "HOUSE OF WONDERS" AND
OTHER ENTERTAINING WOMEN

Three sociable sisters experienced similar neighborly surveillance in the final few years of the eighteenth century and ultimately received the same kind of judicial paternalism despite their neighbors' complaints. Perhaps of approximately the same social rank as Doña María Guadalupe, these ladies occupied their own home, still living with their mother. Allegedly, each of the sisters had a lover and their home functioned as an entertainment venue, so much so that surrounding residents called their abode the "house of wonders." This sobriquet, along with a few other suggestive pieces of data, gives credence to the accusations made in this criminal case, despite the expected denials and assertions of respectability on the part of the accused.[61]

Neighborhood observations and suspicions influenced law enforcement to arrest five individuals carousing in the House of Wonders just after midnight on Christmas Eve of 1797 for concubinage, scandal, and other "excesses." The young women's lawyer did not deny that several gentlemen regularly entered Wonders, spending time there until late at night, in order to relax by singing and playing the guitar. The advocate argued that hardworking people required diversion after a hard day's work and that the sounds of music did not prove that bad conduct went along with it. He went on to advise against inscribing this as immoral: "Infinite individuals of good conduct in this city have visits from gentlemen at all hours and this does not mean that they should be said to live evil or disorderly [lives]."[62] This comment surprisingly suggests a broad toleration for new forms of laxer socializing among both genders, perhaps as a result of the popularity of European-influenced social venues, especially dance halls, theaters, and salons/tertulias. However, neighbors living and working near the House of Wonders did not buy into this lax attitude. They suspected inappropriate behavior resulted with the sisters' frequent male guests.

Several aspects of the sisters' lives, including the fact that men gathered at their house in the evenings, challenged the strictest standards of respectable behavior for viceregal women. The eldest of the three accused sisters was twenty-five and married but with an absent husband; a second sister was a widow at age twenty-two; and the third was a sixteen-year-old doncella who usually attended a Jesuit colegio in Puebla. They lived with their forty-year-old mother, who suffered from asthma and dropsy and could not leave her bed. Neighbors believed that each of the young women had at least one male companion who visited them almost daily for card games, dancing, and music, at all hours of the day and night. Even their mother agreed to these allegations but denied that anything illicit took place during any of the visits.[63]

The neighbors claimed that they witnessed several scandalous activities in the house, besides the frequent male visitors, music (guitars played by men standing on the balcony), and, in general, noise and disorder. Neighbors saw men embracing and kissing the young virgin, Doña Clara. A tailor who went to the house for work purposes witnessed Doña Clara sitting on a cleric's lap. Two of the men arrested were soldiers, and the hostile witnesses declared that they had already received reprimands from their military superiors, but they continued visiting the House of Wonders for card games, gambling, and illicit affairs with the sisters. The young widowed sister allegedly shut herself up alone in a room with one of the soldiers on more than one occasion. Two other tailors who worked across the street testified that they saw many men coming and going, in the manner of visiting a casino. In fact, the husband of the oldest sister had endured a previous arrest for gambling in an illegal casino, and although he no longer lived with his wife, his associates frequented her residence. Notoriously, a handful of witnesses saw a fight take place in the street in front of the house, involving a coachman, the male visitors, and possibly even some of the female residents of the House of Wonders.[64] This incident most likely sparked the occupants' arrest, suggesting that all of the above accusations did not bother the neighbors enough to complain to the authorities until a real public scandal erupted.

In the eighteenth century, investigating authorities paid close attention to financial circumstances when trying to determine female moral propriety. Many cases include witnesses' opinions on a woman's possessions and how she financed them, whether licitly or illicitly.[65] The sisters living in the House of Wonders faced this scrutiny and came up suspiciously prosperous in the opinion of the court. Their house contained a large inventory of religious art, furniture, and a substantial amount of Chinese porcelain, a prized item that wealthy women of this era loved to hoard.[66] How did these four women, who had no male protectors or family members living with them, maintain themselves at this level of elegance? Of course, the ladies claimed innocent sources of income. The two older sisters, Doña Gertrudis and Doña Ana, claimed that they worked daily at the cigarette factory. Their mother said she enjoyed a small legacy from her deceased husband. The young Doña Clara had two clerical patrons who paid for her schooling in Puebla. Why they funded her, no one bothered to explain. Perhaps Doña Clara benefited from this patronage from wealthy Spaniards because they wished to protect respectable but poor maidens from sexual scandal, a charitable inclination akin to those who financed dowries for Spanish orphan girls. But why had neighbors seen her sitting on a cleric's lap? Perhaps an innocent gesture, but evidence suggests that priests and friars should not be held to a very high standard of chaste behavior.[67]

Even the witnesses for the defense managed to complicate this blameless story of the sisters' honest but modest incomes. One of the alleged lovers arrested on Christmas Eve, Don Manuel, admitted to giving gifts to the family. The neighbors believed that Don Manuel, a twenty-nine-year-old married Spaniard from Cadiz, secretly lived with the married but separated Doña Gertrudis, sharing meals regularly, a sign of intimacy. The couple allegedly kissed and hugged in front of witnesses. Don Manuel denied all of the accusations of untoward behavior, but he admitted a few damning facts. Answering questions regarding his marriage, he claimed that he lived apart from his wife only because she was very sick and had to spend her time with her family in Xalapa. He had no funds to reunite with her. However, he pitied the women in the House of Wonders and enjoyed compensating them with gifts and money for the meals and time that he admitted that he spent with them. Don Manuel's interrogators mocked this admission, wondering why, if he had extra money, did he not spend it on visiting or caring for his sick wife instead of enjoying an apparent life of leisure, gambling, music, and dance with three young women?[68]

The prosecution also interrogated the young women directly about their finances and their apparent life of leisure and regular diversions. The young widow, twenty-two-year-old Doña Ana María, faced many probing questions about her lifestyle. She claimed that every day, she and her married sister, Doña Gertrudis, went to the royal cigarette factory and worked as rollers. She also admitted to attending dances, but never causing any scandal. Her prosecutors questioned how she could eat, drink, dress herself (presumably with some degree of luxury), go out dancing, and pay for her housing on the scant three and a half reales that she would earn each day as a cigarette roller. They also reminded her that illness and a shortage of paper (which meant no work for rollers) prevented her and her sister from working on many days.[69]

These questions and comments from the prosecutors suggest that presumed doñas and doncellas simply could not afford to live a comfortable, entertaining life without male financial support and protection. Low-paying factory work for women meant poverty or a corrupt way of life, as the interrogators directly stated: they accused Doña Ana María of living off her visitors' gifts and stated that this proved her "disorderly, evil lifestyle."[70] The court clearly did not believe that the sisters and their mother had inherited enough money to live as well as they did. No one involved in this case, including their own advocate, their mother, and one of their guests, denied that they entertained men in their house for compensation or even that street fights involving their guests took place outside their home. However, their respectable social class allowed them to live this way while still maintaining the ability to assert their good reputations. Their Spanish background, plus the fact that they came from a family that perhaps once had had some modest prosperity to afford their single-family home, protected them from any harsh judicial consequences for their scandalous lifestyles.

Ultimately, the authorities did not choose to reprimand the sisters severely for the accusations of concubinage with their three male visitors. Five respectable Spanish witnesses said that the sisters and their mother always maintained a good reputation as honest women. The witnesses knew of the frequent guests to the

House of Wonders but testified that the women had access to legitimate sources of income.[71] The young ladies successfully argued for their innocence by presenting themselves as appropriate targets for charity due to their poverty and illness, especially after their mother died during the proceedings. In response to their innocent and even pathetic stance, and the support for their characters, they were released from jail, and their confiscated possessions were returned. They may even have escaped paying their court costs, based on their arguments that they had no funds. The sisters received only a warning to avoid all scandal in the future.[72]

The House of Wonders looked like a prosperous abode, but in reality, neighbors viewed it as a brothel. Selling sex also possibly funded María Alberta, a twenty-two-year-old labeled as either an indigenous tributary or a mestiza, who ran a pulquería along the Camino Real ten miles north of Mexico City. She enjoyed protected judicial status when some of the local populace denounced her raucous establishment, where she sold the pulque legally acquired by her brother.[73] The local intendant started an investigation of this tavern in 1789 because several respectable male workers, as well as the foreman on the adjacent *hacienda,* accused María Alberta of a range of scandalous behaviors. They claimed María Alberta had the reputation of a "puta publica [public whore]" and everyone knew her as a "*ramera declarada* [declared whore]." Village authorities tried to discipline her several times by punishing her with imprisonment and banishment, but María Alberta always returned to running her licensed, legal drinking house in a scandalous way. Witnesses observed that she welcomed muleteers and other travelers into her tavern day and night, allowing them to sleep and eat there. Neighbors heard the sounds of guitars and disorderly people coming and going even past midnight.

When the authorities went to the pulquería to arrest her, they found her eating with two men. At twenty-two, María Alberta was still a legal minor. When asked why she lived in her drinking establishment alone and not with her brother or in another honorable house, María Alberta replied that she worked full-time in her tavern and had to reside there in order to keep up her duties. She denied opening her bar at night, other than on special occasions, such as her birthday. In response to her arrest, she called on the protection of the bureaucrat in charge of licensed pulquerías and received his full protection. This administrator personally wrote the viceroy, asking that María Alberta be released and allowed to return to her work. In effect, her arrest threatened his authority and blocked the collection of lucrative taxes on pulquerías. Despite her reputation as a "*mujer sumamente mala* [exceedingly bad woman]" whose morals apparently offended many of her neighbors and local authorities, María Alberta violated only the rules set for running pulquerías, not laws against individual sexual transactions (which still did not formally exist). With discretion, she could sell sex out of her saloon, with the implicit stamp of approval of the administrator of pulque sales. Her manipulation of competing bureaucracies suggests how other women also might have run clan-destine brothels with police toleration, as long as they avoided public scandal, and so might have reinforced the centuries' old Spanish tradition of mixing the sale of alcohol with the sale of sex.

These respectable and semirespectable women sustained their denials despite all of the evidence to the contrary. Usually seeking to maintain business as usual, only when noisy scandals erupted and disturbed their neighbors did they have to record themselves into criminal and church inquiries. Other than that, their indoor affairs could continue without prosecution or documentation. Their patrons, their social and sexual capital, youth, and stable homes or work places caused the courts' lenience, silencing their neighbors' verbiage and making illegible attempts to inscribe them with written labels relating to transactional sex. Their successful scribal seductions actually reinforced the sexual duplicity Sor Juana denounced in her famous poem.

4

Courtesans and Their Lovers

She was then very young, though married, and the mother of two children, and that when he came to visit her mother, she was sitting sewing in a corner where the baron did not perceive her; until talking very earnestly on the subject of cochineal, he inquired if he could visit a certain district where there was a plantation of nopals. "To be sure," said La Güera from her corner; "we can take M. de Humboldt there;" whereupon he first perceiving her, stood amazed, and at length exclaimed, "Valgame Dios! Who is that girl?" Afterwards he was constantly with her, and more captivated, it is said, by her wit than by her beauty, considering her a sort of western Madame de Staël.

FANNY CALDERON DE LA BARCA ON THE MEETING BETWEEN
ALEXANDER VON HUMBOLDT AND MARÍA IGNACIA RODRÍGUEZ[1]

[Josefa de Ordóñez is] one of those actresses who, through her skill or good looks, has been courted and protected by a number of well-known individuals. There is no doubt that they pay for her and fete her, causing both small and large scandal due to the publicity.

LETTER DATED FEBRUARY 9, 1767[2]

In one kind of sexual transaction, all parties involved sought extreme visibility and even overexposure: eighteenth-century courtesans, celebrities in their era, whose status became legendary as the centuries passed. Spanish American cities lacked a king who desired royal mistresses, but the viceroys, wealthy bureaucrats, military men, and aristocrats enjoyed their affairs with cultured, genteel women. As these courtesans seduced the viceregal court and spectacularly shed their plebeian origins, their overweening ambitions sparked the wrath of some (perhaps rejected) men of the same rank as their lovers. Courtesans began the process of writing themselves into the archives as they promenaded on the city streets, with their brash materialism violating the privileges of the hereditary nobility. These public and presumptuous displays set into motion accusations of their disregard of sumptuary laws. Their driving desire to publicize their own sexual capital enraged their contemporaries and prompted scribes to write hundreds of pages of petitions, denunciations, and complaints. Josefa de Ordóñez (1729–1790s) performed her honor as a litigant and deponent, like other women who appeared before the judiciary, but this famous actress had the training and wherewithal to sustain it for decades, with studied dramatic panache and elegant costumes and backdrops.[3]

Ordóñez, as a very successful theater professional, may have envisioned her lifetime of tumultuous interactions with the authorities as her own ongoing dramatic creation, with the purpose of reinscribing herself from a plebeian actress to a grand lady. Courtesans could tell their own stories effectively because of their high level of cultural fluency, their education, and their privileged racial status.[4] They wrote their characters as "a somewhat softer, more decorous, if still impish and unpredictable, figure whose sexual allure does not intrinsically entail a threat to gender roles and male economic control." They seem "more conventionally feminine" than street solicitors (chapter 5).[5] Their elegant, elusive unconventionality and "seductive vagueness" still attracts twenty-first century consumers of their life stories.[6] However, these women also told complex stories with "facades that conceal longings, furies, and not least, suffering."[7] At first glance, their superficial delicacy (the pale skin and white wigs of countless paintings) posed little threat to their male protectors and thus reinforced the gender hierarchies of their day. But viceregal courtesans wrote their unthreatening personas because in reality they walked a dangerous razor's edge between opulence and ostracism.

In retelling Ordóñez's carefully constructed autobiographical drama, I highlight her materialistic, flamboyant milieu and the performance she wrote for herself within it. Setting the stage, first we meet courtesans with a seventeenth-century prelude foreshadowing the important theme of sumptuary laws, the regulations that Ordóñez flaunted in the eighteenth century. Then male patrons enter in supporting roles in their special function as *cortejos,* financial patrons of eighteenth-century women who appeared in official documentation because their neighbors, their lovers' families, or officers of the law condemned their materialism, libertinism, and social ambition. We reach a climax with an in-depth examination of Ordóñez's triumphs and her struggles with the authorities. Frequently initiating her own litigation, she coauthored extensive files now stored in archives in both Mexico City and Seville. The dénouement finds an older Ordóñez as a respectable character, symbolically united with her legendary eighteenth-century peers in Lima and Bogotá, perhaps serving as a model for her nineteenth-century successors such as the aforementioned La Güera Rodríguez. The curtain rises on late-seventeenth-century scandalous ladies.

COURTESANS AND CONSUMPTION

In a 1674 proclamation, the Mexico City high court named twenty-two women as breaking the laws regulating public displays of wealth and status. Most of them were labeled *españolas,* and the rest did not receive racial designations. Sixteen of these women had the honorific title doña, suggesting that they claimed elite status, but even so, the court decree did not concede that they had any socially and morally acceptable justification for behaving like rich noblewomen.[8] From the seventeenth century, travelers to Spanish America, such as Thomas Gage, had noted the surprising opulence of female attire and adornments, but in the eighteenth century, the perception of the social danger of women who dressed extravagantly reached its peak, generating fearful pronouncements about their immorality and how this threatened the broader society.[9] Courtesans flourished in a milieu of libertinism and materialism that gained popularity in seventeenth- and eighteenth-century Spanish America, following trends in European metropolises, most notably Paris and London.[10] Rich men and women in Madrid and Mexico City paraded in lavish carriages, adorned in elegantly tailored clothes, dripping from head to toe in jewels and precious metals.[11] From Mexico City to Lima, fashion gradually provoked more intense fears of both social dislocation and widespread public immorality, leading to the persecution of women like La Ordóñez and her seventeenth-century predecessors.

The women's aliases (perhaps bestowed in childhood by family, or by lovers later in life, or even self-declared nom de guerres) ranged from obscure to crassly humorous to nonsensical: La Chinche, two women called Las Priscas, La Guadalajara, La Sedasito, La Vende Barato, La Lorencilla, La Dijome Dijome, La Algodoncitos, La Manteca, Mundo Nuevo, La Migajita, La Chata, La Molinera, La Gallega, La Cometa, La Torito, La Latinera, and La Chorreada.[12] The choice of the judges to record these women's aliases instead of their formal names in an official document immediately denied their respectability, although it also may have served to distance them from their families to avoid humiliating their relatives. Regardless, with this document, the authorities helped inscribe fictional characters for the accused ladies.

Courtesans' conspicuous consumption disregarded social, legal, and moral codes that allowed only those with honor to possess and display wealth. Because the women discussed in this chapter allegedly did not acquire their expensive clothes, carriages, servants, slaves, jewelry, theater boxes, and furniture through inheritance or the earnings of their legitimate spouses, they infuriated their neighbors. Their accusers labeled them disturbers of the peace for their flaunting of material tokens of wealth. Courtesans disrupted the social hierarchy that placed honorable men and women at the top. According to this schema, only those lucky enough to be born with elite status should enjoy riches and comfort, and thus plebeian but rich courtesans faced censure and prosecution.

To support the connection between honor and materialism, the Spanish monarchs had mandated limitations on consumption and luxury from the medieval era.[13] Phillip III decreed in June of 1600 that "no woman who publicly made her income with her body" could promenade in a carriage or bring cushions or pillows to mass, and that no individual of any rank could go out in a rented carriage. Moving toward the 1623 brothel prohibitions (chapter 2), in 1611, Phillip III decreed that whores could also not wear gold, pearls, and silk.[14] Despite the brothel closures and regulations against the expensive and showy *guardainfantes* and ruffs, eighteenth-century commentators viewed the reign of Phillip IV as a time of degeneracy.[15] Although Charles II ushered French styles into the Spanish realms, his 1674 royal pragmatic recognized the "great danger" of luxurious dress and carriages decorated in fabric, gold, and silver. In the monarch's view (or that of his mother or his advisors, given his incompetency), this ostentation wasted money better spent on maintaining families.[16]

Responding to the royal regulations, in the 1670s, the Mexico City high court tried to make examples of almost two dozen "scandalous women" who offended the public with their "profane dresses" and carriages. The only hints in this file of their occupations or style of living came from the use of the term *escandalosa*, their nicknames listed above, and the denunciation of their materialism. While this document provides scant details on the affairs and material consumption of one of these women, the long list of potential offenders hints at seventeenth-century Mexico City's demimonde, which would grow in complexity in the eighteenth century.

What most disturbed the authorities was the women's ostentatious public display of wealth, despite their having no known claim to rich husbands or family-generated inheritances. The court objected to nonvirtuous, nonnoble women displaying themselves publicly in luxurious clothes and expensive carriages, accompanied by an entourage of slaves or servants in livery, and bringing self-indulgent cushions and lap rugs into church. According to royal sumptuary laws, only "people of quality" could use carriages.[17] These women acted as if they were honorable, but since their wealth was not inherited through their family or provided by their marriage, they were effectively mocking and subverting the honor code and Christian morality. The decree observed that the "republic" in general noted this disregard and viewed this as a harmful situation. These vague accusations meant that the court viewed these immoral women as causing a general sense of disturbance in public life, that is, in the "republic." These women further ridiculed societal values with their use of humorous aliases, thus mocking the great value placed on names in the Iberian world.

The 1674 pronouncement demanded that the aforementioned women would suffer two-year banishments to ten leagues outside of Mexico City if they continued the shameless display of their ill-gotten gains and their dishonest lives. The decree ordered them to dress decently like honest women, avoid traveling in their own or borrowed coaches, not bring ostentatious items to church for their comfort during mass, and overall live honestly. Besides banishment, the authorities also threatened to beat their liveried coachmen with two hundred lashes and send their slaves to a workhouse. When the judicial functionaries went to look for the women on the list at their homes, oddly enough they found only their numerous servants in residence. Many of the women had disappeared already, probably informed by their protectors before the unwelcome visitors came knocking at their doors. Most of these scandalous women escaped punishment and probably continued their previous ways of life after the search trailed off.

One of the targeted women, sixteen-year-old Doña Lorenza de Mendoza, known as La Lorencilla, anticipated the reign of La Ordóñez with her frequent interactions with the authorities. Described as a tall Spaniard with black hair and eyes, La Lorencilla suffered banishment from her house in the Calle de Tacuba because she was said to be a bad example by flaunting her carriage, indecent dresses, and the rugs and cushions that she brought to church. She was sentenced to live in a house of seclusion in Puebla de los Angeles in compliance with the above decree.[18] Four years later, La Lorencilla returned to cause more problems in Mexico, including having ongoing affairs with married men.

During Holy Week of 1678, La Lorencilla sent her page to the house of the forty-year-old Sergeant Major Don Juan de Ortega, with a message requesting a carriage for her to ride in while she viewed the procession in the Plaza Mayor. Several men witnessed this request and the fact that Ortega loaned her his carriage (worth almost five hundred pesos), two black mules with their harnesses and accoutrements, as well as his coachman, a free mulatto.[19] La Lorencilla took advantage of this generous loan and proceeded to promenade around the plaza and the viceregal palace in Ortega's ostentatious conveyance. Three guardsmen on horseback accosted her as she turned around the back of the palace and called out that they had been sent to transport her back to incarceration in Puebla. La Lorencilla began to shout, cry, and otherwise cause a disturbance, objecting to their detaining her.[20] The guards escorted her back to Puebla, where she spent a few days enclosed.

Using a tactic commonly employed by elite men and women who wanted to end their incarcerations, she then complained of illness.[21] As a result, La Lorencilla received the permission of medical doctors to move to a private home in Puebla, where she admitted many visitors and traveled around in fancy borrowed carriages.[22] However, protected by powerful men in Puebla and Mexico City, her advocates argued that she accepted the actions of law enforcement very willingly. They opined that she behaved in this compliant way because she was an important, honorable lady. Those in charge of her incarceration were instructed to care for her with a generous, respectful attitude, given her status.[23] If she threatened social hierarchies, she at the same time buttressed the prevailing standards of elite masculinity, so men flocked to help and defend her. Wealth and elite protectors buffered courtesans such as La Lorencilla from the indignities suffered by other women of lower status who lived outside of sexual moral norms. Lovers stepped in to act in the role of fathers or husbands, shielding their favorites from judicial repercussions, while at the same time making a great deal of effort to protect their own property.[24]

Courtesans received gifts or monetary compensation openly from their protectors and flaunted conventional morals with their nonmonogamous or extramarital affairs.[25] From the perspective of their era, sexual "venality" marked the "highest class of courtesan to the lowest streetwalker."[26] In eighteenth-century France, the definition of courtesan made it clear that contemporary observers saw the difference between courtesans and street solicitors as only a matter of degree: "[A courtesan is] a woman given over to debauchery, especially when she exercises this shameful trade with a kind of charm and decency, and knows how to make *libertinage* appealing in a way that prostitution cannot."[27] The women who attained the status of affluent concubines faced persecution simply for displaying their allegedly ill-gotten gains. In all cases, their accusers presented the courtesan's greed as the abhorrent characteristic that inspired her immoral character. But paradoxically, when it came to elite courtesans, Bourbon reformers acted in a protective and even fatherly way. Since many of them, in fact, privately waited on courtesans or married women as generous male protectors, they often sympathized with ladies of this kind.

Some Bourbon bureaucrats showed their sympathies by officially objecting to their prosecution or incarceration. In 1789, the bishop of Cartagena bought a house that he designated as a home for licentious women. Inspired by the need to "contain the liberty of certain women dragged down by their passions," he formulated a strict set of rules, guards, prayers, and work assignments in line with the recogimiento tradition.[28] Secular authorities arguing against its foundation could not envision worldly courtesans assigned to mundane tasks enclosed in a grim religious prison. They phrased their rejection of this proposal in a language of patronizing familiarity:

> Many of [these ladies] due to their poverty make a living with the despicable surrender of their bodies, and this sensual occupation has endured so long, that it would be harsh and inhumane to enclose them ... due to the whimsical haughtiness or delicacy of some of them, it would not be easy to force them to the suggested work of washing soldiers' clothes or the like.[29]

Protecting elegant, genteel women, even courtesans, from a loss of social status did not challenge the gender roles of these Bourbon bureaucrats. Nonetheless, certain men in power did not believe sexually active women deserved a punishment that obliged these ladies of luxury to labor as servants, or take on a penitential role. Courtesans enjoyed elevated status due to their wealth, sophistication, and connections to elite men, while defying the rhetoric valuing female sexual purity by "surrendering their bodies." This document demonstrates the status ambiguity of these women and the equally ambiguous outlook of elite men who understood the common tale of commercial sex as a last resort for poor and desperate women, but who nonetheless maligned the courtesans' characters by calling them lazy, capricious, and haughty.

SCANDALOUS WOMEN AND CORTEJOS IN THE EIGHTEENTH CENTURY

A particular kind of man paid for the courtesans' lavish lifestyles. This social trend took hold of Mexico City, where some commentators noted its ubiquity.[30] La Ordóñez became a highly successful courtesan through her lifelong exploitation of the *cortejo,* a term that refers to the elite men who funded the luxurious lifestyles of married women. Ordóñez achieved a unique degree of success, enjoying the gifts and protection of at least three rich cortejos simultaneously. Other women reaped more modest material benefits from this kind of thoughtful attendant. The cortejo was common in Madrid, according to Francisco de Goya and other observers; other terms for men of this kind include *chichisbeo* (a name used earlier in the eighteenth century) and *petimetre.*[31] Some observers argue that increased materialism and more open socializing between men and women led to the popularity of cortejos in eighteenth-century Madrid. Carriages, food, drink, and the French and Italian styles of dress and accessorizing became more excessive and ostentatious than they had been in the previous centuries. This trend supported the urban luxury trades of manufacturing gloves, fans, ribbons, slippers, hats, and any number of accessories. All of this tended to bankrupt the average husband, who even may have appreciated how cortejos could pay for some of his wife's expenses of dress and entertaining.[32]

The cortejo took part in a dramatic change in how Spaniards in the Old and New Worlds socialized, conversed, and shaped their public personalities and characters. He crept into all intimate corners of the house, having tête-à-têtes with the lady of the mansion. In fact, the older word for cortejo, in 1730s Spain spelled chichisbeo, refers to the Italian word for "whisper."[33] These men did not just hide in wives' bedrooms and baths. They also took their *amigas* out to the theater and bullfights and on walks, all openly without compromising the lady's reputation. They proliferated to such a degree that a published list of sixty-nine alphabetized and annotated couples (married women with their cortejos) circulated in Madrid in 1768. The list also made reference to the many other adulterous couples that remained secret and to the large number of ladies seeking genteel companions.[34] Of course, clerics and some husbands did not like this new form of socializing and initiated divorce proceedings or other kinds of litigation in protest of certain relationships. Although evidence indicates that some married women openly took lovers from the early days of the Spanish viceroyalties, eighteenth-century observers perceived cortejos as a new, foreign import, either French or Italian. In reality, these men abounded in Spain and the Spanish Americas.

The Venetian playright Carlo Goldoni (1707–1793) made grotesque mockery of *cicisibeos* (the Italian spelling) in his plays *Le Avventure* and *Le Smanie*, in which men of this kind appear as a kind of "doll for the use and consumption of elegant ladies."[35] In Italy, a man of this kind

> ingratiated himself into the family circle. He found a place alongside the husband; indeed he took the husband's place. As a serving gallant he helped the lady of the house with her toilet, took a regular position in her retiring room, went visiting with her and accompanied her to the theatre. He poured out her chocolate, held her powder box and fan, sat beside her in her carriage, and gave orders to her servants. However much the moralists might thunder, . . . the cicisbeo held his ground.[36]

This description fits well with the interpretation of the cortejo in eighteenth-century Mexico City. They were members of the family, acting as doting stepfathers to children whom they may or may not have fathered.[37] It seems that the Italian version acted out a more servile role than such a man had in Spanish America, where gentlemen certainly attended their amigas in their social life, bath, and bedrooms but did not wait on them as lackeys.

In Spanish America, cortejos were mannerly, generous, constant companions in the form of wealthy, elite men, usually bachelors, who openly socialized with elite married women as their recognized personal companions. Married women received a range of donations from their lovers, from small tokens such as jewelry and tobacco to full support for an ostentatious way of life and a luxurious household.[38] This institution worked very well for sociable, elite Creole women who married less wealthy Spanish men on limited salaries, especially soldiers or other petty bureaucrats who had a limited midrange income. The wives wanted to entertain and dress on a level "not possible with their husband's income," a phrasing repeatedly used by witnesses in documentation relating to these cases, in the same way that Ordóñez's detractors used it. If a wife wanted to give a party, the courteous companion could supply and underwrite everything needed for the festivities, down to the silverware.[39]

Eighteenth-century Spanish American husbands usually controlled their violent impulses, but occasionally they exploded and attacked their wives' cortejos. Tension often increased when suspicions arose about the possibility of a woman's having a child with a lover. But in general, husbands put up with the arrangement until, at least in the recorded cases, some incident provoked them and they denounced their wives for adultery, or their peers and neighbors could no longer ignore their disregard for moral rhetoric and the codes of honorable behavior. The ongoing toleration for male companions resembled the general attitudes toward nonmarital, nonmonogamous sex in this society as a whole. In most cases, observers implied, but did not necessarily always have to prove, that an adulterous sexual relationship existed between the cortejo and his amiga.[40] The cortejo was a transatlantic Spanish tradition, albeit one that the more conventionally moral found extremely objectionable.[41]

THE THEATER OF LUXURY AND THE TRIUMPHS OF JOSEFA ORDÓÑEZ

Eighteenth-century viceroys supported the theater as a symbol of European cultural enlightenment and as a potential avenue for educating the illiterate masses. At this time, Mexico City theatergoers could view Spanish classics such as the plays of Lope de Vega and Calderon de la Barca, as well as more burlesque entertainments in the form of popular songs and dances. Viceroy Revillagigedo initiated a golden age in viceregal theater by calling for the reconstruction of the wooden Viejo Coliseo (in existence from 1725 to 1752) and ordering the construction of the stone Nuevo Coliseo (operating from 1753 to 1931), where Ordóñez worked as a manager and a leading actress. With this new theater, Mexico City's elite intellectuals and political leaders hoped their city might strive toward the sophistication of European capitals.[42]

The theater in New Spain had a strong traditional connection to charity and evangelizing indigenous peoples, but despite its religious origins, ecclesiastics noted that actresses in Mexico City had taken lovers notoriously since the seventeenth century.[43] As they did in Europe, young plebeian or middle-class Spanish American women pursued careers in the performing arts in order to find male patronage. Divorce cases prove that men sought mistresses among actresses. Actors attempted to pander their own wives who worked with them in the theater.[44] Both courtesans and their paying companions promoted their very public lives, although in both Europe and New Spain moralizers regularly objected to the financial success of these women.[45]

It should be noted that not all scholars agree with eighteenth-century generalizations about actresses who sought their fortunes as courtesans. According to Thomas Wynn, "This misogynistic conflation of the public actress with the public prostitute was a sure way to denigrate a successful, relatively independent woman; the potentially disruptive character is rendered comprehensible, manageable and safe when reconfigured as a whore, a commodity to be owned and traded."[46] While English women began to gain respectability as actresses in this era, in France the connection between actress and prostitute persisted. Whether or not actresses as a group tended to choose this path purposefully, few attained Ordóñez's status as an elite courtesan. She accomplished this despite the fact that in her era, Bourbon reformers sought to professionalize and regulate New Spain's theaters, to the point of unrealistically expecting performers to conform to sexual norms.[47]

Ultimately, the moral reformers fought a losing battle. Lima also hosted a demimonde where the theater could mean a nonconforming sex life for some young women, including one aristocratic fourteen-year-old who in 1774 fled her violent elderly husband to become an actress supported by her lover.[48] In a similar case in mid-1790s Mexico City, a dancer at the Coliseo abandoned her husband, Roman Zapata Punzalan. The *bailarina* instead chose the benefits of various relationships with wealthy patrons, and the spouses had not reunited even fifteen years later.[49] The wronged husband (a native of the Philippines) described his wife as "freely prostituting herself with various lovers" and *bienhechores* (benefactors), all given the title don, quite similar in status to Ordóñez's protectors. From the husband's point of view, these patrons made a mockery both of him and of the Christian institution of marriage, although his 1809 petition does not go deeply into the fact that his wife had long ago accused him of sodomy.[50] Another late-eighteenth-century bailarina named Micaela del Corral, alias "La Zua," also enjoyed financial support from her lovers. After her arrest in 1795 by the *intendant* of Veracruz for her disruptive sexual behavior with a handful of wealthy military men, La Zua's colleagues in the Mexico City Coliseo successfully petitioned for her release so that she could continue to perform her notoriously scandalous dances and save them from financial ruin. Like Ordóñez, La Zua persisted in defying decrees to moderate her conduct and faced serving time in houses of reclusion.[51]

With the impressive grandeur of her wealth and the nonconformity of her behavior (while still maintaining the loyalty of her powerful patrons), Ordóñez's successes outshone the careers of all other courtesans/performers in eighteenth-century New Spain. We are told that poetasters even wrote scandalous verses in her honor, although unfortunately these have not survived.[52] Born in the province of Granada in 1729, Ordóñez embarked from Cadiz with her parents and siblings when she was a slim, pretty fourteen-year-old of average height, under contract to act at Mexico City's Viejo Coliseo theater. Not long after immigrating, she married Gregorio Panseco, an Italian-born violinist and flautist who came to New Spain on the same ship. When she was barely out of her teens, Ordóñez held the position of production manager of the theater and led its reconstruction, supported by one of her early lovers, a Maecenas who took on the theater's financial risk.[53] As the Nuevo Coliseo's leading actress, Ordóñez earned two thousand pesos annually.[54]

Ordóñez's family of performing artists expected her to interact intimately with wealthy supporters, and they financially depended on her as part of their strategy for economic survival. Such interactions often functioned as the entire purpose for training a girl for a stage career.[55] As the entire family worked as performers, they had no reason to feel shame for this conscious choice of career and its implications for Ordóñez's sexual marketability. Ordóñez's mother and sister lived with her in her luxurious house for much of her life in Mexico City. They helped her during her many litigious travails, earning their keep.

In 1755, ten years after contracting her marriage to Panseco, Ordóñez began litigation for divorce, initiating a series of disputes that various courts continued for virtually the rest of the couples' lives.[56] Even before this, only a few years after her arrival, she had come to the attention of the authorities due to her affairs and an intriguing incident when she shamed Viceroy Revillagigedo's wife during one of her stage performances.[57] No further details explain what Ordóñez did, but her acts reflected the theatrical practices of the time. During performances, actors and actresses often behaved casually, depending heavily on prompters for their lines, talking amongst themselves and to their colleagues backstage, eating and drinking in the wings, as well as signaling openly to audience members.[58]

Her audacity and the official reaction against her grew as she passed into her mid-thirties. The viceroy and the *real sala de crimen* (a royal court in residence in Mexico City) began an investigation into Ordóñez's behavior in 1765, sparked by the private casino that she operated out of her home. She also sold alcohol without a license. Ordóñez's circle of powerful donors included some men who had conflicts with the royal visitor Jose de Galvez, who came to New Spain at precisely this time in an effort to carry out Bourbon reforms.[59] The various investigations and penal sentences made against her never focused directly on her status as a courtesan because this occupation was not specifically prohibited. But the illegal card games and other gaming she allowed in her house did break laws. The concern with these infractions expanded to a broader examination of her way of life in 1766, after Ordóñez caused a public scandal by her bold display of wealth at a bullfight.[60] Her actions allegedly caused discord and disquietude in Mexico City.

Witnesses' statements in these investigations revealed Ordóñez's extensive and prestigious web of male friends as well as her impressive wealth.[61] Her conspicuous consumption highlighted her lovers' munificence. It is likely these men sought to enhance their own status through her. Her lovers were almost all Spanish immigrants and high-ranking royal functionaries, who undoubtedly brought these attitudes of European libertinism with them.[62] Reportedly, Ordóñez started a relationship with her first official patron around 1749. Her early affairs included a relative of Viceroy Fuenclara as well as a captain who also acted as godfather to her third child, born in 1752. Godfather status suggests that this lover fathered Josefa's child, and in fact it was known that she had only one of her four children with Panseco. Her longest-lasting companion and supporter was Don Joseph Gorraez, a notary for the viceroy as well as a local government official in his own right. Observers noticed Ordóñez often visited the notary's house, and he spent a great deal of time in her home. Gorraez served as godfather to Ordóñez's (and his?) son in 1759 and continued to visit her in the 1760s, despite the frequent presence of another generous lover, Don Francisco Casaviella, who came to New Spain in the entourage of the commandant general of the military. Lastly, Ordóñez received luxurious gifts including a billiards table from Don Fernando de Montserrat, the nephew of Viceroy Marquis de Cruillas. These three favorites joined another dozen or more men who frequented Ordóñez's illegal private casino, according to hostile witnesses, and who kept her in astounding luxury.[63] Amongst these protectors was Ordóñez's own legal advocate on retainer to defend her or help her file any judicial petitions she wished to make. Ordóñez could call on rich and powerful supporters to sprint to her aid at a moment's notice. They cherished her as a delicate creature needing their protection, a role she cultivated.

Witnesses spoke scornfully and perhaps even enviously about Ordóñez's immense wealth, which they attributed to over two decades' worth of affairs with wealthy men.[64] While Ordóñez earned a very good salary when she worked at the Nuevo Coliseo as a young woman, by the mid-1760s, her income (enjoyed by her entire extended household) apparently came from her elite male patrons and the gamblers that visited her house, wasting thousands of pesos in a night. At this time, Panseco took in a scant eight hundred pesos a year in salary as a violinist in the cathedral and lived in separate rooms from his wife.[65] One witness observed that Ordóñez had 40,000 pesos' worth of clothing, jewelry, and ornaments and that even a salary of 8,000 pesos could not support her lifestyle.[66] She dined on the most exquisite fish and wine. Gorraez supported her daily household needs, purchasing coal, water, candles, and food. Along with Montserrat, he also supplied her with black slaves and did all the necessary legal paperwork. Her three favorite cortejos also gave her housecoats or robes of taffeta and other expensive fabrics, jewelry sets made of gold, diamonds, and emeralds, and a watch allegedly worth a thousand pesos.

Solid wealth in the form of a well-furnished house distinguished courtesans from lower-income sex workers. For a professional performer, no better stage existed than one's own tasteful palace.[67] In 1766, during their ongoing investigations provoked by her actions at a bullfight, viceregal officials made an inventory of Ordóñez's household goods, cataloguing a breathtaking and overwhelming array of possessions that rivaled those of the wealthiest and most powerful men in the city, although with a more feminine emphasis.[68] This inventory, in fact, listed only those items that she had not stashed with her lovers before the notary came to confiscate her possessions, so it did not include her very valuable dresses and jewels.[69]

Courtesans in Europe influenced the tastes of their contemporaries as they adopted some of the styles of noble interior decorating and architecture, while rejecting others that did not appeal to them. Following the habits of Parisian actresses/courtesans who spent more money than almost anyone else to maintain their beautiful homes and elegant appearances, Ordóñez's personal consumption probably helped sustain certain merchants' entire businesses.[70] Unlike noble wives or even men with a middling income, courtesans had a great deal of freedom when it came to decorating their homes. Because she simultaneously took gifts and income from at least three elite lovers who had their own separate accommodations, Ordóñez could afford to choose items of great value for the sole purpose of highlighting her beauty and sophistication. Her patrons probably did not decide on her specific purchases, so like other courtesans she surrounded herself in exquisite objects and décor bought with their good credit to frame herself in a dazzling setting. Her home functioned to display her attractiveness and to entertain her followers, not as a domestic, private family space.[71] A doctor who visited for many years noted the pristine cleanliness of her home.[72]

Ordóñez's goods came from numerous parts of Mexico, Europe, and China. She adorned her walls with damask hangings in pink, scarlet, and gold. Her doors and windows had lavish damask curtains, and she had rugs on her floors. Ordóñez possessed numerous works of both decorative and religious art, ranging from chandeliers to folding screens (made of glass or painted) to paintings and statues. Her choice of art favored different images of the Virgin as well as a large rendition of the Apocalypse. Her assortment of religious objects grew as she aged. Mirrors and large windows (possibly stained-glass) filled her house with color and light. Ordóñez owned an enormous number of Chinese figurines and other knickknacks. Even this collection followed Parisian trends, as courtesans displayed their superior culture and intelligence by acquiring almost bizarre quantities of artistic, natural, or scientific objects. Eighteenth-century inventories show that "for courtesans, the passion for porcelain verged on a mania."[73]

Ordóñez hosted many visitors, and given her successful career in the theater, her home prominently featured both entertainment and the arts, showcasing guitars, sheet music, elegant desks, books (carefully stored in their own cupboard), and, of course, her extremely well-furnished private casino, with wallpaper depicting scenes from Don Quixote. She might have staged performances in her home, as she possessed chairs for sixty people at least, not to mention sofas and footstools. She also had costumes and accessories used for theatrical performances, including four sets of angel wings. The costumes consisted of a short skirt, jacket, and cloak, all of heavily decorated silk. She could serve her guests food and libations on her hundreds of pieces of various kinds of cups, glasses, plates, bowls, and saucers, including hundreds of more items made of Chinese porcelain, shipped into western New Spain via the Manila Galleon. Her larder contained food in abundance. She served coffee and may have even had tea, or what the inventory called "cha." With the help of her numerous servants and slaves, Ordóñez, her family, and guests enjoyed sanitation in the form of chamber pots and porcelain urinals, two items that were not always present in viceregal inventories. Ordóñez or others in her household may have done some needlework, as she owned a spinet and samplers.

Ordóñez also had many personal items relating to her personal health and beauty concerns, although the inventories do not list her jewelry and expensive outdoor clothes. The intimate items hint at her self-conception as a courtesan. The surprising fact that she retained her cortejos at the age of thirty-seven and beyond confirms her as one of the most successful courtesans in her era, but she may have felt some concerns about maintaining her physical attractions. Most women of her occupation enjoyed male patronage for only a few years in their teens or early twenties, before repeated pregnancies, venereal disease, and harsh medical treatments destroyed their teeth and skin and weakened their overall health and appearance.[74] As simple as Ordóñez's beauty aids might seem today, only very wealthy Spanish Americans had the time and money to spend on such extensive bodily care, especially with imported items. Ordóñez had soap on hand, from both Castile and Puebla. She had a kind of Chinese dye, most likely used for her hair, as it was found with a balm. The odd possession of "Chinese crab eyes" may have served as a homeopathic cure for her ailments. She also used perfumed oils and waters in her hair. Supporting her skin and hair beautification efforts, Ordóñez had on hand a very large number of silk and linen gloves, colorful silk hairnets, fans, buckles, and dozens of stockings, petticoats, slippers, handkerchiefs, and nightgowns. Among her intimate possessions were many small religious items, such as printed images and rosaries.

Ordóñez's books (possibly shared with her husband) included three volumes of the complete works of Sor Juana Inez de la Cruz and one of her plays, religious women's writings, biographies of religious men, instruction in Catholic doctrine, plays by Calderon de la Barca, a Spanish grammar (Nebrija), philosophy, and theology. Ordóñez also had novels and poetry depicting European courtly life and the trials of love and marriage. We cannot know if Ordóñez or her cortejos chose these thoughtful and fitting books, but they suggest that she or one of her friends believed they reflected her way of life. This summary highlights only a fraction of her household goods. Clearly, Ordóñez's possessions confirm her as the leading courtesan of her era, and even a cultural influence.

THE TRIALS OF JOSEFA ORDÓÑEZ

Ordóñez did not hide her lovers from her husband, who lived with her or in a separate apartment in the same building for most of their marriage. As a European-born musician, familiar with her family history, Panseco had to know that actresses and dancers might strive for courtesan status.[75] During their disputes, Panseco openly clashed with her lovers, but at other times he seemed forced by the various official orders and perhaps his own greed to tolerate them. He apparently did not try to kill them, therefore ignoring the dictates of the traditional Spanish honor code. One witness noted that Ordóñez's lovers disregarded her husband's occasional outbursts, asking rhetorically, "Then for what purpose did Panseco take an actress for his wife?"[76] Panseco himself even alluded mysteriously to conflicts over "a certain actress" when discussing a falling out he had with a former friend.

Later, in her sixties, Ordóñez accused Panseco of strange, sacrilegious sexual acts. She also claimed she had always rejected his advances toward her. But at the same time, whenever she found out he was having sex with a particular servant,

Ordóñez fired her.[77] Although Ordóñez offered many good reasons to support her petitions against Panseco for divorce, ecclesiastical divorces at this time did not allow both partners to be at fault. The spouse who filed for divorce required a spotless reputation to succeed in their litigation.[78] So clearly Ordóñez's notorious reputation prevented the success of her various divorce cases.

Her public display of a particular carriage and her ostentatious behavior at a bullfight in 1766 pushed Ordóñez's detractors to begin a formal, secret investigation of her scandalous behavior. The authorities concluded that Ordóñez's supporters allowed her to mock both social and legal norms. The *real sala de crimen* and the viceroy wanted to deter this situation in order to teach both Ordóñez and any potential imitators a lesson about the correct functioning of viceregal hierarchies. The investigation found twelve men and four women who had either attended the bullfight in question or worked at her house, asking them to speak about Ordóñez's way of life, in order to gather evidence for her violation of sumptuary laws.

A royal pragmatic of 1723 decreed that no man or woman could wear cloth decorated with brocade, gold, silver, jewels, pearl buttons, or any other decoration mixed with these luxurious elements. These rulings applied equally to actors performing on stage. Phillip V prohibited wearing any form of false gems and had strict standards for displays of wealth in terms of livery, coachmen, lackeys, and carriages. Coaches could not be oversized and could not have gold, silver, or painted exteriors, or any decoration made of damask, silk, or velvet. Carriage owners had to register their vehicles and could not own them at all if they did not have noble status. Decrees also ruled on wearing luxury items fabricated outside Spain. The late-eighteenth-century commentator Sempere y Guariños interpreted these decrees as motivated by the king's desire to make Spaniards more hardworking and productive. Later royal decrees emphasized the continuing use of opulent carriages, as well as excessively large and flamboyant hats. Contemporary observers especially criticized the magnificence seen in the Indies.[79]

Ordóñez infuriated her detractors by an ostentatious show of wealth and status at an event that functioned as a royal ceremony. Possibly she chose this bullfight, a moment highly charged with assertions of Spanish crown prestige and authority, as a marketing ploy to flaunt her sexual capital to potential new patrons. Of course, bullfights were sexually symbolic performance events, a bloody show of violent masculine prowess.[80] The bullfight in question celebrated the marriage of the heir to the Spanish throne.[81] The viceroy allotted seats of honor for various functionaries in royal service. Ordóñez attended and sat near the official boxes over the course of seven days by the invitation of her cortejo Francisco Casaviella, a high-ranking bureaucrat. They sat in full view of the viceroy and many other courtiers as well as Galvez, the royal inspector. In the presence of these powerful officials, Ordóñez allegedly behaved audaciously during the bullfight. She dressed with a supreme display of wealth, in different expensive ensembles each day. Witnesses especially noted how she sent her seven-year-old son, lavishly dressed, to offer a monetary gift to a famous bullfighter known as "El Andaluz." In a shocking display to those in attendance, Ordóñez distributed more largesse during the bullfight than the viceroy or any other nobleman in attendance.[82] In response to her large tip, El Andaluz dedicated his next kill to the actress, addressing her as *"Vuestra señoria"* or "your grace," a serious etiquette error, considering her plebeian origins. Ordóñez also promenaded throughout the city in a luxurious closed carriage embellished by her lover Gorraez's livery, attended by a young black page wearing a silver necklace and liveried footmen and coachmen. She knew that nothing other than an expensively decorated home could surpass a lavish carriage and servants in terms of public exposure of her sexual capital.[83] As Gorraez willingly loaned it to her, he undoubtedly also relished this exercise in self-promotion.

Witnesses in the 1766 investigation and even the notary involved in the case reported on Ordóñez's displeasing personality.[84] She possessed a direct style that astounded the notary who visited her house in June of 1766 to announce her banishment to the house of seclusion in Puebla and the confiscation of her expensive carriage. As soon as she read the decree, the notary claimed she "screamed" to her servants to call three of her protectors, although he warned her to respect the Real Sala with a more discreet attitude. Almost immediately, Gorraez and Casaviella responded to her summons.[85]

Ordóñez also had the reputation of treating her servants and slaves with cruelty. She allegedly beat Panseco and abused him verbally.[86] She openly cuckolded her husband who could not take vengeance on her powerful lovers. In general, witnesses described her as "audacious," "conceited," and "haughty." Her vanity derived from hearing too much applause when she worked on the stage, according to one witness.[87] She allegedly impoverished her lovers but at the same time treated them despotically and even beat and abused Gorraez if she heard rumors that he had visited another house.

Juggling her role as the boldest, most flamboyant courtesan of her time, Ordóñez also managed to manipulate official pity, despite the prevalence of hostile descriptions of her character. As the authorities pushed her banishment into effect, Ordóñez attempted to organize her huge number of belongings and set out on the carriage journey to Puebla. Before she could leave in late June of 1766, she complained of several terrible ailments, including typhus, tuberculosis, fever, epilepsy, and bloody flux. A doctor warned that if Ordóñez traveled at this moment she would literally die from menstruating while enduring the jostling of carriage travel, as indicated by a huge amount of blood they saw on her clothes, although they did not violate her modesty with further examination of her body.

Instead of beginning a dangerous, if not fatal, journey, the doctors suggested that she should go to the women's institution of the Misericordia in Mexico City, but when they examined the proposed rooms, they found them to be unhealthful. The new construction of Santa Maria Magdalena seemed more suitable, on the condition that Ordóñez would have new windows and partitions installed for her comfort. She should also have two servants in attendance. The Real Sala ordered these renovations for her sake.[88] In spite of all this effort, and many pages of discussion of her health and comfort, Ordóñez was allowed to retire to private houses (with monetary guarantees that she would not flee) after only a very short stay in official confinement in Mexico City.[89]

For a time Ordóñez managed to escape both her spouse and harsh judicial reactions. Unfortunately, though some of her powerful patrons left Mexico City shortly after the 1766 investigation, Ordóñez persisted in acting in an unrepentant way. Only a few years later, the viceroy and bishop decided to send Ordóñez to a stricter, less pleasant reclusion in Santa María Egipciaca in Puebla, a place of incarceration for criminal women as well as those entangled in divorce cases. Ordóñez protested her imprisonment up to the level of King Carlos III himself. For the rest of her life Ordóñez rarely paused in her various methods of complaining against her husband's mistreatment and heresies. In her later years, she continued to associate with and receive patronage from Gorraez, and she also took on at least one new lover.[90] Her date of death is unknown, but Panseco died as a widower in 1802.

ORDÓÑEZ CEDES THE STAGE TO OTHER LEGENDARY COURTESANS

A handful of eighteenth-century Latin American courtesans have achieved legendary status and have become, over the course of the nineteenth and twentieth centuries, national symbols displaying a wide range of emotional expressions ranging from feminine audacity and heroism to bleak denunciations of Spanish late-viceregal debauchery. While these myths are inspirational, patriotic, or simply poignant, they lack the complex humanity that La Ordóñez inscribed into the archives, her own version of her seductive and dramatic life story.

Three famous Spanish American courtesans chose their lovers from the most powerful men of their time and even influenced the course of history themselves, according to a range of literary and folkloric sources, as well as some scholarly history. From the mid-eighteenth century to the early decades of the nineteenth century, women known by the sobriquets of La Perricholi (Lima), Marichuela (Bogotá), and La Güera Rodríguez (Mexico City) were the Pompadours and Du Barrys of Latin America. If we include eighteenth-century Brazil, we cannot forget Xica da Silva, a freed slave who, according to popular legend, inspired by her astounding eroticism, luxuriated in fabulous wealth thanks to her patron's generosity. Taking a closer look at the historical record, most of these women, despite their famous lovers, appeared to have sought nothing more than lives of quiet, pious dignity surrounded by their families.[91] Only in the nineteenth and twentieth centuries did they become bewitching seductresses or objects of pity. They enjoyed (or suffered) some renown during their lifetimes but rose to more widespread fame with their depiction in nineteenth-century folklore, journalistic accounts, or patriotic histories. In the twentieth century, they became the subjects of novels and plays. Most of their gentility and the political/historical context fell away when these women featured in films or *telenovelas* starting in the 1970s.

The Limeña actress and alleged lover of Viceroy Manuel de Amat y Junyent (1704–1782), Miceala Villegas Hurtado, known as La Perricholi (1748–1819), became a symbol of Peru in the works of Ricardo Palma.[92] Like Ordóñez and any number of actresses in European cities, La Perricholi worked in the theater from her early teenage years, possibly with the sole purpose of finding a rich patron in Bourbon Lima's libertine cafés and theaters.[93] Although her son (conceived with Viceroy Amat) was not legitimated, she famously received properties as gifts from her elite lover. La Perricholi married in her late forties, after Viceroy Amat had returned to Spain, and died a wealthy woman with a reputation of piety. In a similar case in Bogotá, literary traditions, especially a 1946 play and a 1944 novel and, more recently, *telenovelas,* assert that Marichuela, or María Lugarda de Ospina, brought down the career of the "Virrey Fraile," Jose Solis Folch de Cardona (1716–1770), leading to his retirement to a Franciscan friary.[94] However, historic accounts, based on a crown visitation assessing Solis's term as well as his formal response, adamantly deny Marichuela's importance in ending his political career.[95]

Lastly, the Mexican aristocrat María Ignacia Rodríguez or "La Güera Rodríguez" (1778–1850) fits into the category of famous courtesans due to her alleged 1799 affair with a teenaged Simón Bolívar and her several cortejos, including perhaps even Alexander von Humboldt.[96] From the age of sixteen, Rodríguez endured a horrible marriage to an abusive aristocrat chronicled in an 1802 surviving divorce case. Although Rodríguez had evidence for abuse, her spouse accused her of adultery, and the case was dismissed. Fortunately for her, he died in 1805.[97] Rodríguez married two more times and enjoyed a long and exciting life at the center of Mexico City's enlightened political and intellectual culture.

The mature, educated Güera (Fair Lady) had an influence on Mexican Independence through her popular tertulia or salon where she hosted political conversations. Agustín de Iturbide, later the first Emperor of Mexico, attended from 1816. He discussed ideas with Rodríguez that influenced Mexican Independence and the Plan de Iguala.[98] Along the way Rodríguez gave birth to seven children, only two surviving by the time she reached her seventies. In 1843, the elderly Güera visited with Fanny Calderon de la Barca, who described her as follows: "La Güera retains a profusion of fair curls without one gray hair, a set of beautiful white teeth, very fine eyes, and great vivacity." She attracted Humboldt who, according to La Güera, said she was "the most beautiful woman he had seen in the whole course of his travels." Although presented in a more patriotic, heroic light, cultural treatments of La Güera roughly follow the pattern of La Perricholi and Marichuela: a mention by Guillermo Prieto in the nineteenth century, a biographic novel in the mid-twentieth century (still in print), and a movie in 1978.[99] Both La Güera, a born aristocrat and cultural force, and La Ordóñez, a plebeian with pretensions to the pinnacle of viceregal society, can be ranked among the most important courtesans of Mexican history.

Perched at the pinnacle of the pyramid of sexual entrepreneurs, courtesans perfected the high art of transactional sex. They effectively marketed their sexual capital and at the same time represented a public and tangible display of their lovers' wealth and high social status, a very desirable outcome for an elite man.[100] This show might enrage other men, especially frustrated suitors and solemn reformers, who then opened investigations of these women, or tried to send them into seclusion. But accusations of sumptuary violations benefited courtesans because they sought to advertise their own audacious materialism and carefully write their feminine delicacy and dignity into their case files. Ordóñez purposefully embroiled herself in various kinds of adjudication for decades. On the judicial stage, she practiced her skills as a consummate, highly intelligent actress, even admitting that she worked as a courtesan when it suited her.[101] She succeeded in acquiring status as she aged, so she could record herself as a doña in her later litigations. This final act documents how, after a lifetime of writing herself into the archives, she successfully seduced her scribes into telling her version of her story.

5

Streetwalkers and the Police

When asked if she has heard anyone blaspheming: she responded that her friend Pancha "the Butcher" will curse her soul, and her father and her mother's souls, when she is drunk in the street, and on one occasion when they went out for a stroll together, she said damn your whoring [puta] soul, but she never blasphemes against God or the Virgin.

TESTIMONY OF JOSEPHA VELASCO (AKA CHATA LA HERRERA), AGE TWENTY-TWO[1]

[Arrested women] María Ana Ortega, Spanish woman from Mexico, widow, age forty. María Micaela Sánchez, Spanish woman from Mexico, age twenty.

At nine pm, they were arrested for scandalous behavior, one guard lost his cape, another his hat, and they ripped his shirt. . . . The arrested women denied that they were drunk and said that they had only bought a half- real of aguardiente. . . . In jail, La Ortega bit the alcaide Soto, and he still has a scar on his hand. They also beat the prison matron, and having separated them to calm them, they became more agitated . . . they put up such a fight that it took the guards more than a half-hour to subdue them, and at that time they had to call for reinforcements.

They were corrected with twenty-five lashes and three days' incarceration for drunkenness and paid twenty reales for the damages that they caused to the guards. Released.

MEXICO CITY POLICE LOGBOOK, FEBRUARY 29, 1796[2]

In 1776, according to statements presented before inquisitors, a woman known as Pancha "the Butcher" had worked as a "ramera publica [public whore]" for ten years. She appeared to be Spanish, "white and Mexican." No one knew her exact age or real surname, but she looked older than twenty-five. Witnesses reported that Pancha's mother was a "public prostitute" and that her father was an Indian butcher and the inspiration for her nickname. Pancha's face had marks of previous cuts, inspiring her other alias, Scarface (a loose translation of *La Cara Cortada*).

She had a reputation for frequent arrests, skipping mass even on holidays, and drinking and wandering the parks with soldiers.

The witnesses in this investigation of alleged blasphemy were nine men who loitered around vinaterías (taverns selling hard liquor or *aguardiente*) during the hours that Pancha spent on the street.[3] They voluntarily confessed to the Holy Office that they had heard Pancha speak any number of scandalous words in public settings. Three witnesses claimed that she said *"se chingaba en dios."* Other men testified that she went so far as to exclaim *"me cago en los santos* [I defecate on the saints]" as well as *"que se jodia en dios y en María santísima y los santos* [screw god, the most blessed virgin, and the saints]." Witnesses alleged that she tried to beat some statues of saints with a stick and also declaimed against the nuns in the Saint Joseph convent during a night that she spent enraged loitering around their cemetery. Pancha engaged in street fights, attacking men who rejected her or spoke badly of her or her younger sister. Men responded with violence to her dissolute, *"endiablada* [wicked or diabolical]" temperament and actions. One of her lovers, a silversmith in his mid- to late twenties, testified that he had warned her to stop blaspheming, confronting her the morning after a rant. Pancha began to cry and said she only spoke that way *"de los dientes para fuera* [to show her teeth]." This witness opined that no amount of beatings would ever make Pancha submit.

The men's anecdotes, Pancha's own rants, and her scarred face inscribe her as an undisciplined, violent woman. But other evidence complicates her way of life: Pancha worked surrounded by family, friends, and roommates willing to stand by her. She solicited on the street with her younger sister and walked around with her brother. She also interacted with her parents, albeit usually in the form of loud arguments. Hostile witnesses did not provide her real name to the inquisitors, and as far as these documents indicate, Pancha impenitently eluded their questioning. Although secondhand accounts testify that the secular authorities had prosecuted her for unspecified crimes, the Holy Office did not have the jurisdiction to investigate or punish her for selling sex. This Inquisition investigation does not even contain any clear repercussions in response to her publicly irreligious persona. Because street-level policing and record keeping increased in the late eighteenth century, it is easy to see how Pancha and the other plebeian streetwalkers introduced in this chapter seduced historians with scribal tracings of their sexual entrepreneurialism. However, these women succeeded in evading both our efforts to retell their experiences and even the growing surveillance in their own era.

BUENA POLICIA IN THE BOURBON ERA

Bourbon scribes recorded arrests made and the magistrates' decisions regarding these offenses in a nightly diary known as the *libros de reos* ("books of arrested individuals"). This chapter analyzes the entries in six of these books dating from

July of 1794 to the end of 1798. Short (sometimes only one line) summaries of dozens of arrests of women working or simply present on the streets reduced them to nothing more than momentary low-level judicial exchanges written with only a modicum of attention paid to sum up their identities and crimes. This new and more quantitative documentation actually caused more evasiveness on the part of both those under arrest and those doing the arresting. In the 1790s, law enforcement inscribed only a handful of women arrested for brothel work and a few dozen public sex acts. The number of female offenders grows precipitously when we take into account the women who were incarcerated because the nightly patrols encountered them doing nothing more than going out in public at night or interacting with men in suspicious circumstances. In these latter cases, the authorities never mentioned anything to do with sex. It was unacknowledged and thus remains illegible. Despite nightly entries, many official pronouncements regarding changing plebeian street culture, and a greater presence of authority figures on the street, law enforcement, judicial notaries, and the women taken into custody made a conscious effort to avoid recording transactional sex.[4]

In the late eighteenth century, Mexico City experienced significant temporary population increases as rural dwellers emigrated into the metropolis during periodic agricultural crises.[5] Crown reformers chronicled their fear of this mass of bodies and the effluences of the approximately one hundred thousand underemployed plebeians (often called *léperos* in the nineteenth century) who resided in the capital. Historians argue that the greater attention the judiciary paid to the bodies and bodily functions of the poor "allowed elites to widen the cultural boundaries between themselves and the lower classes."[6] Reformers interpreted the public display of plebeian bodies as moral degradation, a sentiment that they expressed through their commentaries and ordinances against bathing in fountains, littering, unlicensed vending, street nudity, and public defecation, urination, and sex.[7] The majority of the nonelite bodies who ran afoul of these prohibitions had indigenous or African physical traits, which reinforced the Enlightenment categorizations and rankings of races.[8]

Consistent, state-mandated, nocturnal law-enforcement patrols were a new development in Spanish imperial rule, a validation of the idea of *buena policia*, or "good government" manifested as order in the city's thoroughfares, markets, and other public spaces. In past centuries, most criminal investigations grew out of complaints made by viceregal subjects. Watchmen walked the streets with some regularity, but they possessed a limited intimidation factor, and only a few courts were available in each locale to prosecute petty crimes. In 1745, the Mexican Viceroy Fuenclara decreed that three police deputies would report to the city cabildo (town council). The *Acordada* court, created in 1719 to crack down on rural banditry, had patrolmen on the street from 1756, but without consistency.[9] In the 1770s, viceroys issued decrees on the need for "buena policia" in the sense of order and cleanliness.[10] In the 1780s and 1790s, reformers reorganized and increased neighborhood-level courts in Mexico City and instituted a new set of guards in charge of lighting the new streetlights and policing the streets at night.[11] The modern police force grew out of elite reactions to urban population growth as well as well-justified fears of violent mass revolution. The creation of a corps of men to "police" cities suggests the development of an increasingly invasive state. Rulers were obliged to explain why these (very lightly, by today's standards) armed men were walking around as enforcers of government authority.[12] "Public good" offered a useful justification for militarizing the urban milieu.[13]

The Mexico City police, or *ronda,* often referred to as *serenos* or *guardafaroleros* ("lantern guards"), patrolled the streets, armed with a whistle and a *chuzo* (pike), at night after igniting the public lanterns. They did not carry guns or wear military-style uniforms, but their cloaks had some significance for the populace, who did attempt to rip them on occasion. On any night, approximately ninety-two of these men walked the beat, maintaining over one thousand lanterns.[14] The patrolmen made a wage of about eight pesos a month, and therefore, they had to live among the people they policed.[15] Their duties extended beyond arresting criminals to overseeing trash collection, sanitation, markets, and even cemeteries.

In the eighteenth century, sex on the street was a scandalous offense against morality and the new ideas of good city government, as well as a justification for the disgust that the elite expounded toward poor bodies and their base physicality. But despite all of this righteous rhetoric, prostitution still remained a hazy transgression in terms of the law. In criminalizing transactional sex more broadly in 1623 and 1661, Phillip IV expanded the judicial focus from procurers to brothels (chapter 2). Brothel suppression meant that the authorities could not only target bawds and ruffians but had some justification (via the seventeenth-century royal mandates) for prosecuting women selling sex out of any building where they lived and entertained male visitors. However, the crown made no new decrees prohibiting prostitution or clarifying the parameters of closing brothels in the eighteenth century.[16]

Since legislation did not clearly define the regulation of prostitution, nor decriminalize it entirely, street-level police had the power to control the judicial treatment of prostitutes.[17] This legal equivocation placed a great deal of power in the hands of patrolmen.[18] If they observed a woman soliciting sex publicly, the guards made a personal choice each time they either arrested her or let her remain working in public. The patrols might even pass their time on duty in visiting tolerated brothels or talking to street solicitors. Scribes reinforced the evasiveness of this personalized policing by their vague, abbreviated entries in the police dockets. All of these prevarications served the interest of the arrested women by avoiding a recorded label that marked their immorality.

The lantern guards arrested women whom they encountered having sex or soliciting sexual transactions in public places, including the streets and pulquerías.

The problem with their behavior was its public nature, its obvious gross physicality that shamed the reformed Bourbon streets, not the transaction involved. Only very rarely do the records mention an exchange of money because these men did not use entrapment as police do today.[19] Because no clearly worded law forbade prostitution or prescribed precise judicial sanctions (in contrast to pandering), only two very short records use the term *prostitute* or the older word for whore (*ramera*). In one case, the magistrates sent the accused woman back to her home village, and the other refers to women taken into custody to testify against other women accused of working as "panderers and whores [*leonas y rameras*]."[20]

Although ambiguous in recording specific acts of transactional sex, the dockets provide evidence of thousands of detained individuals. These books function like a census of all those criminalized city dwellers who had the misfortune to be caught in the act or to have provoked a complaint by a neighbor that led to a formal investigation. The books specify the detained individual's age, occupation, marital status, race, place of origin, and punishment received, although not always what crime caused the arrest. Hundreds of women were recorded in the *libro de reos* dating from 1794 to 1798, although men represent the vast majority of the offenders. More than half of the arrested women in Mexico City migrated from nearby regions and rural villages. These migrants did not travel from remote, isolated hamlets and innocently fall victim to urban corruption. They were adult women who left their homes or their marriages or both in hopes of improving their lives. Most of the women arrested for infractions relating to sex were older than twenty. Over 40 percent of these women appeared Spanish to the scribes, with "Indian" representing the next most common label.[21] The woman most likely to go up on charges implying her involvement in transactional sex in the late eighteenth century was an unmarried woman of European ancestry between the ages of twenty and twenty-nine, hailing from a nearby provincial town or village.

Two historians have made a serious statistical study of these dockets, eighteenth-century law, and crime. First, Michael Scardaville in the 1970s counted and analyzed all the existing arrest records from the late colonial era, resulting in an in-depth study of 7,067 recorded crimes from 1794 to 1807. More recently, José Sánchez-Arcilla Bernal tabulated the records found in the existing books dating from 1794 to 1798, the same ones that I refer to in this chapter. Sánchez-Arcilla found a total of 7,029 arrests.[22] Even this set of over seven thousand records does not include all arrests, because many of the record books have not survived. Nor does it accurately represent all illegal acts committed in Mexico City in those years. Of course, many intimate sexual crimes, often of the kind that most affect women, went unreported, in contrast to the typical highly legible (read as) masculine infractions of murder, brawling, or robbery.

Because the police of the time obscured the causes for detaining streetwalkers, and the women almost never confirmed any particular label or crime, even what

TABLE 5.1 Incidents of women arrested in transactional sex-related offenses, 1794 to 1798[a]

Lewd acts (sex in public)	21
Lewd acts in a pulquería (including "sleeping with" a man)	8
Prostitution/brothel/pandering	11
With a man/men/soldier(s) in public in suspicious circumstances (including pulquerías)	70
Private transactional sex acts, gatherings, or relationships	31
Insults relating to prostitution or pandering	5
Loitering	62
Total	208

[a]AGN, Mexico, "Libros de Reos," Vol. 73, Exps. 45–50, 1794 to 1798. I counted by incident, not by individual arrestee, following Sánchez-Arcilla's methodology.

historians choose to interpret as an arrest for prostitution remains open to debate.[23] The abbreviated entries in the arrest records cannot express the complexity of transactional sex, which involves an implicit, unspoken understanding of reputation, circumstances, and negotiation far more complex than can be captured in a few lines summarizing a momentary interaction between a street patrolman and a woman caught in a suspicious act.[24] Criminal suspects lied and always had an excuse ready to explain their location and activities. A wide range of illicit interactions falls in that difficult-to-document grey zone of nonmonogamous, nonmarital sex, whether for pay or for pleasure, or a combination of both.[25] My breakdown of arrests relating to transactional sex is summarized in table 5.1.

But despite its illegibility and ambiguity in the written records, transactional sex featured all over the cityscape, in busy streets, secluded parlors, and modest apartment buildings. Sánchez-Arcilla blames "the permissiveness of viceregal authorities themselves" for the lack of clearly stated arrests for prostitution.[26] Scardaville agrees with this assessment and observes,

> The police mounted no campaign to rid the city of prostitutes. As long as the brothels were congregated in specific self-contained streets and did not cause any public disturbances, the authorities allowed prostitutes to ply their trade. . . . Even the courts readily acknowledged that prostitutes worked on all the city's streets and alleys.[27]

Streetwalkers worked on many streets of the city, but they shared the goals of the patrolmen: obscuring the records and avoiding the written notation of a permanent label. The police scribes wrote of solicitation in the Alleyway of the Holy Spirit, in the Plazuela of Jesus, underneath the bullfighting ring, in the Alleyway of La Barca, beneath or on bridges including La Misericordia and Our Lady of Anguish, in cemeteries, in the Plaza de Armas, and at the Portal of the Augustinian friars. Sex workers remained a part of the urban landscape because, in the late eighteenth century, reformers viewed drunkenness as a far more serious vice and threat to the public good and urban buena policia than transactional sex. As this inscription of indigenous bodies played a role in constructing late colonial racial hierarchies, Bourbon-era law enforcement spent an enormous amount of time and energy recording the huge incidence of public drunkenness and illegal pulque selling but generally left women trading in sex alone.[28]

SEX IN PULQUERÍAS

From the sixteenth century, church and state created an enduring stereotype of indigenous barbarity based on a culturally biased interpretation of native alcohol consumption.[29] The frequency of this excuse in a judicial context only compounded the eighteenth century's highly racialized interpretation that blamed drunkenness for a general lack of discipline that weakened the plebeian classes (especially indigenous individuals), causing them to waste their time and money, destroy their families, and fill the streets with ragged, unpleasant bodies and bodily functions. Other than monitoring urban illumination, the new police force primarily functioned to remove drunks from the streets, as well as to keep a wary eye on the poor and their public actions.[30] More than two thousand people, or around 3 percent of the adult population, found themselves in police custody for public intoxication in 1798. Street patrols had to haul away drunks by the cartload, as the average Mexico City resident over the age of fifteen consumed close to two hundred gallons of pulque annually. Drinkers could imbibe at any of 1,600 legal and illegal pulquerías, which hosted an estimated 62,000 customers each night.[31] The viceregal bureaucracy made a significant income off taxing pulque and aguardiente, so the colonial rulers never considered outlawing these intoxicants even though they pontificated against their dangers. In contrast to the elusiveness of sex crimes, the dockets clearly and repetitively inscribe indigenous degradation.

Pulquerías offered a popular setting for plebeian socializing and buying and selling sex. Most of these taverns were unlicensed, run by women, providing food and a gender-mixed social setting where families and single people met and interacted. How Mexico City's poor viewed their local street taverns probably differed greatly from official perceptions of their threatening, dark, dirty, criminal ambiance. Licensed saloons were supposed to have one wall open to allow greater police surveillance, although pulquerías seldom followed this ordinance.[32] Hundreds of astute businesswomen exploited the lucrative but illegal business of selling pulque on the street or in makeshift stands, risking arrest and suppression.[33]

From 1796 to 1798, surviving arrest records show that the night patrols arrested six women and their male partners for having sex inside pulquerías. Selling sex alongside alcohol hearkens back to the practices of medieval taverns in and around legal brothels in Spain that provided clandestinas to their paying customers (chapter 1). In contemporary Madrid, law enforcement interpreted "women sitting in taverns" as prostitutes and fined the owners of the establishments that allowed this practice.[34] The same infraction in Mexico City might result in twenty-five lashings and a jail sentence for some women, but most of those caught in this act disguised its transactionality with careful word choice and creative explanations.[35]

Couples who had sex in Mexico City pulquerías may have chosen this venue to hide their exchanges, possibly in a partitioned area or in a bar illegally closed to street viewing. But occasionally, a zealous watchman peered into one of these humble establishments. For example, the guards caught two migrants from outside Mexico City, Florentino Paris (an unmarried mestizo, age twenty-four) and Maria Andrea Flores (an indigenous soltera, age eighteen), in an act that they described as "*mezclandose* [mixing themselves]" in the "*rinconada* [corner] *de la pulquería*" at 8:30 p.m. one evening in May of 1796.[36] Both individuals lacked spouses, but they managed to convince the judge that they would soon marry and thus avoided imprisonment or lashings. Unfortunately, this explanation did not succeed for the castiza named Gertrudis Miranda (age twenty-four), caught in an "*acto torpe* [lewd act]" with an indigenous man five years her junior in the notoriously scandalous Pulquería de la Florida.[37] Because they were both single, Miranda's claims that she had sex in this public setting "with the promise of matrimony" might have lessened her punishment, but her partner would not confirm their engagement. Both culprits received twenty-five lashings, and Miranda was sent to serve in a respectable house, a common sentence applied to women whom the court viewed as delinquent.[38] The references to a potential marriage erased the illicit nature of the sex act.

Marriage could also underline a written notation of immorality. After midnight one night in January of 1798, a patrolman arrested an indigenous man (age thirty-three) and woman (age twenty-five) having sex. Again, this lewd act took place in the bawdy pulquería de la Florida.[39] The woman tried to explain that she used to have an illicit relationship with this particular man, but they had separated, due to the fact that both of them were married to other people. Having reunited that very day in the pulquería, they decided to have sex again. This simple explanation of their public sex act did not prevent them from receiving twenty-five lashes each. In other cases, even if just one of the lovers were married, the courts sentenced the woman harshly, regardless of the creativity of their excuses or the veracity of their tales. For example, an indigenous widow, age thirty, received a sentence of eight days in jail for sex and drunkenness in a pulquería with a thirty-five-year-old married Spaniard.[40]

Some *reos* lacked ready verbal skills to expunge their public transactional sex acts from the records. The authorities reacted incredulously when the patrolmen found two indigenous paramours in their early twenties having sex around midnight in the Pulquería del Palacio.[41] Although only the young woman labeled herself married, both received twenty-five lashings, despite their excuse: they were cousins, out drinking together, and the guard happened to enter just when the man was picking up the woman after a drunken fall.[42] Another couple, a married man, age twenty-three, and a slightly older widow, both labeled castizos, who were arrested for the vague offense of "sinning" also used the "I just fell on top of her" excuse while drinking at a fandango.[43] The magistrate again doubted the validity of this tale and sentenced the man to ten days of forced labor and the woman to lashings and three days in jail. An over-forty Spanish widow also caught in the act did not claim a previous relationship with her partner in crime, a man who fled the scene when law enforcement entered another pulquería around midnight in April of 1798. The widow said that she had met this stranger that day while she walked home to her house. They went out drinking together at a pulquería and proceeded to engage in a "lewd act" before the guard entered. She received eight days in jail for her crime.[44]

Illicit acts are implied when night watchmen arrested women for offenses described evasively as "finding" them "with a man" in a pulquería. In one case of this kind, a man showed his guilty conscience by fleeing when the patrolman "found" him with a thirty-year-old married indigenous woman "underneath the shack of the pulquería de Palacio" after 2:00 a.m. The married woman received no punishment. A single indigenous woman, age eighteen, spent eight days in jail after the night watchman "found" her with a married indigenous servant in the Pulquería de las Maravillas after midnight. The man admitted he met her by chance there and planned to have sex with her. A woman labeled a mulata widow (age nineteen) endured twelve lashings after an encounter with a married Spanish cigarrero (age thirty-eight), whom she also claimed to meet by chance in a pulquería.[45]

The intentional ambiguity in documenting saloon sex as "found with a man" mirrors popular prevarications such as the euphemistic "sleeping with." Only the judicial sentence clarifies the difference between the criminal acts described as "sleeping with" a man versus "passed out with a man" in a pulquería. Of course, sleeping is not the same as passing out in a drunken stupor. Every night, the patrolmen arrested individuals whom they found passed out on the streets or in pulquerías, incarcerating them for the night as they "slept off" their drinking. At least five incidents of this kind involved a couple, "drunk and passed out," an offense that resulted in an eight-day jail sentence for the woman, in line with the common punishment for drunkenness, and therefore not of real interest here.[46] On the other hand, "acostados [sleeping]" with seems to imply a sex act in the current sense of the phrase. For example, at 1:00 a.m., a patrolman found a married Spanish woman, age thirty-five, and a fifty-year-old widowed indigenous cigarette roller "sleeping together" in the Pulquería de la Bola. Both received twenty-five lashings for their crime. Another Spanish woman, this time unmarried, received only a very strong warning and a sentence to return to her native Texcoco, when the ronda found her "sleeping" with a thirty-year-old Spaniard in, once again, the pulquería de la Florida, where they admitted they went "with the goal of having sex *[el fin de mezclarse]*."[47] In the same manner as "sleeping with" or "found" with a man, the euphemistic term *"mezclar"* helped disguise that this pulquería operated as a public brothel. The authorities could not record and thus make legible the ongoing illegality of this establishment because that would mean that, unless they immediately shut the place down, they were ignoring the royal decree closing all brothels. As the classic viceregal maxim stated: *obedezco pero no cumplo* (I obey but I do not carry out). Therefore, the raunchy pulquería de la Florida stayed in business until at least 1811.[48]

BROTHELS, PROSTITUTION, PANDERING, AND TRANSACTIONAL RELATIONSHIPS

Paradoxically, the increasing recognition of the open secret of monetized sexual relationships and brothels by eighteenth-century Mexico City residents and law-enforcement officials coincided with a lack of interest in using specific language to record these arrangements or establishments. In fact, transactional sex is inherently ambiguous and, as can be seen in the examples in this section, does not fit into clear categories. How could giving or withholding a material or monetary gift prove a crime? How did a house party prove that a building had become a brothel? What living arrangements involving more than two people in a monogamous/ heterosexual couple equate to a pandering situation? These unavoidable prevarications produce an "evidentiary paradox: a known prevalence of the crime, and an equally know rarity of its documentation."[49] Viceregal transactional sex outside marriage was so prevalent that it did not necessitate written recording. When it did appear in writing, vocabulary varied in its evasiveness or clarity, depending on the purpose and shape of the judicial record.

Despite elusive verbiage, the written tone of documenting certain incidents clearly acknowledges the commonplace nature of exchanging sex for cash. In January of 1798, at 10:45 p.m., a corporal found two migrants from outside Mexico City having a dispute over payment for two sex acts. The culprits were an unmarried indigenous woman (age twenty-five) and an indigenous widower (age thirty).[50] As was common, drinking played a role in the exchange. Mariana Ignacia Vertiz had solicited her client, who worked at the cigarette factory, from her house, asking if he would give her a half real for pulque. Later they had sex (euphemistically recorded as "mezclar"), but since the cigarrero could not pay, Vertiz said that he offered her his sheet, although the client said she had stolen it.

Due only to the deponents' goals in furthering their cases, two marriage disputes in the 1790s led to a clear recording of acts of prostitution and pandering in the traditional forms of brothels or rufianismo. In 1795, a soldier called Domingo Lara petitioned for divorce because he accused his wife, Maria Josepha Larranaga, of working a few nights in a brothel and haunting pulquerías in the company of a known bawd.[51] He had petitioned for divorce in the past, but his efforts led only to two failed reunions with his wife. After one of their attempts at reuniting, Lara caught Maria Larranaga walking out of a brothel, bragging that she went there to "fornicate." For her part, Maria Josepha Larranaga claimed that she entered the brothel only to ask for a half-real for cigarettes, but her husband still insisted on cutting her head with his sword. In 1796, another man requested the arrest of his wife, Ana Ladron de Guevara (an española, age twenty). The husband disguised his motivations, claiming that he caught her "with a soldier."[52] Guevara for her part avoided further prosecution with very clear, accusatory language: she left her marriage because her husband "whored her out on a daily basis [aputeandola diariamente]," solid justification supporting her petition for divorce.

More subtle verbiage appears when written records refer to enduring transactional relationships, including those that were rather pricey for the payer. In the case of Maria Fernandez, a seventeen-year-old taken into custody for sexual "incontinence," along with her twenty-five-year-old lover, a married Spaniard, the magistrate dictated that the man pay Maria Fernandez's mother twenty-five pesos, in weekly installments of four reales (or half of a peso).[53] An arrest for "living in sin" documented how a soldier paid another young Spanish woman, the eighteen-year-old Modesta Adrian, a sum of two reales for her daily maintenance a year after their short affair ended.[54] A young lady named Doña Tomasa Henriquez, taken into custody for "living in sin," enjoyed the highest paid transactional relationship that appears in the surviving dockets—an income of a peso a day from a priest, and possibly more from a soldier.[55]

Law enforcement avoided raiding alleged establishments that hosted transactional sex until neighbors complained and in the process named the buildings as brothels. At this point, public recognition prompted the creation of written records. In 1795 and 1798, the logbooks indicate that the police made a halfhearted effort to close brothels, with a total of five investigations peaking in the summer of 1795. Due to complaints from unspecified individuals, on June 20, the guards entered a suspected lupanar (brothel) due to the frequent sightings of men entering the establishment.[56] Inside, they found a fifty-four-year-old married Spaniard employed in the tobacco factory, and two young Spanish women, age fifteen and twenty. The man said that he had entered the house with the goal of "soliciting a girl." Only a week later, surrounding residents complained about a certain asesoría where men and women gathered and provoked a scandal.[57] This time, the guards arrested four women: the manager, a forty-year-old mestiza from Puebla, and three employees. These latter women were much younger than the brothel keeper: two were sixteen (an india and an india cacique), and one was nineteen (another mestiza). The watchmen found the women drunk, wandering in the street, and entertaining a soldier "for gain [por interes]" but never used the terms prostitution or brothel. In July of 1795, the parents of Maria Gertrudis Avila, a fifteen-year-old indigenous girl from Pachuca, sent a Spaniard to Mexico City to investigate the disappearance of their daughter, who had left home two months previously.[58] The authorities found her living in a house of ill repute in the Callejon de San Antonio. Later in the fall of 1795, law enforcement took six men and women under the age of twenty into custody for a suspected "*congal* [brothel]," located in an *asesorita* connected to the Pulquería de la Nana.[59] Only one of the men, a Spanish shoemaker, was married, and the other male offenders (described as *indios*), worked as cigarette rollers. All three women (two *indias* and one *parda*) claimed soltera status. The men said that they entered the house of Eusebia Miranda (a parda, age nineteen) and observed that "there appeared to be nothing evil about the house, although they presumed that it was a *congal* because many soldiers and women congregated there." The women denied any wrongdoing other than sex outside of marriage, and they received no punishment, other than returning to their families or serving in an honorable house. In the same year, a corporal raided a house because he heard about "a scandal on his beat" involving a known brothel.[60] He entered a house and found seven women there, several beds, and two guards cavorting *(retozando)* with the women. The *cabo* arrested only three individuals, including a mulato man who claimed he was the spouse of one of the women (later found to be a lie), and two twenty-year-old women, described as an unmarried india and a married mulata. Despite all of the evidence, law enforcement denied that any crime had been committed and released the women with a strong warning.

In other incidents, typically inspired by neighbors' complaints, the police raided less formal parties, vaguely described as "gatherings of men and women" or places where both genders notoriously caused "scandal." The term translated as "gathering *[concurrencia]*" in this context suggests sexual contact and, in some of these complaints, also can imply procuring.[61] In one arrest involving two couples, the men mentioned that they met two women at a vinatería before agreeing to go home with them for sex, and in another foursome, the men said the women "grabbed them *[los estiraron]*, and, having entered [a dark room], they went to have sex."[62] The pickup lines might also go in the opposite direction, as in the case of two couples arrested when the watchman "found" them together. In this case, the women said the men made the first move as the women were walking by them. All involved received twenty-five lashings.[63]

The new night watchmen had very little effect on either the established or more impromptu brothel business, and they also did not suppress the older tradition of female intermediaries in affairs. The authorities arrested only four procuresses in the 1790s, although lawmakers had criminalized this occupation for centuries. However, bawds ran such subtle operations that the magistrates struggled to prove accusations against them. For example, in 1798, a lieutenant arrested three individuals: an eighteen-year old single castiza, a married Spanish man, age twenty-five, and their landlady, a thirty-year-old mulata.[64] The older woman allegedly served as the couples' tercera, a suspicion sparked when the guardsman found the Spaniard and the castiza alone in a room at 11:00 p.m. The man received twelve lashings, and the young woman had to serve in an honorable house, but the landlady was released without consequences.

Sometimes a confused night watchman took individuals into custody for private and subtler transactional relationships. In March of 1798, a lieutenant of the guard found three Spaniards together in a rented room at 2:00 a.m.[65] They were gathered together suspiciously, but no one was actually having sex at that moment. The triad, a nineteen-year-old woman from Puebla, a nineteen-year-old barber, and a thirty-one-year-old silversmith, admitted that they all met in the room, which they rented for this sole purpose, every few days for sex. The authorities did not see anything worth punishing here, but they did not like the lack of monogamous structure in this arrangement, so they rearranged it to fit their paternalistic vision of social hierarchies. They sent the girl back to her mother, sent the silversmith back to his master, and set the barber free without penalty.[66]

Sex for sale permeated the city, but both the authorities and the perpetrators usually had good reasons to keep it unrecorded, most importantly that the actual monetized exchange between a man and a woman was not a crime and could almost never be proven with the kinds of surveillance available in this era. Generally, no one (especially the perpetrators) wanted to record transactional relationships, so official intervention attempted to further erase it. But these scattered, ambiguously worded prosecutions suggest a variegated and active world of indoor transactional sex and even communities of enterprising women working alone or in pairs or with procuresses.

SEX ON THE STREET

Policing public lewd acts demonstrated how crown reformers hoped to curtail plebeian bodies and intimate physical behaviors that spilled out into public. In 1793, Viceroy Revillagigedo took strong measures to stop gender mixing in bathhouse changing rooms and in the baths themselves, in response to complaints about men and women bathing and drinking to excess together while bathing in public establishments.[67] Allegedly, some shockingly bold or desperate plebeians even took advantage of the privacy of dark corners in churches. Scardaville reports that "sexual orgies were commonplace in public steam baths and in the public toilets constructed next to the pulquerías."[68] Some residents of Mexico City did not have access to a private location for sex, which could lead to sex on the street, as was very common in other large and growing metropolises in this era.[69] Surviving dockets record twenty-one incidents, variously labeled as an *"acto carnal," "acto torpe," "mezclando carnalmente,"* or *"acto venéreo."* Punishments ranged widely, including lashings (between five and fifty), eight days in jail, supervised servitude, forced return to marital cohabitation or family life, or just a warning. For all but five of the women arrested for public lewd acts, the court scribe included a paternalistic coda in his summary about who would supervise them after their release.[70] This verbiage calling for proper familial surveillance functioned to confirm that, despite the forced written acknowledgment and recording of public sexual disorder, the authorities had acted to resolve the issue and prevent further publicizing of these events.

This rhetorical gesture made little practical sense for the accused. Whether done on a steady basis or only as an occasional solution during times of extreme hardship, working-class women turned to selling sex to augment their tiny legal incomes.[71] They could not or did not want to depend on a husband's income or on a paltry wage in typically female occupations. But after their arrests, paternalistic law enforcement forced them back into precisely these economically untenable or otherwise unbearable situations. One case from 1795 made a mockery of bureaucratic efforts to reorder one teenager's life. A patrolman arrested a seventeen-year-old labeled a mestiza actually having public sex in her *depósito* (a kind of safe house where women went allegedly for the protection of their honor and that of their male guardians when they were involved in sex-related litigation, including divorce). Her sentence: to go right back into depósito.[72]

Other than the believability of their excuses and the status of their male companions, the scant information available makes it difficult to determine why certain women received cruel punishments and others left their incarceration with only a warning. The court evaluated certain women as disreputable, possibly repeat offenders who had received verbal warnings in the past, and punished them harshly as street solicitors, while judging other women as hapless victims. For example, an entry from January of 1798 recorded a woman called Gertrudis Pérez as a prostitute, a very rare example of a clear accusation of selling sex. Later in the month, the night watchmen arrested a thirty-year-old married indigenous woman called Maria Gertrudis Pérez for a public sex act near San Lazaro with a slightly younger unmarried indigenous button maker.[73] They offered an excuse of drunkenness, but perhaps due to her previous offense, Perez received twenty-five lashings, and the court compelled her to return to her husband's custody. Even with the written specificity of her offense, Pérez obfuscated her identity by using slight variations in her name, one of the most common and timeless techniques in the sex-work realm.

Harsher sentences did not always coincide with racial profiling—these records rarely mention women designated as of African ancestry incarcerated for street solicitation.[74] However, one woman (no age or marital status given) described as a mulata caught in a carnal act with a soldier in 1794 (time of day unknown) received the harshest sentence encountered in all of these records: fifty lashings and release to her aunt.[75] In 1798, another mulata (unmarried, age forty) left police custody with only a warning.[76] The guards caught the latter offender in a "lewd act" with a

Spanish widower, age fifty-seven. The culprits denied any guilt, and apparently, they convinced the court of their innocence. Most likely, sex with a soldier clearly suggested prostitution to the authorities, leading to lashings. An indigenous widow named Isabel Santollo (age twenty-five) also received a harsh judicial reaction when the guards found her engaged in a "venereal act" with a soldier in the wee hours of the morning.[77] Santollo admitted only drunkenness and denied any further crimes, but the court sentenced her to twenty-five lashings and eight days in jail, after which they released her into her sister's custody. Of course, the scribe did not record any details regarding the soldiers involved with the woman arrested, because the men enjoyed the juridical erasure of military fuero.

Spaniards rarely received lashings for street solicitation. The police took three Spanish women into custody for public sex in the 1790s, and only one of them potentially had to endure a paltry five lashings. In this particular case, a Spanish girl (age sixteen) fled her husband, who complained to the authorities that he had found her in a lewd act with another man and demanded her arrest.[78] The husband then backed off on his vindictiveness and requested that his young wife not receive corporal punishment. The sentence included her return into her husband's custody, a phrase also seen in the sentence of an española (age unknown) arrested in a lewd act with a forty-six-year-old indigenous man who worked at the cigarette factory.[79] The woman claimed that she chose to drink aguardiente with this man because she knew him as a servant employed at a house that she visited. Both culprits said that they were too drunk to remember what happened next. While the female partner only had to go back to her marriage, with the warning that she improve her conduct, the cigarrero suffered fifteen days calzado (in leg irons). The judiciary shifted into paternalistic mode in reaction to the arrest of a twenty-four-year-old Spanish widow for "carnally mixing" with an unmarried Spanish man on a patio one evening just after eight.[80] Although the culprits would admit only to having a conversation, the young woman had to spend eight days in jail, and then, as seen in many sentences, she had to go to an honorable house where her conduct would be monitored. Her partner received eight days of forced labor.

Offenders attempted to mitigate their punishments and erase the record of their transactions with a variety of excuses and pretenses. If both persons involved could claim unmarried status, they could convince law enforcement to set them free under the promise that their public lewdness represented nothing more than a prelude to their celebrating the bonds of holy matrimony. This ruse worked for four individuals arrested for public sex, women labeled indias and mestizas between the ages of fifteen and twenty-eight who endured no further punishment beyond forced marriage to their street lovers.[81] Although it decreed no other sentence, the court expressed doubt that these marriages would come to fruition. In the case of a seventeen-year-old labeled a mestiza arrested "in between the legs of" a Spaniard at 8:45 p.m., the authorities threatened imprisonment if the promised marriage did not happen. While these women had the bad luck of encountering a watchman on the beat while having sex openly in a public place, a clear offense against Bourbon sensibilities, other women faced incarceration for nothing more than walking the streets at night.

WOMEN ON THE STREET

In their legal codes, late-eighteenth-century jurists grouped together street solicitors and unmarried women walking on the street without a defined occupation and proposed the punishment of imprisonment in a women's jail.[82] The dockets document over sixty incidents of women arrested for an ambiguous offense recorded as "found on the street" or "found on [the guard's] patrol," descriptions that I sum up as loitering (see table 5.1). This vanishingly vague wording served as an excuse to round up select streetwalkers without having to record a written reference to sex. My tally in table 5.1 does not include women who were apparently arrested just for public drunkenness because I see a clear distinction between alcohol-related entries and inscribing prostitution permanently into the police logbooks. Although reformers in Spain in this era equated the offenses of drinking to excess, vagrancy, and solicitation, in Mexico City, Bourbon bureaucrats associated drunkenness more with colonial racial differentiation than sexual immorality. Including drunk women, this figure would increase to one hundred women arrested annually simply for walking on the Mexico City streets at night or falling asleep outside in a public place, whether or not they had been drinking.[83] The "found on the street" arrests protected the guards from involving themselves in more serious accusations and allowed the women to more easily erase their transgressions.

Vagrancy concerned the authorities in Spain from the mid-eighteenth century. The Spanish king defined vagrants in 1745 as

> those who lack an occupation, benefice, estate, or income, living without knowing how to earn their income by licit and honest means. Those who have a patrimony or emolument, or are sons of a family, but lack any other occupation than gathering often at gambling houses, with individuals of bad reputation, or frequenting suspicious places.... The beggar that is youthful, healthy, and strong, but has an injury that does not impede him from working.[84]

The royal description goes on to include men who do not work but only gamble, drink, socialize, and have affairs; semi-employed day laborers; wandering performers and peddlers; youths who beg; and those who sleep outside at night, or in taverns or gambling houses. This description defines vagrants as men, but women, of course, also lived itinerant lives. In both Madrid and Paris, the late-eighteenth-century judiciary saw little difference between vagabond women and prostitutes and perceived the urban problem of female criminals as increasing precipitously.[85] In contrast to Mexico City, where the patrolmen dedicated most of their time and energy to incarcerating drunks, in Madrid, reformers founded city patrols to rid the streets of vagrants and beggars.[86] In the case of a woman living on the street, outside the control of any patriarchal figure (father, employer, guardian), Spanish authorities of this era criminalized her, even while acknowledging that outside factors such as poverty or war contributed to rising eighteenth-century homelessness.[87]

In the elite perception, vagrancy and homelessness made public spaces chaotic, ugly, and filthy.[88] A hospice created in 1774 served to house a certain number of homeless poor. Bourbon reformers in Spain worried about vagrancy and street crime in general, but in 1790s Mexico City, the Spanish rulers dedicated more nightly patrols and verbiage to drunkenness, racializing plebeians as deficient in their faculties, as well as their poverty.[89] Despite migration into the capital and underemployment of the poor, only twenty-one incidents noted in the arrest records specifically targeted male and female vagrancy (often associated with another crime, such as drunkenness or adultery) out of a total of over seven thousand entries. Scardaville assigns this crime to only 1 percent of the arrests he tabulated.[90] At least according to the dockets, the night watchmen rarely arrested vagrants.[91] Only two women received the label of *vaga* or *vagamunda*.

The criminalization of women follows gender norms with sexuality as the interpretative lens—all female delinquency must be sexual.[92] Therefore, when law enforcement arrested women loitering at night, the law interpreted them as prostitutes. However, the scribes and even the arresting guards did not want to record them officially as such but wanted instead to paternalistically guide them and remove them from exposure to this label. Permitting unsupervised women to wander the streets at night would suggest that men within this society had little control or authority over their female family members and dependents and that the authorities did not care about public immorality.[93] In an effort to reassert the proper gendered order, the courts punished loitering women by mandating their return back into a family setting or into domestic servitude.[94] For example, the watchmen took Ana María Lopez, a fifteen-year-old unmarried girl, into custody as a vaga in 1795. The scribe described her as "libertine and badly behaved," noting a clear association between vagrancy and her sexual activity. The court released her into her brother's guardianship and exhorted him to make her attend mass and to keep an eye on her decorum and associates.[95] A second woman, labeled an indigenous widow, age twenty, faced arrest due to the complaint of her alleged lover's wife. Feliciana Sandoval denied the accusations of adultery; however, the scribe also accused her of cross-dressing: "According to the Alcalde Rio Frio, she is a provocative and vagrant drunk that nightly goes about with the vagabonds of the Tarasquillo Barrio to [attend] wakes and dances, disguising herself as a man with sleeves and hat. She denies these particulars."[96] Feliciana Sandoval received the sentence of service in an obraje.[97]

Although Spanish law as well as general elite perceptions equated women on the streets to prostitutes, Mexico City law enforcement did not specifically refer to transactional sex when they took women into custody for the "offense" of walking the streets at night. Sánchez-Arcilla and Scardaville assume that the guards arrested these women for breaking the curfew, although they disagree on when it came into effect: either 10:00 p.m. or 8:00 p.m.[98] Even as vague as this assumption is, curfew violation does not make sense in every case of nighttime arrest. For example, the court sentenced the married indigenous woman Maria Josepha Nara (age twenty-five) to eight days in jail for no other stated crime than her presence on the street at 7:30 p.m.[99] In fact, the scribes never wrote the word *curfew* in all of the sixty-two cases that I have labeled "loitering." Why would they deem it necessary to erase such a mundane transgression?

Instead, the guards, judges, and scribes most likely believed that most of these women were outside soliciting the thousands of men drinking in pulquerías or seeking sex partners on any given night. Among those women who did not inspire a sentence of jail or lashings, in twenty-five cases, the magistrates released the offenders with a warning, threatening them with an investigation of their "life and conduct," or advising the women or their guardians to "take care of their conduct."[100] This encoded coda signifies that the authorities interpreted their presence on the street as sexual delinquency and in need of supervision, without specifically naming them as prostitutes.

Because the description of the offense is so vague, only the harshness of the punishments offers a way to differentiate women on believable nighttime errands from known street solicitors. Of the sixty-two incidents of women arrested for no other crime than their physical presence on a public street, three served eight days in jail, and five received twenty-five lashings. Why were these particular women singled out for an offense that otherwise almost always led to immediate release from police custody? Again, racial designation did not guarantee the court's leniency. A Spanish Doña Petra Soto endured twenty-five lashings for no other stated crime than her presence on the street late at night.[101] Was she soliciting or a recidivist? In two cases, the judge explained why he imposed a harsher punishment. A sentence of twenty-five lashings makes sense as a harsh response to street solicitation after a guard caught an eighteen-year-old española sitting in the doorway of a military barracks before 4:00 a.m.[102] Any contact with soldiers implied solicitation and prostitution. The court directed this young woman to return to her parents' care so that they could monitor her conduct. In another case resulting in twenty-five lashings, the scribe noted that the woman arrested after one in the morning, a twenty-two-year-old india, was a repeat offender but did not specify her crime.[103]

Other possible repeat offenders received lighter punishments the second time around. On January 5, 1796, the police incarcerated and administered twelve lashings to a Leandra Ramona, described as a sixteen-year-old indigenous virgin, for wandering on the street at 11:00 p.m. The offender said that she had no father and did not know her mother's location, so she lived with her aunt. Then, six months later, the night watch rounded up a Maria Leandra Ramona, also a virgin, but this time described as a nineteen-year-old mestiza, found on the street at 1:15 a.m. This time Leandra Ramona (most likely the same woman, given the fluidity of race labeling and the rarity of her name as well as the unusual doncella status) said that she fought with her female employer. Her mother said she would not take her in because she could not "subjugate" her, so the girl had to go live with her uncle. She received no other punishment.[104]

Sometimes the scanty records documenting how loitering women interacted with law enforcement allow a light sketch of their short careers on the streets. In May of 1798, the guards arrested Maria Francisca Medrana, described as a twenty-six-year-old mestiza from Jalapa, at four in the morning for sleeping in an asesoría—apparently in a semipublic location where she did not belong. Medrana said she found the building open and sought shelter after her husband abandoned her. The court sentenced her to service in an honorable house. Seven months later, the ronda re-arrested her, now labeling her as a twenty-seven-year-old mulata from Jalapa, while she was "removing a sleeve" (her own or her companion's) in an encounter with a drunk, married, indigenous man in his late thirties in the alleyway of the Holy Spirit (see chapter 7 for more on this location). This time, Medrana spent eight days in jail.[105]

Multiple arrests might inspire a woman to shift the written record away her own offenses and instead write the patrolman as the offender. In June of 1796, a guard caught thirty-year-old Spanish widow Maria Coronel out at three in the morning, with no good excuse other than visiting friends. The magistrate released her to her creditors and warned her to take better care of her conduct. One month later, the night watchman took her into custody at 10:30 p.m., when she claimed she went out for medical reasons. Although the guard denied it, Coronel claimed that he grabbed her, pushed her, and hit her with his pike on her forehead, causing a small mark. This tactic worked, and Coronel left incarceration immediately with nothing more than a warning.[106]

The notoriously harsh Spanish nun Sor Magdalena de San Jerónimo observed that all loitering women claimed that they had an honorable reason for their presence on the streets. If they were carrying a jar or basket, they could explain that they went out to buy a necessary item, most often tallow for candles.[107] In most loitering cases (fifty-six of the total), arrested women convinced the courts that they had a good reason for going out at night. Their verbal acuity effectively erased their sexual criminality entirely from the records, and they avoided lashings or imprisonment.

Mexico City women, ranging from age fifteen to forty-five, described as mestizas, indias, españolas, castizas, mulatas, and moriscas, widows, maidens, single women, and married women, used Sor Magdalena's typical excuses to avoid lashings or jail time. They explained their presence on the street as late as 4:30 a.m. was due to visiting family or friends, going to wakes, returning from dances or mass, caring for the sick, watching fireworks, or finding a drink of water.[108] About one-third of the alleged loiterers left the jail immediately after processing, with no warning or any particular person designated to oversee their future conduct.

One case fits well with Sor Magdalena's suggestions: a fifteen-year-old maiden out with a thirty-year-old widow buying candle wax at 1:15 a.m., a classic setup for street solicitation (see chapter 7 for similar incidents). They left the jail with only a warning.[109] In a similar case, the patrol arrested another two indigenous women, an unmarried girl, age fifteen, and another thirty-year-old widow, for walking the streets together after midnight.[110] The authorities released them but said they had to return to their native villages. Women caught "sitting in a door" had to think of more believable explanations for why they deserved immediate release from incarceration after the guards caught them in this position, a seemingly timeless bodily configuration that implied sexual availability. One Spanish maiden (age forty) claimed that she waited in a doorway at midnight simply out of fear of entering. An indigenous married woman (age twenty-five) strenuously denied that the watchman had found her in a door. She explained that she had instead done nothing more than go outside to the toilet to exercise her body.[111]

Women "found with" or "talking to" soldiers on the street could not explain away this extremely visible act of solicitation or erase themselves from the logs with innocent-sounding excuses. In response, the magistrates released most of the women into the custody of a family member or an employer, usually with a strong warning to improve their conduct. A variety of women sought a military clientele: from two twenty-year old mestiza virgins caught drinking with five men at the Vinatería de la Santa Veracruz, to a forty-year-old Spanish widow.[112] Two Spanish women in their mid-twenties faced eight days' incarceration and then service in an honorable house, after the police found them with a group of soldiers at 10:00 p.m.[113] Maria Sánchez, a thirty-year-old indigenous widow, received the harshest sentence of twenty-five lashings, probably due to the fact that a guard "found her" with a soldier in an alley, most likely engaged in a sex act. Even if the police found them in flagrante delicto, the arrestees verbally protested by claiming that the soldiers were their relatives or, on the contrary, that they had nothing whatsoever to do with them.[114] Women also might react physically to efforts to police their public sex acts. A guard caught Maria Trinidad Fernandez from Otupa, no age or race given, in a "venereal act" with a soldier.[115] In her rage at this intervention in her street activities, Fernandez broke the guard's pike, resulting in an encounter with his corporal, twenty-five lashings, a sentence to servitude, and an investigation into her life and habits. Unlike other loiterers, women who solicited soldiers lacked a viable excuse to explain away their suspicious contacts and thus endured a notation in the dockets, a scolding, and sometimes a physical punishment and an assignment to domestic work. However, both the scribes and the perpetrators refused to specify that prostitution took place, further obscuring the written record of transactional sex.

Bourbon bureaucrats wrote new kinds of records in the last three decades of Spanish rule as they sought to document their efforts to achieve urban cleanliness and ordered thoroughfares. Paradoxically, their verbiage about erasing plebeian physicality from the Mexico City streets, especially in the form of indigenous drinking customs, made it very visible. Sex work also balanced between the poles of greater exposure and further erasure. When they illuminated the streets, the guards shined a light on women who were loitering, soliciting, drinking with men, and having sex in public. These public women and their acts certainly did not conform to their supervisors' talk of orderly and rational ideals, so the patrolmen took some of the offenders into custody. However, the judiciary did not want to record hundreds of prostitutes in their dockets. Noting indigenous barbarity served a clear imperial purpose, and in Madrid, the Bourbons feared female vagrancy and sexual disorder, but exposing sex for sale was not an official priority for 1790s Mexico City. The age of regulation had just barely begun (see conclusion). Instead, the guards, scribes, and streetwalkers worked together to hide its existence, even as notaries wrote thousands of written entries that, when organized as statistical evidence, tell a tale of an ultimately losing struggle for elite control of the city streets. At no time could the authorities suppress transactional sex, and usually they did not even try. It became ever more difficult to patrol the streets after mass insurrection began.

6

Multiple Prostitute Identities

If a woman has a little bit of respectability, then she is judged a public woman. . . . If she speaks to men, it is evil. If one or two young men enter her house, then she has prostituted herself. What excellent logic!

If I sew for a living, I am judged as practicing an illicit business. If I work as a servant, they judge me for having an affair with my master. Everything I do is a crime, and I have no other resources than to abandon myself to the desperation I encounter at the hands of my cruel and destructive starvation.

My respectability (it certainly shames me to give it this name) is a paper doll that disappears on closer examination.

STATEMENT MADE BY MARIANA LÓPEZ ORTEGA (ALSO KNOWN AS LA SARGENTA) DECEMBER 24, 1802[1]

In the early nineteenth century, for the first time in New Spain's archives, the word *prostitution* appears frequently, as deponents on all sides of judicial inquiries manipulated its deprecatory tone. The use of this word strengthened their accusations and denials by recording allegedly depraved, professionally sexual women. In response to this hardening scribal category, the women in this chapter reacted by multiplying their identities when they came before the court accused of prostitution or running a brothel. They wielded the terminology of prostitution with the purpose of differentiating themselves from the label. In their notarized words, these women consistently denied that they were prostitutes, meanwhile acknowledging that such an occupation did exist and thus helping strengthen a new vocabulary of female deviance.

The first woman examined here, Mariana López Ortega, known as *La Sargenta* ("Sergeant Lady" or "the Sergeant's Woman"), pushed the boundaries of conventional behavior and her own dueling identities in the early nineteenth century as she literally battled for her autonomous way of life. The second half of the chapter presents the case of María Manuela González Castrejón, a brothel manager who staged an elaborate occupational disguise involving several witnesses to her trial. López Ortega and González Castrejón refused to label themselves as prostitutes, in the understanding of prostitutes as bad women. Trial documents do not capture all of the roles that these two defendants played, as the goal of their statements was simply to write themselves as moral, respected, and financially independent women. We can read nothing more than an enticing hint of the multiplicity of changeable identities embodied by sexually active women such as these in the final decades of the Viceroyalty of New Spain. The label of prostitute emerged as an ever more solid opponent to their shifting personas, even as they reaffirmed it with their denials of its applicability to themselves. At the same time, notaries and judges began to inscribe a new and very seductive label in this era: the "prostituted girl," an innocent victim of corrupting and evil influences.

Case studies continue to complicate clear categorizations. In a series of late-colonial cases, both the old (whore or public woman) and the new (prostitute) vocabulary carried very little weight in court. For example, a husband in 1807 responded to his wife's petition for divorce by saying that she only wanted to be free of him to squander her life in libidinous and libertine prostitution.[2] But all of the witnesses in the case denied these exaggerated accusations, and the scribe declared that the wife's prostitution had not been effectively proven, despite her illegitimate child. In 1810, a woman tried to denounce a royal official for living with (using the older term) a public woman as his *comadre,* but it appears that her complaint aroused very little reaction.[3] In 1816, Manuel Gomez, chained up in a jail cell for unknown crimes, requested that the authorities examine the life and habits of his lover, Casimira Pinzon, whom he simply referred to as a prostitute. It seemed that his imprisonment may have had to do with acts of vengeance that she perpe-trated after their breakup, and Gomez felt it unjust that she walked free.[4] Again, no evidence indicates if the use of this modern label resulted in any actions on the part of the judiciary.

One potential husband in 1802 denied that his fiancée's past history of prostitu-tion would deter him from marrying her.[5] In the face of his brother's accusations and attempts to prevent his marriage to Doña María Petra Colocia, Don Ramon Huidobro commented that calling his fiancée a "public woman" presented no legal impediments to marriage. He added that he knew his wife had committed only one "fragility," and he believed that "if one of a betrothed pair had a weakness in [com-mitting] a carnal crime, this would only unravel the marriage if they continued the same life [after marriage] but not otherwise." The open-minded Don Ramon hoped that marriage would give Doña Petra a "tranquil spirit," stating that this was an important motivation for fulfilling his promise to her.[6] The social venues where genders had begun to mix publicly in the eighteenth century, for drinking, danc-ing, and just talking, had lost their taint of scandal. Don Ramon and his elite peers understood that women might have their "weak" moments, but this did not change their suitability as wives. This casual attitude toward nonmarital sex fits with the fact that the authorities also possessed a general disinterest in prosecuting public women. In many cases, the authorities sympathized with women affected by war, especially young women working in brothels and poor wives abandoned by their soldier husbands. These women were the nineteenth-century descendants of the sisters of the House of Wonders or other semirespectable women discussed in chapter 3. Against the odds, the courts tried to reunite even alleged public women/separated wives with their husbands but did not attempt any other punishments.

This was the suggested resolution for a dispute between two "prostitutes" that a royal notary tried to mediate in 1813. A woman called Doña María Josefa Romana, known as La Marquina, brought a jewelry box full of diamond-encrusted trinkets to show the notary in an effort to clear her name and deny that she had stolen them.[7] Another woman, Petra Arellano, had implicated La Marquina as a possible thief of items stolen from a Señor Conde de Santiago. La Marquina's accusation that perhaps Arellano was the actual thief led to a long altercation between the two women, in the presence of the notary. The argument revealed that La Marquina could not have afforded to buy the jewelry with the very limited salary her soldier husband earned, especially since they had lived apart for two years. Arellano observed that La Marquina maintained herself through the efforts of a "distinguished subject" who served as her patron (cortejo) and that she also "prostituted herself" to other decent men.[8] The authorities advised her to end her life of "vicious prostitution" and return to her husband's side, where she could fulfill her duties as a married woman. The rest of this case has scattered, which is unfortunate, because it might have revealed more about how poor soldiers' wives managed to make a living on their own in Mexico City, even finding themselves in possession of expensive jewelry, and to avoid prosecution by appealing to the judge's pity and paternalism.

WHO CREATES THE TEXTUAL RECORD?: "LA SARGENTA" VS. DOÑA MARIANA LÓPEZ ORTEGA

Neighborly complaints to law enforcement led to the 1802 arrest of a young Spanish woman known as La Sargenta. The authorities labeled her as *"la reo mujer cabada,"* which might also refer to her soldierlike status if *"cabada"* alludes to the word *cabo.*[9] Loosely translated, this alias means "the arrested corporal woman." These noms de guerre affiliated her with the military. Her real name was Maríana López Ortega. Trial documents reveal that La Sargenta/López Ortega had at least two distinct but overlapping identities—as a scandalous streetwalker and as a paid but respectable domestic servant. I will use her two names interchangeably but carefully here, in an effort to acknowledge that she simultaneously inscribed herself as both of these women in her criminal investigation. I choose to use one or the other or both names depending on which character the scribe wrote in that particular paragraph, page, or statement. Neither name is stable or permanent or revealing of her real sense of self but instead shows nothing more than what the authorities wanted to label her as, and how she responded, in the textual skirmish between these two characters. To clarify, within her case file, hostile witnesses identified her as La Sargenta, while family knew her as Mariana López Ortega. The two identities battled each other as the case proceeded, and this shifting back and forth may confuse the reader, as it may have perplexed those making a judgment on the case and even the protagonist herself. In the end, the defendant worded her statements effectively so that López Ortega erased La Sargenta, at least according to what the documents tell us. La Sargenta/López Ortega looks like a tough survivor, and she was, very literally, a fighter. But in contrast to her strong actions against her persecutors, the rhetorical self-characterizations that she performed in the court context show her as an abused woman who innocently socialized with and worked for many different soldiers, forging a modest living through their payments for her domestic labor. She even referred to herself as a doña. While López Ortega narrated her good repute, her enemies wrote La Sargenta as a rowdy, drunk, violent prostitute.

La Sargenta saw opportunities to make a living off soldiers, in her own urban interpretation of the camp follower.[10] Although her arrest took place eight years before the Grito de Dolores, she lived and worked in a militarized Mexico City. Bourbon viceroys had sought to reform the military, which had previously depended on local militias, from the mid-eighteenth century.[11] The number of regular army troops tripled in New Spain from 1758 to 1810.[12] Certain strategic areas of New Spain, including the capital, also retained a royalist militia that grew in numbers into the era of insurgency.[13] By the late eighteenth century, the Spanish crown realized that a greater military presence in their empire would lead to an increase in sex for sale. The military fuero—which meant that soldiers did not come under the jurisdiction of criminal courts—made it difficult to police the serious crime of pandering within the military. In 1798, King Charles IV attempted to put into effect stricter judicial control over soldiers, publishing a royal decree stating that military men who committed very serious crimes, such as lenocinio (pandering), would lose their privilege of protection from criminal prosecution.[14] Whether they were aiding and hosting royalists or patriots, women whose work combined cooking and clothes washing with sexual relationships with soldiers faced prosecution. It is not surprising that, within the viceregal justice system, the women who helped insurgents received less toleration than royalist female supporters.[15]

The records do not provide La Sargenta/López Ortega's age. Because she had a sixteen-year-old sister, possibly she was around twenty during the events narrated in her case file, although she might have been a few years older or a little younger. She and her sister were born in Mexico City. She was married, but her soldier husband had run away to Queretaro four years before her arrest in 1802.[16] During those years, she was officially separated from him and claimed that she had filed for divorce. Among her possessions, López Ortega stored the papers relating to her divorce petition or possibly a criminal case against her husband. Her neighbors had the understanding that she had submitted a petition for divorce and was waiting for a decision.[17]

Because she was a married woman in this state of limbo, La Sargenta's neighbors did not approve of her living outside a court-sanctioned "safe house [depósito]." In other words, they did not think that she should live independently without the protection of an appropriate man of honor. But despite attempts at reconciliation, La Sargenta/López Ortega refused to live with her husband. At one point after her husband left her, his commanding officer had ordered her to a house of female reclusion, but she did not submit to his mandates either.[18] With these acts, La Sargenta/López Ortega indicated that she did not want to live either as a wife or as an officially fallen or protected woman. Sharing her neighbors' condemnation of La Sargenta's independence as well as the desire to enclose her, the authorities accused her of fleeing her husband so she could live a libertine life and indulge her vices.[19] But in her own version of her marriage, López Ortega presented herself as abandoned by her husband when he left for Queretaro. Various authorities had attempted to find her husband for four years beginning in 1799, without success. He moved from place to place, working at different haciendas, avoiding apprehension for years. He even succeeded in hiding from his military superiors.[20] In 1802 and 1803, she did not know his whereabouts. She admitted that she still did not want to reunite with him.

In the written statements submitted to the court by her advocate, López Ortega claimed that the *mala vida* that her husband gave her had led to her arrests for excessive public drinking and even her prostitution. She alleged that her husband never even provided food for her, instead robbing her. She accused him of giving her a venereal disease and acting as her panderer, in the "scandalous *lenocinio* with which he prostituted me."[21] Her sophisticated written statement transformed her from public nuisance in her neighborhood to a victim of an abusive man, inscribing herself with the López Ortega identity. To support this transformation, throughout her defense, she always referred to herself by her real name and avoided the suggestion of disrepute by not acknowledging the alias used by the authorities and hostile witnesses.

Despite the fact that she had separated from her husband in the late 1790s, López Ortega continued to socialize regularly with his military colleagues and the officers of the "crown regiment" based in the viceregal capital. Taking advantage of these connections, she organized quite a good living by cooking and sewing for several men, according to the very elegantly argued statement that she made via her advocate. She claimed that one officer (also referred to as a cadet) paid her a generous twenty-five pesos a month to wash his linens, do his darning, and cook his meals.[22] This fastidious young gentleman apparently disliked the "reheated" food made by his aide-de-camp, and he found his regimental mess hours inconvenient. Avoiding all of this unpleasant hassle, he chose instead to stop by her flat for most of his meals, other than when he dined out at "distinguished houses" where he visited his friends. Rumors had circulated that she lived as his concubine and that the cadet actually rented her accommodations in his name. López Ortega denied this, asking rhetorically that if she did cohabitate as the mistress of such a young, rich, respectable man, was it credible that he would also allow her to "prostitute herself" with the many other individuals that entered her home?[23] As a good woman here, she implicitly insulted promiscuous women and the dishonorable men that might tolerate their behavior, confirming the attitudes that inspired her accusers.

López Ortega claimed that other men came to visit her because she did their sewing for them. These soldiers visited her flat because they knew her husband.[24] While their visits may have appeared suspicious, she denied that she committed illicit acts with any of these men. Because of the cooking and mending services that she provided, and the fact that it all took place behind closed doors, López Ortega could assert that she was respectably employed with some degree of feasibility. No one, not law enforcement nor her neighbors, could positively know what went on in the privacy of her rooms.[25] As long as she cooked and sewed for them, she could deny that she also had sex with her visitors. She explained that the money she earned in this manner was the only income that prevented her from dying of hunger, and she expressed dismay that the authorities and her neighbors found such innocent acts suspicious.[26] Simultaneously, La Sargenta was a scandalous prostitute whose visitors were clients only seeking to trade in sex. Witnesses narrated her domestic activities as lurid and even violent.

At the time of her arrest in October of 1802, López Ortega had escaped from her depósito because she had told the man in charge of it that she had to leave it in order to care for her sick sister.[27] She had been living for four months with her sixteen-year-old sister and an Indian maid in a mezzanine flat next to and owned by the Regina convent. A thirty-three-year-old Spaniard who lived in the same building with his family labeled La Sargenta as a "woman of evil life" and a "scandalous public woman."[28] According to this don, many men came to her flat continuously, and he heard them speaking only the most obscene words. He claimed that he had heard one cadet beating her. The neighbor feared that he would start a fight in response to the disruptions and dishonor his family, so he had complained to the convent majordomo to force La Sargenta to move.

The guards who made their rounds near her house also knew about these disturbances in her living quarters.[29] A twenty-two-year-old patrolman named Rafael Rodríguez, while walking his beat, testified that he saw La Sargenta frequently trying to enter the local bar to drink aguardiente. He observed that she usually had a man with her and at times appeared drunk. He listed the male companions that went to drink with her: "a *paisano*, a cadet, a sergeant, a soldier." Rodríguez claimed that she referred to all of these different men as her husbands. Sometimes the *vinatero* shut his door, preventing her entry, suggesting that she did not even possess the respectability to enter his drinking house.[30] In response, López Ortega asserted her respectable identity, via her advocate, and denied or belittled all of the above characterizations. She refuted that the soldiers who visited her caused any scandal in her neighborhood and explained away their noise as nothing more than normal behavior for rowdy young men. She said that they amused themselves in an aggressive way, play fighting in and around her room and patio, simply because they served in the military. She criticized the suspiciousness that converted any visit she had from a young man into proof that she "prostituted herself."[31]

In her defense, López Ortega refused to categorize herself as a plebeian woman seen drunk on the streets, causing public scandal. While still living with her husband in around 1798, La Sargenta had served time in jail for public drunkenness and disorderly behavior, causing a "great scandal in the street." She said that on this occasion she had drunk aguardiente by accident, implying that her husband forced her to drink it. However, with scribal suggestions of La Sargenta, López Ortega also admitted that she still enjoyed going out at all hours to enjoy some aguardiente with her *compañeras* but said she had no tendency to the vice of drunkenness.[32] She did not submit to this vice daily, or even weekly, but only rarely in an effort to endure her insomnia, and she claimed that she never lost her senses while drinking.[33]

Reminding the court of the lack of support she received from her husband, López Ortega tried to explain away every hint of disreputable behavior in the statements that she made in her defense. She also discussed how the general public tended to harshly criticize and exaggerate the faults and misdeed of any unfortunate woman, no matter what she did.[34] However, López Ortega/La Sargenta could find not a single character witness willing to back up her claims and testify to her good reputation. And despite the respectable portrait that she painted of herself, the authorities discovered her in a very scandalous position one night at midnight, an event that challenges the López Ortega archival inscription. This incident caused her second arrest and time served in jail to await the result of the investigation into her behavior.

Each witness to and participant in these events narrated a slightly different story. The circumstances leading up to La Sargenta's second arrest took place in a bakery owned by an *alcalde* named Don Agustín and his wife, Doña Ana. During the month of October 1802, Doña Ana heard from her servants and employees that the man who worked as the bakery's doorman and night watchman, a *chino* (Filipino) called Tomas Angulo, had spread the rumor that he was La Sargenta's *cortejo*.[35] He bragged that he had arranged to have sex with La Sargenta in the bakery during his nightshift. Hearing these reports, Doña Ana asked her servants to watch out for any disturbances late at night in her bakery. On the night of October 27, they reported that La Sargenta had knocked at the door at 11:00 p.m., but then no one heard any more suspicious noises. The next night, the same thing happened, this time at midnight. Doña Ana called from her balcony to the street patrolman Rodríguez, commanding him to accost La Sargenta in the bakery. He and other guards barged in and claimed they caught her in flagrante delicto with the doorman.[36]

Despite Doña Ana's attempt to frame La Sargenta, she, along with her servant and a soldier who were waiting for her outside the bakery, convinced the guards not to arrest her on the spot. But Doña Ana would not let her get away with her midnight interaction with the porter, so she woke up her husband. The alcalde/baker ordered the guards to arrest La Sargenta that night. Due to her identity as an alleged whore, the patrolmen knew where to find La Sargenta. They came to the flat that she shared with her sister and her servant in the darkest hours of the next morning. La Sargenta's sister opened the door, recognizing the alcalde Don Agustín among the group of men. The guards then entered the women's lodgings and found La Sargenta fast asleep in bed. They took her into custody with great violence and against her will. When the police took La Sargenta from her bed, she wore only a *camisa* and *enaguas,* or a nightshirt and petticoats. They grabbed her and dragged her toward the steps. Only her vehement protests compelled them to allow her to return to her room for some clothes before going into the street. She managed to hurl a rock at the arresting officers as they yanked her away from her house to the jail. The men literally dragged La Sargenta kicking and screaming to jail, incarcerating her at around four in the morning. The night jailers on duty witnessed the prisoner in a dangerous rage, hiding a knife in her underclothes and swearing at the alcalde, calling him a range of offensive names, to be discussed further below. The jail attendants quieted her and confiscated her knife from inside her clothes.[37] The bakery doorman Angulo, La Sargenta's sister, and their servant also had to spend time in jail.

It should come as no surprise that López Ortega and her compañeras vocalized their own version of these events, explaining away the violence and sexuality essential to La Sargenta's identity and the justification for her cruel treatment by the guards. The arrested woman and her india servant (also incarcerated) both said that López Ortega stopped by the bakery only to buy bread, after an evening spent standing in the doorway or arch *(portal)* that led to a plaza. The servant said that López Ortega had picked up the soldier just to have someone to walk her home and did not explain why they had stood outside until 11:00 p.m. The servant and the soldier waited outside while López Ortega went in for the bread by herself. López Ortega denied that she had been caught in the act with Angulo and admitted to knowing the porter only slightly, just enough to greet each other on the street.

López Ortega and her sister portrayed the arrest as a shocking invasion of her home and bodily privacy. Since the time of her separation from her abusive husband, perhaps López Ortega/La Sargenta had become used to defining her own use of her body without having to submit to any men unless she chose to on her terms. The forced touching by the men who arrested her enraged her, leading to an explosive reaction. Her sister said that the guards woke up López Ortega/La Sargenta and rushed her out the door. She explained that her sister had a "violent temper," which, along with the fact that the guards woke her up suddenly and forced her outside "almost nude," explained her "insolent words" and her resistance to arrest. López Ortega/La Sargenta admitted that she was "blind with rage" from the sudden disruption of her sleep and alleged threats from the alcalde's sword, which led to her swearing and insulting the alcalde. One of the arresting patrolmen, as well as the female guard at the jail, possibly searched her "between the legs" to find the knife she hid there, another cause of her violent resistance.[38]

The specific words that La Sargenta used to insult the alcalde Don Agustín as she entered the jail mattered a great deal because they meant that she faced accusations of disrespecting an arresting officer and a representative of crown justice.[39] Observers disputed what she actually said. The nightshift guards at the jail testified that she told Don Agustín to go to "*la mierda* [shit]" and that he was a "*carajo* [slang for penis]." A patrolman said she called Don Agustín *mulato, chivato,* and *sordo* (deaf, possibly meaning to her protests). López Ortega, in the statement submitted by her legal advocate, denied remembering saying any insults. She defined *chivato* as a vulgar word for alcahuete, which would suggest that she called Don Agustín a panderer.[40]

López Ortega could not deny that she swore but justified why she did it, the level of insults she chose, and how the words did not accurately represent her as a scofflaw. Critically, she did not use the "five illegal words," as defined by the Novísima Recopilación. These criminal words were: *sodomítico* (sodomite), *cornudo* (cuckold), *traidor* (traitor), *hereje* (heretic), and *puta* (whore) (the law specified that this was an illegal word when used for a married woman).[41] Chivato and mulato, relatively mild insults in contrast, fell far out of the range of these slanderous, fighting words. López Ortega, in her advocate's prepared statement, explained that obviously she said these words only due to her passionate rage at the way the guards wrenched her nude from her bed and that she did not mean them literally or as slanderous insults. She claimed that she did not know whom she was addressing because at that moment she was still hiding under her blanket. Her advocate argued that, of course, López Ortega did not consider Don Agustín a procurer but, in fact, knew him to be a decent man of good reputation. It was also argued that obviously she also did not know his parents, so she could not make a judgment on his lineage.[42] The charges for slander and disrespect of authority could not possibly detain her in jail, especially since she had not harmed the alcalde physically and had no intention for these words to be taken literally as pointed insults or disrespect for an important authority figure. The long statement made in López Ortega's name offers a surprising justification of the use of profanities as perfectly natural and expected when circumstances lead to aroused and agitated passions. Her advocate argued that in the same way that some words are used as empty courtesies (such as "*Beso a Vuestra Merced la mano* [I kiss your grace's hand]"), other words said in anger are just spontaneous reactions in the moment. Both men and women swear in this way when they are fighting or enraged, and this should not be taken as intentional slander.[43]

In other sections of her defense statement, López Ortega represented herself as a poor, humble woman, despite the fact that if she earned what she claimed, twenty-five pesos a month, her income ranked her far above laborers who scraped by on only thirty-four pesos annually. With this income, she could have supported a household with five dependents.[44] She certainly fit into the middle class of Mexico City residents, those who could afford at least one servant. In fact, her servant testified that López Ortega promised her two pesos a month in salary.[45] Contrary to this evidence and the rumors spread by her neighbors that she lived a life of luxury, López Ortega described her possessions as ragged and scanty in her attempts to argue that she did not receive any support from illicit lovers. Specifically, gossips said that the mantilla she wore to church probably had a value of five hundred pesos. The accused said that it was of local make, barely worth twenty pesos. She claimed she owned little more than a bed, a few chairs, a few kitchen items, and clothes that she had to pay off weekly. All of her clothes could fit into a very small chest. She said that only her cleanliness and pride hid the pitiful poverty of her life, and this paltry wealth proved that no one either protected her or gave her gifts.[46] It seems likely that her primary lover, the cadet who paid her a set sum to do his domestic tasks, actually paid for the advocate who submitted the lengthy petition defending her against the accusations and attempting to formulate her good reputation. If he could afford to pay a domestic servant such a generous salary, he certainly possessed great wealth himself.

While López Ortega's statement in her defense went on for many pages, with many different arguments in her favor, her alleged lover did not seek out extensive legal help. Describing himself as a forty-year-old married *"chino de Manila,"* Angulo readily admitted to his crimes shortly after his incarceration. He explained that he had known La Sargenta for ten days when she came to visit him the night in question, actually her third visit to him while he worked. According to his boss, Doña Ana, this short relationship led Angulo to brag that he was La Sargenta's cortejo. He explained that due to his "weakness *[fragilidad]*" he flirted with her and attempted to seduce her, although he said that they had never met in private at each other's rooms.[47]

On the night when they were both arrested, La Sargenta knocked on the bakery door at midnight, asking for a real's worth of bread. After he let her in, Angulo confessed that they engaged in an "acto torpe," and in his opinion, La Sargenta willingly had sex with him until the guards interrupted them, barging in through the bakery door with their lances and lanterns.[48] Angulo claimed that he did not know that she was married. López Ortega denied that they had sex that night, or that they even knew each other beyond a casual greeting in the street, although she did admit visiting the bakery three times late at night. Given the traditional pattern of women's utter denial of selling sex, it seems likely that La Sargenta went to Angulo for bread after a late night out with her servant and her friends and that they both agreed to have sex as part of this exchange. Their very petty acts of sexual commerce probably would have passed unnoticed, without any public scandal, if the baker's wife had not sent for the guards. It also did not help that La Sargenta already had a bad reputation of frequent drunkenness, disturbing the peace, and earning her living independently as a domestic worker and a possible sexual partner for hire for the soldiers who visited her room.

La Sargenta's alleged client succeeded in negotiating his way out of jail by portraying himself in his testimonies as penitent and regretful. In a statement made a few weeks after his arrest, Angulo contradicted his previous confession and denied that he had sex with La Sargenta on the night of their arrest, claiming that the guards had entered the bakery before they had the opportunity. A married man who did not know his spouse's current location, Angulo admitted that he only vaguely knew that he had last heard that his wife lived in Chalco with her relatives. He expressed that he felt ashamed that he had disrespected his employers by opening the door to La Sargenta on three different occasions and begged their pardon. He confessed that his wife left him because he wasted away his principal and could not support her. He promised the authorities that he would reunite with her within fifteen days, so they let him out of jail with no further punishment or admonitions.[49] Angulo successfully maneuvered within the criminal system by denying his act of adultery and taking on a penitent attitude. Conveniently, with Angulo's denial of a sexual act, La Sargenta also appeared less guilty. Angulo's later retraction might have served as a way to reduce his alleged lover's blame as well.

Late in 1802, while various officials continued trying to find her husband, a judge with the titles of *alcalde, regidor,* and *corregidor* determined that La Sargenta/López Ortega had served enough time in jail. He decided that the appropriate punishment for her would be confinement in an honorable house. He forbade her to walk alone in the street or have any contact with the cadet who had paid her such a lavish salary. She also had to attend mass regularly, at the risk of imprisonment.[50] With these proclamations, the judge tried to shape La Sargenta's full transformation to López Ortega, but the woman in question insisted on effecting this change on her own terms. Evidence suggests that López Ortega continued to use the courts in her struggle for autonomy on her own terms. By April of 1803, going by honorable name of Doña Mariana López, she petitioned once more for release from her last "safe house" so that she could find ways to support herself, possibly with the help of her relatives in Xalapa.[51] After four years of searching, still no one had found her husband. As the case ends here, we can only hope that she left confinement permanently and had more freedom to live her various identities according to her needs and desires.

This may well have happened, because during the Era of Insurgency, individuals who served in the armed forces or had any connection to the military especially disregarded efforts to control the public sale of sex. For example, in 1815, Don Manuel Martin Mansilla complained to Viceroy Felix Calleja that one night around 11:00 p.m., while he was patrolling with two other *comisarios,* he passed by the café next to the Coliseo theater.[52] There he encountered several of what he called *mujeres de mal vivir* (women of evil life), passing their time with two officers from Zamora and three artillery sergeants. At this hour of the night, the soldiers were breaking curfew, as well as associating with known whores.[53] Don Manuel sought help from a sergeant major stationed in a nearby plaza, in an effort to drag the women off to jail. When the law-enforcement officials tried to pull the woman away, the five soldiers ganged up on the police and violently attempted to set the women free. Don Manuel would not let go, so the soldiers pulled out their firearms, threatening the patrolmen. Don Manuel and his four assistants could not challenge this threat, so they gave up the struggle. This ineffectiveness led to Don Manuel's petition to the viceroy, humbly requesting that soldiers at least pay some regard to Mexico City judicial officials, even to just show the appropriate respect and consideration. In 1819, toward the end of the insurgent era, a similar disregard for the authorities took place when an alcalde tried to warn a royalist soldier before arresting his wife for her occupation of selling sex.[54] The alcalde called her a *"mujer muy prostituta"* and claimed that her husband supported her ventures. As a result, the soldier sought out and threatened the alcalde, who then called on his well-armed deputies for aid. The husband ran away and successfully escaped the five men armed with pistols.

THE GONZÁLEZ CASTREJÓN BROTHEL INVESTIGATION

Bawds also inscribed themselves with a variety of identities into criminal records in the early nineteenth century. Brothels remained a tolerated site for transactional sex, only sporadically prosecuted by street patrols or complaining neighbors. Runaway girls so often ended up at these establishments seeking shelter and a way to make money that their relatives knew to look for them there.[55] More and more after 1800, an avuncular pity saturated some of the official depictions of certain girls: namely, young, delicate Spanish doñas in distress. Condescending to forgive these presumably innocent victims meant that their corrupters—that is, bawds and others who pushed the girls into nonmarital sex—had to shoulder the blame for crimes committed.

María Manuela González Castrejón faced the high court in 1809 with the charge of running a brothel and prostituting her own daughter, Francisca, along with several other very young women.[56] In this case, an older bawd received the brunt of the castigation while her younger employees emerged from the proceedings almost with impunity, even when the brothel manager tried to paint some of their lives as viciously corrupt. The court viewed forty-year-old González Castrejón, in contrast to her employees, as irredeemable. Allegedly a repeat offender, despite all evidence to the contrary, she could not shake her reputation as a hardened criminal whose every act seemed suspicious. In her defense, the bawd asserted her good reputation as working in a legitimate career as a used-clothes dealer, an occupation that blended extremely well with managing brothel workers. She may very well have made money in this legal fashion, but the authorities could not forget her previous confessions of managing a brothel.

Like La Sargenta, González Castrejón had at least two identities, but in this case, the bawd wanted to prove that she had changed her persona over time. She could not deny that she had run a brothel in 1808, but this person no longer existed in 1809. In her second trial, González Castrejón argued vehemently that she had reformed after the first guilty conviction. But the respectable guise did not succeed in submerging the illegal activities of the past. Ultimately, the authorities believed the rumors about González Castrejón, as well as the physical evidence at hand, and found her guilty of running a brothel for the second time. However, they took a more lenient attitude toward the young women who allegedly worked for her, focusing not on punishment but on arranging what they understood as a more protected situation for them.[57] The rest of this chapter will examine how the older, experienced woman, notwithstanding her utter denials and several supportive witnesses, suffered more serious legal prejudices than the allegedly inexperienced and naïve young "victims" of the bawd's corrupting influences.

Born in 1769, by the first decade of the nineteenth century, González Castrejón was married with four children and an absent plebeian Spanish husband. The first indications of disrepute in the life of the future convicted madam emerge from a 1798 police docket, which documents that a patrolman arrested María Manuela Castrejóna (labeled a castiza) for public loitering on the street at night with two mestiza women and a morisca.[58] At twenty-nine years old, she fit well within the average age range for a streetwalker. After another decade had passed, she had moved her operations indoors, causing officials to take action and remove a girl from her premises and imprison the older woman. At this time, her husband was in jail, and she had sole responsibility for her family's well-being.

In 1808, the alcaldes placed a sixteen-year-old Spaniard named María Gertrudis Riojano with her aunts because they had evidence that she had worked in González Castrejón's brothel.[59] During this trial, the bawd's accusers claimed that she allocated men to women and girls in her house and took a commission off of what the men paid them for sex. Her employees gave her approximately 25 percent of the income that they earned from their assignations. Allegedly, the costs for men who came to visit González Castrejón's brothel ranged from one to three pesos per client. She also asked her employees for two reales a day for their food and may have provided them with *túnicos* (nightgowns or loose undergarments) and stockings. González Castrejón admitted that she did have men in her house "carnally mixing" with Riojano, and blamed her own "extreme fragility" for these misdeeds.[60] Riojano herself said that she only washed clothes at González Castrejón's house but that she did see others frequently engaging in prostitution there.[61]

In 1809, law enforcement returned again to investigate González Castrejón's brothel, which they believed still operated despite her previous trial and brief incarceration. The authorities stated that they had heard many complaints that she "with great scandal, prostituted several young girls with individuals of different classes." According to three of her neighbors, many "decent" men and women entered these houses at all hours of the night and day. At around nine on an evening in June, an alcalde named Don Agustín Coronel investigated two alleged brothels (lupanares) in the Callejon de la Condesa, bringing over law enforcement to arrest several of the women and the male patrons present.[62] The authorities now had another strong case against her for bawdry based on this suspicious nighttime activity, reports made by hostile witnesses, and the precedent of her 1808 confession and guilty sentence.

Approaching González Castrejón's house on the night of the raid, the alcalde and patrolmen found two young soldiers' wives standing in the doorway. Inside, they encountered a group of five women that included mestizas and Spaniards, as well as the bawd's sixteen-year-old castiza daughter. The girls were all between the ages of fourteen and seventeen. The patrolmen also came upon two married men who worked at a *fabrica* in Guadalupe, one of whom toiled as a bookkeeper and the other as an *interventor,* a supervisor or inspector. The male visitors also included a nineteen-year-old waiter from Trieste, whom the guards found holding a pair of pants in his hands.[63] The alcalde mayor and his sergeant immediately arrested all of the women and the Italian waiter, even though the young man protested that he had only stepped into the *accesoria* looking for a pair of his stolen pants. Later, he was allowed to leave the jail in order to continue his work in the café. In contrast to this brief incarceration of a single man, the authorities immediately let the married men go, to quickly erase their names from a criminal record.

González Castrejón's respectable persona provided a convenient protective umbrella under which the arrested girls could hide any alleged illicit acts. In their numerous statements and interrogations, each young lady swept up in the raid claimed a good reason for visiting these rooms at night, referring to the defendant's legitimate work as a clothes dealer. Since the bawd did make money at this time by selling clothing and other items, most of the visitors claimed that they came to her house in the evening to buy and sell goods. Some professed to work as seamstresses themselves. Others claimed that they just happened to be walking by when the alcalde made the sting. Two of the girls who made these excuses had been caught at the brothel in the presence of their mothers. The mothers were Spanish widows, over forty years old, who said that their income came from sewing or embroidery, despite the interrogators' insistence that they had brought their daughters to the establishment to prostitute them.[64] Three of the girls testified that they simply worked as servants in the house. In their statements, all of the arrested young women who already had reputations as solteras, or sexually active unmarried women, portrayed themselves as victims of predatory men who falsely had promised them marriage. By now this widely accepted story could function as a believable excuse for selling sex as long as young women portrayed their occupation as short term and nonvoluntary.[65]

Regardless of the girls' protestations of innocence supported by the existence of a legal business, three of González Castrejón's neighbors had serious complaints to make against her. They told the authorities that they saw so much disorder going on at her house that they avoided peeking out their windows. The owner of a nearby tavern noticed that González Castrejón left her door open until 11:00 p.m. or as late as 1:00 a.m. He saw both men and women entering, even at dawn. He also observed González Castrejón and another woman standing on the balcony, each wearing nothing more than one of the numerous tunics in their possession. Another neighbor (a widow around fifty years old) testified that men and women constantly entered this house, a place of "bad behavior [mala conducta]." A third neighbor (another widow) said that she had known González Castrejón for eighteen years and expressed amazement at her newfound riches, a dramatic change from her days as a washerwoman. Due to her wealth, and the frequent visits by men and women to her house, González Castrejón retained her bawdy reputation.[66] The authorities admitted that they had no more witnesses other than these three neighbors. Few people observed what went on at the brothel because González Castrejón's house actually had quite a hidden location behind the walls of other edifices. This privacy might serve the brothel's clientele well, as well as prevent its inscription into the archives as a criminal space.

The bawd's prosecutors expressed dismay that she had fallen back into this career after they had set her free after her previous trial, with only a warning to amend herself. Now she deserved a more rigorous judicial reaction.[67] But González Castrejón claimed that she had lived up to their demands, and she repudiated any claim that she was anything but a respectable businesswoman living in an honorable home. She utterly denied the validity of all accusations in her second prosecution and inscribed herself as a good mother, concerned about her children's welfare, and as an effective, respected businesswoman involved only in legal dealings.

González Castrejón argued that she made a very good income, up to an impressive four pesos a day, as a dealer in used clothing and ornaments *(alhajas)*. To support her claims, she presented five Spanish character witnesses to write her into the records as a successful, trusted clothing peddler. The witnesses described her as a trader who bought and sold from house to house, in her own home, as well as in the *Parián* market and other public markets. Two of these witnesses were Spanish men who claimed the same occupation, so undoubtedly González Castrejón did buy, sell, and accept pawned clothing and other items to provide at least some of her income. Her allies explained that she had worked her way up to this profitable profession from poverty by laboring as an in-house washerwoman for elite homes, and also ran an *atolería* along the way.[68] The witnesses testified that she had employed herself dealing in clothes for at least a year, perhaps since her last conviction for brothel keeping, although none of them mentioned this illicit occupation. Judging from her witnesses' statements, González Castrejón epitomized a versatile, hard-working Mexico City female plebeian.

No different from most other poor women, she may have explored more than one path to financial stability. Brothels in this era in Paris, and most likely other major metropolises, functioned as banks for small loans backed up by personal property as collateral. Professional madams bought, sold, loaned, and took in pawned goods, especially clothing and all other types of accessories useful for female adornment.[69] The proper wardrobe always coexisted with sexual transactions and the exploitation of one's sexual capital.[70] While independent sex workers had to acquire their all-important clothing and jewelry via personal gifts, by buying used items, or by making their own, madams might provide their charges with the essential clothing and luxurious ornamentation. Successful madams brokered in clothes and personal adornments in order to run their own brothels properly and with the expected degree of elegance.

Clothes, in fact, came up in minor but suggestive concerns in both of González Castrejón's trials. In 1808, her employee María Gertrudis Riojano complained that she had suffered while incarcerated because she had no clothes. Perhaps without the support of her former employer, the young girl lacked the ability or funds to outfit herself appropriately.[71] In the later 1809 trial, the bawd argued that two of her employees testified against her because they owed her fourteen pesos for clothes she had provided. Without her help, González Castrejón claimed that these girls would have gone around almost naked.[72] Why would this canny businesswoman loan out clothes to young girls who had no chance of paying her back? Although she claimed to be a charitable woman, in truth González Castrejón had four children of her own to support.

Inventories of González Castrejón's possessions support the hypothesis that she both dealt in clothes and ran a brothel and that these two trades worked together very conveniently. The authorities confiscated a large supply of female underclothes at her lodgings. Almost no outdoor clothing appeared in the inventory. The closest items that González Castrejón and her daughter Francisca possessed to outdoor clothing were six bodices or *armadores*, but this term might also refer to women's underclothes only for private indoor use. Their lodgings also contained eight pairs of stockings made of either silk or cotton. The other small items listed in these inventories also leave open the possibility of coquettish indoor activities in the house: several fans and decorative hair combs. The authorities found a large amount of clothing of the size that they believed fitted a young woman's body. They inventoried in the range of fourteen petticoats of a wide variety of fabric, but apparently no outdoor skirts. The women's clothing also included seven *túnicos*, or loose sleeveless garments. Added together, this seems a huge quantity of indoor clothing for one young woman. If González Castrejón truly earned her income just off selling clothes, it appears that she ran a lingerie store. This seems a very unlikely coincidence in the context of her previous guilty sentence for bawdry. Viceregal women usually prioritized owning ostentatious outdoor clothes, hats, and jewelry, not just underclothes, so it defies belief that González Castrejón could make a good income from selling only nightgowns.[73]

In line with this interpretation of their belongings, other inventories indicated that the mother and daughter lived in quite a luxurious setting that seemed very appropriate for an unpretentious but comfortable brothel. Their décor included five sofas, four chairs, various tables including small corner tables, a dressing table with a mirror, another stand-alone mirror, and comfortable beds with sheets and blankets. They had a well-stocked kitchen, with all the basics for cooking, as well as numerous cups and glasses. While the officials noted that some of the goods were old and worn out, other pieces of furniture were of elegant make and material. Their lodgings did not rival Josefa Ordoñez's sumptuous quarters (González Castrejón had only four pieces of Chinese porcelain), but someone had put thought and money into its ornamentation. The presence of several tin candlesticks and copper wall lamps suggests that lighting and atmosphere mattered here. As usual, religious themes dominated the artwork, which included eleven small paintings of saints and larger renditions of San Luis Gonzaga and the Virgins of Guadalupe and *la Purísima*. The inventory also mentioned a handful of religious books.[74] González Castrejón and her character witnesses had to explain to the court why she had even this modest degree of wealth and why men and women often visited at odd hours of the day and night. The accused and her allies asserted over and over again that all of these possessions and the frequent activity derived only from her business dealing in clothes and ornaments.

While the alleged bawd worked hard to convince the court of her good reputation and respectable career, two young sisters found in her brothel quickly received the authorities' pity, due to their age, appearance, and even their own persuasive statements. Two of the girls arrested in the sting in June of 1809 were a soltera called María Hilaria Ximénes, who looked around fifteen, and her sister Clara, a doncella who appeared thirteen. The alcalde who led the initial raid, Coronel, expressed great concern for these "two very good looking little Spanish girls [*muchachas españolitas muy bien parecidas*]." Coronel hinted that he had run into them before in their checkered past. Despite their youth, the Ximénes sisters already had lived under the protection of thieves and a procurer within their own family. The girls' brother, a soldier, also "very good looking, but very lazy and a real panderer [*muy bien parecido pero muy flojo y muy lenon*]," had left them to survive on their own, moving from house to house, or even actively working as their procurer.[75] Coronel hoped that he could find a decent home for these young, attractive girls to avoid their further "disgrace."

Why would Coronel choose to inscribe the appearance of these siblings into this file? This comment represents a scribal seduction, a purposeful inscription of the allure of a deponent to shape the readers' narrative and emotional reactions.[76] Usually, the notaries and other viceregal writers asserted the status of their subjects not via their aesthetically pleasing bodily features but, instead, through tangible factors such as their dress, employment, family and social connections, behavior, housing, horses, entourage, and expensive belongings. Of course, race labeling also involved an assessment of the superiority of certain kinds of skin color and features. This inscription of beauty hints at a categorization of Spaniards according to subjective views of their attractiveness, a rating of their appearance as a factor in the official determination of their value as individuals.

The only other person in this book who received this kind of assessment was Josefa Ordóñez, whom the authorities viewed as a woman who seduced her lucrative protectors with her physical appeal. A few decades before Clara and María Hilaría's birth, comments regarding beauty contributed to a judgment of Ordóñez as sexually suspect, despite her Spanish origins and her pretentions to status. With his odd description, Coronel may have wished to stress Clara and María Hilaría's vulnerability to falling into the life of kept women, because clearly in his opinion men found them sexually desirable. Describing them as "little Spanish girls" suggests that he perceived them as delicate youngsters. He wanted to record the sisters as the type of vulnerable but ladylike Spaniards whom the authorities felt obligated to protect. On the contrary, surely these worries about inherent fragility did not apply to their good-looking military brother/panderer. Instead, here Coronel perhaps wanted to underscore that the brother had a natural ability to use his looks as part of his hustle, as did La Ordóñez. Commenting on the family's appearance supported a moral judgment of them as either worthy of paternalistic protection, or corrupt and irredeemable.

In their statements, Clara and María Hilaría went along with the effort to tap into protective emotions and presented themselves as innocent children. They proffered a few hints suggesting that they knew that González Castrejón ran a brothel, but they stated that this sort of sinfulness was beyond their comprehension. They said that they were orphans, but their deceased mother had known the bawd. The scribes recorded their naïve voices as they retold rumors about visitors who came to the house with their faces covered to take part in vaguely evil activities that the girls did not understand. María Hilaría also spoke of a man who had betrayed her with a false marriage promise. This incident meant that she now had the reputation of a sexually active single woman. The older sister said that she and her young sister had worked in the kitchen near the brothel for six weeks until their brother took them away for their own protection. Then they sought work in the tobacco factory.[77]

After they left their kitchen work, the older sister, María Hilaría, claimed that González Castrejón had visited them twice to convince them not to waste their efforts working in the factory for a petty few reales a day. The bawd had attempted to seduce them with new clothes and an income of three or four pesos a day if they came to work in her house. María Hilaría claimed that they had refused, knowing that it was a "bad" place where men and women went for "bad" reasons.[78] Due to the alleged immorality in this house, they rejected the offer. Following their brother's and a cleric's advice, María Hilaría professed that they would never set a single foot in the brothel. Clara, the younger sister who held onto her reputation as sexually inexperienced, repeated this information in an even more childish tone. When they worked near the brothel, the girls hid in the adjacent kitchen, protecting their innocence, according to a nearby tavern keeper who pitied them.[79] The sisters offered no more specifics, but it seemed clear to the judges that González Castrejón's offers of money and clothes constituted an act of procuring young girls. The girls defended their testimonies in a face-to-face legal encounter with the bawd (a *careo*).[80]

María Hilaría and Clara did a very good job of inscribing themselves as uninformed children, a pose that played right into the authorities' paternalistic understanding of their own role as protectors of the weak, especially women and children. But other testimonies on the side of the defense contradicted this innocent self-representation. González Castrejón's daughter said that the sisters had known about the raid in June 1809 and had warned their maid of it before it took place.[81] Other witnesses for the defense asserted that María Hilaría and Clara were actually independent prostitutes working out of their own rooms, without needing any encouragement from the clothes dealer. González Castrejón herself maintained that she had never even heard of the sisters before their arrest.[82] She denied offering them money and clothes to work for her.

The questions prepared by the defense asked witnesses if they knew María Hilaría and Clara as "women of evil lives, known as public prostitutes, and for how long." The first witness, a married Spanish woman, testified that she lived near the sisters for two months. In that time, she saw soldiers come and go from their rooms, and she also saw the sisters often in pulquerías. These acts caused the surrounding barrio to label them as prostitutes.[83] The defense also called on Clara and María Hilaría's landlady, a forty-year-old Spanish widow, to describe how they lived. She said that the girls rented with her for a month, occupying a "high interior room" in a house known as *del ahorcado.*" At this time, the sisters lived with a soldier and a boy, both of whom they called their brothers. The landlady disapproved of their disruptive way of life, coming and going all day long, not returning home until nine or ten at night. The sisters had plenty of money to pay their rent, but their landlady did not believe that they worked at the tobacco factory because she had seen them on the street and at home frequently during the workday. She had even decided that her daughter should not associate with these disreputable tenants.[84]

The landlady's fifteen-year-old daughter, Octaviana, backed up this version of Clara and María Hilaría's suspicious lifestyle with more explicit details. Octaviana said that she visited their room in her mother's lodgings in order to learn how to make cigars. Instead of learning a useful trade, the teenager observed that during the night, soldiers, along with other decent as well as shameless men, came to their room. The men spent time alone with both sisters in their bedroom. On one occasion, Octaviana said that she heard their bed creaking a great deal after Clara, the younger sister, had gone into the bedroom with a man. This event enraged her, so she left their lodgings and never went back to see them again. Octaviana agreed with her mother in that she also saw Clara and María Hilaría on the street frequently, both day and night, so she did not believe that they worked as cigarette rollers. She observed them in the company of their brother, who went around drunk. Octaviana explained that a *señor* maintained them, as well as the other men she saw in their room. Another young man who testified for the defense also accused Clara and María Hilaría of prostitution because he had seen them in the presence of "shameless men," and he witnessed them frequently going to the palace, perhaps a known circuit for public women.[85]

Despite her supportive character witnesses and her strong protestations of innocence, González Castrejón received a harsh sentence of public humiliation and six years' incarceration. Clearly, the judges believed that even if González Castrejón dealt legitimately in clothing and other accessories, she *also* ran a brothel. Her ultimate sentence in December of 1809 was less harsh: four years in reclusion, confiscation of her property, and payment of all court costs. As of 1812, González Castrejón remained in jail. She had never left her incarceration from the time of her trial. However, by this time, the new Spanish constitution might have changed her status.[86] Other than her daughter, all of the other girls and men found in the alleged brothel endured no punishment other than a brief incarceration during the investigation.

Religious, intellectual, and juridical rhetoric excoriated bawds as shockingly corrupt sinners: women who tempted young women into nonmarital, nonmonogamous sex. As was the case since the sixteenth century, both law and custom differentiated between bawds and whores. This distinction grew in the nineteenth century, as the judiciary became very sympathetic to young, white, attractive women, especially when older family members acted as their procurers. Although La Sargenta/López Ortega and the Ximénes sisters had reputations as sexually active women, their tactics before the court diverged. La Sargenta told her story as a mature, dignified domestic servant, victimized by her husband, following the accepted rhetoric of divorce proceedings. Clara and María Hilaría testified in a childlike way that confirmed the magistrates' pity for their youth, beauty, and appearance of (fallen) innocence. But as an older, experienced career sex worker and successful businesswoman possibly with African ancestry, González Castrejón inspired no judicial paternalism. Her identities merged into one unsympathetic character, and she could not write herself into the archive as innocent or redeemable.

Selling Sex, Saving the Family

When she was asked who brings the men or how her sister facilitates men coming for her to sin with, she said: that [her sister] makes her stand in the doorway, and when a man passes, the deponent has to speak with him, and when she disobeys, she is beaten, so she has to submit, and she has to go to the bedroom with the men whom she is allotted. Other nights, her sister Bartola is in the doorway, and she chooses the men who are locked up with the deponent in the bedroom, or they go in with [the older sister, Bartola]. Afterwards, her sister dealt with the procuress [named] "La Poblana," who brings various men at night, sometimes three. . . . If she does not do it, or does not show pleasure in it, [her sister] beats her with a stick or the first thing that she can find.

TESTIMONY OF DOÑA MARÍA DOLORES RODRÍGUEZ, AGE SIXTEEN

When he was asked what happens at the apartment under the Holy Spirit portal: he said that . . . La Poblana brings different men every night, he does not know any of them and up to four [men] come . . . some of them go with his aunt Mariquita [Bartola], the wife of don Ermendildo Alcocer, while the others stay in the parlor with the deponent; his aunt Dolores will leave with one of them and another will enter, until one by one all of them have been with his aunts, and he does not know what they do.

TESTIMONY OF ANTONIO TRINIDAD ESCAMILLA, AGE NINE[1]

In May of 1801, an alcalde in Mexico City received a complaint from a sixteen-year-old Spanish woman named Doña María Dolores Rodríguez, who accused her sister Doña María Bartola de Vivar, a twenty-six-year-old married woman, of making money from the younger woman's sex acts for two years. In her first statement, Rodríguez explained to the alcalde that shortly after she left her mother's care in the countryside, her sister organized her defloration for compensation. After this initial act, Vivar invited men to visit their lodgings nightly for sex with either her or her sister. After a year, Vivar arranged for a professional procuress known as La Poblana to send more men to their rooms in the Portal del Espíritu Santo.

Rodríguez feared that Vivar would beat or abuse her if she resisted, and she anticipated a terrible punishment for denouncing her sister. But the girl also claimed that she could no longer endure this situation, especially because she could not take communion, and as a result she could not go to confession. Rodríguez asked to return to her mother's care.[2] The authorities respected the words of the complainant (who disappeared during the course of the deliberations). As a result, this investigation reestablished a patriarchal family by encouraging the older sister's surrender to her husband's leadership.[3]

The alleged deflowerer, Don Manuel Duran y Otero, a Spaniard, age twenty-four, who administered a workshop (obraje) at the Salto de Agua, described his experience with the sisters as an elaborate con, masterminded by Vivar. He said that he met the two women sitting in a doorway while he strolled in the Holy Spirit alleyway one evening. They propositioned him, so he went into their rooms, had sex with Rodríguez, and gave her older sister four pesos. On his way out, Vivar begged for more money, saying that her sister had been a virgin. Don Manuel responded with disbelief because, in his words, Rodríguez "had offered herself easily, and the house was a brothel." The older sister threatened to produce bloodstained linens, so he promised that he would compensate her with a significant present of cloth and more money. Vivar took his expensive watch as an advance on the payment. Later, the sisters went to his family home and explained the situation to his mother. Again, Vivar led the dialogue. The offended mother kicked the women out, calling them names ("moth-eaten sows of the republic *[unas puercas polillas de la republica]*").

While describing Vivar with the medieval term *alcahueta* (bawd), judicial officials and witnesses also spoke of prostitution. Her husband, Don Ermengildo de Alcocer, a squadron corporal based in Mexico City, deployed all of the terms, both ancient and contemporary, that he could call on to berate his wife:

> She is in jail for adulterous public prostitution and pandering [lenocinio] . . . with people of low character, all classes of men . . . she is a whore, extremely lewd and ribald. . . . Even the most barbarous, uncivilized nations detest and severely punish this offense. For her prostitution, my adulterous consort deserves ten years secluded in the harshest reclusion, but she also acted as her sister's bawd. This is shocking and depraved *rufianería!* . . . Although whoring women have been permitted and tolerated by the constitution and circumstance of the times, with certain precautions, it is most detestable that a married woman give herself to prostitution, and even more so, to the occupation of a ruffian.

Despite the seriousness of the crime, the husband argued that his wife should not suffer public humiliation but seclusion. He added that he had considered starting a divorce petition.

Vivar narrated her defense along conventional terms: she wrote herself as an abused, abandoned wife subject to the philandering Alcocer, and her sister as a victim of sexual violation who had not received the appropriate monetary compensation from her deflowerer, Duran y Otero. The older sister ended her sentence of enforced seclusion by writing a passionate, penitential letter to her estranged husband, begging him to take her back and swearing that she would in future behave with total wifely obedience and humility. He agreed with reluctance, with the following conditions: she must go to confession regularly; she could not go to a store or tavern without his permission; she must submit to his will, or that of his mother; she must fulfill her domestic duties as suited to her sex and her state as a married woman; and she must carry out the obligations of matrimony. On the surface, the court reestablished the familial, monogamous status quo, and all was well.

By the early nineteenth century, the viceregal archive of prostitution had grown and become much more legible due to the labeling and categorizing of prostituted girls as victims of evil procurers.[4] As can be read in the last few pages of this book's text, multiple voices from within the files argued for acknowledgment and recognition of their choice of accusatory labels, but the deciding judges listened most closely to the complaining girls and how they described their panderers. Scribes recorded the women's denunciations at length and in detail, inscribing long tales of their exploitation. These thorough accounts make selling sex findable and readable for historians, so we can write our own narrations and continue the process of scribally seducing our readers. However, exchanging sex for instant cash remained a verbal con, and even these more decipherable cases overflow the margins with deceptions, fabrications, and prevarications, spoken by the multiple deponents whose words cover hundreds of parchment pages.

Mexican courts continued to investigate cases of what law enforcement called outrageous and scandalous prostitution in the decades leading up to and even during the Wars of Independence from Spain. The term *prostitute* implies a criminalization of the women or girls who had sex for money, even though their legal status remained vague in Mexico until 1867 (see conclusion). Procurers still suffered the most judicial retribution. In the examples given in this chapter, older women received most of the blame from both complainants and the authorities as bawds. This chapter discusses five examples of sex transacted among family members and within the home itself, concluding with a long and exhaustive high-court investigation into a family brothel.

These families were inscribed into the archives only because their daughters used the courts as a way to quit their jobs as sources of sexual capital within familial economic-survival strategies. These cases took place within families that already belied the notion that fathers and husbands should protect and hide young women's sexual resources.[5] Concerns over honor receded when families were obliged to prioritize their survival and their immediate financial needs. But young women betrayed filial loyalty and domestic hierarchies when they spoke as plaintiffs to denounce their sisters, mothers, or fathers for involving them in selling sex.[6] In response to the complaints (the daughters' disobedience to their familial superiors), the late viceregal state stepped in to preserve traditional ideas of family as a sexual sanctuary for protected daughters.[7]

This analysis rejects both the "deviant" or liberating understanding of sex work that writes it as operating in an individualistic context outside of the traditional family structure. Some studies of sex work continue to emphasize negative conditions or choices or even "immorality" (whether directly stated or indirectly implied) that isolates individuals from their (dysfunctional) families as the context for making money through sex.[8] However, despite this misconception, across the globe, individuals take on this occupation to fulfill their filial duties and their obligations to their parents.[9] This chapter stresses that sex work could fit within the "continuity with the forms of domination and protection that exist within the family." The daughters here acted as loyal family members, until they complained to the authorities.[10]

Viceregal economies operated within a gendered hierarchy in which women and girls could earn very little income without male patronage. To maximize their financial stability, parents or guardians attempted to negotiate legitimate marriages. Since girls often married at approximately the age of fourteen, daughters' wishes might not have greatly influenced the choice of spouse, although formally the Catholic Church required their consent.[11] In the final years of Spanish rule and the insurgency era, fiscally secure church-sanctioned marriages might have appeared a hopeless goal for many poor young women. Men paying large sums for their virginity or maintaining them as mistresses offered an attainable income source. On-the-spot compensation for sex could replace the more traditional and court-mandated payments for breach of promise or support for illegitimate children when families needed money quickly in periods of extreme political or economic crisis.[12] Ultimately, family members intended that earning money instantly by selling a daughter's virginity or by having her engage in sex acts or ongoing sexual relationships would preserve their families more effectively than marriage or the maintenance of a patina of family honor. These economic strategies involving young women's sexuality remained entirely within a domestic setting until the courts intervened. In four out of five of the cases documented here, doncellas or solteras demonstrated a verbal acuity and strategic use of judicial entities. In response, the courts found their comfort zone by reinforcing parental and gender roles. The judiciary understood that although selling sex within the home weakened the honor of the male head of household (if he existed), they proposed solutions that created new families, perhaps with more effective men in charge to avoid further public scandal. They did not "rescue" young women without at least attempting to find a new family for them to join.[13]

Selling sex enforced gender and age hierarchies within the family.[14] Mothers and sisters accused of bawdry created a self-defense that revolved around invoking pity and justified procuring their children and younger sisters due to poverty and desperation.[15] One father discussed below also attempted to inspire mercy from the court when he made the convoluted claim that he resorted to pandering his children as a way to support all of his dependents. Women received lenience in response to their claims of victim status, but the court took a stricter, critical, and more judgmental tone in reaction to what it viewed as the father's immoral wastefulness of household funds. A man who denied his duty to protect his daughter's sexual purity, even in financial desperation, greatly offended the judges. The court labeled this kind of man an anomaly and a monster, while mothers more successfully asserted their victimhood to protect themselves from the harshest punishments. This judicial gender bias and the alienation of pandering, deadbeat fathers from the human moral and ethical community allowed internal or external threats to the family to exist without demolishing it.

FAMILY PANDERING AS MATCHMAKING

The family-based procuring that took place in New Spain around 1800 might shade toward motherly matchmaking because these schemes did not always rule out the hope of an arranged, lucrative marriage within the church. But mothers also put into practice the related strategy of trying to arrange their daughters' careers as kept women. Juana Munguia, a mulata resident of Acapulco in 1799, could not resist this temptation. However, Munguia's plan did not work because her own daughter reported her and another bawd to the military and civil authorities (one and the same in this location).[16] In this case, by calling on an officer of the law, the daughter thwarted her mother's economic strategy for the family, in a sense quitting her job as a dutiful daughter and severing herself from her mother's influence, all with the support of the local judiciary.

Munguia had given birth to her daughter when she was around sixteen years old. The daughter, named Teodora Josefa, knew her father's identity despite her designation within the records as a "*bastarda.*" When Teodora Josefa was around eighteen years old, shortly after they had relocated to Acapulco, her mother started forcing her to go to the local Castillo (the port fortifications) to talk to Lieutenant Don Pedro Antonio Velez while he was on duty. For two months, Munguia pushed Teodora Josefa into soliciting the officer, until the girl made her complaints to the authorities. Calling herself a doncella, Teodora Josefa claimed that she resisted visiting the military headquarters but that her mother dragged her there. Her mother also forced her daughter to visit Velez's house to ask him to loan her money. Teodora Josefa complained that she endured verbal abuse when she refused to obey her mother. The daughter explained the kinds of insults she suffered, testifying that her mother tried to tempt her with the suggestion that if she chose to go with "another black or mulatto man of her class," she missed out on "remedying her poverty and improving her reputation."[17] These words of advice indicated that Munguia saw sexual liaisons not as personal rewards of individualistic affection but as steps in upward mobility for her daughter and perhaps herself.

Teodora Josefa said that she could not prove that her mother pushed her toward prostitution because they had always discussed this issue in private. However, the girl had other ways to prove her claims against her mother. When visiting the fort, Teodora Josefa endured more cruel words, this time from a man called Rafael Guerrero. This soldier, also labeled a mulato, allegedly called Munguia "an enormous bawd." He said that the mother lacked both shame and scruples because she forced Teodora Josefa to come with her to talk to Velez in front of all of the troops. In his own statement, Guerrero did not admit to saying these words other than as a joke, but he did reveal that Velez complained to him about Munguia's overtures.[18] Teodora Josefa cited both men's disapproval of her mother's ambitions for her.

The daughter also accused her mother of calling on a fifty-year-old bawd named María Rafaela "La Petateca" to parley with them at their house. The two older women pulled Teodora Josefa into their *corralito*, where La Petateca tried to persuade the girl to prostitute herself (the daughter's exact words as recorded in the documentation) with Velez. If she did, the professional bawd promised Teodora Josefa that she and her mother would receive a little house and clothes, as well as maintenance from the lieutenant. This discussion again resulted in verbal attacks against the young girl. La Petateca called her a *"boba"* (an idiot or a fool) if she chose to lose this opportunity and instead have a relationship with an "unlucky poor working man."[19] Teodora Josefa testified that she cut off the conversation at this point and went inside. Her mother then asked her about the talk with the bawd and added that La Petateca had arranged for Velez to give her ten pesos as an additional incentive. Despite all of the material temptations, the daughter continued to reject the older women's propositions.

Thirty-four-year-old Munguia's statements reveal a socially ambitious and well-developed moneymaking strategy for her daughter that would benefit the mother as well. Munguia denied her daughter's accusations, but in telling their story, she could not hide her schemes for their financial betterment. In the first hint that she had a definite plan in mind, Munguia explained that the family had resided in Acapulco for only four months. Given the timing of the campaign to form a lucrative relationship between Velez and her daughter, Munguia probably moved from her village with clear economic goals in mind. Their more isolated natal village was located several days' travel on the coast to the north of the port. Relocating to Acapulco meant that the women could more effectively take advantage of military men stationed there.

Munguia articulated her ideas regarding her daughter's behavior and future in response to her interrogator's leading and judgmental questions. Her responses gelled with her goals of carefully promoting the girl's sexual capital. When asked if in the last two months Teodora Josefa had lived honestly and preserved her honor, Munguia admitted that her daughter did not have the slightest inclination toward jeopardizing her own virtue. This seems accurate given the girl's protests to the authorities. Munguia responded carefully and deceptively when asked if she acted as a good mother by advising her daughter to live as a Christian. The accused bawd assured the court that she supported her daughter's own god-fearing efforts to continue her good thoughts and customs.[20] Notwithstanding the usual rhetoric that required her to assert her own innocence, Munguia did well to testify to her daughter's virtue, continuing her strategy to find a good financial match even during her interrogation. Testifying to military and judicial officials provided Munguia with a potentially prosperous venue to discuss her daughter's good qualities. Speaking to the judge and scribe, Munguia promoted Teodora Josefa's status as an eligible, moral young girl ready for a higher-status husband. When asked about their communication with Velez, Munguia claimed that he had visited them (not vice versa) and only with the best of intentions. With this bragging assertion, the mother implied, however falsely, that Velez had considered marrying Teodora Josefa. Presenting her daughter as desirable to a Spanish officer functioned as an ongoing marketing strategy for her daughter's high-value sexual capital.[21]

When confronted with allegations that La Petateca tried to tempt her daughter with ten pesos from Velez, a scheme that presented a crude contrast to the more refined prospect of marriage, the mother did not deny that the other woman was an alcahueta. Instead, Munguia simply brushed off her daughter's claims regarding these plans, dismissing the older professional bawd as a drunk who talked nonsense. However, La Petateca, otherwise known as Rafaela Navarro, described as a mulata from Apantzingan who had lived in Acapulco for ten years, admitted her efforts to serve as an intermediary between Velez and Teodora Josefa. La Petateca claimed that Velez had reached out to her to "solicit Teodora Josefa's agreement" to a sexual relationship in exchange for gifts, a house, and clothes. Although both mother and daughter painted her as a coarse woman, La Petateca knew her business well. She explained that she presented Velez's offers to Teodora Josefa "without forcing her . . . because she is the mistress [dueña] of her own body to do with it as she wishes, I only put forward the intentions and offers of Don Pedro."[22] Unlike Munguia, La Petateca did not force Teodora Josefa. Instead, she persuaded her clients in the ancient alcahueta tradition, practicing a specialized trade that differed from those of a matchmaking mother, a brothel keeper, or a violent and coercive panderer. Her orchestrated couples had to come together by their own free will. They just needed the extra push of La Petateca's scheming words. She must have had a good reputation as a successful bawd because local men of importance like Velez allegedly sought her out when they wanted to pay for sex or find a woman to maintain over the short or long term.

The single mother's performance of upwardly mobile strategies wavered slightly when the court asked Munguia questions that forced her to reveal how she disciplined her daughter. A long and detailed question probed if Munguia had sent Teodoro Josefa to ask to borrow money from Velez, and how the mother had responded when her daughter refused. As mentioned above, the daughter testified that her mother verbally attacked her, saying that if she did not go to the Castillo, she would live a life of misery and shame with a black man or a mulatto like herself. Munguia admitted that she did chastise her daughter with threats of this kind, but for a different reason. According to the mother, it enraged her that her daughter "put on a very bad face *[le pusiste muy mala cara]*" when Velez visited them. Munguia chided her daughter by asking why she did such a thing. She added that if the visitor had been "another black rascal *[zaragate]* like yourself, you would have shown a very good face and you would have been ready to frolic *[retozar]* with him."[23] In this revealing confession, Munguia expressed anger that her daughter did not value the practical benefits of associating with a wealthier, Spanish man, whom the mother described as "a man of respect *[un sugeto de estimación].*" She understood that Teodoro Josefa felt more sexual attraction to another kind of lover, but practicalities outweighed romance in the older woman's plans. Munguia sought to channel her daughter's desires away from a man of her own class and race to a man that would help both of them economically and socially.

Due to the use of criminal labels such as *alcahueta* and forms of *prostituir,* this case of routine motherly matchmaking almost resulted in serious consequences for Munguia and La Petateca. Fortunately for them, a more sophisticated, sympathetic voice intervened amongst the mocking jeers of local soldiers and the daughter's betrayal (both carefully noted by scribes). Initially, the Acapulco authorities sentenced Munguia to two months in prison and then sent the case to the viceroy for his perusal. In late 1799, Viceroy Azanza agreed with the decision to send Teodora Josefa to live with her grandmother and to imprison Munguia for two months. However, he did not concur with the accusation that the two older women were *lenonas.* The viceroy used this feminine form of the Latin term for procurer, *leno.* He explained his opinion with a clarification of the terms used in the investigation: "Their persuasions had not succeeded, and because in order to commit this crime, it is required that they have a house of prostitution where men and women meet for vile ends *[torpeza].*"[24] Viceroy Azanza insisted that Munguia amend herself and behave as a better mother in the future. His subtler approach to the definition of *lenona* may have derived from his familiarity with professionally run brothels that, as we have seen in chapters 5 and 6, were common in Mexico City in this era. In the viceroy's opinion, a matchmaking mother, even one who seemed greedy and lacked concern for arranging an actual marriage, did not have the same criminal status as a brothel manager. The viceroy saw no need to inscribe Munguia with such a negative word since she did not run a brothel and sought nothing more than her own family's financial security and her daughter's obedience to her plans for this goal. It should come as no surprise that Munguia's ambitions failed because, other than the most skilled courtesans such as those introduced in chapter 4, public women had the most success when they targeted men of their own social class.[25] Teodora Josefa lacked the drive, family loyalty, and personal sophistication to rise above her plebeian status, as her own mother noted in mocking the girl's desires for casta men.

COMPLICIT MOTHERS

Despite Viceroy Azanza's fine distinctions regarding vice, other residents of Mexico City in the late eighteenth century did voice a censorious perception of procuring mothers. Demonstrating an even stronger tendency toward lucrative schemes, another mother in this era allegedly continued procuring for her daughter in the militarized viceregal capital even after the younger woman married.[26] In 1798, Juan Jose Gandara made a criminal complaint to the local corregidor that his wife of two years, Juana Victoria Chamorro, frequently left their home in Tacubaya to work as a prostitute in Mexico City, accompanied by her mother, Rosalia Oviedo. The corregidor designated all of the individuals involved in this case as indios. Because all of their statements took place within the context of a marriage dispute, extremely vindictive language colored all of the rhetoric. For example, Gandara accused his wife of a "vicious inclination to carnal commerce, with all classes of men, especially the troops." The disgruntled husband claimed that the two women went so far as to disguise their trips to work in Mexico City with false plans of making a pilgrimage to the Virgin of Guadalupe's shrine north of the city. While there, the women attended dances, promenaded through the streets, visited the barracks, and took part in other "illicit diversions" without even covering their faces to hide their identities.[27] Gandara found several witnesses willing to testify that his mother-in-law was a known whore who pandered her two daughters.[28] According to witnesses, the women worked out of pulquerías and their own home, catering to soldiers and coachmen. Witnesses said that the mother and married daughter often drank to excess and made a shameful public spectacle of themselves.

Although Gandara had witnesses to back up his claims, and all of the statements accurately represent late-colonial plebeian prostitution, these kinds of accusations lost credibility when they were made within an acrimonious conflict between spouses. In her short statement concluding this file, Juana Chamorro counterattacked in the most effective way possible. She accused her husband of abuse and neglect.[29] In fact, Gandara had initiated the petition from jail, where he remained due to his wife's complaints. Chamorro did not explicitly deny that she worked as a prostitute, but she did make it clear that her husband did not provide for her. Divorce petitions could only have one wrongdoer and one innocent party, but unfortunately, no further evidence exists to back up either spouse's allegations. Regardless, the statements made by Gandara and his allies, if nothing else, confirm that Mexicans of this era did understand that prostitution could exist within families, possibly as an occupation handed down from mother to daughter.

Thus far in this chapter, men, in the form of a husband or a court official, represented the voice of morality and social order, speaking out against mothers presented as immoral. This gendered moral stance also functions within another late-eighteenth-century case in Valladolid (now Morelia). In 1792, an indigenous cacique complained to the local alcalde about a young woman who had agitated the personal life of his eighteen-year-old son.[30] Manuel Gaspar Rodríguez and the witnesses in his complaint claimed that a mulata named María Gertrudis Romualda refused to marry his son, preferring her libertine life as a "public whore" and a "provocative street walker [mujer callejera provocative]." Another witness described her as "muy prostituta," meeting any number of men in the streets. Her mother consented to all of these activities as her daughter's alcahueta, not minding that Romualda allegedly interacted with "soldiers, recruits, and any man at all."[31] Within this text, Romualda sacrificed all of her femininity to support the father's accusations. Race and gender stereotypes intertwined as the father and witnesses claimed that Romualda was "more muscular [membruda]" than his son and thus often abused him physically. She also possessed the traits of "daring and boastfulness," refusing to carry out her proposed marriage to the cacique's son.[32] While the witnesses decried family pandering as a scandalous, immoral, and debauched lifestyle, apparently some men did not worry about the family connection, and a clientele existed for mothers and daughters who worked together as plebeian public women. This short file does not deeply explore this phenomenon, but a longer case goes deeper into procuring within the familial context.

FATHERS AS PANDERERS

Court officials expressed real or feigned discomfort and surprise when they happened upon a family-run brothel, but this morally appalled reaction did not stop one particular early-nineteenth-century family from making money off of their male clientele. The Mexican high court adjudicated on this domestic brothel in 1814.[33] In this case of a stepfather's prostituting (the term used in the file, so I will use it throughout this section) his own wife and stepdaughters, an abused girl succeeded in breaking up her family, with the help of the authorities.[34] The mother, Doña María Sánchez, allowed the prostitution of her own child, a girl named Doña María de Jesus Ferra, as a remedy for poverty, hunger, and family survival. Although both women were victims of the stepfather, Sánchez also faced sanctions from the court for prostituting her daughter. While she was a victim of her husband, the mother was also a perpetrator, according to Spanish justice. After listening to and recording dozens of pages of contradictory and deceptive statements, the authorities ultimately intervened in this family's financial strategies and imposed the officially accepted value system of domestic monogamy, however economically inconvenient.

The case began in June of 1814, motivated by information that a "decent" man had turned his family home in the Espiritu Santo alley into a "scandalous brothel." The court notary and two deputies went to the neighborhood one night to investigate. There they observed a young girl standing in the doorway of an accesoria, wearing a scarlet shawl. This person was later identified as Doña María de Jesus Ferra. At around 8:00 p.m., a man in a black hat approached and spoke to the girl. She immediately allowed him to enter her room. The officials then followed the client, barging into the house after the couple. Upon entering, they observed the man sitting on the bed, talking and holding hands with the young girl in the shawl. Sánchez sat on a sofa cradling a newborn baby in her arms, alongside another man wearing a cape and a white hat. Just then a third man and a twelve-year-old girl came out of the bedroom. This man said that he was the owner of the house and gave his name as Don Domingo Ximénez. The man in the black hat immediately confessed that he had entered the room to "mezclarse carnalmente [carnally mix]" with Doña María de Jesus, as he had already done once before, because she was a known prostitute. In the tradition of rarely arresting the paying clients, the authorities allowed the two male visitors (military men whose fuero protected them from further prosecution by a secular court and allowed them erasure from the file) to leave and began questioning the family.[35]

Throughout this investigation, the judicial officials never relented in expressing their moral outrage and disgust toward this couple's prostituting their own children. For their part, both parents made continuous appeals to the court's pity and mercy for the family's extreme poverty. Ultimately, only the daughters succeeded with these tactics and received no punitive sentences. While women accused of having sex for money (not procuring others) seldom received judicial punishment up to this point because of the lack of laws against them, by the nineteenth century, New Spain's courts had taken on the "new sentimental construction of the prostitute" that took its place alongside a "new ideal of domestic femininity." Doña María Dolores Rodríguez (whose case starts this chapter) also succeeded in manipulating the role of the victim in her complaint against her older sister. These young women wrote themselves as "objects of passive distress" and pity, "victim[s] of a corrupting seducer," in order to escape their own families and reorder their lives.[36] The nineteenth-century rhetoric of defendants' justifying prostitution by piteous tales of abused innocence was now fully accepted as the appropriate way for public women to respond to criminal accusations.

The mother and daughter made spontaneous declarations after the raid, blaming the father, Ximénez, for the prostitution of Doña María de Jesus and her mother.

At this moment, caught in the act, Sánchez did not yet have time to construct a narrative of affronted honor and dignity to bolster her adherence to official moral codes in spite of her actions under duress. For fear of Ximénez's rage, according to Sánchez's first confession, mother and daughter regularly walked out in search of clients for sex in the streets or, more often, in the bed of their shared family lodgings. The women said that this occupation had sustained the family for four months. Following the centuries-old ruffian tradition, the fifteen-year-old Doña María de Jesus passed many nights enduring her thirty-year-old stepfather's angry curses while she stood at the door attempting to solicit two or three men a night. On other nights, Ximénez went out to gamble until 11:00 p.m. The distraught mother claimed that her husband had even considered sending out the younger daughter, Doña María Rosa, on to the streets. At this stage, the preteen earned only a peso for hugging and kissing men she met on the street or in their home. After hearing these initial accounts, the court expeditiously put both of the girls into protective custody in a house of seclusion and imprisoned their stepfather. The mother stayed at home in bed due to illness.[37]

The judge questioned Ximénez next, uncovering more details of his pathetic family situation. Born in Ayacapixtlo (possibly Yecapixtla?), he claimed Spanish ancestry and signed his name with confidence. Two weeks before his arrest, he said that his wife had given birth to her seventh child. In terms of his occupation, Ximénez stated only that he had worked in "commerce" and had served as a halberdier. He took up this military position as a judicially mandated punishment for his wife's previous complaints against him, to be discussed below. For the last six months before his arrest, he had found no gainful employment or income and had also fallen ill. One morning a few months before, he claimed that his family had no money in the house. None of the eight of them had eaten any breakfast even after 10:00 a.m. Ximénez testified that only the dire need of that moment made him decide that his eldest stepdaughter should earn their household income through prostitution. He also explained that this plan began only when a man offered to give them a thousand pesos to marry Doña María de Jesus and then abandoned her without paying them after taking her virginity.[38]

The content of Ximénez's initial statements focused on family survival, mundane details, and material needs. As a guilty party, he could not invoke the morally outraged tone used by the mother or the court officials. Instead, he tried to present himself in a straightforward way as a father who had found a way to support his family. In describing how his family brothel operated, the stepfather explained a few practicalities in his first statement. He said that every night, Doña María de Jesus stood in the doorway from around 9:00 p.m. She admitted two or three men a night, whom he called "decent men that appeared acceptable to her [los hombres decentes que a ella le parecian bien]," men such as captains, lieutenants, and colonels.[39] She could have allowed many others to enter, but if she judged them old or poor, she rejected them. She charged two pesos and up for a half hour with her. Approximately six pesos a day represented an immense income for a woman in this era and even a generous pay for most men, especially in this time of severe hardship. Clearly, these high-ranking military officials who came to visit the family brothel had money to spare. Potential clients who could not manage that sum, whom Ximénez called "oficialitos," received a discount and had sex with her for one peso. As far as other kinds of hospitality that a brothel might provide, the family gave the clients fruit or cigars.

Ximénez offered these acts as the only way they could afford food, and as a caretaking parent, he demonstrated that he took control of the family income. As her "ruffian," in the understanding of this word as a man who collects a woman's pay, Doña María de Jesus's stepfather took all of her earnings, claiming to use them on the family's needs. This was the only money that came into their household. Therefore, the parents had to figure out what new schemes might result in more money for the six children and two adults that Doña María de Jesus singlehandedly supported. In this desperate situation, Doña María de Jesus and both of her parents worked together on various phases of their plan to market the fifteen-year-old. These included luring in men and deceiving them into thinking that she was a virgin whose sexual innocence had great monetary value.[40] At least two men confessed to falling for the "doncella" hoax when it came to Doña María de Jesus's sexual status.

Both of Doña María de Jesus's parents retained some sense of their personal reputations, however low their standards were for their own behavior. In court, as time passed, they pushed more and more for a certain "not so bad" vision of themselves as victims of poverty and/or spousal abuse. In their self-characterizations, they were admitted procurers but otherwise quite respectable people. Note that the entire family maintained the use of the honorifics don and doña. The parents' dishonest scheming also included each parent's refusing to admit that they had done anything "worse" than live off of their eldest daughter. But the fact remains that both of them had committed many other acts that they could not bear to confess into the archived file at the risk of shattering their very tenuous claims to decent reputations. For the mother's part, the fact that she might have also sold sex threatened her claims of victim status, even if she did it under her husband's coercion.

Sánchez claimed Spanish ancestry, and she was born in Mexico City sometime before 1784. As a sickly woman who had just given birth to her seventh or possibly eighth child, Sánchez made her second statement from her sickbed at home. She explained that Ximénez was her second spouse, whom she had married two years after her first husband died in 1807. Until approximately 1810, this now pitiful woman bragged that she enjoyed a very respectable reputation and even some degree of prosperity. She ran a shop independently and had employees and servants to assist her in her home and business. She allegedly educated her daughters well, encouraging them to read morality tales such as one about a wolf who ate up women who kissed men. Her eldest son lived in Xalapa as a Franciscan friar.[41] In the context of selling sex as a filial duty, these confessions suggest that the work of Doña María de Jesus aided her brother in sustaining his religious career without the family's fiscal desperation forcing him to support his mother and younger siblings with a less prestigious but more lucrative career.[42]

Sánchez blamed all of her problems on her second husband, Ximénez. After her marriage to this con man, all of her wealth trickled away, wasted on his "dissipations." She complained that he cheated on her, treated her badly, and presented a terrible example to her family as a whole. Fed up with his abuses, Doña María Sanchez filed for divorce in 1810, after only one year of marriage. The ecclesiastical court granted it to her without hesitation. But then, she admitted, she had the weakness to forgive him and seek a reunion, a move she deeply regretted in retrospect.[43] Taking into account the timing, it seems very likely that, as a woman with many children who had lost her wealth and a decent first husband (described as an "hombre de bien"), Sánchez felt vulnerable to the threat of war and widespread rebellion in the autumn of 1810. These severe dislocations perhaps contributed to her succumbing to such an awful choice of husband and then taking him back after initiating divorce proceedings.

Sánchez understood that, as a woman admittedly caught in consenting to her own daughter's prostitution, she had to appear as passive and victimized as possible to gain any sympathy from the authorities, although she also offered several examples of how she took decisive legal actions to protect them. Doña María Sanchez claimed that one night a few months back when her family was in dire need, a *gachupín* called Don Joaquín followed her and Doña María de Jesus home. He met with Ximénez, and they discussed a concubinage arrangement that would eventually lead to marriage with the fifteen-year-old. Allegedly, Don Joaquín promised to pay two hundred pesos for Doña María de Jesus to be his mistress, and later he would marry her and pay eight hundred more pesos. Her mother claimed that she did not believe this scheme would come to fruition, so she tried to stop it.[44] A few months later, the same gachupín caught Doña María de Jesus alone in the house and allegedly "violated her virginity." After that, according to the mother, Doña María de Jesus stood at the door nightly and anywhere from one to three men "made love to her" for between one and eight pesos each. Some nights the girl faked sickness, and other nights she really was too sick to work. Ximénez kept watch over all of the proceedings (even spying on their acts in the bedroom) to prevent men from "committing an outrage" with Doña María de Jesus. The mother stated that she allowed this activity only because they were so poor. When she objected, her husband cursed her and forced the daughter to continue.[45]

Doña María de Jesus's statement echoed her mother's account with a little more detail, delicately writing a fine line between accuracy and complete fabrication. She repeated the story about Don Joaquín, who allegedly promised her money and marriage but then abandoned her after raping her. This act inspired her stepfather to prostitute her to other men or, as she put it, "with all men [con todos los hombres]." Of the eight pesos that she said she earned per night, Doña María de Jesus said that her father took six to waste on gambling.[46] He compelled her to walk the streets at night, seeking out men that "parecian bien [appeared fine]" to have sex with her. Her stepfather used these words also, and they suggest that Doña María de Jesus could reject some potential clients that did not attract her for whatever reason. Regarding her twelve-year-old sister, Doña María Rosa, Doña María de Jesus said that one man, known as "the fat mister" [el señor gordo], came regularly and kissed and hugged the young girl, leaving them with a peso that they gave to Ximénez. Doña María Rosa confirmed this point and complained that kissing men scared her, due to the aforementioned story that she had read about a wolf eating women who kissed men, a story that took on a symbolic importance as the focus of this family's former moral code and claims to respectability. The twelve-year-old also said that her sister was now a "bad woman" because she stood in the doorway, allowed men to flirt with her, and admitted them into the bedroom.[47]

As the case became more complicated, the court tracked down the men involved in the negotiation of Doña María de Jesus's virginity. Of course, their stories differed from those offered by the family. The first potential client was Don Joaquín Arteaga, a thirty-two-year-old married man of Spanish descent born in Xilotepec (clearly not a gachupín), who worked at the Royal Mint as a polisher (limador). Before he married, one night in November of 1813, Don Joaquín recounted that he was strolling around the city after 7:00 p.m. He testified that he accidentally encountered the accused mother and daughter, women whom he had never met before, and greeted them, in hopes of seducing one of them. He asked them where they were going, a confession that indicated his admission that he sought to solicit sex on the street that night. Sánchez responded that her husband had sent them out to find a man that might pay a significant amount of money to have sex with her virgin daughter, or maybe marry her. As they chatted, they approached the family lodgings. Don Joaquín said that he feared entering, but the mother assured him that her husband approved of their solicitation.[48]

After entering the rooms, Ximénez confirmed that Don Joaquín should not be shocked because, as the father explained, the family simply had to find a way to fight their miserable economic situation. In pity, Don Joaquín said that he gave the father a peso. He promised that he would give them two hundred pesos to marry their daughter. Ximénez suggested that he could also just have her as his mistress, maintaining her in a casita. Don Joaquín noticed that the mother seemed to agree to all of this, but Doña María de Jesus hid herself in a corner, distant from the negotiations. When he came back the next day, he talked to Sánchez alone, and the mother agreed to the conditions of concubinage that they had already discussed. He observed that still the daughter did not participate in the conversation, which might signify her silent obedience.[49] These observations regarding Doña María de Jesus may have functioned in the court setting to ameliorate her possible guilt in this transaction, or also to highlight that her parents ignored her consent both in terms of sex and her potential spouse.[50]

A week or so later, Don Joaquín confessed, he returned to the house in the afternoon and found Doña María de Jesus on her own. When he asked about her becoming his mistress, she said that she had to ask her mother. Becoming aggressive, he put her on his lap and began to fondle her breasts. He begged and supplicated her with many endearments to surrender her virginity to him, but she resisted, assuring him that she was a virgin and that his advances were wrong. This enraged him, so he claimed that he gave up entirely on his plan of attack for seducing her. He said he stormed out of the house without ever "having a carnal act" with her.

Don Joaquín did not speak to the girl again until around April of 1814, when he saw Doña María de Jesus standing in her own doorway. At this time, she worked soliciting men, as her father ordered her to do, allegedly since the gachupín (misidentifying Don Joaquín?) had deflowered her. When he met her standing in her doorway, Don Joaquín said that he asked her, "Who was the happy man who had deflowered her?" Despite her suggestive position standing in her doorway, she replied that no one had. She said that she was still a virgin. Don Joaquín claimed that this was the sum total of his dealing with this family and that he had never given any of them more than the one peso in alms that he offered on the first night that he had talked to the father.[51]

The second known target for the virgin con was Don Blas de Villanueva, who was a twenty-nine-year-old Spanish-descended dealer in wheat and a cavalryman fighting on the side of the patriots. In his statement, Don Blas claimed that the previous year (December of 1813), he encountered Doña María de Jesus and her mother standing in a doorway at around ten in the evening. He followed the women to their lodgings. There he met a halberdier, whose name he could not recall, who offered both his wife and his daughter for sex. Don Blas chose Doña María de Jesus and gave the father a peso, all the money that he had with him. He said that the mother, father, and daughter all claimed that she was still a virgin. This information seemed to dissuade Don Blas from carrying out the transaction. Perhaps he viewed sex with a virgin as a violation, and he wanted to have sex with a more experienced woman. Or he may have feared the standard procedure of deflowered women's using the courts to seek longer-term compensation for breach of the "*palabra de casamiento* [marriage promise]." As we learned in the first example in this chapter, Don Manuel Duran y Otero found himself in an awkward situation for just such a mistake made in an unwise, lustful moment. In response to Don Blas's rejection, Ximénez again suggested his wife instead. Don Blas said that he thought it was not a good idea for him to sleep with another man's wife, especially if the two men were friends. Don Blas claimed that the negotiations then changed, and all of them admitted that Doña María de Jesus was not a doncella, to counter his disinclination to pay for sex with a virgin.[52] They also stated that both she and her mother slept with men for four pesos. In the end, Don Blas claimed that he left the family brothel without paying for or receiving any sex at all. Sánchez confirmed this version of the story, denying that she knew anything about negotiating for her daughter's virginity. On other hand, Ximénez asserted that Don Blas had slept with his stepdaughter and that he had found her a virgin at this time.[53]

It is possible that both Don Blas and Don Joaquín lied in their statements to disguise or diminish the fact that they undoubtedly passed their evenings in walking the city streets looking for sex, or even to deny their acts of rape. They accepted the plaintiffs' solicitations with enthusiasm while they strolled around the city at night. But Ximénez and his wife also lied, both to these potential clients and in court, in the ongoing scam to sell their daughter's alleged virginity as many times as they could for the best possible payment. In the case of the so-called gachupín Don Joaquín, they even suggested that marriage might come of the transaction.

The sad truth behind these efforts to sell Doña María de Jesus's virginity is the fact that other evidence contradicts this verbalized sexual status. In a later statement made after Doña María de Jesus accused one of her potential clients of taking her virginity, she changed her testimony, instead accusing her stepfather of this act. Regardless of their schemes to market her virginity to at least two men, mother and daughter made a strong legal case against Ximénez in 1811 for rape of the then-thirteen-year-old girl. This act took place two years before Doña María de Jesus began working openly as a prostitute. According to the victim herself, her stepfather attempted to rape her from age nine, when he had taken her to San Lázaro, on the outskirts of Mexico City, and dragged her into a drainage ditch. On this occasion, a passing man saved her. Ximénez continued his sexual attacks four years later, when he took her out with the pretext of buying her new shoes. Doña María de Jesus said that this time he tied her hands to a tree and violated her. Some references suggest that a friend of hers passed by and possibly stopped the rape in the act. Ximénez threatened to kill her and her mother if she reported him.[54]

Doña María de Jesus and her mother had witnesses to back up their accusations, including a young cousin and a midwife. The cousin testified that Ximénez had taken the two girls on a walk and then grabbed his stepdaughter and carried her away screaming. The witness did not know what happened next, but she knew the mother and daughter had complained to the viceroy.[55] The justices also found the midwife, a woman named Maria Rita Castillo, known as "La Zambrano," described as a mulata widow over age forty. La Zambrano had an official license from the *protomedicato* to work as a midwife. She testified that she remembered Sánchez and her daughter's coming to see her in 1812, when the girl was thirteen years old. Upon examination, the midwife found her "recently and completely violated." La Zambrano remembered that the mother and daughter admitted that Ximénez had raped her the day before the exam.[56] Sánchez complained to the authorities, who then imprisoned Ximénez. However, he petitioned for his release in order to take care of her and her seven children, which then allowed him to carry out his plan of pandering his eldest stepdaughter, with her mother's complicity.[57]

Of course, the stepfather denied these horrific accusations in a face-to-face *careo* (a conversation in court about the accusations) with his stepdaughter. In his rage at this court-orchestrated confrontation and the allegations of rape and incest against him, Ximénez retaliated by accusing his wife of prostitution with various men. He did admit that she made an income this way with his consent and knowledge, even before involving her oldest daughter. Ximénez said that his wife's involvement in the sex trade had taken place several years ago, when the family had its first struggle with desperate poverty. He named two of her military clients and claimed that she saw three or four men daily.[58] At this time, all of the daughters were children, so only the mother worked selling sex. He also accused his wife of agreeing to the potential sale of the virginity of their next eldest daughter, the preteen Doña María Rosa.[59] Even with all of the heinous charges against him, Ximénez tried to write a less nefarious image for himself, despite his ready admission of guilt in the charge of running a brothel in his home. He willingly inscribed himself as a ruffian who pandered his wife and stepdaughter, but nothing more.[60]

Although he received no sympathy from the court whatsoever, Ximénez continued his efforts to reshape his image throughout the case. In a later testimony, he retracted his allegations of prostitution against his wife, admitting that he had tried to defame her in this way only out of vengeance for the rape accusations. He denied the validity of the heinous charges against him, observing that the women's descriptions of the assault had numerous irresolvable internal contradictions and gaps. The court reacted with censorious statements, appalled by the fact that "satisfying his brutal appetite" led to "such a horrific crime" of "first degree incest."[61] The justices pointed out that even if he was not an incestuous rapist, they still viewed Ximénez as a panderer who greedily took part in commercial sex to fund his own vices, referring back to his stepdaughter's claims that he gambled away her earnings. At this point, Ximénez tried to whitewash his gambling, claiming that it was his way of trying to contribute some small pittance to the pitiful family income and to purchase clothes for Doña María de Jesus.[62] Even gambling offered an opportunity for him to try to record himself as a good father who wanted to take care of his family's needs.

The mother of the family combated the court's view of her as an evil mother and morally suspect wife. In her original statements, made when the authorities barged into the family's home and caught them prostituting Doña María de Jesus in flagrante delicto, Sánchez confessed that her husband had compelled her, even as a mother, to solicit men on the streets. The two male clients described above also observed that Ximénez offered sex with either his wife or his daughter to them when they visited the home brothel. These pieces of evidence combined with Ximénez's words solidify the likelihood that the mother did sell sex. However, over the course of the investigation, Sánchez denied that she had participated in the sex trade.[63] She reformulated her self-presentation to remain within the helpless-victim model, alluding to traces of personal dignity and honor.

While this tactic usually gained judicial sympathy, in this case the court expressed repugnance toward her attempts at respectability, similar to their disgust at her husband's efforts to shore up his reputation. Official statements expressed doubts about her claims that she had not worked as a prostitute herself. During her interrogations, Sánchez endured harsh condemnations and exhortations that "she maintained a scandalous brothel without fear of God or respect for justice" and that, as a mother, she offered a bad example to her daughters. The justices belittled her expressions of fear of her husband's beatings if she did not agree to prostitute her daughter, pontificating that

> neither persuasions nor threats from her husband allowed such disgusting acts. . . .
> She should prevent her daughter from carnally mixing with any man, but she allowed
> it for four months, knowing that it was not only with one man, but that she had sex
> [se mezclaba] with many men every night. She permitted this along with her criminal
> husband dissipating in vice what that poor unhappy young girl earned through
> the prostitution that her barbaric parents drove her to. . . . Their alleged poverty
> does not exculpate [Doña María Sánchez], because it could not be so extreme
> if [Ximénez] had enough to gamble. . . . When she is a bawd for her daughter, she
> sacrifices her soul, her honor, her reputation, and the happiness of that poor unfor-
> tunate girl who has lost everything because her own parents disgraced her and
> caused her unhappiness.[64]

In response to this lecture, Sánchez begged for the court's pity and mercy, still refusing to confess that she worked as a prostitute herself. She did admit that Ximénez violently intimidated her enough that she agreed that another military man would "violate the virginity" of the young Doña María Rosa. However, the mother said she planned to stop the act before it happened.[65] Despite the harsh words, ultimately, the mother avoided punishment to the full extent of the law against bawds.

While the court emphasized that parents had to take moral responsibility for their children by protecting girls from sex with men for cash, the accused couple asserted that prostituting their daughters offered them the only source of income they could find. In effect, the parents tried to argue that organizing and managing this occupation for Doña María de Jesus and eventually her younger sister represented the best way for them to protect and support their family. From their perspective, both parents wanted to do what they viewed as right and necessary: feed their children and keep the family together. As Ximénez argued, his children were crying with hunger, and that forced a father to do anything he can to help them.[66]

Doña María de Jesus emerged from her parents' exploitation and entered what appeared to be a conventional marriage. Her husband was a young man who loved her for many years and did not openly denigrate her short career as a prostitute. As of April 1815, documentation attests that Doña María de Jesus lived with her husband and sister Doña María Rosa.[67] This arrangement meant that neither of the two girls had to reside in a house of reclusion, which had been a possible fate for both of them. The story of her marriage offers an appealing, if idealized, end to Doña María de Jesus's traumatic teenage years. Apparently, a young Spaniard named Don Manuel Ronderos had worked for Sánchez as the cashier in her store when the family lived respectably. In this capacity, he met Doña María de Jesus when she was only ten years old. Over the years, he decided that he wanted to marry her and received permission from his relatives to carry out his intentions. By this time, he was serving as a cadet in the San Luis regiment, so he had also asked for, and received, agreement from his superior officers to the marriage. However, in one of his typical cruel schemes, Ximénez had snitched on Don Manuel to his commander, reporting that he had committed some unmentioned crimes. As a result, the young man had to leave the city for a year.

For her part, Doña María de Jesus complained that her stepfather had prevented this marriage, with the pretext that her suitor was not an "hombre de bien."[68] Both Doña María de Jesus and her mother testified that Ximénez had both raped and prostituted her in order to prevent her marrying anyone. As stated above, he initiated his attempts to violate her when she was only nine years old, but circumstances prevented the rape for four years.[69] Practically, he may have believed that he could profit from marketing her virginity more effectively if she did not have a known suitor, a man like Ronderos who, due to the affection the young man seemed to feel for Doña María de Jesus, would "waste" the financial benefit that the stepfather could reap if he controlled her sexual activity himself.[70] If her virginity was a valuable commodity that would help the family survive in hard times, Ximénez wanted to control it in order to make a profitable sale.

Ximénez advanced the erroneous view that men would marry only a virgin. On the young suitor's return, Ximénez continued his nefarious plot, telling Don Manuel that his stepdaughter had lost her virginity to a European merchant. Contrary to the stepfather's expectations, Don Manuel did not let this report deter his desires to marry Doña María de Jesus. He rationalized that he had only heard that she had experienced a single carnal act, and it had been a rape. He blamed

Ximénez for any other "immoral acts" committed by Doña María de Jesus.[71] His statements suggest that his love for her and desire to marry her persisted as long as he could envision her as a victim of abuse, not a sexually active woman who pursued this occupation for pay. The court also viewed Doña María de Jesus as an innocent victim of her stepfather's "shocking depravity." Her advocate argued that once she left the clutches of this "infamous monster," who did not even deserve to be called a man, she would never again number among the "public prostitutes."[72]

As a postscript to this apparently happy, if conventional, end to Doña María de Jesus's story, Ximénez caused continuing annoyances for the authorities. Disgusted by his behavior, the court sentenced him to ten years' hard labor on the Acapulco fort. Over the years of Mexico's insurgency wars, Ximénez continued to pester the viceregal authorities, who had far more pressing worries, with his complaints of the unendurable heat of Acapulco. He begged to go to work in a cooler region.[73] Sadly, he dragged his wife and younger children with him on his banishment and his ongoing criminal activity, including time spent in jail in 1817 and 1818 for desertion. Sánchez received a sentence of six years in a house of seclusion but did not carry out this punishment.[74] Therefore, Ximénez's self-representation to the court as a provider was ineffective, but his wife's persona as a victim of his abuse, albeit one that always returned to him, succeeded after the dismissal of her original sentence.

In their negotiations with potential male clients, Ximénez and his wife carried on a Spanish tradition of faking virginity and virgin brokering that dated back at least to the medieval era. La Celestina herself, the most notorious Spanish bawd, included thousands of hymen repairs among her many achievements, faking many women's virginity several times.[75] The most useful and profitable context for selling and faking virginity was, of course, not sex work but marriage itself. Because Iberian women in both Spain and the New World commonly sued men for breach of promise or defloration without carrying out their promises of marriage with the goal of monetary compensation, virginity was already monetized in this social and historic context.[76] It required only a slight adjustment from marriage to a straightforward sale to try to make fast cash out of this valuable commodity.

While Spanish America at this time does not seem to have had a large market for virgins (other than as potential wives), in eighteenth-century libertine France, mothers sought out professional female brokers to find the highest possible bidders for their daughters' virginity. These women sought to make as much money as possible on the exchange. Successful madams in this era and even into the twenty-first century also sold some girls' virginity many times over, in the same con that Ximénez and Sánchez practiced. The idea of brokering young women's sexuality was such a normal part of the business of arranging a marriage that selling virginity in Paris did not arouse police attention. In Paris, bawds had wealthy interested parties in mind and could more discreetly match them with the young girls offered by their mothers. These arrangements happened in private, not on the street.[77]

If professional virgin brokers (outside of conventional marriage and match-making) existed in early-nineteenth-century Mexico City, clearly Ximénez and Sánchez, as well as Doña Bartola in the first case, did not know about them. If they did, the parents and sister would not have needed to solicit such an expensive resource in such a crude fashion on the street. In more recent contexts, virgin brokering occurs within the environment of family, friends, and work colleagues, with a period of apprenticeship and negotiation for the young women involved.[78] While virginity can demand a high price depending on the vagaries of context, it is sold within a certain accepted and familiar social context, similar to the marriage market.

The young age of Doña María Dolores, Doña María de Jesus, and her younger sister Doña María Rosa makes all of them, by our standards, victims of despicable nonconsensual sex crimes, and their stories inevitably evoke our pity and disgust with their selfish and abusive relatives. However, in this historic context, even young family members had to contribute to the household income. Other money-making options earned only a tiny fraction of what they made in this occupation and thus would not save their families from dire poverty. The six girls discussed here (Teodoro Josepha, Chamorro, Romualda, Doña María Rosa, Doña María Dolores Rodríguez, and Doña María de Jesus) all in some way took part in sex for sale to help their families. Doña María de Jesus even became an active con artist in selling her own virginity by presenting herself as a virgin to Don Joaquín and per-haps other men. Her rejection and effective protest of his aggressive harassment indicate that not only did she not want to have sex when her parents were not there in the home to supervise the transaction (with the presumption that he would rape her, as she said, and not compensate her according to the system the family had set up to fund their needs), but that she also did not want to disabuse him of the fic-tion of her virginity. Her efforts to reject Don Joaquín and continue the potentially lucrative deception shows that she made choices about her participation in the family business.

Emphasizing their extreme poverty, all of the family leaders mentioned here claimed that they could no longer fulfill their provider duties.[79] Therefore, Doña María de Jesus and Doña María Dolores Rodríguez sold sex to conserve and sup-port their families, not weaken them.[80] Filial duty motivated Doña María de Jesus and Rodríguez in the months when they walked the streets with their mother or sister or solicited in their doorways. This changed when they realized that the authorities could separate them from their panderers. So the young women rejected and reorganized their families by filing complaints. In the process, they became disobedient and disloyal daughters who forced their mothers and sisters into worse economic situations, a vagrant life, and ongoing spousal abuse. The pages of these cases offer almost endless ways to interpret and retell their fractured and evasive tales of exploitation, manipulation, and deception. Again, only the victims' use of clearly criminalizing labels caused scribes to capture their narratives for posterity and allow historians to find them within the archive, but our resulting writings do not necessarily need to coalesce or harden into a "charmed account" or "straight story."[81]

Conclusion

Santa found a pool of shadow on the sidewalk and stayed in it until she was able to hail an empty rental coach and direct it to the well-known brothel.

"Hop right in, my patrona*," said the coachman, lighting the lamps as he listened to the address. "Okay, I know where, Elvira's house."*

Santa abandoned herself, mind and body, to what she supposed to be forces beyond her control, and finding herself back in the brothel, she breathed easier and wrapped herself in ignominy as if wrapping herself in cashmere and silk. She would not try to change; she would continue being bad. . . . She would behave the same way. With her caresses she would calm the men who thirsted for her body, calm all who wanted it. There was enough for everybody.[1]

The seduced, abandoned, and doomed Santa steps out of the pages of an early twentieth-century Mexican novel to embody the conscious-struck fallen woman. Throughout this book, I have re-narrated textual inscriptions of selling sex over the course of three centuries. A key aspect of archival understandings of transactional sex was the gradual emergence of the word *prostitute* over the course of the eighteenth century. From Australia to France, this new terminology invoked perceptions of criminalization and professionalization. In New Spain, the authorities used the newer term in relation to women's victimization. Labeling a woman a whore asserted that she had made a personal choice to follow a path of immorality and promiscuity, for pay or not. In contrast, innocent women and girls could be "prostituted" and rescued. Globally, government officials also equated prostitution with disease, an association that began around the mid-sixteenth century and that contributes to the whore stigma to this day.

Notwithstanding a few petitions and licenses in the first decades of settlement, the legal institution of the brothel did not appear often in New World archives. Instead, the documentary record suggests that even older customary and informal practices such as female bawdry and domestic transactional sex persisted from the Iberian medieval context into the nineteenth century. Although sparse, sixteenth-century litigation in Mexico City subjected women to defamation for trading in sex but also offered them an opportunity to assert themselves as victims of abusive ruffians in the form of their pandering husbands. Before 1623, these women may have sinfully sought to exchange sex for money, but they did not break any laws in the process. This differed from the situation in Spain, where municipalities financially benefited from prosperous brothels and an income of legal fines for a variety of transgressions against their regulations.

In the New World, African and indigenous participation in whoring and bawdry provoked fearful inquisitors to link transactional sex and companionship with exotic and dangerous sorcery and erotic magic. While the Holy Office also made this connection in Iberia, Old World suspicions did not affiliate witchcraft, spells, and divination with a more serious fear of racially motivated rebellions. Instead, a horror of syphilis and a church/state shift, post-Trent, toward enclosing women perceived as morally dangerous and as a negative influence on respectable ladies, inspired more restrictive regulations against bawds, brothels, and whores in the late sixteenth and early seventeenth centuries. These broad trends increased stigmatization in general, which sometimes resulted in violence.

Emerging from this milieu of increasing illegality, the words *prostituir, prostitución,* and *prostituta* appeared in Mexico City documentation by the early eighteenth century. Litigants and the judiciary associated this term with moneymaking as well as victim status of those women who were "prostituted."[2] But even as the judicial angle changed, rich and poor women continued to benefit from acts of male sexual patronage, on a petty scale (buying a drink of pulque) or grandly (funding a palatial home). Although street-level surveillance and documented prosecutions increased exponentially in this era, men of all classes continued to take advantage of sex for sale at whatever level they could afford. Laws and policing, as always, had very little effect on suppressing transactional sex.

As noted by Marie Kelleher for fourteenth-century Catalonia, "with the legal boundaries so imprecisely defined but the stakes so high, a woman's representation of her own sexuality took on great importance."[3] Before the nineteenth century, in response to accusations of whoring or bawdry, women created a dignified, reputable, Christian identity for themselves, other than in cases of victimized wives' seeking to escape their ruffian husbands. The latter situation conformed to rhetorical juridical formulas common to divorce petitions, which required an unequivocal victim-versus-abuser dichotomy. However, archival records from Mexico City between 1800 and 1815 include statements made by very young women asserting their claims in court with a performance of victimization endured in the context of their own family homes.

In this era of political and military uprising, domestic brothels represented a group economic-survival strategy rather than moral deviance. Not sympathizing with their panderer's desperation, the judiciary responded by removing the girls from the custody of their siblings or parents. These actions showed that the state now doubted whether or not some families could provide their daughters with stability and conventional morality or facilitate their role in social reproduction. The authorities might restructure families that took part in domestic pandering by approving of the insertion of a man into the group to serve as an effective husband and guardian or patriarch. When women stressed their sexual victimization within their family homes, they exercised a useful tactic for representing an unthreatening femininity to both judges and potential husbands. They petitioned themselves into accepted gender roles and disguised their sexual transactions with the proper textual notation of monogamous marriage.[4]

The early decades of the nineteenth century severely disrupted the lives of colonial subjects. When the dust settled, in Mexico, Europe, and regions around the world under European colonial rule, commercial sex took place in an environment of increasing government intervention, a phase in the history of sexuality that extends into the twenty-first century. The concern about disease control took on a more scientific, sanitary tone in the eighteenth century. This discourse remained critical to sex-work law, as it does to the present day. Through prolific regulations, scientific studies, works of literature, and statements made by sex workers themselves, the nineteenth and twentieth centuries saw an enormous increase in the archiving and inscribing of women who sold sex. But their roles remained the same: either pathetic victims (usually of nonwhites or non-Christians or other feared populations), lascivious and scandalous disturbers of the peace, or dehumanized and horrific threats to public health. Empire-building and international conceptions of race/gender difference led to increasing government regulation in locations as dispersed as the disappearing Spanish American viceroyalties, extending outward to Europe, Asia, and Oceania.

Enlightenment-era commentators in Spain complained of plebeian prostitution as an unending, uncontrollable problem even after almost two hundred years of crown attempts at suppression. They interpreted the "countless whores [*infinitas rameras*]" who walked the Madrid streets as symbols of the "triumph of vice."[5] Increasing militarization of ports and cities in the Napoleonic and Independence eras inspired enlightened Spaniards to theoretically entertain a return to legalized and regulated sex work. In the opinions of some health reformers, prostitutes shouldered the blame for any perceived decline in the physical, mental, or emotional strength of soldiers. Inspired by concerns regarding military health and effectiveness, the short-lived 1822 Penal Code implied a return to legalization and governmental brothel regulation, but its repeal in 1823 quickly ended this trajectory. Crown and dispersed municipal regulation of brothels finally returned under the legal reforms of Isabel II, who ruled from 1833 to 1868.[6]

Over the course of the century, Spanish American prostitution regulations often followed the French model, which set the pattern for Mexico during the rule of Maximilian.[7] In Old Regime France, no specific laws directly outlawed whoring, although the Paris police maintained ongoing surveillance of "kept women" for decades before the Revolution. Similar to Spain's, French laws in the late eighteenth century focused on the military and gestured toward sex work as an illicit occupation done in a criminal milieu. Laws that danced around the periphery of prostitution introduced various restrictions without definitively formulating laws to suppress it. Regulations dating from the 1770s to 1790s called for the arrest of prostitutes found in soldiers' encampments, forbade tavern keepers to allow sexual transactions in their bars, and permitted the police to raid scandalous houses. Early in the nineteenth century, France reinitiated the era (previously tried in sixteenth-century Spain) of registration and medical exams, justified by modern ideas of sanitation. This policy medicalized all women who sold sex and criminalized those who resisted invasive exams. Enforcement operated on a street level and thus ignored the middle- and upper-class kept women and courtesans. From 1830, certain bawds or "madams" received licenses to run legal brothels or "tolerated houses."[8]

Mexico adopted and reformed versions of the French laws from 1865 to 1872. Before this time, viceregal policies remained in place, especially in the 1830s, with efforts to solidify street-level policing.[9] The laws regulating prostitution that came to Mexico with the French Intervention focused on disease control, the authority of the brothel manageress, and the age and sexual status of prostitutes. Mexican law legalized prostitution for sexually active women over age fourteen who chose this occupation of their own free will. Their clients had to be older than fifteen and disease free. While these laws derived from French influences, by designating a powerful whorehouse "madam," they perpetuated early-modern Spanish regulations as well as the even older Iberian traditions of bawdry in a domestic setting. In 1898, the minimum age for legal prostitution changed to sixteen years old. In the Revolutionary Era, Mexican law continued to modify specific regulations for how prostitutes should behave, dress, and act and where they could legally work, again with an emphasis on toleration within certain geographic parameters.[10]

Throughout the era of Mexican efforts to conform to modernizing French and British regulatory moments, and then later, as national regulations disappeared in an even more "modern" attempt to domesticate female sexuality in the mid-twentieth century, documentation retained a late-viceregal tone. Archives preserve examples of how calling a woman a prostitute still meant abuse of her reputation, her essential public self. Written reports continued to disguise elusive transactionality. Before and after the Mexican Revolution, reformers reinscribed familiar and very seductive tales of female victimization, failed families, and pathologically abusive men for new political purposes.[11]

Argentina also followed the French model by legalizing and regulating prostitution in 1875, with an emphasis on containing sex workers in licensed brothels, keeping them off the street, out of the public gaze, and away from criminal male control. Disease control did not emerge as a focus until later in the century. Government intervention, especially the famous "Ley Palacios" of 1913, continued steadily in the decades to follow. A global perception of Buenos Aires as a center for the "white slave trade" became popular in the early twentieth century, a vision that ran parallel to similar ideas in the United States.[12] The paranoia about international prostitution rings disguised gendered fears of women's immigration and insertion into the urban industrial workforce.

Britain and its empire developed the most influential approach to sex work on a global scale in the second half of the nineteenth century, embracing a racist and elitist conception of epidemic disease that continues to affect former colonies into the twenty-first century. The introduction of lock hospitals in mid-eighteenth-century London marked the beginning of the British linking of sanitation, sex work, and state control.[13] The Vagrancy, Municipal Corporations, and Poor Laws of the 1820s and 1830s opened up an avenue for criminalizing poor women soliciting on city streets within Britain. Vague accusations or perceptions of idleness, disorder, or disturbing the peace justified harassment from the new police forces. The Contagious Disease (CD) Acts of 1864 further empowered law enforcement to arrest streetwalkers and force them to register and endure genital exams. Other laws in this era governed the management of brothels.[14] Some perceived this regulation as in effect turning the state into a panderer. The CD Acts provoked a passionate feminist response against compulsory medical exams, leading to their repeal in 1886. However, the closure of hundreds of London brothels by "purity" reformers in 1888 meant that many more women had to turn to streetwalking and cheap nightly lodging, necessary preconditions for the legendary gruesome killings of "Jack the Ripper."[15]

Outposts of the British Empire faced the CD Acts and their consequences for decades, beginning with Hong Kong in 1857. Each colony, from Australia, to India, to Canada, implemented a different interpretation of the CD Acts. Factors that shaped their implementation included local labor patterns and the racial makeup of workers; the presence or absence of the British military; and most importantly, the perceived agency of women in the region. For example, imperial authorities viewed white European prostitutes as consciously choosing to immigrate to Australia in order to continue their profession but denied that free volition to Asian women, whom they viewed as voiceless and nameless. According to their race, some women under British imperial rule were perceived as more hygienic (Japanese), others more subject to abusive men (Indian women), and others dirtier, less sanitary, and doomed to extinction via venereal disease. Although the Colonial Office ordered the repeal of the CD Acts in 1887, tolerated prostitution continued throughout the British Empire, and the obsession with disease control reared up again during the twentieth-century world wars.[16]

Similar fears to those seen in Buenos Aires, London, and Mexico City sprang up in the United States. Here, accounts of "fallen women" emphasized the dangers faced by country girls who, inspired by their greed for luxuries (especially clothes), ventured into the cities to work.[17] Brothels dominated the urban sex trade in a tolerated but illegal position, with the authorities shaping how sex work operated in any given locale. Often, as in the British Empire, the suppression of prostitution coincided with attempts to monitor and control nonwhite races. For example, city ordinances in San Francisco called for brothel closure starting from the 1850s, targeting Chinese "Houses of Ill Fame." Chicago had a tradition of both black and white women's catering to a wide range of male leisure/entertainment desires by managing "parlor houses," less expensive boarding houses, and "buffet flats." In the first decades of the twentieth century, sex work in Chicago moved toward more informal and dangerous street solicitation, often in the hands of powerful local gangs, as a result of zoning regulations forcing brothel closures and shifting the location of the "red light districts." These efforts at suppression and control overlapped with purity movements that sparked paranoia of the "white slave trade" and immigration restrictions at the national level.[18]

Historians cite Victorian-era and turn-of-the-century American reform, rescue, and "purity" movements and fears of the "white slave trade" as the genesis of the idea that women "were more passive and dependent than they had ever been."[19] Not only does this particular vision of "unqualified passivity" have a specific historic setting, but it also applied only to women of certain races, classes, and religions, in an effort to demonize others who lacked the "civilized" nature of domesticated women.[20]

Motivated by their ineffectiveness in reducing sexually transmitted disease, nationalistic goals of ridding the country of its reputation as a vice-tourism destination, and many other complications, Mexico abolished its sex work regulations in 1940 and shut official brothels in the *zona de tolerancia*. This led to the immediate criminalization of women who had previously worked as legal and registered prostitutes and a permanent inscription of them as disease vectors.[21] Since then, cities such as Tijuana have retained regulations with a quasilegal status for lucrative high-status female (mainly heterosexual) prostitution, quite similar to viceregal approaches that protected courtesans viewed as having high sexual capital. The ongoing violence and danger proves that newer laws have not addressed the key issues of safety, disease, and especially the injustices and hierarchies within the broader social and economic context, which are perilously amplified in the border region. Even as subjects of very recent studies, sex workers, however stigmatized, retain their elusiveness from official control and resist documentation.[22]

The late-nineteenth- and early-twentieth–century popular narratives of sexual predators reflected concerns over young women's mobility and immigration to cities or away from their native lands. These gendered worries about migration continue into the present day, with the prevalence of an ongoing understanding that "consent in the context of prostitution is impossible," even when it involves voluntary migration.[23] This view takes away women's abilities to make good economic choices and also requires a villainous character to seduce or force women into sex work. It also questions the moral worth of families making this choice for their daughters. Historians have complicated this global story with evidence that economic conditions, not "immoral influences," led to women's involvement in sex work. For example, Donna Guy's classic work on prostitution in Buenos Aires notes that "fears of white slavery in Buenos Aires were directly linked to disapproval of female migration," but most women claimed that poverty, not manipulative panderers, drove them to work in brothels.[24] In her acclaimed study of twentieth-century sex work in Nairobi, Luise White emphasizes that African women sold sex within a variety of domestic settings "as a way to prosper," not as an act of financial desperation. Benson Tong argues that migrant Chinese women in San Francisco, who entered prostitution via abduction or sale by their parents, were "active, thinking, indentured workers" who "rose to the challenge of adapting to a circumscribed life."[25] Despite their differing interpretations of the economic preconditions, all of these authors acknowledge sex work as an economic decision that offered women a range of reactions and options, and all of them avoid the trap of "isolating women in the categories of deviancy and subculture."[26]

A useful insight for historians from recent sex-work-activism literature is the idea that sex workers were and are "experts in their own lives" and exercise human agency within their sometimes very limited options.[27] Some of the women documented in this book took the opportunity to start litigation, speak up in court when on trial, or physically challenge law enforcement. Their actions demonstrate conscious choices to survive and sometimes even prosper within the narrow economic parameters available to them. In a more recent context, sex-work scholars deemphasize the importance of the debate of whether or not women choose sex work and take the stance that "very few workers truly exercise unfettered choice in the modern labor market."[28] The currently available choices for poor women's labor (domestic menials, low-paying factory work, street vending) resemble those on offer for the women in this book. But even within a barren field of job options, or in scenarios where families sell their young daughters to brothels, women can resist medical exams, avoid official registration as a legal prostitute, lead or take part in riots inside of carceral institutions, form open or secret communities to protect one another, and, of course, complain to the authorities about various forms of exploitation or mistreatment.[29]

Concluding this survey of increasing regulation in the last five hundred years, our own era shows that criminalization causes ever more violence against those individuals we choose to marginalize with law codes that inscribe gender and sex biases. Sex work, conceived of as nonnormative, nonmonogamous, nonhetero, and unsafe to one's health, fits into the category of a threat. This inscription is far from new. Despite the limitations and evasions of the written record, historical examples help contextualize the global "sex wars" as continuous rewritings of enduring verbal debates.[30] Sex-work activist Melissa Gira Grant notes, "It's impossible to come to a politics of sex work without referring back to the prostitutes and whores who came before," a comment that I interpret as approving of and encouraging historical studies as valid contributions to this ongoing discussion.[31]

NOTES

INTRODUCTION

1. Francisco Delicado, *Retrato de la Lozana Andaluza* (Venice, 1528). English version: *Portrait of Lozana*, trans. Bruno M. Damiani (Potomac, MD: Scripta Humanistica, 1987), 90–92. I added "northern whores," left out in the Damiani translation of this passage. The full quote in Spanish is as follows: "Mirá, hay putas graciosas más que hermosas, y putas que son putas antes que muchachas. Hay putas apasionadas, putas estregadas, afeitadas, putas esclarecidas, putas reputadas, reprobadas. Hay putas mozárabes de Zocodover, putas carcaveras. Hay putas de cabo de ronda, putas ursinas, putas güelfas, gibelinas, putas injuínas, putas de Rapalo rapaínas. Hay putas de simiente, putas de botón griñimón, nocturnas, diurnas, putas de cintura y marca mayor. Hay putas orilladas, bigarradas, putas combatidas, vencidas y no acabadas, putas devotas y reprochadas de Oriente a Poniente y Septentrión; putas convertidas, arrepentidas, putas viejas, lavanderas porfiadas, que siempre han quince años como Elena; putas meridianas, occidentales, putas máscaras enmascaradas, putas trincadas, putas calladas, putas antes de su madre y después de su tía, putas de subientes e descendientes, putas con virgo, putas sin virgo, putas el día del domingo, putas que guardan el sábado hasta que han jabonado, putas feriales, putas a la candela, putas reformadas, putas jaqueadas, travestidas, formadas, estrionas de Tesalia. Putas avispadas, putas terceronas, aseadas, apuradas, gloriosas, putas buenas y putas malas, y malas putas. Putas enteresales, putas secretas y públicas, putas jubiladas, putas casadas, reputadas, putas beatas, y beatas putas, putas mozas, putas viejas, y viejas putas de trintín y botín. Putas alcagüetas, y alcahuetas putas, putas modernas, machuchas, inmortales, y otras que se retraen a buen vivir en burdeles secretos y públiques honestos que tornan de principio a su menester." See digital edition based on Antonio Pérez Gómez, *Retrato de la Lozana Andaluza* (Valencia: Tipografía Moderna, 1950), accessed March 29, 2016, www.cervantesvirtual.com/nd/ark:/59851/bmcok284.

2. *Portrait of Lozana,* 38. The scene with the quoted list starts on 89, a postcoital conversation that took place while Lozana's lover "basks in glory." For the historical context, see Tessa Storey, *Carnal Commerce in Counter-Reformation Rome* (Cambridge, UK: Cambridge University Press, 2008). As an Andalusian immigrant earning her fortune in early-modern Rome, La Lozana's career alluded to the growing Spanish influence over the Papal State and the Americas. See Thomas James Dandelet, *Spanish Rome, 1500–1700* (New Haven, CT: Yale University Press, 2008). Angus MacKay focuses on the language used for sex work in *La Lozana,* and La Lozana as a *conversa.* See MacKay, "Women on the Margins," in *Love, Religion and Politics in Fifteenth-Century Spain,* ed. Ian Macpherson and Angus MacKay (Leiden, Netherlands: Brill, 1998), 28–42. For more on La Lozana, see Carmen Yu-Chuh Hsu, "Courtesans in the Literature of the Spanish Golden Age" (PhD diss.: University of Michigan, 2002), 91–103.

3. Melissa Gira Grant, *Playing the Whore: The Work of Sex Work* (London: Verso, 2014), 19; Chi Adanna Mgbako, *To Live Freely in This World: Sex Worker Activism in Africa* (New York: New York University Press, 2016), 23–24. On these pages, Mgbako discusses how a single story of victimhood "erases the voices and experiences of those who don't fit that universalized narrative" that presents "sex workers as simple objects of pity and potential rescue incapable of speaking for themselves."

4. Jorge Cañizares Esguerra, *Puritan Conquistadors: Iberianizing the Atlantic, 1550–1700* (Stanford, CA: Stanford University Press, 2006), 215–33, provides an excellent historiographic essay on this issue. Cañizares Esguerra points out that, in terms of religious ideology, political innovation, scientific research, literary production, the history of ideas, and "cultural and racial hybridization of global proportions . . . the Iberian empires . . . first set into motion the processes . . . that typify our modern world." The quote comes from 219. James E. Sanders, *The Vanguard of the Atlantic World: Creating Modernity, Nation, and Democracy in Nineteenth-Century Latin America* (Durham, NC: Duke University Press, 2014). See also "Forum: Entangled Empires in the Atlantic World," *American Historical Review* vol.112, no. 3 (June 2007): 710–99.

5. Cañizares Esguerra, *Puritan Conquistadors,* 219: Anjali Arondekar, *For the Record: On Sexuality and the Colonial Archive in India* (Durham, NC: Duke University Press, 2009), 4.

6. *Portrait of Lozana,* 21–22, 77.

7. Ibid., 23, 105–7, 138. The quotes I cite here show the complexity of La Lozana's sexual persona; however, I do not deny that Delicado may have deeper goals in his story: a denunciation of traditional female healing and of the disease-ridden early-modern whore. See Jean Dangler, *Mediating Fictions: Literature, Women Healers, and the Go-Between in Medieval and Early Modern Iberia* (Lewisburg, PA: Bucknell University Press, 2001), 128–72.

8. Laura Ann Stoler, *Along the Archival Grain: Epistemic Anxieties and Colonial Common Sense* (Princeton, NJ: Princeton University Press, 2009), 252. Italics in original.

9. Walter Johnson, "On Agency," *Journal of Social History* 37, 1 (2003): 113–24. Historians have proven definitively how women effectively used the courts to achieve their own goals. Two examples are: Kimberly Gauderman, *Women's Lives in Colonial Quito: Gender, Law, and Economy in Spanish America* (Austin: University of Texas Press, 2003); and Chad Thomas Black, *The Limits of Gender Domination: Women, the Law, and Political Crisis in Quito, 1765–1830* (Albuquerque: University of New Mexico Press, 2010).

10. Kathryn Burns, *Into the Archive: Writing and Power in Colonial Peru* (Durham, NC: Duke University Press, 2010), 2–3, 22, 39, 89, 93–94, 127, 134–35. Burns points out that notaries were not omnipotent in writing archives. Their clients, and perhaps the judiciary, also duped them. See 97.

11. Carolyn Steedman, *Dust: The Archive and Cultural History* (New Brunswick, NJ: Rutgers University Press, 2001), 70. Italics in original.

12. Elizabeth Grosz, *Volatile Bodies: Toward a Corporeal Feminism* (Bloomington and Indianapolis: University of Indiana Press, 1994), x, 18, 27. See also 60–61, 116–21, 136–37.

13. Steedman, *Dust,* 1–2, 68. Stoler, *Along the Archival Grain,* 1–2, 5, 19, 21, 33.

14. Arlette Farge, *The Allure of the Archives,* trans. Thomas Scott-Railton (New Haven, CT: Yale University Press, 2013), 26–29.

15. See Arondekar, *For the Record*; Stoler, *Along the Archival Grain,* 53; Burns, *Into the Archive,* 24, 34; Zeb Tortorici, "Archival Seduction: Indexical Absences and Historiographical Ghosts," *Archive Journal* Issue 5, accessed January 26, 2017, http://www.archivejournal .net/issue/5/archives-remixed/archival-seduction; Zeb Tortorici, "Visceral Archives of the Body: Consuming the Dead, Digesting the Divine," *GLQ* 20, no. 4 (2014): 407–38; Daniel Marshall, Kevin P. Murphy, and Zeb Tortorici, "Editors' Introduction," *Radical History Review* 122 (2015): 1–10. To explore the connections between historians' subjects and our own desires, see Zeb Tortorici, "Auto/ethno/pornography," *Porn Studies* 2 (2015): 265–68.

16. Steedman, *Dust,* 75, 77, 78, 81. Also observed in Farge, *The Allure of the Archives,* 7–9.

17. Stoler, *Along the Archival Grain,* 3, 255.

18. D. A. Brading, *The First America: The Spanish Monarchy, Creole Patriots, and the Liberal State, 1492–1867* (Cambridge: Cambridge University Press, 1991), 526–32.

19. For the literature of "transactional sex," a term that has especially been applied in Africa, see Mark Hunter, *Love in the Time of AIDS: Inequality, Gender, and Rights in South Africa* (Bloomington: Indiana University Press, 2010), 16, 28, 178–82, 233n23. Using the term *transactional sex* agrees with Ruth Mazo Karras's assertion that "the fact that a category of analysis was not in use at the time does not obviate its usefulness for historians." See Karras, "Women's Labors: Reproduction and Sex Work in Medieval Europe," *Journal of Women's History* vol. 15, 4 (2004): 153–58, 153.

20. Stoler, *Along the Archival Grain,* 40–41, 57–59, 71.

21. For *The Book of Good Love,* see chapter 1. For the *Tragicomedy of Calisto and Melibea,* also known as Fernando de Rojas, *Celestina,* ed. and trans. Dorothy Sherman Severin and James Mabbe (Warminster, Wiltshire: Aris & Phillips, 1987), see chapter 2. The bulk of the archival evidence comes from the Archivo General de la Nación, Mexico City; but acknowledging the context of the Spanish Empire, I also use sources from the Archivo General de Indias (Seville). I model my archival narratives on Natalie Zemon Davis, *Fiction in the Archives: Pardon Tales and Their Tellers in Sixteenth-Century France* (Stanford, CA: Stanford University Press, 1987), and the idea of a rhetorical self in a court setting from Stephen Greenblatt, *Renaissance Self-Fashioning: From More to Shakespeare* (Chicago: University of Chicago Press, 2005). Overall, I emphasize narrative and biographical detail over statistics. As noted by Mark Hunter, "Since sex money exchanges are saturated with questions of morality, in-depth qualitative research has been much better than quantitative research in picking up the extent of exchanges that link money and sex." Hunter, *Love in the Time of AIDS,* 233n23.

22. "What makes literature valuable to the historian of sex is not its representativeness but its expressiveness"; stories place "moral commandments within the patterns of social life [and show] . . . its tensions and its silences." Kyle Harper, *From Shame to Sin: The Christian Transformation of Sexual Morality in Late Antiquity* (Cambridge, MA: Harvard University Press, 2013), 10. See also Stoler, *Along the Archival Grain,* 145, for how literature fits within the colonial program.

23. Laura J. Rosenthal, "Introduction," in *Nightwalkers: Prostitute Narratives from the Eighteenth Century,* ed. Laura J. Rosenthal (Peterborough, Ontario: Broadview Press, 2008), ix–xxix.

24. Judith Walkowitz, *City of Dreadful Delight: Narratives of Sexual Danger in Late Victorian London* (Chicago: University of Chicago Press, 1999), 85–101, 201, 244–45. Walkowitz labels late-nineteenth-century journalism that repeated the "old story of the seduction of poor girls by vicious aristocrats" in order to appeal to middle-class feminist readers, as "political melodrama." At the same time, extremely explicit exposés of abusive prostitution provoked their readers' titillation. These first-hand accounts published in wildly popular periodicals closely resembled the violent pornography of the era. Walkowitz also shows how the newspaper coverage of (and our ongoing fascination with) Jack the Ripper and his allegedly prostitute victims fits into the melodramatic genre of corrupt fallen women receiving their well-deserved, horrible fate. She ties this to the more recent "Yorkshire Ripper" and warns us to avoid perpetuating female victimization, as "the forces of political reaction . . . are only too delighted to cast women in the roles of victims requiring male protection and control."

25. In the United States, the stories told in early-nineteenth-century sentimental novels provided a narrative structure for describing criminalized women, especially female factory workers discussed in real-world court cases. Following the typical novelistic denouement, lawyers stated that these women deserved to die for their immoral sexuality. Jeanne Elders DeWaard, "The Crime of Womanhood: Ambivalent Intersections of Sentiment and Law in Nineteenth-Century American Culture" (Ph.D. diss., University of Miami, 2003), 36–42. See also Zabrina Zee Zahariades, "The Great Social Evil: Images of Fallen Women and Prostitutes in American Literature from 1872 to 1952" (MA thesis, California State University, Northridge, 2012). Decades later, the ideologies of purity crusaders mirrored movie plots from the early twentieth century, which portrayed naïve and passive young country girls falling victim to urban tricks such as drugged drinks, only to wake up and find themselves prisoners in a brothel. Taking a moral stance allowed these films to portray a great deal of explicit material to draw in ticket buyers. Leslie Fishbein, "From Sodom to Salvation: The Image of New York City in Films about Fallen Women," *New York History* (April 1989): 171–90.

26. This important historical variation suggests that we should question our broad and essentializing presuppositions about sad or abused victims of sex for sale, who might also be diseased, damaged, and pathologically promiscuous, without, at the same time, falling into the trap of the equally superficial libertine, self-empowering story. Historical scholarship for decades has provided useful contextualization through listening to a variety of women's voices from the past. However, the popular debate on sex work today continues to map onto libertine-versus-victimized dichotomies, which do not represent indisputable facts or even useful analytical categories. For anthropological perspectives on essentializing

gender roles, such as the pervasive stereotype of the Mexican macho, see Matthew C. Gutmann, *The Meanings of Macho: Being a Man in Mexico City* (Los Angeles and Berkeley: University of California Press, 2006), 20–21, 246–53. Luise White, *Comforts of Home: Prostitution in Colonial Nairobi* (Chicago: University of Chicago Press, 1993), 1–7, addresses the stereotypes of criminalization, decline, and degradation casually introduced into so many discussions of sex work.

27. Steedman, *Dust,* 48, 55. See also 142–55.

28. On this dichotomy, see Annie Sprinkle, "We've Come A Long Way—and We're Exhausted," in *Whores and Other Feminists,* ed. Jill Nagle (New York: Routledge, 1997), 66; Matthew H. Sommer, "Foreword," in Amy Stanley, *Selling Women: Prostitution, Markets, and the Household in Early Modern Japan* (Berkeley and Los Angeles: University of California Press, 2012), xiii. For the use of activism in historical scholarship, see Zeb Tortorici, "Introduction," in *Sexuality and the Unnatural in Colonial Latin America,* ed. Zeb Tortorici (Berkeley and Los Angeles: University of California Press, 2016), 8–10.

29. Stoler, *Along the Archival Grain,* 20, 44–53; Burns, *Into the Archive,* 125–35.

30. Given the limits of my sources, I do not discuss men who sold sex. For insights into possible venues for gay transactional sex in New Spain, see Zeb Tortorici, "'Heran Todos Putos': Sodomitical Subcultures and Disordered Desire in Early Colonial Mexico," *Ethnohistory* 54,1 (Winter, 2007): 35–67. Tortorici's dissertation and forthcoming book also highlight the possibilities of consensual exchange in unequal sexual encounters between men. See Zeb Tortorici, "Contra Natura: Sin, Crime, and 'Unnatural' Sexuality in Colonial Mexico, 1530–1821" (PhD diss., University of California, Los Angeles, 2010).

31. Gira Grant, *Playing the Whore,* 9, 33. Nagle, "Introduction," in *Whores,* ed. Nagle, 6.

32. This parallels studies of contemporary sex workers, who do not obsess over morality but instead dwell on economic concerns, stigmatization, and their fears of law enforcement and its abuses. Adanna Mgbako, *To Live Freely in This World,* 11.

33. Arondekar, *For the Record,* 33–36, quote on 36.

34. Harper, *From Shame to Sin.* After pride, greed was viewed as the evilest of the seven deadly sins because it indicated an individual's concern with materialism not spirituality. See Stanford M. Lyman, *The Seven Deadly Sins: Society and Evil* (Lanham, MD: General Hall, 1989), 136, 232–33. For the complex Christian understanding of symbolic whore/saints, see Ruth Mazo Karras, "Holy Harlots: Prostitute Saints in Medieval Legend," *Journal of the History of Sexuality* vol. 1, 1 (1990): 2–25.

35. Adanna Mgbako, *To Live Freely,* 16.

36. Philippa Levine, *Prostitution, Race, and Politics: Policing Venereal Disease in the British Empire* (New York: Routledge, 2003), 191. For an example of a recent law, see Oregon Laws, accessed May 13, 2016, http://www.oregonlaws.org/ors/167.007: "A person commits the crime of prostitution if the person engages in, or offers or agrees to engage in, sexual conduct or sexual contact in return for a fee."

37. Thomas Elyot, *The Dictionary of Syr Thomas Eliot Knyght* (London: Thomas Bertheleti, 1538), accessed April 15, 2016, http://quod.lib.umich.edu/e/eebogroup. For the complexity of medieval and early-modern terms in English, see Ruth Mazo Karras, *Common Women: Prostitution and Sexuality in Medieval England* (Oxford: Oxford University Press, 1996), 10–13. Karras uses "whore" as a translation for her sources' use of *meretrix,* 147n35. She notes that women called whores, strumpets, etc. were not "the same thing

as what we today call a prostitute." This changing terminology relates to changing ideas of the law.

38. Gira Grant, *Playing the Whore*, 15; Levine, *Prostitution, Race, and Politics*, 178.

39. Gail Pheterson, "Not Repeating History," in *A Vindication of the Rights of Whores*, ed. Gail Pheterson (Seattle: Seal Press, 1989), 3–4; Nagle, "Introduction," 4; Gira Grant, *Playing the Whore*, 112, 126. Selling sex can be viewed as a "queer act," as sex work very consciously "destabilize[s] heteronormativity." Further, "sex work stands at the crossroads of feminism and queer theory, providing a unique vantage point from which to critique . . . the norm of white procreative heterosexuality." Eva Pendleton, "Love for Sale: Queering Heterosexuality," in *Whores and Other Feminists*, ed. Jill Nagle (New York: Routledge, 1997), 73. Although controversial, sex workers and activists have embraced the term *whore*, and even "whore feminism," for decades, in an effort to "identify with all those branded persons and demand rights as whores." This movement publishes books with "whore" in the title, has gathered in "World Whores' Congresses" starting in the 1980s, and, even further back, created a feminist organization called "Whores, Housewives, Others" (a combination that defies belief today).

40. Kirsten Pullen, *Actresses and Whores: On Stage and in Society* (Cambridge: Cambridge University Press, 2005), 5–6, notes that in some historical work, authors contrast the righteousness of women mislabeled as whores and the "real" whores, miserable poor women lurking on the streets. That "sorting error" is not my point here either. Pullen also argues for the reclaiming of *whore* as a "new way to understand accusations and labels." On "whore" or "slut" as a "sorting error" (an insult that a woman has to contradict/correct— "No, I am not a whore!"), see Gira Grant, *Playing the Whore*, 75–78. Not unlike when historians write about race, our choice of terminology reveals our contemporary political ideologies. Sex work suggests agency and the ability of participants to argue for their own human rights, along with other global laborers. Its inventor, Carol Leigh, felt embarrassed, judged, and objectified when she attended a panel at a feminist conference in the late 1970s entitled "Sex Use Industry." She suggested a change to "Sex Work Industry" in order to "create a discourse about the sex trades that could be inclusive of women working in the trades," such as herself. Carol Leigh, aka Scarlot Harlot, "Inventing Sex Work," in *Whores and Other Feminists*, 229–30; Gira Grant, *Playing the Whore*, 89. For the antiprostitution movement, see Adanna Mgbako, *To Live Freely*, 22–24; Gira Grant, *Playing the Whore*, 20–21; Laura Maria Agustin, *Sex at the Margins: Migration, Labour Markets, and the Rescue Industry* (London: Zed Books, 2007).

41. Before Carol Leigh invented the term *sex work*, historians struggled with terminology, applying the term *prostitute* to premodern or even ancient non-Western women. Vern Bullough and Bonnie Bullough, *Women and Prostitution: A Social History* (Buffalo, NY: Prometheus Books, 1987), x–xiv. Gira Grant, *Playing the Whore*, 125–26.

42. Jesús Padilla González and José Manuel Escobar Camacho, "La Mancebía de Córdoba en la Baja Edad Media," in *Coloquio de Historia Medieval Andaluza: La Sociedad Medieval Andaluza: Grupos no Privilegiados* (Jaén, Spain: Diputación Provincial de Jaén, 1984), 289.

43. See Ana María Atondo Rodríguez, *El amor venal y la condición femenina en el México colonial* (Mexico City: Instituto Nacional de Antropología y Historia, 1992), 153, 257, 265, 267, for the use of this phrase.

44. For the idea of performance and the complexity of relationships between sex workers and their clients ("bounded authenticity"), see Elizabeth Bernstein, *Temporarily Yours: Intimacy, Authenticity, and the Commerce of Sex* (Chicago: University of Chicago Press, 2007), 100–106, 119–30.

45. Yasmina Katsulis, *Sex Work and the City: The Social Geography of Health in Tijuana, Mexico* (Austin: University of Texas Press, 2008), 7–8, clearly explains that sex work operates on a huge, vague continuum, and the reasoning for focusing more tightly on criminalized sex workers.

46. Stoler also recommends the "unsettling space that spans knowing and not knowing." Stoler, *Along the Archival Grain*, 50, 187, 249.

47. Eukene Lacarra Lanz, ed., *Marriage and Sexuality in Medieval and Early Modern Iberia* (New York: Routledge, 2002), 170; Harper, *From Shame to Sin*, 3.

48. Timothy Gilfoyle notes that before 1980, beyond an older "salacious" historiography, mainly "government control" has interested historians. Only later did the "social history of prostitution" begin to shape scholarship. Timothy J. Gilfoyle, "Prostitutes in the Archives: Problems and Possibilities in Documenting the History of Sexuality," *The American Archivist* 57 (1994): 514–27. For the Spanish viceroyalties, see Nancy van Deusen, *Between the Sacred and the Worldly: The Institutional and Cultural Practice of "Recogimiento" in Colonial Lima* (Stanford, CA: Stanford University Press, 2001); Karen Viera Powers, *Women in the Crucible of Conquest: The Gendered Genesis of Spanish American Society* (Albuquerque: University of New Mexico Press, 2005), 136–41. Van Deusen presents *recogimientos* in Lima as a focus for authorities who, after 1580, imagined that women designated as "lost" or "of a bad life" could repent and reform. The labels given created a group of women who did not fit into a post-Tridentine model of enclosure and morality. As cities expanded rapidly in sixteenth-century Spanish America, viceroys and other authorities began to complain about a moral chaos. They discussed and attempted to make legislation in an effort to control what already they could not control (van Deusen, *Between the Sacred and the Wordly*, 59, 64–65, 144). For general works, see Aida Martínez and Pablo Rodríguez, eds. *Placer, dinero, y pecado: Historia de la prostitución en Colombia* (Bogotá: Aguilar, 2002). For modern Latin America, see Guy, *Sex and Danger*, and Katherine Bliss, *Compromised Positions: Prostitution, Revolution, and Social Reform in Mexico City, 1918–1940* (University Park: Pennsylvania State University Press, 2001). See also Brennan, *What's Love Got to Do with It? Transnational Desires and Sex Tourism in the Dominican Republic* (Durham, NC: Duke University Press, 2004); Annick Prieur, *Mema's House: On Transvestites, Queers, and Machos* (Chicago: University of Chicago Press, 1998). See chapter 1 for references to the historiography of sex work in early-modern Spain.

49. Treva B. Lindsey and Jessica Marie Johnson, "Searching for Climax: Black Erotic Lives in Slavery and Freedom," *Meridians: Feminism, Race, Transnationalism* vol. 12, 2 (Fall, 2014): 169–93. The authors propose the idea that we can think about the sexual agency of canonical figures such as Harriet Tubman and "take seriously the erotic subjectivities of black women during slavery," 172. Some radical feminists judge women who sell sex as either collaborators in misogyny or passive sexual slaves. See the infamous quote from Julie Burchill, *Damaged Gods: Cults and Heroes Reappraised* (London: Arrow Books, 1987):

Prostitution reinforces all the old dumb clichés about women's sexuality; that they are not built to enjoy sex and are little more than walking masturbation aids, things to be DONE TO, things so sensually null and void that they have to be paid to indulge in fornication, that women can be had, bought, as often as not sold from one man to another. When the sex war is won prostitutes should be shot as collaborators for their terrible betrayal of all women.

Feminist historians of Spanish America have honored the humanity and agency of women in the viceroyalties for decades, so the avoidance of researching whores and prostitutes may have more to do with perceptions of sex workers in the twentieth and twenty-first centuries.

50. Stoler, *Along the Archival Grain,* 33, 151.

51. "The commodification of sexuality . . . is *anything but* deviant. . . ." Katsulis, *Sex Work and the City,* x. Italics in original.

52. Nina Kushner, *Erotic Exchanges: Elite Prostitution in Eighteenth-Century Paris* (Ithaca, NY: Cornell University Press, 2013), 222, for the concept of sexual capital. See Nicole von Germeten, *Violent Delights, Violent Ends: Sex, Race, and Honor in Colonial Cartagena de Indias* (Albuquerque: University of New Mexico Press, 2013), 87–90, for an example of a couple that married for love, risking financial support.

53. Van Deusen, *Between the Sacred,* 105–9; Asunción Lavrín, "In Search of Colonial Women in Mexico: The Seventeenth and Eighteenth Centuries," in *Latin American Women: Historical Perspectives,* ed. Asunción Lavrín (Westport, CT: Greenwood Press, 1978), 34–35.

54. Catherine Hakim, *Erotic Capital: The Power of Attraction in the Boardroom and the Bedroom* (Philadelphia: Basic Books, 2001), takes credit for inventing the term "erotic capital," but missing the point of Pierre Bourdieu's original essay, she believes that sexual attractiveness can help women attain upward mobility. For numerous examples of men paying in defloration suits, see Renato Barahona, *Sex Crimes, Honour, and the Law in Early Modern Spain: Vizcaya, 1528–1735* (Toronto: University of Toronto Press, 2003), 4, 6, 35, 44, 82, 130, 151–53.

55. The ongoing controversy around transactional sex could exist partially because "sex workers provide a powerful indictment of gender roles by demanding payment for playing them" and avoiding the social and religious dictates of marriage and monogamy. Or even that sex for sale detracts from the "presumed innate sacredness" of sex, which is really about "social anxieties about nonsanctioned female sexual activity that transcend all cultures." Pendleton, "Love for Sale," 81; Annie Sprinkle, "Feminism: Crunch Point," in *A Vindication of the Rights of Whores,* ed. Gail Pheterson (Seattle: Seal Press, 1989), 160–63; and Tawnya Dudash, "Peepshow Feminism," in *Whores and Other Feminists,* ed. Nagle, 116, on how commodifying one's own body increases a sense of agency. While scholars and activists have moved beyond interpreting sex workers as revolutionaries, those labeled prostitutes today still risk social norms with every sexual transaction they undertake. As Gail Sheehy argued in the early 1970s, "there is no more defiant denial of one man's ability to possess one woman exclusively than the prostitute who refuses to be redeemed." Gail Sheehy, *Hustling: Prostitution in Our Wide-Open Society* (New York: Delacorte Press, 1971), 26. See also Adanna Mgbako, *To Live Freely,* 30–33, 38, 46–47, quote on 51.

56. European (especially non-Iberian) travelers expressed disdain for the laxness and luxury that they perceived as common in the New World. Fernanda Núñez Becerra,

La Prostitución y su Represión en la Ciudad de México, Siglo XIX: Prácticas y Representaciones (Barcelona: Gedisa Editorial, 2002), 26.

57. Bawds and (to use a more recent term) madams have made a good living over the centuries. In racially stratified societies, this occupation involved many nonwhite women who might otherwise have suffered poverty and marginalization. See Benson Tong, *Unsubmissive Women: Chinese Prostitutes in Nineteenth-Century San Francisco* (Norman: University of Oklahoma Press, 1994), 6–8; and Cynthia M. Blair, *I've Got to Make My Livin': Black Women's Sex Work in Turn-of-the-Century Chicago* (Chicago: University of Chicago Press, 2010), 39–43, 57–67.

58. For the essential chronology of regulation and criminalization, see Katherine Norberg, "The Body of the Prostitute: Medieval to Modern," in *The Routledge History of Sex and the Body: 1500 to the Present,* eds. Sarah Toulalan and Kate Fisher (London: Routledge, 2013), 393–408. For this process in Spain, see Margaret E. Boyle's *Unruly Women: Performance, Penitence, and Punishment in Early Modern Spain* (Toronto: University of Toronto Press, 2014).

59. Unlike in contemporary France, Spanish American magistrates did not yet dehumanize them as disease vectors, criminals, or "repulsive figure[s] who threaten[ed] to corrupt the very core of bourgeois society." Norberg, "From Courtesan to Prostitute: Mercenary Sex and Venereal Disease, 1730–1802," in *The Secret Malady: Venereal Disease in Eighteenth-Century Britain and France,* ed. Linda E. Merians (Lexington: University Press of Kentucky, 1996), 34–50.

60. Theater and sex also overlap in Boyle's *Unruly Women,* 3, 8–9, 26–27.

61. For an overview of this process, with a very effective emphasis on how institutional ideals did not work in practice, see Silvia Marina Arrom, *Containing the Poor: The Mexico City Poor House, 1774–1871* (Durham, NC: Duke University Press, 2004), 5–33.

62. For studies of the spectacle of female sexuality and the stage ("suffering as sexual spectacle"), see Jean I. Marsden, *Fatal Desire: Women, Sexuality, and the English Stage, 1660–1720* (Ithaca, NY: Cornell University Press, 2006), 60–76, 94–95, quotes on 60 and 73. While depriving women of agency, the spectacle of female sexual suffering makes the ravished heroines objects of the male gaze and the center of attention and drama, thus appealing to female audience members. The eighteenth and nineteenth centuries' sickly, pitiful, self-sacrificing whore "with a heart of gold" continues to entrance us and plays into the "stereotyping of contemporary sex workers." Pullen, *Actresses and Whores,* 176n6. Pullen skillfully explores performance, labeling, and sex work throughout this book.

63. Whether due to this change in legal perceptions or the increasing instability of viceregal life in the insurgency era, this chapter offers my only documented examples of sexual abuse. Adanna Mgbako, *To Live Freely in This World,* 13, argues that scholars should not narrate "stories simply to elicit an emotional response from the reader . . . participating in the cynical selling of suffering."

64. Pullen, *Actresses and Whores,* 182n10.

65. Levine, *Prostitution, Race, Politics,* 323–28, notes that AIDS and debates in the last few decades over the decriminalization of homosexuality revisited the obsessions she traces in her book about the late-nineteenth- and early-twentieth–century British Empire. More recently, Amnesty International's recommendation to decriminalize sex work, in an effort to promote human rights, caused moral indignation and protest on the part of high-profile

commentators: accessed May 20, 2016, https://www.amnesty.org/en/qa-policy-to-protect-the-human-rights-of-sex-workers/.

66. Kushner, *Erotic Exchanges*, 38–39, 88.

67. Ann Twinam, *Public Lives, Private Secrets: Gender, Honor, Sexuality, and Illegitimacy in Colonial Spanish America* (Stanford, CA: Stanford University Press, 1999), 61–63, 282.

68. Karras, "Prostitution and the Question of Sexual Identity," 161–62.

69. Pullen, *Actresses and Whores*, 3.

70. Nagle, "Introduction," *Whores and Other Feminists*, 2–6.

CHAPTER 1

1. Juan Ruiz, *The Book of Good Love*, trans. Rigo Mignani and Mario A. Di Cesare (Albany: State University of New York Press, 1970), 113, 187–88, 259.

2. Leyla Rouhi, *Mediation and Love: A Study of the Medieval Go-Between in Key Romance and Near Eastern Texts* (Boston: Brill Publishers, 1999), 206–8, 225, 236–45.

3. Josefina Muriel, *Los recogimientos de mujeres: respuesta a una problemática social novohispana* (Mexico City: Instituto de Investigaciones Históricas, 1974), 29.

4. Marie Kelleher, *The Measure of a Woman: Law and Female Identity in the Crown of Aragon* (Philadelphia: University of Pennsylvania Press, 2010), 99–101.

5. Hsu, "Courtesans in the Literature of the Spanish Golden Age," 65–66.

6. *Mancebía* derives from the word *manceba*, which an early Castillian/Arabic dictionary simply defined as puta or "whore." Ultimately, both words come from the Latin word *mancipus* or "slave." See http://dle.rae.es/?id=O8D4nM1; and Fray Pedro de Alcalá, *Vocabulista arávigo en letra castellana. En Arte para ligeramente saber la lengua aráviga* (Granada, Spain: Juan Varela, 1505), accessed February 12, 2017, http://ntlle.rae.es.

7. Pilar Jaramillo de Zuleta, "Las 'arrepentidas,'" in *Placer, dinero y pecado,* ed. Martínez and Rodríguez, 92.

8. James A. Brundage, *Law, Sex, and Christian Society in Medieval Europe* (Chicago: University of Chicago Press, 1987), 45–46, 105–6, 120–23, 133; Harper, *Shame to Sin,* 46–51.

9. Francisco Tomas y Valiente, *El Derecho Penal de la Monarquía absoluta (siglos XVI–XVII–XVIII)* (Madrid: Editorial Tecnos, 1969), 23–28.

10. Brundage, *Law, Sex, and Christian Society,* 210–11, 390–95, 462–68; Manlio Bellomo, *The Common Legal Past of Europe, 1000–1800* (Washington, D.C.: Catholic University of America Press, 1995), 97–101.

11. Valiente, *Derecho Penal,* 212–18.

12. Translating putería as "prostitution" is not correct. Prostitution by definition is a modern legal criminal status. Selling sex (in a regulated way) was not illegal in Spain until 1623 (see chapter 2). On the contrary, the Siete Partidas gave whoring legal status. Note the mistranslation of this word in Samuel Parsons Scott, *Las Siete Partidas* (Chicago and New York: American Bar Association, 1931), cited in Mary Elizabeth Perry, "Deviant Insiders: Legalized Prostitutes and Consciousness of Women in Early Modern Seville," *Comparative Studies in Society and History* 27 (1985): 140.

13. Kelleher, *Measure of a Woman,* 103.

14. Tomas y Valiente, *Derecho Penal,* 47, speaks of a "general horror al matrimonio."

15. Grace E. Coolidge, "'A Vile and Abject Woman': Noble Mistresses, Legal Power, and the Family in Early Modern Spain," *Journal of Family History* vol. 32, 3 (2007): 196, 201, 209.

16. Alfonso el Sabio, *Las siete partidas: Selección* (Barcelona: Linkgua Ediciones, 2009), 145. Also see note 6 in this chapter. Their sexual status also meant that these women could not claim protection by starting an *estupro* case for seduction, a kind of legal protection for women who often received compensation from the violators. See Poska, *Women and Authority*.

17. Marie Kelleher, "Like Man and Wife: Clerics' Concubines in the Diocese of Barcelona," *Journal of Medieval History* vol. 28, 4 (2002): 351, 357; Heath Dillard, *Daughters of the Reconquest: Women in Castilian Town Society*, 1100–1300 (Cambridge, UK, Cambridge University Press, 1984), 12747.

18. Dillard, *Daughters of the Reconquest*, 196–97.

19. Although it is tempting to use it here instead of ruffian, the sex workers' rights movement has recognized the inherently racist history and use of the word *pimp*, which is usually applied to African American men. For the popular use of this word, see Christina and Richard Milner, *Black Players: The Secret World of Black Pimps* (Boston: Little, Brown, and Company, 1972), and Robert Beck (Iceberg Slim), *Pimp: The Story of My Life* (Los Angeles: Holloway House, 1967).

20. "Leno en latín tanto quiere decir en romance como alcahuete; y tal hombre como este, bien sea que tenga sus siervas u otras mujeres libres en su casa mandándoles hacer maldad de sus cuerpos por dinero . . . es infamado por ello." Alfonso el Sabio, *Las siete partidas*, 214.

21. In early-modern English, the term *bawd* in fact signified both men and women.

22. Carmen Peris, "La Prostitución Valenciana en la Segunda Mitad del Siglo XIV," *Revista de Historia Medieval* vol. 1 (1990): 193–95; Ruth Mazo Karras, "The Regulation of Brothels in Later Medieval England," *Signs* vol. 14, 2 (1989): 413; Kelleher, *Measure of a Woman*, 104; Dillard, *Daughters of the Reconquista*, 199–201.

23. Alfonso el Sabio, *Las siete partidas*, 214.

24. See the *Nuevo tesoro lexicográfico de la lengua española*, accessed via the Real Academia Española at http://lema.rae.es/drae/.

25. Eukene Lacarra Lanz, "El Fenómeno de la Prostitución y sus Conexiones con 'La Celestina,'" in *Historias y Ficciones: Coloquio Sobre la Literatura del Siglo XV*, ed. Valles Lavador et al. (Valencia: Universitat de Valencia, 1992), 271; Denis Menjot, "Prostitutas y Rufianes en las Ciudades Castellanas a Fines de la Edad Media," *Temas Medievales* vol. 4 (1994): 199.

26. Eukene Lacarra Lanz, "Legal and Clandestine Prostitution in Medieval Spain," *Bulletin of Hispanic Studies* vol. 79, 3 (2002): 271, 278.

27. *Nuevo tesoro lexicográfico de la lengua española* online. In the English 1591 dictionary, ramera appears as "whoore, strumpet."

28. Jaramilla de Zuleta, "Las 'arrepentidas,'" 94; Muriel, *Los Recogimientos,* 36–37; Hsu, *Courtesans in the Literature,* 64–65.

29. María del Carmen García Herrero, "El Mundo de la Prostitución en las Ciudades Bajomedievales," *Cuadernos del Centro de Estudios Medievales y Renacentistas* vol. 4 (1996): 80; Iñaki Bazán Díaz, "El Estupro: Sexualidad Delictiva en la Baja Edad media y Primera Edad Moderna," in *Matrimonio y Sexualidad: Normas, Prácticas, y Transgresiones en la*

Edad Media y Principios de la Época Moderna, ed. Martine Charageat (Madrid: Casa de Velázquez, 2003), 28.

30. Mary Elizabeth Perry, *Gender and Disorder in Early Modern Seville* (Princeton, NJ: Princeton University Press, 1990), 48–49.

31. García Herrero, "El mundo bajomedieval," 80.

32. Hsu, *Courtesans in the Literature,* 65–66.

33. Pablo Rodríguez, "Las Mancebías Españolas," in *Placer, Dinero, y Pecado,* ed. Martínez and Rodríguez, 39–65.

34. Eukene Lacarra Lanz, "Changing Boundaries of Licit and Illicit Unions: Concubinage and Prostitution," in *Marriage and Sexuality in Medieval and Early Modern Iberia,* ed. Eukene Lacarra Lanz (New York: Routledge, 2002), 173; García Herrera, "El mundo bajomedieval," 72.

35. Denis Merjot, "Prostitutas y rufianes en las ciudades castellanas," 195–96; García Herrera, "El mundo bajomedieval," 78.

36. Kelleher, *Measure of a Woman,* 103–4.

37. García Herrera, "El mundo bajomedieval," 72–73.

38. Lacarra Lanz, "Legal and Clandestine Prostitution," 272.

39. For statistics see Lacarra Lanz, "Changing Boundaries," 182.

40. García Herrera, "El mundo bajomedieval," 79.

41. Karras, "The Regulation of Brothels in Later Medieval England," 423–24.

42. Kelleher, *Measure of a Woman,* 104–5 Brundage, *Law, Sex, and Christian Society,* 521–30.

43. Stuart B. Schwartz, *All Can Be Saved: Religious Tolerance and Salvation in the Iberian Atlantic World* (New Haven, CT: Yale University Press, 2008), 26–33.

44. Alain Saint-Saëns, "It Is Not a Sin!: Making Love According to the Spaniards in Early Modern Spain," in *Sex and Love in Golden Age Spain,* ed. Alain Saint-Saëns (New Orleans: University Press of the South, 1996), 11–26.

45. García Herrera, "El mundo bajomedieval," 100.

46. This sounds oddly similar to today's strip clubs. See Stacey Reed, "All Stripped Off," in *Whores and Other Feminists,* edited by Jill Nagle (New York: Routledge, 1997), 185–86. Contemporary accounts suggest the same sensation of danger in early-modern sex tourism to Amsterdam. See Lotte Van de Pol, *The Burgher and the Whore: Prostitution in Early Modern Amsterdam* (Oxford: Oxford University Press, 2011), 232–34.

47. García Herrera, "El mundo bajomedieval," 76–77.

48. Mary Elizabeth Perry, "Deviant Insiders: Legalized Prostitutes and a Consciousness of Women in Early Modern Seville," *Comparative Studies in Society and History* vol. 27, 1 (1985): 145, 147.

49. Pablo Pérez García, "Un Aspecto de la Delincuencia Común en la Valencia Pre-Agermana: La 'Prostitución Clandestina' (1479–1518)," *Revista de Historia Moderna* vol. 10 (1991): 19.

50. Ibid., 17.

51. Lacarra Lanz, "Legal and Clandestine Prostitution," 274.

52. Antonio Collantes de Terán Sánchez, "Actitudas Ante la Marginación Social: Malhechores y Rufianes en Sevilla," in *Actas del Coloquio de Historia Medieval Andaluza: La Sociedad Medieval Andaluza: Grupos No Privilegiados*[is there an editor? no] (Jaén, Spain: Diputación Provincial de Jaén, 1984), 293–96, 302.

53. Lacarra Lanz, "Legal and Clandestine Prostitution," 274–76.

54. García Herrera, "El mundo bajomedieval," 88.

55. *Novísima Recopilación de la Leyes de España*, Tomo V (Madrid: Imprenta de Sancha, 1805), 423.

56. Peris, "La prostitución valenciana en la segunda mitad del siglo XIV," 185; Pérez García, "Un aspecto de delincuencia," 23–26, 33.

57. Lacarra Lanz, "Legal and Clandestine Prostitution in Medieval Spain," 278; Hsu, *Courtesans in the Literature*, 68–69.

58. García Herrera, "El mundo bajomedieval," 89–90.

59. See the entry for alcahuete in the Real Academia Española's online *Diccionario de lengua española* at http://lema.rae.es/drae/.

60. Rouhi, *Mediation and Love*, 154–58. The word used for the female mediator in medieval Spain was *ajuz*, literally meaning "old woman."

61. Ibid., 213, 217.

62. Hsu, *Courtesans in the Literature*, 129–31.

63. AGI, Seville, Indiferente 421, Legajo 11, foja 104 recto. See also Muriel, *Los recogimientos*, 33–36.

64. AGI, Seville, Indiferente 421, Legajo 11, foja 140 verso.

65. AGI, Seville, Real Cedula, Mexico 1088, Legajo 3, foja 152.

66. Germeten, *Violent Delights*, 41.

67. Without regulated sex work, illegal, illicit transactions will always boom. See Karras, "The Regulation of Brothels in Later Medieval England," 405.

68. Núñez Becerra, *Prostitución y su Represión*, 25–28.

69. *Novísima Recopilación*, 423. One case survives, demonstrating this law in action: AGI, Seville, 1601, Indiferente 427, Legajo 31, "Real Cédula a Pedro de Morales, conmutándole los cuatro años de galeras a que había sido condenado por rufián, por cuatro años de servicios de artillero sin sueldo, en el presidio de San Juan de Puerto Rico, ordenando al mismo tiempo a los oficiales de la Casa de la Contratación, lo pongan en libertad y lo envíen en la primera ocasión propicia, a la citada isla," 153v–154r. Pedro de Morales was originally sentenced to ten years' rowing for the king without pay, but his sentence was reduced out of pity for his wife and five children. Note that despite the fact that Morales apparently needed to support his family in Spain, he was moved to Puerto Rico to carry out his sentence.

70. AGI, Seville, Indiferente 427, Legajo 30, 326–27.

71. Ibid., 348–49.

72. Hermann Bennett, *Colonial Blackness: A History of Afro-Mexico* (Bloomington: University of Indiana Press, 2011), 19, 40–41, 138–39, 201; María Emma Mannarelli, *Private Passions and Public Sins: Men and Women in Seventeenth-Century Lima*, trans. Sidney Evans and Meredith D. Dodge (Albuquerque: University of New Mexico Press, 2007), 75, 135.

73. The term *consentidor* does not appear in early-modern dictionaries with a sexual tone. However, in the late seventeenth century, *tercera para malos tratos* is defined in Latin as *lenocinari*. See Baltasar Henríquez, *Thesaurus utriusque linguae hispanae et latinae* (Madrid: Ioannis Garcia Infançon, 1679), accessed February 12, 2017, http://ntlle.rae.es.

74. AGN, Mexico, 1555, Clero Regular y Secular Caja 5428, Exp. 62, "Juicio criminal seguido por Francisco de Saavedra, alguacil del Arzobispado de México contra María india presa en la cárcel eclesiástica por alcahueta," 1–15.

75. AGN, Mexico, 1567, Clero Regular y Secular Caja 2275, Exp. 11, "Autos hechos contra Luisa de Espinosa por alcahueta de amancebados," 1–6.

76. AGN, Mexico, 1577–1578, Indiferente virreinal, Criminal, caja 5568, exp. 40, "Denuncias que hace Luis de León fiscal del arzobispado sobre escándalos que han propiciado la conducta de algunos individuos como el predicaren las noches, hacer alboroto en una iglesia, y la alcahuetería de una mujer para con sus hijas."

77. AGN, Mexico, 1582, Clero Regular y Secular Caja 2307, Exp. 9, "Alcahueta de su hija," 1–30.

78. Rollon said Alameda was his stepdaughter and that she had fled his home to live with her aunt at the time of the investigation. "Alcahueta de su hija," 5.

79. Ibid., 6.

80. Ibid., 14, 20.

81. Abigail Dyer, "Seduction by Promise of Marriage: Law, Sex, and Culture in Seventeenth-Century Spain," *The Sixteenth Century Journal* vol. 34, 2 (2003): 440.

82. AGN, Mexico, Bienes Nacionales, Vol. 497, Exp. 28, "Contra Antonio Temiño, por el delito de lenoncino," 1571. Unfortunately, many pages of this file are severely damaged by water and are almost impossible to read. Only a few leaves could be seen in their entirety.

83. Ibid., 21.

84. Ibid., 12.

85. In the positive self-fashioning manner typical of any sex-related adjudication started by Spanish women to redeem their own honor. See Dyer, "Seduction by Promise of Marriage," 441, 448.

86. AGN, Mexico, 1570, Bienes Nacionales, Vol. 497, Exp. 7, "Contra Catalina García por alcahueta," 1–26.

87. Ibid., 5, 10, 14, 15.

88. Ibid., 1.

89. Ibid., 2–3.

90. Ibid., all accusations on 2–5.

91. Ibid., 5–7.

92. Ibid., 11.

93. Ibid., 18.

94. Ibid., 19–26. The witnesses explained Rojas's dishonest accusations as acts of vengeance against García for two reasons. First, the women had fought, perhaps even physically, over García's husband because Rojas was also his lover. Second, allegedly, García had helped put one of Rojas's lovers in jail for concubinage.

95. Karras, "Holy Harlots," 1990, and "Prostitution and the Question of Sexual Identity," 167.

96. "Contra Catalina García por alcahueta," 19, 21, 22, 24, 25.

97. Ibid., 22.

98. While domestic transactional sex perhaps dominated, it was not the only option, in contrast to the observations in some previous historiography. See Pablo Rodríguez, "Servidumbre sexual: la Prostitución en los siglos XV–XVIII," in *Placer, Dinero, y Pecado*, ed. Martínez and Rodríguez, 67–88.

99. AGN, Mexico, Bienes Nacionales, 1577, Vol. 1072, Exp. 15, "Contra Martin de Vildosola por lenocinio."

100. Ibid., 2–7.

101. Atondo, *Amor venal,* 74–80; "Contra Martin de Vildosola por lenocinio," 8–9.

102. "Contra Martin de Vildosola por lenocinio," 2.

103. Ibid., 6–9.

104. Atondo, *Amor venal,* 81–83.

105. "Contra Martin de Vildosola por lenocinio," 10.

106. Atondo, *Amor venal,* 83–84.

107. The cases in this chapter and throughout this book suggest that some viceregal subjects also understood sex very differently from what their priests preached or what was written in theological treatises or confession manuals. Textual sources weigh heavily toward proscription, but popular ideas diverged drastically from intellectual and religious propaganda.

William Reddy argues that what many now view as an unbreakable link between love and sexual exclusivity—that our love for one special person elevates our sexual desires to a higher plain, above animalistic instincts—may have emerged as a quiet rebellion against medieval church reforms promoting chastity. Several other civilizations have taken a completely different approach to sensuality and sex without creating an opposing concept of the spiritual. Reddy, *The Making of Romantic Love: Longing and Sexuality in Europe, South Asia, and Japan, 900–1200 CE* (Chicago: University of Chicago Press, 2012), 1–6. Ana Maria Atondo gleans clues from certain women's testimonies that the witnesses speaking in the case were also sex workers living a "relaxed life," observing the details they reported in court because they were "enjoying themselves *[holgarse],*" in the company of the married couple and Rodríguez's lovers. Atondo, *Amor venal,* 73.

108. Atondo, *Amor venal,* 83–84.

CHATPER 2

1. Fernando de Rojas, *Celestina,* trans. Margaret Sayers Peden, ed. Roberto González Echevarría (New Haven, CT: Yale University Press, 2009), 52–53, 55, 74, 134. Italics added.

2. AGN, Mexico, Matrimonios 4834, "Demanda de divorcio de doña Melchora de Rivera Cabeza de Vaca de Sotomayor contra su marido don Gaspar Ortiz de Ávila por malos tratos, por tratarla de puta y amenazarla," 1677, 1–2, where the complainant accuses her husband of insulting her in this way for the slightest interaction with men; AGN, Mexico, Inquisición 525, Exp. 3, "María Nieto por sus escándalos y haberle inquietado a una negrita su esclava," 1691, "puta" used on 36, 39, 46, including the insult "*perra puta alcahueta* [bitch whore procuress]."

3. Martha Few, *Women Who Live Evil Lives: Gender, Religion, and the Politics of Power in Colonial Guatemala* (Austin: University of Texas Press, 2002).

4. Faramerz Dabhoiwala, *The Origins of Sex: A History of the First Sexual Revolution* (New York: Oxford University Press, 2012), 270–71.

5. See *Nuevo tesoro lexicográfico de la lengua española,* accessed March 21, 2016, http:// ntlle.rae.es.

6. Jean Dangler, *Mediating Fictions: Literature, Women Healers, and the Go-Between in Medieval and Early Modern Iberia* (Lewisburg, PA: Bucknell University Press, 2001), 84–127.

7. Peter Stallybrass, "Patriarchal Territories: The Body Enclosed," in *Rewriting the Renaissance: The Discourses of Sexual Difference in Early Modern Europe*, ed. Margaret W. Ferguson, Maureen Quilligan, and Nancy J. Vickers (Chicago: University of Chicago Press, 1986), 127.

8. Rouhi, *Mediation and Love*, 256–85.

9. For these alliances across viceregal racial designations, see Few, *Women Who Live Evil Lives*.

10. Martin Nesvig, *Ideology and Inquisition: The World of the Censors in Early Mexico* (New Haven, CT: Yale University Press, 2009), 2–3; Kathryn Joy McKnight, "'En Su Tierra Lo Aprendió': An African Curandero's Defense before the Cartagena Inquisition," *Colonial Latin American Review* 12,1 (2003): 63–84. See also Germeten, *Violent Delights, Violent Ends*, chapters 6, 7, and 8.

11. AGN, Mexico, Inquisición Vol. 314, Exp. 8, "Contra Isabel de San Miguel mestiza por otro nombre Isabel Guixarro y Jerónima de Mendoza negra y demás culpados sobre ser alcahuetas y embusteros," 377–85.

12. In contemporary London, theatergoers also customarily made the rounds of whorehouses in an evening out. See Pullen, *Actresses and Whores*, 38.

13. Atondo, *Amor venal*, 125–26.

14. Ibid., 125–33.

15. AGN, Mexico, Bienes Nacionales 14, Vol. 207, Exp. 18, 1621, "El fiscal del arzobispado contra Ana Bautista por alcahueta y amancebada."

16. These institutions were begun in the late sixteenth century, around the time that Phillip II introduced stricter brothel regulation. They targeted women viewed as whores. This transition, from *recogimientos* as "safe houses" to a form of female incarceration, parallels the increasing criminalization of sex work in the era. See Muriel, *Los recogimientos*, 41–58; and Gabriel Haslip-Viera, *Crime and Punishment in Late Colonial Mexico City, 1692–1810* (Albuquerque: University of New Mexico Press, 1999), 127.

17. "Contra Ana Bautista," 1–4.

18. Assuming the more modern framework of sex work as an indication of deviance or marginality, Atondo argues for Bautista's passive "fall" into this career after her husband's death, not that the bawd might have had the economic sense to anticipate a decline in income and organize other methods of making money on purpose. She also states that the women who worked for Bautista had to commit this "transgression of the norms" due to poverty. Atondo, *Amor venal*, 97, 100–101.

19. "Contra Ana Bautista," 2; Atondo, *Amor venal*, 104–14.

20. "Contra Ana Bautista," 8; Atondo, *Amor venal*, 111–15.

21. Blair, *I've Got to Make My Livin'*, 57, 60–69.

22. Arguably, the social status of her clients notably improved as her career as a bawd progressed. Atondo, *Amor venal*, 100.

23. "Contra Ana Bautista," 10.

24. Ibid., 12–26; Atondo, *Amor venal*, 101.

25. "Contra Ana Bautista," 24, 40.

26. Dyer, "Seduction by Promise of Marriage," 440; "Contra Ana Bautista," 8.

27. This case coincided precisely with the dismissal of the Marquis de Guadalcazar and the beginning of the viceregal term of the Marquis de Gelves, as well as the influence of Olivares in Spain. See Atondo, *Amor Venal*, 121–22; "Contra Ana Bautista," 44.

28. Atondo, *Amor Venal,* 147–48; Simón Pedro Izcara Palacios, *Mujer y Cambio de Valores en el Madrid del Siglo XVIII* (Ciudad Victoria, Mexico: Universidad Nacional Autónoma de Tamaulipas, 2004), 87–91.

29. Andrés J. Moreno Mengíbar, "El Crepúsculo de la Mancebías: El Caso de Sevilla," in *"Mal Menor": Políticas y Representaciones de la Prostitución (Siglos XVI–XIX),* ed. Francisco Vázquez García (Cádiz, Spain: Universidad de Cádiz, 1998), 51–54, 70.

30. The debate continues unresolved whether syphilis was an Old or New World disease. While some emphasize syphilis's connection to yaws, it may have first appeared in Lisbon with sailors and indigenous captives from the Caribbean who arrived there in 1493. See Ian Michael, "*Celestina* and the Great Pox," *Bulletin of Hispanic Studies* LXXVII (2001): 103–38, for the first medical and literary references to syphilis in Europe. Geoffrey Parker argues that the French Pox caused many medical discharges in the Spanish forces as well as significant expense. Geoffrey Parker, *The Army of Flanders and the Spanish Road, 1567–1659* (Cambridge[UK?]: Cambridge University Press, 2004), 143. Various governments' worries over syphilis and soldiers strongly affected brothel regulation into the nineteenth century (conclusion).

31. Perry, "Deviant Insiders," 148; *Gender and Disorder,* 137–39. Syphilis eventually had the same effect in France in the nineteenth century. See Jill Harsin, *Policing Prostitution in Nineteenth-Century Paris* (Princeton, NJ: Princeton University Press, 1985), 64–66.

32. See Harsin, *Policing Prostitution,* 16–18, for how elite French kept women avoided mandatory inspections.

33. Condoms have been documented in Europe since the seventeenth century, at least. Made of sheep's guts or bladders, they could be purchased in sex-toy emporiums in eighteenth-century London and were on offer in some brothels. Apparently, some street prostitutes carried them in eighteenth-century London, or so some clients assumed. Lynn Hunt, "Introduction," in *The Invention of Pornography, 1500–1800: Obscenity and the Origins of Modernity,* ed. Lynn Hunt (New York: Zone Books, 1993), 30; Cruickshank, *London's Sinful Secret,* 170, 209–11. For syphilis, see Michael, "*Celestina,*" 134–35.

34. Mengíbar, "El crepúsculo de las mancebías," 66; Vázquez García and Moreno Mengíbar, "El universo asistencial," 143–48. See also the humorous "Paradoxa en loor de las bubas" in *Poder y prostitución en Sevilla,* eds. Vázquez García and Moreno Mengíbar, 206–15.

35. Delicado, *Portrait of Lozana,* 23. See introduction.

36. Thank you to Kristen Block for this information. See Francisco Guerra, *El Hospital en Hispanoamérica y Filipinas, 1492–1898* (Madrid: Ministerio de Sanidad y Consumo, 1994), 72–73, 104–5, 216, 229, 348–49, 377–79, 441–43, 479, 540, 555, 581, 583, 588; and María del Carmen Sánchez Uriarte, "El Hospital de San Lázaro de la Ciudad de México y los leprosos novohispanos durante la segunda mitad del siglo XVIII," *Estudios de Historia Novohispana* 42, 1 (2010): 81–113.

37. María Luz López Terrada, "El Tratamiento de Sífilis en un Hospital Renacentista: La Sala del Mal de Siment del Hospital General de Valencia," *Asclepio* vol. 41, 2 (1989): 21, 35, 36, 38.

38. Vázquez García and Moreno Mengíbar, "El universo asistencial," in *Poder y prostitución en Sevilla: Siglos XIV al XX,* eds. Vázquez García and Moreno Mengíbar (Sevilla: Universidad de Sevilla, 1995), 151–54.

39. The Society of Jesus took an interest in whores from the early years of Ignatius's missions in Rome, where the Jesuits founded a reformatory for women. See John Patrick Donnelly, *Ignatius of Loyola: Founder of the Jesuits* (New York: Pearson, 2003), 121–23; John M. McManamon, *The Texts and Contexts of Ignatius Loyola's "Autobiography"* (New York: Fordham University Press, 2013), 84–86, 93–96, 126.

40. Mengibar, "Crepusculo de las mancebías," 47–64, 73–76, 84–94; Perry, "Deviant Insiders," 138, 152–56. The regulations also decreed that no boys under age fourteen could visit the brothel.

41. Isabel Ramos Vázquez, "La Represión de la Prostitución en la Castilla del Siglo XVII," *Historia. Instituciones. Documentos* vol. 32 (2005): 282–84.

42. Philip's corrupt court is humorously portrayed with a moralizing tone by Martin Andrew Sharp Hume, *The Court of Philip IV: Spain in Decadence* (New York: Putnam, 1907), 55–56, 132, 146–49, 356, 406, 445–46.

43. *Novísima Recopilación de las leyes de España, Tomo V* (Madrid: Imprenta de Sancha, 1805), 421–22.

44. Mengibar, "Crepusculo de las mancebías," 48.

45. Izcara Palacios, *Mujer y cambio,* 110, 126–28. At least a hundred unregulated brothels flourished in Madrid in the eighteenth century. See *Obras de Don Francisco de Quevedo Villegas,* vol. 3, ed. Florencio Janer (Madrid: Rivadeneyra, 1877), 107–9.

46. José Deleito y Piñuela, *La mala vida en la España de Felipe IV* (Madrid: Espasa-Calpe, 1967), 10–27, 37–38.

47. Atondo, *Amor venal,* 147–48; Izcara Palacios, *Mujer y cambio,* 90n123; María Luisa Meijide Pardo, "Mendicidad, Vagancia, y Prostitución en la España del Siglo XVIII: La Casa Galera y los Departamentos de Corrección de Mujeres" (PhD diss., Universidad Complutense de Madrid, 1992), 4, 359–60.

48. Founded by Philip III in 1608. Ramos Vásquez, "La represión," 279.

49. Ibid., 286.

50. Muriel, *Los recogimientos,* 110–23; Ana Laura Torres Hernández, "Pecado, Recogimiento, y Conversión: Un Proyecto Contra la Prostitución Femenina en la Ciudad de México del Siglo XVII," *Boletín de Monumentos Históricos* vol. 29 (2013). This article discusses how an understanding of penitent, reformed women emanates from the late-seventeenth-century painting by Juan Correa, *La conversión de Santa María Magdalena.* See also Van Deusen, *Between the Sacred and the Worldly* for other kinds of enclosure in the Americas. This was also the era that produced Sor Juana Inez de la Cruz's beloved proto-feminist poem "Foolish Men" (chapter 3), decrying male sexual hypocrisy in New Spain.

51. AGI, Seville, Audiencia de Guadalajara 230, Libro 3, f. 304, 1665.

52. Ibid., f. 307, 1679; Audiencia de Guadalajara 231, Libro 5, fs.10–11, 20–21, 1679.

53. AGI, Seville, Audiencia de Guadalajara 231, Libro 5, fs. 83–85, 117 184–85, 1681–1682; Audiencia de Guadalajara 232, Libro 9, fs. 187–88, 1703. See similar futile efforts in Adanna Mgbako, *To Live Freely,* 164–70. A cotton workshop also existed in Mexico City's Santa Maria Magdalena. Muriel, *Los recogimientos,* 120.

54. AGI, Seville, Audiencia de Guadalajara 231, Libro 5, fs. 287–88, 1685; Libro 6, fs. 124–28, 1685.

55. Ibid., Libro 4, fs. 383–85, 1677; Audiencia de Guadalajara 232, Libro 8, fs. 75–77, 1696.

56. AGN México, Inquisición, Vol. 758, 1714, "Contra doña Nicolasa de Guzman española por alcahueta supersticiosa," 378–96.

57. Atondo, *Amor venal*, 306–17. As usual, Atondo presents Guzman's employees as poverty-stricken victims. See *Amor venal*, 309, 312.

58. "Contra doña Nicolasa de Guzman," 378.

59. Ibid.

60. Despite her indigenous heritage, Guzman had climbed the social and racial ladder to attain the honorific title (doña), usually reserved for elite Spanish women. Ibid., 386–87.

61. Ibid., 396.

62. Ibid., 384–89; Atondo, *Amor venal*, 314–15. Later in the century, an inquisition investigation mentions a teenage girl of African descent whose virginity was allegedly sold for only four pesos by a female slave in a neighboring house. AGN, Mexico, Inquisición 525, Exp. 3, "María Nieto por sus escándalos y haberle inquietado a una negrita su esclava," 1691, 83–100.

63. "Contra doña Nicolasa de Guzman," 386.

CHATPER 3

1. Alan S. Trueblood, *A Sor Juana Anthology* (Cambridge, MA: Harvard University Press, 1988), 111–13.

2. More recent sex workers choose this career precisely to avoid a working-class life and the paltry wages and poor work conditions of factory or domestic servitude. Yu Ding and Petula Sik Ying Ho, "Sex Work in China's Pearl River Delta: Accumulating Sexual Capital as a Life-Advancement Strategy," *Sexualities* vol. 26, 1 (2013): 44–46; and White, *Prostitution in Colonial Nairobi*, 98–101.

3. These chapters follow historians' rough conception of colonial cities as having elite-, middle-, and lower-class populations at this time. Haslip Viera, *Crime and Punishment*, 23–25.

4. Dan Cruickshank, *London's Sinful Secret: The Bawdy History and Very Public Passions of London's Georgian Age* (New York: St. Martin's Press, 2010), 126. These distinctions overlap in some ways with the more modern differentiation between indoor and outdoor workers, those "on the stroll" who solicit men in cars, brothel workers, and those who use marketing methods (from traditional "call girls" working out of agencies advertised in the telephone book, then websites) to see clients only in private. For the wide variety of sex-worker experience in the early twenty-first century, see Bernstein, *Temporarily Yours*, 2007. See Pullen, *Actresses and Whores*, 192n7, for the negative bias that turns all sex workers into streetwalkers.

5. Cruickshank, *London's Sinful Secret*, 126.

6. Van Deusen, *Between the Sacred and the Worldly*, 156.

7. Tomas y Valiente, *Derecho Penal*, 219–35.

8. Germeten, *Violent Delights*, 141–43. See also Muriel, *Los recogimientos*, 123–25, for changing perceptions of sociability and sexuality in this era.

9. Amparo Sevilla, "Historia Social de los Salones del Baile," in *Las Espacios Públicos de la Ciudad, Siglos XVIII y XIX*, ed. Carlos Aguirre Anaya, Marcela Dávalos, María Amparo Ros Torres, et al. (Mexico City: Instituto de Cultura de la Ciudad de México, 2002), 152–53.

10. Juan Pedro Viqueira Albán, *Propriety and Permissiveness in Bourbon Mexico,* trans. Sonya Lipsett-Rivera and Sergio Rivera Ayala (Wilmington, DE: Scholarly Resources, 1999), 118–28. Theatrical dances were also viewed as entertaining for only the crudest audiences, 44–49, 64–68.

11. See Sergio Rivera Ayala, "Dance of the People: The Chuchumbé," in *Colonial Lives: Documents on Latin American History, 1550–1850,* eds. Richard E. Boyer and Geoffrey Spurling (New York: Oxford University Press, 2000), which criticizes Bourbon church and state authority figures, including military inspectors.

12. AGN, Mexico, Virreinal bandos, Vol. 11, Exp. 5, 1779, "Bando para corregir los abusos de concurrencia de ambos sexos en las de esta capital."

13. Norberg, "The Body of the Prostitute," 393–408. For other examples of the term *prostitute* in eighteenth-century Mexico see Lee Penyak, "Criminal Sexuality in Central Mexico, 1750–1850" (PhD diss., University of Connecticut, 1993), 58.

14. In eighteenth-century European metropolises, commercial sex stimulated the economy through conspicuous consumption of luxury goods and entertainment and even inspired urban development and architectural creativity. During London's Georgian building boom, with inexpensive constructions rapidly thrown up to maximize profits, sex workers of all levels represented some of the most readily available and profitable renters. Allegedly, tens of thousands of London women moved between sex work and domestic servitude. The *List* emphasized that certain neighborhoods revolved around the sex trade, creating a geographic focus for sex workers in the metropolis. Edinburgh also had a similar guide. Cruickshank, *London's Sinful Secret,* xi, 38, 51, 128, 132, 180–87.

15. Ann Lewis, "Classifying the Prostitute in Eighteenth-Century France," in *Prostitution and Eighteenth-Century Culture: Sex, Commerce, and Morality,* ed. Ann Lewis (London: Pickering & Chatto, 2012), 19–20. Early pornography also circulated in Mexico City. Penyak, "Criminal Sexuality in Central Mexico," 24–34. In Spain, an anonymous author published an extensive and scatalogical list of sixty-five whores in 1519, called the *Carajicomedia.* See Hsu, "Courtesans in the Literature of the Spanish Golden Age," 82–90.

16. AGN, Mexico, Inquisition, Caja 5013, Exp. 82, 1784, and Caja 5018, Exp. 48, 1785.

17. AGN, Mexico, Clero Regular y Secular Caja 1958, Exp. 5, 1713, "El Provisorato oficial y el Vicario General sobre la denuncia que hace Doña Josepha María de Navarro de su hijo, el bachiller don Diego de Vergara Gabiria, clérigo de menores ordenes," 1–16.

18. AGN, Mexico, Cárceles y Presidios Caja 1058, Exp. 5, 1796, "Expediente de María Guerrero española, para que se liberara a su hijo Marcelo Sanchez, preso por golpear a una mujer mundana," 1–6.

19. AGN, Mexico, Real Audiencia Caja 2334, Exp. 5, 1799, "Don Juan Domingo Gonzáles, sobre que su moso Joseph Ambrosio a tenido amistad ilícita con una prostituta con la cual tiene un hijo y quiere impedir se case con ella," 1–8.

20. Silvia Marina Arrom, *The Women of Mexico City, 1790–1857* (Stanford, CA: Stanford University Press, 1985), 207–10, 230.

21. Ibid., 220–24.

22. AGN, Mexico, Criminal Caja 5202, Exp. 8, 1788, "Autos de Alonso Gavidia contra su mujer Ana María Sáenz, por libertina, escandalosa vida y ninguna subordinación," 1–4.

23. AGN, Mexico, Clero Regular y Secular Caja 5249, Exp. 38, 1788, "Real Provisión de ruego para que el Provisor del Obispado de Valladolid remitiera a la Real Audiencia los

autos de Doña Anna María Sanchez Revollo, mujer legítima de Alonzo Gavidia, acusada de adúltera y prostituta," 1–8. Other men might make vaguer accusations against their wives for simply associating with particular men in public, with the implication of adultery or prostitution. See AGN, Mexico, Clero Regular y Secular Caja 4881, Exp. 60, 1784, "Denuncia de Antonio Graduño contra su mujer Joachina Velasquez por andar en malos pasos y no esta con él," 1–17.

24. AGN, Mexico, Bienes Nacionales Caja 5236, Exp. 92, 1757, "Solicitud de divorcio promovida por Joseph Prieto, mando de Rosa García. Expone la conducta escandalosa de su mujer," 1–2. AGN, Mexico, Criminal Caja 1434, Exp. 3, "Autos criminales a pedimento de Francisco Martínez, español, contra Isabel Manzano, su legitima mujer para divorciarse por su mal carácter," 1–82.

25. AGN, Mexico, Matrimonios Caja 31, Exp. 38, 1785, "Solicita se recluya a su mujer en la Misericordia por no poder sujetarla de su mal comportamiento," 172–77.

26. Germeten, *Violent Delights,* chapter 10.

27. Haslip Viera, *Crime and Punishment,* 127–29; Muriel, *Los recogimientos,* 41–158 [page range ok?].

28. Chad T. Black, *The Limits of Gender Domination: Women, the Law, and Political Crisis in Quito, 1765–1830* (Albuquerque: University of New Mexico Press, 2010), 79–80.

29. AGN, Mexico, Matrimonios vol. 99, "Testimonio de los autos que sigue Jacinto Rodriguez," 1744, 327–463. *"Meretriz"* used on 330.

30. This case predates by three decades the real pragmática, a crown decree that allowed parents a legal forum to object to marriages of social or racial unequals, but it takes the tone of cases made in the name of this late-eighteenth-century policy. Patricia Seed, *To Love, Honor, and Obey in Colonial Mexico: Conflicts over Marriage Choice, 1574–1821* (Stanford, CA: 1988), 205–26.

31. "Autos que sigue Jacinto Rodríguez," 329–33, 346, 351.

32. Ibid., 341.

33. Ibid., 355.

34. Ibid., 334, 344.

35. Olsson, "'A First-Rate Whore,'" 72. In these renditions, La Tafolla embodied the stereotypical bad-tempered women of African descent depicted in some eighteenth-century *pinturas de castas.*

36. "Autos que sigue Jacinto Rodríguez," 336, 338, 340, 342, 345, 347, 348.

37. From the perspective of the higher levels of viceregal society in this particular era, these aggressive characteristics defined a courtesan who catered to elite men. La Tafolla's denunciations resemble characterizations of courtesans of the highest rank in Paris: "At the top of the ladder you see the ambitious and haughty women, who aim always at the highest. . . . They are cold, [with] calculating brains to note a weakness and turn it to their own account." See Lewis, "Classifying the Prostitute," 22.

38. "Autos que sigue Jacinto Rodríguez," 442.

39. Meijide Pardo, "Mendicidad, Vagancia, y Prostitución," prologo.

40. Black, *Limits,* 74–75.

41. "El señor provisor don Joseph Ruiz de Conesares juez provisor vicario general de este arzobispado contra una mujer quien esta metiéndole hombres," Rosenbach collection, 1778.

42. Ibid., 8–9.

43. Ibid., 17.

44. Ibid., 2.

45. Ibid., 3–5.

46. Ibid., 2, 4, 5.

47. Ibid., 18–20, 34–35. After several months in jail, Ayala complained that he had suffered more than enough punishment for a short period of incontinence. He felt very repentant and promised to go to confession regularly and not to fall into temptation again. His foster father, Joseph del Castillo, also demanded his freedom.

48. Ibid., 38–42. As punishment for his relationship with Castillo, the ecclesiastical court put Ayala in an *obraje* (workshop) that made shoes and demanded that he take communion twice a day for two weeks, as well as say a rosary on his knees. He was not to restart his relationship, and the religious authorities advised against the couple's marrying, due to their youth.

49. AGN, Mexico, Criminal, Caja 32B, Exp. 108, 1792, "Querella por practicar la prostitución," 1–14.

50. Ibid., 3–4.

51. Ibid., 9.

52. See *Nuevo tesoro lexicográfico de la lengua española,* accessed December 3, 2014, www.rae.es.

53. "Querella por practicar la prostitución," 4–5.

54. A man called Don Fernando did not testify because he lived in distant Real de Catorce, working as a miner. Witnesses had also mentioned lovers called Don Juan and Don George, but these men did not come in for questioning. Doña María herself claimed she knew nothing of Don George and Don Fernando beyond saying "Good morning" to them. Ibid., 4–6, 9.

55. Ibid., 7.

56. Ibid., 6–7, 9, 11.

57. Ibid., 8.

58. Eric Van Young, *The Other Rebellion: Popular Violence, Ideology, and the Mexican Struggle for Independence, 1810–1821* (Stanford, CA: Stanford University Press, 2001), 273, 344. Van Young mentions a *"meson del Chino"* existing in 1809, where revolutionary talk took place; see 262–63. All of these descriptions of leisure activities come from "Querella por practicar la prostitución," 7–11.

59. Their lives mirror those of many of the unwed mothers discussed by Twinam, *Public Lives, Private Secrets,* including the women's claims of fragility in the face of seduction.

60. "Querella por practicar la prostitución," 7, 12–14.

61. AGN, Mexico, Alcaldes ordinarios, Criminal, Caja 35B, Exp. 55, 1797, "Incontinencia, escándalos y otros excesos en una casa situada en la calle de San Pedro y San Pablo."

62. Ibid., 53.

63. Ibid., 27.

64. Ibid., 2–3, 25–26, 33, 52.

65. Germeten, *Violent Delights,* chapter 11, and also see chapter 4 of this book.

66. "Incontinencia, escándalos," 20–21.

67. Ibid., 10, 27, 34.

68. Ibid., 3, 29–32.

69. Ibid., 33–34. Haslip-Viera documents one roller working only twelve days in a month. *Crime and Punishment*, 29–30. See also Susan Deans-Smith, *Bureaucrats, Planters, and Workers: The Making of the Tobacco Monopoly in Bourbon Mexico* (Austin: University of Texas Press, 1992).

70. "Incontinencia, escándalos," 33–34.

71. Ibid., 47–51.

72. Ibid., 56–59.

73. AGN, Mexico, Real Audiencia, Criminal Contenedor 45, Vol. 177, Exp. 12, 230–44, 1789, "Causa de oficio contra María Alberta sobre lo que dentro se expresa."

CHAPTER 4

1. Meeting between "La Güera" Rodríguez and Alexander von Humboldt in 1800, as told by Fanny Calderon de la Barca, *Life in Mexico, during a Residence of Two Years in that Country* (London: Chapman and Hall, 1843), 72. Calderon de la Barca related an interesting undated anecdote from Rodríguez about a ballet dancer who had received a beautiful, opulent, expensive gown as a gift from a cleric, not knowing it had been both the wedding dress and the burial shroud of a deceased aristocrat. She was shamed on stage for her shocking choice of costume. This anecdote, however obscure, supports the link between the Mexican theater and well-paid love affairs.

2. For the complete case, see AGI, Seville, Audiencia de Mexico, 1707, Leg. 28, "Expediente de la cómica [Josefa] María Ordóñez," 1766–1767. This file does not have consistent pagination, so I will cite documents by date hereafter.

3. Linda A. Curcio-Nagy, "Josefa Ordoñez: The Scandalous Adventures of a Colonial Courtesan," in *The Human Tradition in Mexico*, ed. Jeffrey M. Pilcher (Wilmington, Del.: SR Books, 2003), 5.

4. Martha Feldman and Bonnie Gordon, "Introduction," in *The Courtesan's Arts: Cross-Cultural Perspectives*, eds. Martha Feldman and Bonnie Gordon (New York: Oxford University Press, 2006), 6.

5. Lena Olsson, "'A First-Rate Whore': Prostitution and Empowerment in the Early Eighteenth Century," in *Prostitution and Eighteenth-Century Culture: Sex, Commerce, and Morality*, eds. Markham Ellis and Ann Lewis (London: Pickering and Chatto, 2012), 75.

6. Feldman and Gordon, "Introduction," 5. Among the most popular biographies of this kind are: Jo Manning, *My Lady Scandalous: The Amazing Life and Outrageous Times of Grace Dalrymple Elliott, Royal Courtesan* (New York: Simon & Schuster, 2005); Joan Haslip, *Madame Du Barry: The Wages of Beauty* (New York: Grove Weidenfeld, 1992); Christine Pevitt, *Madame De Pompadour: Mistress of France* (New York: Grove Press, 2002).

7. Feldman and Gordon, "Introduction," 9. Also see Pullen, *Actresses and Whores* for an extensive study of sex work and performance over the last four centuries.

8. Atondo, *Amor Venal*, 187–88.

9. Charles F. Walker, *Shaky Colonialism: The 1746 Earthquake-Tsunami in Lima, Peru, and Its Long Aftermath* (Durham, NC: Duke University Press, 2008), 150–55. I also closely examined the significance of clothing in Germeten, *Violent Delights, Violent Ends*, chapters 8 and 11.

10. Catherine Cusset, *Libertinage and Modernity* (New Haven, CT: Yale University Press, 1998); Kushner, *Erotic Exchanges;* Cruickshank, *London's Sinful Secret.*

11. María del Carmen Vázquez Mantecón, *Los Días de Josefa Ordoñez* (Mexico City: Universidad Nacional Autónoma de México, 2005), 49–50.

12. Although this list is not a fictional/creative document but a threat of judicial punishment, the list of women reminds the reader of the mania for cataloguing sex workers in contemporary European cities. See chapter 3.

13. In the eighteenth century, sumptuary laws were interpreted as an inheritance of Roman Law. This can be seen in the overall structure of the 1788 study by Juan Sempere y Guariños, *Historia del Luxo* 2 vols. (Madrid: Atlas, 1973).

14. Sempere y Guariños, *Historia del Luxo,* Vol. 2, 101–4.

15. Ibid., 124–32.

16. Ibid., 13–15.

17. Atondo, *Amor Venal,* 185–86.

18. La Lorencilla's physical description is on AGI, Seville, Audiencia de Mexico, Legajo 84, Ramo 2, Number 64, "Autos en q los señores de la real sala de crimen mandaron q las mujeres publicas no trajesen trajes profanos ni anduviesen en coches," 13.

19. "Autos contra las mujeres publicas," 19, 21–26.

20. Ibid., 14–19.

21. Germeten, *Violent Delights,* 51, 175–76; and see below for Ordóñez and the same ploys.

22. "Autos contra las mujeres publicas," 38–42.

23. Atondo, *Amor Venal,* 190–92.

24. The majority of the case is dedicated not to denouncing La Lorencilla but to handling male financial concerns including Ortega's need to have his carriage, mules, and driver returned to him after their confiscation (and possible whipping) by the authorities, as well as the compensation owed to the men who drove La Lorencilla to Puebla. This is why a great stress was put on the fact that she borrowed the carriage, driver, mules, and other expensive equipment. See "Autos contra las mujeres publicas," 15–28, 32–36.

25. Still a point of dispute in the twenty-first century. Vázquez Mantecón, *Los días,* 127, rejects Atondo's description of Ordóñez as an "elite prostitute."

26. Lewis, "Classifying the Prostitute," 21.

27. Ibid., 18.

28. AGN, Bogotá, Colonia, Policia, Leg. 2, 1790, "Obispo y cabildo fundan una casa de reclusión para cortesanas y casadas mal avenidas en sus matrimonios," 250–69.

29. Ibid., 269. These statements also confirm that men of this era, although they discussed them in a jovial, patronizing tone, viewed public women as lazy, a common stereotype throughout history.

30. Arrom, *Women of Mexico City,* 242–44.

31. Simon Pedro Izcara Palacios, *Mujer y cambio de valores en el Madrid del siglo XVIII,* 36.

32. Ibid., 19–35, 68–69.

33. Ibid., 39–40.

34. Ibid., 41, 66–68.

35. Juli Leal, and J. Inés Rodríguez Gómez, eds., *Carlo Goldoni: Una vida para el teatro: Coloquio internacional, bicentenario Carlo Goldoni* (Valencia: Universitat de València, Departament de Filologia Francesa i Italiana, 1996), 76–77.

36. Colin Bingham, *The Affairs of Women; A Modern Miscellany* (Sydney: Currawong, 1969), 182, heavily citing Paul Hazard's *La pensée européenne au XVIIIe siècle de Montesquieu à Lessing* (Paris: Boivin et Cie, 1946). See also Hazard, *European Thought in the Eighteenth Century, From Montesquieu to Lessing*, trans. J. Lewis May (Gloucester, MA: Peter Smith, 1973), 257. Bingham makes it very clear that although these men bore some resemblance to gigolos, they would have felt great shame in accepting money or gifts from their ladies.

37. Germeten, *Violent Delights*, 199–201.

38. Ibid., 198–202.

39. Ibid., 216, 223–24.

40. Even if commentators blamed the phenomenon on foreigners, this kind of arrangement definitely existed in Spain as well, causing, in one case, a dramatic response when an archdeacon returned from Cuzco to his hometown of Cadiz in the 1770s. To his horror, he discovered that his married sister openly lived with her lover, a rich and powerful notary. Scorning her unemployed husband's limited means, she luxuriated in a very well appointed household, and her ostentation extended even to enjoying the notary's box at the theater. Nobody, not even their parish priest, seemed all that concerned about this blatant disregard of marriage vows. They preferred to ignore the adulterous arrangement, a clear example of the reconciliation between "public lives" and "private secrets," until the clerical brother arrived home, loudly protesting about his violated honor. AGI, Cuzco, 68, "Expedientes eclesiásticos tramitados en el consejo y cámara de indias y en la vía reservada: recursos de Simon Jiménez de Villaba, archidiácono de Cuzco, contra su hermana por conducta escandalosa (1778–1779 y 1797); testimonios sueltos (1757 y 1763) y cartas (1795)." See also Twinam, *Public Lives, Private Secrets,* 34.

41. In the 1750s, Doña Luisa de Llerena, a woman descended from Cartagena's local Creole military elite, suffered a period of persecution, surveillance, and scathing criticism of her private life. Llerena allegedly had several lovers that waited on her in her home and in public and supplied her with luxury items. She ate with them and cared for them in illness. They visited each other's houses wearing informal clothes. These prosperous men allegedly supported her stylish dress and occasional parties. However, Llerena had also inherited money, property, and slaves and organized her own enterprises, making money off renting out her slaves and even running a candy-making business in her home. In defending themselves, Llerena and her husband asserted that either her parents or Piñero paternalistically supervised all her income, adornments, and expenses, while at the same time acknowledging that she intelligently and profitably managed her own resources. The internal contradiction did not seem to disturb those who supported the couple, as long as they could prove that Llerena enacted her gender role as overseen by men in her family, without receiving any gifts from other men. Her husband's colleagues in the local troops denounced her due to the insult her behavior caused to his honor and, by extension, to the honor of their battalion. Llerena's detractors voiced their judgments using the typical character assessments seen throughout this chapter, while her supporters portrayed her in more euphemistic terms as a proud woman who would not submit to any kind of humiliation. But among her

deficiencies was the fact that Llerena dressed and entertained too lavishly given the salary of Captain Don Francisco Piñero, her peninsular Spanish husband. In terms of personality, her friends viewed her as a vibrant sociable woman of passion and a bold defender of her honor. However, more importantly, her enemies (especially a certain clèric and the governor's wife) slandered her with vocabulary invoking the most public and degraded of all categories of women. They alleged, and persuaded Piñero's colleagues to believe, that Doña Luisa acted as a common whore, even claiming that her social inferiors mocked her as a "puta." Her husband's enemies claimed that Piñero had the reputation of a "*leno* [panderer]" and cuckold who lived off his wife's lovers. On the one hand, she enjoyed one difference from even the scandalously rich Ordóñez: Llerena occupied a position very close to the absolute pinnacle of her local society. No one could call her a social climber. On the other hand, she suffered far worse accusations in terms of sexual immorality than those endured by Ordóñez and some of the other courtesans. Llerena claimed to have nothing more than "spiritual friendships" with her alleged lovers, but her enemies called her a puta, a ramera, and a publicly acknowledged manceba, which underlines the power of public opinion to shape outcomes. Ultimately, the scandal died down when Piñero left Cartagena with his battalion. Llerena's daughter had enough honor to marry a respectable man, and Llerena herself petitioned for her husband's pension later in the century. Germeten, *Violent Delights*, chapter 11. The "Virrey Fraile," Jose Solis Folch de Cardona (mentioned in this chapter in the context of his own scandal), even contributed to the documentation of this controversy.

42. Until Independence, Bourbon reformers continued to intervene in the theater, issuing a set of regulations in 1786 that regulated plays' content, scenery, costumes, audience behavior, the performers' personal lives, and even the placement of a board at the front of the stage to block the view of the actresses' feet. This intervention ultimately made the theater less appealing to the masses and, therefore, less profitable. Viqueira Albán, *Propriety and Permissiveness*, 27–95.

43. Atondo, *Amor Venal*, 242–44.

44. Viqueira Albán, *Propriety and Permissiveness*, 61–62.

45. Kathryn Norberg, "Salon as Stage: Actresses/Courtesans and Their Homes in Late Eighteenth-Century Paris," in *Architectural Space in Eighteenth-Century Europe: Constructing Identities and Interiors*, eds. Baxter and Martin[first names?] (Farnham, UK: Ashgate, 2010), 106–8.

46. Thomas Wynn, "Prostitutes and Erotic Performances in Eighteenth-Century Paris," in *Prostitution and Eighteenth-Century Culture: Sex, Commerce, and Morality*, ed. Lewis[first name?] (London: Pickering & Chatto, 2012), 89.

47. Curcio-Nagy, "Josefa Ordóñez," 14–15.

48. Richard Chuhue Huamán, "Plebe, Prostitución, y Conducta Sexual en Lima del Siglo XVIII: Apuntes Sobre la Sexualidad en Lima Borbónica," in *Historia de Lima: XVII Coloquio de Historia de Lima, 2010*, ed. [first name?]Estrada (Lima: Centro Cultural de San Marcos, 2010), 131–35.

49. AGN Mexico, Judicial Vol. 32, 1809, "Román Punzalan Zapata en pleito por su mujer Ana María Sendejas," 396–410.

50. Ibid., 397–98, 402. The case ended favorably for the estranged wife, who possibly received financial support from her husband because the divorce was never finalized. Roman, however, returned to the Philippines.

51. AGN, Mexico, Criminal, Vol. 383, Exp. 5, 134–41; Ana Patricia Quiroz Sandoval, "El Sacerdote, el Alcalde, y el Testigo. Tres formas de juzgar el fenómeno de la prostitución en la Ciudad de México (1777–1818)," Tesis por licenciada en Historia, Universidad Nacional Autónoma de México, 2007, 40–41, 47–48, 59, 74.

52. "Expediente de la cómica," document dated June 3, 1766.

53. Curcio-Nagy, "Josefa Ordóñez," 6–7. A handful of women held similar leadership positions from the late seventeenth century, but their opportunities dried out in the second half of the eighteenth century with the Bourbon reforms of the theater. Viqueira Albán, *Propriety and Permissiveness,* 58.

54. Vázquez Mantecón, *Los días,* 19, 21–22.

55. Kushner, *Erotic Exchanges,* 64, 74, 92–93, 158, 160.

56. Curcio-Nagy, "Josefa Ordóñez," 7–13, does an excellent job of summarizing this confusing history: the couples' constant conflicts, the various times Ordóñez suffered incarceration, and the ever stranger path their accusations took later in life when they came before the Holy Office.

57. Atondo, *Amor venal,* 261. "Expediente de la cómica," testimony dated May 27, 1766.

58. Viqueira Albán, *Propriety and Permissiveness,* 45.

59. Vázquez Mantecón, *Los días,* 28–31.

60. Ibid., 27–69, discusses these years in depth. Again I am focusing on Ordóñez as a courtesan, but see Vázquez Mantecón, *Los días,* for a discussion of the viceregal court rivalries that may have inspired the investigations.

61. While possibly surprising, it has been common throughout history for courtesans to peacefully and openly have affairs with several men simultaneously. See Guido Ruggiero, "Who's Afraid of Giuliana Napolitana? Pleasure, Fear, and Imagining the Arts of the Renaissance Courtesan," in *The Courtesan's Arts,* eds. Feldman and Gordon, 283.

62. One dancer and kept woman in Paris, active in 1765, also had a Spaniard as a patron. Kushner, *Erotic Exchanges,* 148–49, 187.

63. Vázquez Mantecón, *Los días,* 44–46.

64. Ibid., 38–40.

65. "Expediente de la cómica," document dated July 24, 1766. Panseco left the Coliseo to work as first violinist in the Cathedral choir in 1761. See Vázquez Mantecón, *Los días,* 169.

66. "Expediente de la cómica," testimony dated May 27, 1766.

67. Norberg, "Salon as Stage," 106–7.

68. For the complete inventory, see Vázquez Mantecón, *Los días,* 59–61 (summary), 145–63 (books), 185–92 (inventory).

69. Curcio-Nagy, "Josefa Ordóñez," 9.

70. Kathryn Norberg, "Goddesses of Taste: Courtesans and Their Furniture in Late-Eighteenth-Century Paris," in *Furnishing the Eighteenth-Century: What Furniture Can Tell Us about the European and American Past,* eds. Dena Goodman and Kathryn Norbert (New York: Routledge, 2007), 98–107.

71. Ibid., 100, 105, 109.

72. Atondo, *Amor Venal,* 257.

73. Norberg, "Goddesses of Taste," 108.

74. Kushner, *Erotic Exchanges,* 203, 223.

75. Ibid., 199.

76. "Expediente de la cómica," testimony dated May 27, 1766.

77. Curcio-Nagy, "Josefa Ordóñez," 12–13.

78. Arrom, *Women of Mexico City,* 209.

79. Sempere y Guariños, *Historia del Luxo,* Vol. 2, 140–61, 169–74.

80. Atondo, *Amor Venal,* 259–60.

81. Vázquez Mantecón, *Los días,* 31–40, details this event.

82. "Expediente de la cómica," July 24, 1776.

83. Norberg, "Salon as Stage," 108–9.

84. With a focus on the courtesan, here I will not detail Panseco's far more horrible personal traits, although Ordóñez tried to use them against her spouse whenever possible to achieve her goals or possibly just to continue their decades' long disputes.

85. Vázquez Mantecón, *Los días,* 52–53. "Expediente de la cómica," document dated June 6, 1766. Gorraez claimed the carriage was his and thus protested its confiscation. Ultimately, it was sold for 460 pesos. See "Expediente de la cómica," document dated July 7, 1766.

86. "Expediente de la cómica," testimony dated June 28, 1766.

87. Ibid., testimony dated May 30, 1766.

88. Ibid., documents dated July 11, 1766, and July 21, 1766.

89. Vázquez Mantecón, *Los días,* 56–58, 61–62, 175.

90. Due to the ongoing conflicts with her husband, and the fact that both of them expressed a desire to return to Spain, the couple ended up in prison for two years in the 1770s in San Juan de Ulua in Veracruz. They eventually swore to return to married life in Mexico City, but they never lived together in peace. Vázquez Mantecón, *Los días,* 69, 84, 175, 177–81.

91. Junía Ferreira Furtado, *Chica da Silva: A Brazilian Slave of the Eighteenth-Century* (Cambridge, UK: Cambridge University Press, 2009). This book is the model for a deep historical contextualization of a famous scandalous woman, including an in-depth historiographic essay.

92. Ricardo Palma, "Genialidades de 'la Perricholi,'" in *Tradiciones Peruanas Completas,* edited by Ricardo Palma (Lima: PEISA, 1976), 616–21; Bonnie Korns, "The Life of Micaela Villegas, La Perricholi and Her Influence on the Social Life of Her Time, with Special Reference to Spanish Colonial Lima" (MA thesis, Claremont College, 1947).

93. Chuhue Huaman, "Plebe, prostitución, y conducta sexual," 127–51. The author states, "El hecho de que la prostitución estuviera bastante difundida en Lima es algo innegable" (146).

94. Alberto Miramón, *El Secreto del Virrey Fraile* (Bogotá: Librería Siglo XX, 1944); Antonio Álvarez Lleras, *El Virrey Solís: drama histórico en cuatro actos divididos en nueve cuadros* (Bogotá: Editorial Minerva), 1947.

95. Javier Ocampo López, *Leyendas populares colombianas* (Bogotá: Plaza & Janes, 1996), 66–68.

96. Montserrat Galí i Boadella, *Historias del bello sexo: la introducción del romanticismo en México* (Mexico City: Universidad Nacional Autónoma de México, Instituto de Investigaciones Estéticas, 2002), 37–55; Mark Burkholder, *Spaniards in the Colonial Empire: Creoles vs. Peninsulares?* (Malden, MA: John Wiley and Sons, 2013).

97. Arrom, *Women of Mexico City,* 127, 215, 238, 248, 342n54.

98. Jaime E. Rodríguez O., "The Transition from Colony to Nation: New Spain, 1820–1821," in *Mexico in the Age of Democratic Revolutions, 1750-1850*, ed. Jaime E. Rodríguez O. (Boulder, CO: Lynne Rienner, 1994), 116.

99. Artemio de Valle-Arizpe, *La Güerra Rodríguez* (Mexico City: Libreria de Manuel Porrua, 1950).

100. Kushner, *Erotic Exchanges*, 166, 187.

101. Curcio-Nagy, "Josefa Ordóñez," 12–13.

CHAPTER 5

1. AGN, Mexico, Inquisición, Vol. 1157, Exp. 8, "Proceso contra Pancha *la carnicera* por blasfemia," 1777, 7.

2. AGN, Mexico, "Libro de Reos," Vol. 73, Exp. 46, February 29, 1796.

3. Scholars of sex work observe that this area of inquiry offers an opportunity to explore masculine identity, but few researchers seem to have an interest in it. The nine men who testified were all Spanish men between twenty and fifty years old. Five were single, and four were married. Their occupations included high-level trades such as a silversmith, as well as more plebeian occupations (a weaver and a tailor), business owners, and professional men (a tavern keeper, a schoolteacher, and a petty merchant).

4. Statistical analysis suggests a modern desire to control data and provides insight into the worldview of Bourbon reformers, but not the mindset of the people over whom they ruled. Even in the twentieth century, colonial rulers projected an impression of having far more control over statistics and data than they really had at a grassroots level, or beyond a small urban area. Keren Weitzberg, "The Unaccountable Census: Colonial Enumeration and Its Implications for the Somali People of Kenya," *Journal of African History* vol. 56, 3 (November 2015): 409–28.

5. Haslip-Viera, *Crime and Punishment*, 18–22.

6. Amy C. Hamman, "Eyeing Alameda Park: Topographies of Culture, Class, and Cleanliness in Bourbon Mexico City, 1700–1800" (PhD diss., University of Arizona, 2015), 26. On *léperos*, see Hamman, "Eyeing Alameda Park," 145–46; Sharon Bailey Glasco, "A City in Disarray: Public Health, City Planning, and the Politics of Power in Late Colonial Mexico City" (PhD diss., University of Arizona, 2002), 68–70; Michael Scardaville, "Crime and Urban Poor: Mexico City in the Late Colonial Period" (PhD diss., University of Florida, 1977), 16–23.

7. Sharon Bailey Glasco, *Constructing Mexico City: Colonial Conflicts over Culture, Space, and Authority* (New York: Palgrave, 2010), 82–99, 109–17, 139, 149.

8. As we see in the *pinturas de castas*. Ilona Katzew, *Casta Painting: Images of Race in Eighteenth-Century Mexico* (New Haven, CT: Yale University Press, 2004).

9. Scardaville, "Crime and Urban Poor," 12, 272–73; José María Sánchez-Arcilla, "La Administración de Justicia Inferior en la Ciudad de México a Finales de la Época Colonial. I. La punición de la Embriaguez en los Libros de Reos," *Cuadernos de Historia del Derecho* vol. 7 (2000): 340; Sánchez-Arcilla, "Delincuencia femenina," 117–18; Haslip-Viera, *Crime and Punishment*, 45–48, 88.

10. Jorge Nacif Mina, *La Policía en la Historia de la Ciudad de México, 1524–1928* (Mexico City: Departamento del Distrito Federal, 1986), 19–24.

11. Michael Scardaville, "Justice by Paperwork: A Day in the Life of a Court Scribe in Bourbon Mexico City," *Journal of Social History* 36, 4 (2003): 979–1007.

12. In contemporary Europe, the word *police* also meant "governance," especially over urban areas. In London, reformers criminalized the poor, spreading tales of crime waves to dispel popular resistance to the new concept of militarized street patrols that operated under a more centralized authority than the traditional parish or neighborhood watches. As in the Americas, what the ruling elite most feared was street-level mass unrest. A growth in internal surveillance accompanied the creation of concern for "security," an intangible, nebulous condition that the poor or nonwhites could potentially threaten. But many decades would pass before the common man and woman peacefully acquiesced to uniformed men overseeing their daily street activities. In both Mexico City and London (the latter with more enduring success), it was not until the 1820s that reformers accelerated their efforts to institutionalize and standardize urban police forces, including the use of uniforms. Paul Lawrence et al., "Introduction," in *The Making of the Modern Police, 1780–1914*, vol. 1, ed. Francis Dodsworth (London: Pickering & Chatto, 2014), viii–xi; Elaine A. Reynolds, *Before the Bobbies: The Night Watch and Police Reform in Metropolitan London, 1720–1830* (Stanford, CA: Stanford University Press, 1998), 1, 4–6, 20, 29, 43–44, 46, 59, 69, 77.

13. Historians have different interpretations of the meaning and effectiveness of increased surveillance and bureaucratization. Pamela Voekel highlights the concept of the "public good," unknown in previous eras, when the authorities had used a rhetoric of sin in discussing their surveillance and castigation of plebeian viceregal subjects. Pamela Voekel, "Peeing on the Palace: Bodily Resistance to Bourbon Reforms in Mexico City," *Journal of Historical Sociology* vol. 5, 2 (1992): 183–84.

14. José Arturo Yánez Romero, *Policía Mexicana: cultura política, (in)seguridad y orden publico en el gobierno del Distrito Federal, 1821–1876* (Mexico City: Universidad Autónoma Metropolitana, 1999), 61–81; Scardaville, "Crime and Urban Poor," 3; Sánchez-Arcilla, "Administración de justicia inferior," 354, and "Delincuencia femenina," 116. The guardafaroleros would be punished by their superiors if they did not light the street illumination on time. Sánchez-Arcilla, "Administración de justicia inferior," 396n310.

15. Bailey Glasco, "City in Disarray," 169, 242; Scardaville, "Justice by Paperwork," 998–999n33, 1005n76, 1007n87.

16. Only very late in the century did the crown attempt to oversee the prosecution of pandering within the armed forces. See chapter 6 and *Novísima Recopilación*, 423.

17. This was similar to contemporary Paris, where, likewise, no official law existed:

> By the simplest definition, tolerance meant that, although prostitution could be regarded as illegal (if not in itself, then in certain aspects inseparably related to it) the authorities would not bring the force of the law to bear upon it; they could however, at any moment choose to exercise their power.

Harsin, *Policing Prostitution in Nineteenth-Century Paris*, 95. See also 80–81 and Susan P. Conner, "Politics, Prostitution, and the Pox in Revolutionary Paris, 1789–1799," *Journal of Social History* vol. 22, 4 (1989): 723.

18. Who may have been poorly trained and/or drunk on duty. Scardaville, "Crime and Urban Poor," 248.

19. Ibid., 190n114.

20. AGN, Mexico, "Libros de reos," Vol. 73, Exp. 50, July 19, 1798, and Exp. 49, January 3, 1798.

21. Scardaville, "Crime and Urban Poor," 164, 178–80, 205–7; Haslip-Viera, *Crime and Punishment,* 27. In Europe, the first defined subculture of plebeian prostitutes who consciously defined themselves as such appeared in this era, discarding the pretense that they made most of their income from other menial occupations. Conner, "Politics, Prostitution, and the Pox" 714–18; Harsin, *Policing Prostitution,* 103–4, 114.

22. Sánchez-Arcilla gives this total in "La delincuencia femenina en la Ciudad de México," his article dealing with crimes committed by women, although he is also familiar with the later libros de reos, some of which have disappeared. He explains in detail why he and Scardaville have different totals and the basic statistics of each libro de reo in "Fondos del Archivo General de la Nación de la Ciudad de Mexico," 162–68. For a scholarly study of early-nineteenth-century arrest records, see Teresa Lozano Armendares, *La Criminalidad en la Ciudad de Mexico, 1800–1821* (Mexico City: Universidad Nacional Autónoma de Mexico, 1987).

23. Sánchez-Arcilla Bernal, "La delincuencia femenina," 107, 124, 131–34, 153. In his quantification of the libros de reos from 1794 to 1798, Sánchez-Arcilla notes only four cases of clearly stated prostitution or brothel-keeping, with only one of those four brought to trial (see above). He found three more cases involving accusations of alcahuetería or lenocinio. Sánchez-Arcilla categorizes just over 21 percent of the arrests of women for "carnal crimes," or *"crimenes de incontinencia"*—a total of 355 records of the 1,791 female crimes documented in total. Sexual incontinence (concubinage or adultery) does not necessarily imply sex for sale, unless the plaintiffs purposely chose to call it prostitution. Sánchez-Arcilla also puts public sex acts within his category of "carnal crimes" and analyzes them in the context of drunkenness or as a prelude to the sacrament of marriage. Sánchez-Arcilla, "Administración de justicia inferior," 434–41.

24. Scardaville, "Crime and Urban Poor," 8–10, 141. In the years 1794 to 1807, Scardaville found 180 extant reported arrests for female prostitution, less than half of 1 percent of the total number of arrests of both men and women. Why these two historians, both of whom seemingly did careful statistical analysis, differ so dramatically in their numbers is difficult to ascertain. Two possibilities include that Scardaville interprets other crimes (especially those committed by women arrested for "actos torpes" or caught in the act on the street) as prostitution, or that the later books (after 1798) and Scardaville's other sources had many more records of prostitution. In sharp disagreement with Sánchez-Arcilla's approach, Scardaville argues that the hundreds of arrests for "illicit interactions *[tratarse ilicitamente],"* 6.3 percent of his total, really represent, in his words, "sexual promiscuity . . . or nonprofessional prostitution," i.e., transactional sex. Scardaville argues that selling sex was among the most hidden of all acts that the patrols might target, especially for those women who did not solicit or have sex on the streets or in pulquerías.

25. Mark Hunter, "The Materiality of Everyday Sex: Thinking Beyond Prostitution," *African Studies* vol. 61, 1 (2002): 101, observes that the dichotomies of transactional versus nontransactional sex may not always be useful or accurate.

26. Sánchez-Arcilla Bernal, "La delincuencia femenina," 132.

27. Scardaville, "Crime and Urban Poor," 178.

28. Michael C. Scardaville, "Alcohol Abuse and Tavern Reform in Late Colonial Mexico City," *Hispanic American Historical Review* vol. 60, 4 (1980), 634–71. These reos most often came from the indigenous group of migrants.

29. William B. Taylor, *Drinking, Homicide, and Rebellion in Colonial Mexican Villages* (Stanford, CA: Stanford University Press, 1979), 64–65, 94–97, 104–5. In Madrid, the authorities also equated drinking to increasing urban crime, so this stereotype encompassed the urbanized poor in general. See Meijide Pardo, "Mendicidad, vagancia y prostitución," 576–78, 591. The huge number of plebeian men incarcerated for drunkenness provided an important forced-labor pool for the viceregal authorities. This may have actually cleaned up the city significantly. Haslip Viera, *Crime and Punishment*, 98–99, 102–3, 116.

30. Hamman, "Eyeing Alameda Park," 149–50, 184–94.

31. Scardaville, "Alcohol Abuse and Tavern Reform," 645–46, 645n7; "Crime and Urban Poor," 209.

32. Scardaville, "Alcohol Abuse and Tavern Reform," 647–48.

33. The ubiquity of plebeian women making money in a semitolerated, informal street market runs parallel to negotiating transactional sex. See Christian Groes-Green, "'To Put Men in a Bottle': Eroticism, Kinship, Female Power and Transactional Sex in Maputo, Mozambique," *American Ethnologist* vol. 40, 1 (2013): 104; Scardaville, "Crime and Urban Poor," 211, 227–28, 249–50. Note the following response to a ban on "women selling tortillas and tamales from baskets or portable stalls":

> Within three days of the viceregal decree, the alcaldes de barrio had removed most of these establishments. Although most owners offered no complaints, some women protested bitterly, explaining that the only "respectable" way to support themselves and their families was to sell food to the pulquería customers. As a means to stress their inability to provide for their children if the order remained enforced, a group of women went as far as to give their offspring to the police officials. Concerned with the precarious financial status of the women who sold food from their apartments or stores, Revillagigedo permitted them to return to their former places of residence and prohibited only the sale of food by itinerant vendors (235).

The street vendors' protest, cleverly appealing to socially sanctioned ideas of sexual honor and children's welfare and the shame of other female occupations, actually worked.

34. Meijide Pardo, "Mendicidad, vagancia y prostitución," 589–90.

35. AGN, Mexico, "Libro de Reos," Vol. 73, Exp. 50, December 3, 1798. While punishments were set for various crimes, Haslip-Viera argues that "there is considerable evidence to suggest that corrective measures and punishments were applied in a discretionary manner." *Crime and Punishment*, 97–98.

36. AGN, Mexico, "Libro de Reos," Vol. 73, Exp. 46, May 14, 1796.

37. Ibid., Exp. 50, April 29, 1798.

38. Haslip-Viera views this forced domestic service as parallel to the physical labor endured by male convicts. See *Crime and Punishment*, 126–31.

39. AGN, Mexico, "Libro de Reos," Vol. 73, Exp. 50, January 14, 1798.

40. Ibid., July 7, 1798. See Haslip-Viera, *Crime and Punishment*, 88–96, for descriptions of contemporary jails and women's experiences of them.

41. An institution near the viceregal palace that gave its name to the alleyway where it was located. Maria Aurea Toxqui Garay, "'El recreo de los amigos.' Mexico City's Pulquerías during the Liberal Republic (1856–1911)" (PhD diss., University of Arizona, 2008), 96.

42. AGN, Mexico, "Libro de Reos," Vol. 73, Exp. 50, August 15, 1798.

43. Ibid., Exp. 46, September 26, 1796.

44. Ibid., Exp. 50, April 30, 1798.

45. Ibid., Exp. 46, June 21, 1796; Exp. 50, April 24 and July 3, 1798.

46. Ibid., Exp. 46, March 28, July 17, and August 15, 1796; Exp. 50, January 6 and January 18, 1798.

47. Ibid., Exp. 50, January 17 and November 11, 1798.

48. Located on the nineteenth-century Calle de Buena Muerta, now San Jeronimo. See http://aguadetusverdesmatas.blogspot.com/2011/12/directorio-de-pulquerías-del-siglo-xix .html, accessed December 9, 2015. See also *Mexico dividida en quarteles mayores y menores* (Mexico City: Manuel Antonio Valdez, 1811), 35. Brian Hamnett, *The Mexican Bureaucracy before the Bourbon Reforms, 1700–1770: A Study in the Limitations of Absolutism* (Glasgow: Institute of Latin American Studies, University of Glasgow, 1979), 3.

49. Arondekar, *For the Record*, 10.

50. AGN, Mexico, "Libro de Reos," Vol. 73, Exp. 50, January 23, 1798. As a result, law enforcement briefly imprisoned the accused, then gave each of them twenty-five lashes and ordered them back to their home villages.

51. AGN, Mexico, Matrimonios, Vol. 114, "Petition of Domingo Lara," 121–24, 1795. The wife implied that she needed money due to her husband's stinginess in dispersing his earnings to her. Lara objected to the different houses where his wife had gone for her depósito during the divorce process, because apparently she and some of her relatives all lived as women of *"malas costumbres[bad habits]."* Living with them meant that she would continue her vicious ways, in Lara's view.

52. AGN, Mexico, "Libro de Reos," Vol. 73, Exp. 46, March 22, 1796.

53. Ibid., Exp. 50, May 28, 1798. Along with payment, the girl had to return to her mother's custody, with the warning that she take better care of her daughter's conduct.

54. Ibid., Exp. 48, April 16, 1798. The man faced no repercussions outside of the military court, and his lover faced no punishment other than a sentence to serve in an honorable house.

55. Ibid., April 17, 1798. Scardaville, "Crime and Urban Poor," 176. The court returned her to her brother's care, and then recommended that she move to the poorhouse.

56. AGN, Mexico, "Libro de Reos," Vol. 73, Exp. 47, June 20, 1795. See also Sánchez-Arcilla, "Delincuencia femenina," 131–33. Due to the fact that all were married, the culprits received no punishments except reuniting with their spouses.

57. AGN, Mexico, "Libro de Reos," Vol. 73, Exp. 47, June 29, 1795. The judge sentenced the women to a penitential punishment of serving in the Hospital de San Juan de Dios until such time as they could confess and take communion.

58. Ibid., July 15, 1795. Avila said that a man called Pepe el Fraile forced her into this life by raping her one morning in the Alameda Park, under the promise of marriage. The investigating officers could not find Avila's roommates nor her attacker and decided to give the girl twelve lashings and release her into the custody of the Spaniard sent by her parents.

59. Ibid., Exp. 46, September 28, 1795.

60. Ibid., Exp. 50, January 22, 1798.

61. Sánchez-Arcilla, "La delicuencia feminina," 134n106. See examples in AGN, Mexico, "Libros de Reos," Vol. 73, Exp. 50, November 17, 1798; Exp. 47, November 14 and July 23, 1795. For a gathering interpreted as "lenocinio," see Sánchez-Arcilla, "La delicuencia feminina," 118n63.

62. AGN, Mexico, "Libros de Reos," Vol. 73, Exp. 50, September 6, 1798, and Exp. 49, April 7, 1798.

63. Ibid., Exp. 50, November 26, 1798.

64. Ibid., May 15, 1798. Another situation where a woman hosted a couple is in Vol. 48, April 28, 1798, in this case involving a twenty-five-year-old single indigenous woman, a mulato coachman of the same age, and an older indigenous landlady. See also Sánchez-Arcilla, "La delicuencia feminina," 133–34.

65. AGN, Mexico, "Libro de Reos," Vol. 73, Exp. 50, March 7, 1798.

66. Ibid., March 12, 1798. On the other hand, when law enforcement passed by a scene of "spouse swapping" in progress, the magistrates' reactions suggest that they felt this particular lack of respect for monogamy went a little too far and deserved a response of judicially sanctioned violence. One evening in 1798, two couples decided to drink together in a rented room. One couple consisted of an indigenous tailor (age forty) and his india wife (over twenty-five years old), and the other was a mestizo baker (bizcochero) and his Spanish wife (ages unknown). All of these individuals were born and raised in Mexico City. The revelers left the door open while the older indigenous man and the Spanish woman dozed off to sleep. Around midnight, the mestizo man started having sex with the intoxicated indigenous woman, just at the very moment when a corporal passed the open door. Although the guard caught them in the act, none of the participants could remember anything, due to their alleged drunkenness. There was no way to enforce marital monogamy among this group because none of them had abandoned their partnerships—or had even left the room during the act of adultery. The confounded authorities decided that everyone deserved twenty-five lashes and set them all free. In both of the above cases, the criminal courts resorted to their typical punishments and desultory efforts to reorder the nonmonogamous pairings into conventional couples.

67. Glasco, "Constructing Mexico City," 34, 93–94.

68. Scardaville, "Crime and Urban Poor," 190n112.

69. Dabhoiwala, Origins of Sex, 70–71.

70. Kushner, Erotic Exchanges, 222–23. These statements assumed that transactional sex threatened the ideal male-led family by rejecting monogamous marriage or the status of honorable male guardians.

71. Scardaville, "Crime and Urban Poor," 178–80.

72. AGN, Mexico, "Libro de Reos," Vol. 73, Exp. 47, July 25, 1795.

73. Ibid., Exp. 50, January 31, 1798, and Exp. 49, January 3, 1798.

74. Scardaville, "Crime and Urban Poor," 206.

75. AGN, Mexico, "Libro de Reos," Vol. 73, Exp. 45, November 6, 1794.

76. Ibid., Exp. 50, August 19, 1798.

77. Ibid., October 25, 1798.

78. Ibid., Exp. 47, July 5, 1795.

79. Ibid., Exp. 50, May 9, 1798.

80. Ibid., Exp. 46, July 3, 1796.

81. Ibid., Exp. 46, April 11, 1796; Exp. 50, February 18, 1798; Exp. 50, October 27, 1798; and Exp. 50, January 8, 1798. In the February 18, 1798, case, the male lover changed his mind about the proposed marriage and instead went back to his master.

82. Sánchez-Arcilla, "Delicuencia feminina," 130n98.

83. Scardaville, "Crime and Urban Poor," 15. Scardaville oddly interprets this as an attempt to prevent almost certain female deaths on the dangerous streets. But it seems more likely these women were loitering in search of clients. As noted in his own data, hundreds of female food and pulque sellers survived by working on the streets nightly.

84. Sánchez-Arcilla, "La administracion de justicia," 360n128. Law enforcement began to seriously target vagrants for reform in the 1760s, in both Madrid and New Spain. Haslip-Viera, *Crime and Punishment,* 41–42.

85. Susan P. Conner, "Public Virtue and Public Women: Prostitution in Revolutionary Paris, 1793–1794," *Eighteenth-Century Studies* vol. 28, no. 2 (Winter, 1994–1995): 227. Meijide Pardo, "Mendicidad, vagancia, y prostitución," 571–72.

86. Meijide Pardo, "Mendicidad, vagancia, y prostitución," 366–67, 386, 411–12, 421, 481–82.

87. Ibid., 4–5, 158, 361, 428–29, 451–53.

88. Bailey Glasco, "A City in Disarray," 18, 20, 26, 37, 61–62, 204, 210, 213, 221, 232, 239.

89. Sánchez-Arcilla argues that *novohispano* reformers did not worry about vagrancy, in contrast to Spain: "Delicuencia femenina," 120n71; "La administracion de justicia," 359. For the historiography of vagrancy in Mexico City, see Hamman, "Eyeing Alameda Park," 166n1.

90. Sánchez-Arcilla, "La administracion de justicia," 362n130, 437; Scardaville, "Crime and Urban Poor," 10–11, 62.

91. Scardaville, "Justice by Paperwork," 1000n52, 1004n77. However, periodically in the 1790s, the authorities rounded up hundreds of vagrants to force them into military service. See Eva Maria Mehl, "Mexican Recruits and Vagrants in Late Eighteenth-Century Philippines: Empire, Social Order, and Bourbon Reforms in the Spanish Pacific World," *Hispanic American Historical Review* vol. 94, 4 (2014), 547–79.

92. Joan M. McDermott and Sarah Blackstone, "White Slavery Plays of the 1910s: Fear of Victimization and the Social Control of Sexuality," *Theatre History Studies* vol. 16 (1996): 145.

93. Jeffrey S. Adler, "Streetwalkers, Degraded Outcasts, and Good-for-Nothing Huzzies: Women and the Dangerous Class in Antebellum St. Louis," *Journal of Social History* vol. 25, 4 (1992): 737–44.

94. Scardaville, "Crime and Urban Poor," 181; Meijide Pardo, "Mendicidad, vagancia, y prostitución," 571–73.

95. AGN, Mexico, "Libro de Reos," Vol. 73, Exp. 47, June 30, 1795.

96. Ibid., March 5, 1795.

97. Ibid., Exp. 50, October 19, 1798. Although transvestism could theoretically incur a serious judicial reaction, in another case of a woman arrested for this offense, the court sentenced the cross-dresser to nothing more than an investigation of her life and customs. The patrol found the seventeen-year-old Spanish doncella Maria Robles Villaverde sitting on a bench outside the Coliseo Theater one night at 9:00 p.m. "dressed as a man" and took her into custody, but released her without any further punishment.

98. Sánchez-Arcilla, "La delincuencia femenina," 117, 147–49, 153; Scardaville, "Crime and Urban Poor," 60.

99. AGN, Mexico, "Libro de Reos," Vol. 73, Exp. 50, January 11, 1798.

100. Ibid., Exp. 45, August 8, September 17, September 30, October 6, October 21, October 23, November 4, November 22, December 1, December 4, and December 10, 1794; Exp. 46, January 16, June 20, July 23, August 15, 1796; Exp. 50, January 9, January 11, April 25, June 26, September 23, November 6, December 6, and December 7, 1798.

101. Ibid., Exp. 45, August 30, 1794.

102. Ibid., Exp. 50, November 17, 1798.

103. Ibid., December 10, 1798.

104. Ibid., Exp. 46, January 5, 1796, and July 6, 1796.

105. Ibid., Exp. 50, May 2, 1798, and December 12, 1798.

106. Ibid., Exp. 46, June 22 and July 23, 1796.

107. Meijide Pardo, "Mendicidad, vagancia, y prostitución," 358–59, 484.

108. AGN, Mexico, "Libro de Reos," Vol. 73, Exp. 46, January 16 and June 21, 1796; Exp. 50, January 9, April 7, April 25, June 24, December 4, December 6, 1798.

109. Ibid., Exp. 46, August 15, 1796.

110. Ibid., August 20, 1796.

111. Ibid., Exp. 50, May 1 and November 18, 1798.

112. Ibid., Exp. 48, June 20, 1798; and Exp. 50, November 12, 1798. In all of these cases, the soldiers never even gave their names because they did not fall under the jurisdiction of the arresting officers.

113. In four of these incidents, the women demonstrated a sense of professional self-care, in that they worked with a female companion of their own age. Ibid., Exp. 48, February 23, 1798; Exp. 45, September 14, 1794; Exp. 48, May 17, 1795; Exp. 50, March 7, 1798.

114. Ibid. Exp. 50, July 27, 1798. For other arrests involving public contact with soldiers, see Exp. 46, July 16, 1796; Exp. 47, June 15 and July 23, 1795; Exp. 49, May 7, 1798; Exp. 50, February 17, March 18, November 2, November 12, and December 29, 1798.

115. Ibid., Exp. 45, September 1, 1794.

CHATPER 6

1. AGN, Mexico, Corregidores Criminal, Caja 17B, Exp. 96, 1802, "Contra Mariana López Ortega, álias la sargenta," 28, 25, 37.

2. AGN, Mexico, Matrimonios, Vol. 217, Exp. 8, 1807, "Prueba dada por Jose Luciano Cisneros con María Josefa Rivera," 9 fojas.

3. AGN, Mexico, Acordada Caja 4778, Exp. 83, 1810, "Denuncia de doña María Dolores Quiñones contra el teniente de la Acordada Antonio Montes por haber mantenido en su casa un mujer pública en calidad de comadre y otros irregulares procedimientos," 1–6.

4. AGN, Mexico, Indiferente Virreinal, Criminal Caja 1151, Exp. 3, 1816.

5. AGN, Mexico, 1802, "Expediente seguido por don Guillermo José Huidobro sobre disenso al matrimonio q intenta contraer su hermano don Ramón Huidobro con Petra Colosia," 1–18. A similar case comes from the Isla de Carmen, dated 1809 to 1810. See AGN, Mexico, Matrimonios 3852, Caja 1, 1809–1810, "Expediente que expresa el diseño de don Felipe Montero en el matrimonio que pretende contraer su hijo, José María Montero con

María de la Concepción Ximénez, alias la diabla, señalada como prostituta, ramera, y mujer publica," 1–86. In this case, the familial objection raised issues of sexual reputation, although the more relevant complaint was the potential bride's race. The authorities ignored the allegations regarding the woman's alleged prostitution and focused on the plebeian and racially mixed family of the husband. This couple also already had two illegitimate children.

6. "Expediente seguido por don Guillermo José Huidobro," 5–18. Despite the fact that Don Ramon's family had a number of complaints against Doña Petra, her potential spouse and his supporters felt able to defend her good reputation. Don Ramon's sister confirmed that her potential sister-in-law had a child with a married soldier who happened to be her brother's close friend. She also reported that all of the members of this love triangle had fled justice after a violent incident at a fandango held at a house run by sisters known as Las Maniteras. The brother raised another objection: that Doña Petra's stepfather was a mulatto and had received a sentence of public shaming for bigamy. This meant that Doña Petra's mother had an illegitimate child (since her marriage did not exist if her second husband were already married); therefore, in the brother's opinion, both daughter and mother were "libidinous . . . public whores [rameras públicas]." As these issues with Doña Petra's character piled up, all of the witnesses in favor of the marriage dismissed the incidents as just a passing "weakness [fragilidad]." In the case of the stepfather's bigamy, the couple's supporters argued that they had no reflection on Doña Petra's character as an upstanding Spanish doña. Although these dismissals of the objections to this marriage came from distinguished professionals, Don Ramon's brother responded that he had decided to change his last name so that he would have no affiliation with Doña Petra.

7. AGN, Mexico, Juzgados especiales, Serie Libros y expedientes diversos, Cuadernos sueltos, Caja 97, Exp. 7, 1813, "Certificación por medio de la cual se hace constar que ni María Josefa Romana Marquina, ni Petra Arellano son ladronas," 1–3.

8. Ibid., 2.

9. "Contra Mariana López Ortega, álias la sargenta," 1–48. This name is used on 7.

10. Elizabeth Salas, *Soldaderas in the Mexican Military: Myth and History* (Austin: University of Texas Press, 1990), 25–28, emphasizes the actual military participation of particular heroic women in the Independence Era, although the domestic services that women provided also represent an important and necessary facet of supporting the military.

11. Lyle N. McAlister, "The Reorganization of the Army in New Spain: 1763–1766," *Hispanic American Historical Review* vol. 33, 1 (1953): 28–29.

12. Jorge Dominguez, "International War and Government Militarization: The Military—A Case Study," in *Rank and Privilege: The Military and Society in Latin America*, ed. Linda Alexander Rodríguez (Oxford: Scholarly Resources, 1994), 2–3.

13. Christon I. Archer, *The Army in Bourbon Mexico, 1760–1810* (Albuquerque: University of New Mexico Press, 1977), 22–23, 110–11.

14. AGN, Mexico, Reales Cedulas Originales, 4237, vol. 169, 1798.

15. Van Young gives an example of a forty-year-old woman who hosted and partnered with a string of rebels at her home between 1810 and 1816. Witnesses called her a drunk, lascivious prostitute, and the viceregal authorities punished her with two years' recogimiento in Guadalajara. *The Other Rebellion*, 97–98. In the field, the insurgents often traveled to battles with their families, as well as unmarried women companions; 95–96.

16. "Contra Mariana López Ortega, álias la sargenta." La Sargenta gave these basic biographic facts on 8.

17. Ibid., 10.

18. Ibid.,22.

19. Ibid.,

20. Ibid., 7–8, 15, 43–48.

21. Ibid., 22, 29.

22. Ibid., 34.

23. Ibid., 10, 21, 34–35.

24. Ibid., 21–22, 35.

25. Ibid., 28.

26. López Ortega's domestic labors, which may or may not have had a sexual facet, done for men who visited her at various hours of the night and day in her home, sound very similar to the "Malaya form" of prostitution practiced about a century later in colonial Nairobi. Luise White, using oral accounts from the women themselves, explains that Malaya practitioners in early-twentieth-century Nairobi provided "an extensive set of domestic services," including food, baths, company, conversation, and breakfast for men who knocked on their doors and then spent the night in their homes. Relatively prosperous salary-earning African men craved this inclusive range of homely comforts, so the women kept their rooms clean and ready for visitors. They hospitably offered tea and other amenities to earn the men's extra pennies and loyalty as steady clientele. Malaya women never solicited in public but waited in their rooms for these men to appear. In this way they avoided arrest for solicitation on the street. Although they risked secret acts of violence or men's refusal to pay behind their closed doors, they also had the choice of rejecting potential clients by not answering their knocks. Malaya women integrated themselves in their neighborhoods with the intention of staying, unlike the rural women working in Nairobi who wanted to earn money fast before returning to their family homes. Malaya women tried to avoid fights with neighbors and sat home quietly like wives or widows, waiting for their visitors. Women who took up the Malaya form of sex for sale did not have ties to family outside of the city and sought to establish themselves as a new urban petty bourgeoisie. White, *Comforts of Home,* 14–16, 56–67. Due to the elusiveness of historical sources in the voices of sex workers themselves, White's book has great utility for hearing the extreme practicality of these women's words. The women that White interviewed stressed practicalities, interactions with their friends and neighbors, concerns about their rented rooms, and making money, not moral concerns. In the colonial system White discusses, soliciting was illegal, but prostitution was not.

27. "Contra Mariana López Ortega, álias la sargenta," 11.

28. Ibid., 14–15.

29. Ibid., 19.

30. Ibid., 9.

31. Ibid., 28, 37.

32. Ibid., 19, 21, 30.

33. Ibid., 35.

34. Ibid., 27.

35. See Tatiana Seijas, *Asian Slaves in Colonial Mexico: From Chinos to Indians* (New York: Cambridge University Press, 2014), for the history of Filipinos in New Spain.

36. "Contra Mariana López Ortega, álias la sargenta," 2, 9.

37. Ibid., 1–6, 14.

38. Ibid., 2, 4–5, 6, 8, 13, 20.

39. Ibid., 20.

40. Ibid., 4, 14, 33.

41. *Novísima Recopilación*, Libro 21, Titulo 25, ley 3. The five words had been picked out as the most slanderous and offensive by a royal fuero in 1380 and reiterated in 1566 by Philip II, with punishment of a fine for their use. In 1788, with even greater concern for public scandal and disruptions, Carlos III again repeated the illegality of these words.

42. "Contra Mariana López Ortega, álias la sargenta," 32–33.

43. Ibid., 30–32.

44. Scardaville, "Crime and Urban Poor," 67–68, 88–89.

45. "Contra Mariana López Ortega, álias la sargenta," 4; for class breakdown, see Arrom, *Women of Mexico City*, 221.

46. "Contra Mariana López Ortega, álias la sargenta," 37.

47. Ibid., 6.

48. Ibid.,

49. Ibid., 22–26.

50. Ibid., 42.

51. Ibid., 43–49.

52. AGN, Mexico, Indiferente Virreinal, Caja 4973, Exp. 39, 1815, 1–4.

53. Certain neighborhoods were known for pulquerías activities of this kind and were sometimes viewed as being a potential source of political revolt. See Van Young, *The Other Rebellion*, 341.

54. AGN, Mexico, Indiferente Virreinal, Policia y Empedrados, Caja 5443, Exp. 29, 1819, 1–3.

55. Scardaville, "Crime and Urban Poor," 179.

56. AGN, Mexico, Criminal, Vol. 89, Exp. 1, and Criminal, Vol. 84, Exps. 13 and 14. "Delito: tener un prostíbulo, ejercer la prostitución y prostituir a jóvenes menores de catorce años; acusadas: María Manuela González Castrejón y su hija Francisca." Although the daughter was involved, this was not a family brothel, according to surviving evidence.

57. Ana Patricia Quiroz Sandoval, "El Sacerdote, el Alcalde y el Testigo: Tres formas de juzgar el fenómeno de la prostitución en la Ciudad de México (1777–1818)" (thesis, Universidad Nacional Autónoma de Mexico, 2007), 41–42, 52, 56–57, 60, 66–67.

58. Sánchez-Arcilla, "La delincuencia feminina," 148–49. The accused conveniently forgot this previous arrest in her efforts to strengthen her reputation. AGN, Mexico, Criminal, Vol. 89, "Contra María Manuela González Castrejón por tener un prostíbulo, ejercer la prostitución y prostituir a jóvenes menores de 14 años," 49.

59. AGN, Mexico, Criminal, Vol. 89, "Por tener un prostíbulo," 1–62, summary of the 1808 trial on 2–3.

60. AGN, Mexico, Criminal, Vol. 84, "Prueba dada por Manuela Castrejón González en la causa q[ok?] se le ha formado por lenocinio,"49.

61. AGN, Mexico, Criminal, Vol. 89, "Contra María Manuela Castrejón por tener un prostíbulo," 3. Sending Riojano to her aunts did not work out as a useful solution in terms of protecting the girl from sexual immorality. The authorities quickly discovered that the

young girl's aunts also lived in sin with their lovers. The judges attempted to rectify their error with a stricter seclusion but apparently released the madam to her own devices.

62. Ibid.,Castrejón 5–8. A "very rude and proud" deaf and crippled woman apparently managed one of the alleged brothels, and González Castrejón operated the other one.

63. Atondo, *Amor Venal*, 301–2. AGN, Mexico, Criminal 89, "Contra María Manuela Castrejón por tener un prostíbulo," 8–18.

64. AGN, Mexico, Criminal, Vol. 89, "Contra María Manuela Castrejón por tener un prostíbulo," 12–14, 16–18, 31–36.

65. Clare A. Lyons, *Sex among the Rabble: An Intimate History of Gender and Power in the Age of Revolution, Philadelphia, 1730–1830* (Chapel Hill: University of North Carolina Press, 2006), 315–17, 332.

66. AGN, Mexico, Criminal, Vol. 89, "Contra María Manuela Castrejón por tener un prostíbulo," 19–20.

67. Ibid., Castrejón 48–49.

68. AGN, Mexico, Criminales 84, Exp. 14, "Prueba dada . . .," 210–17.

69. Kathryn Norberg, "In Her Own Words: An Eighteenth-Century Madam Tells Her Story," in *Prostitution and Eighteenth-Century Culture: Sex, Commerce, and Morality*, ed. Ann Lewis (London: Pickering & Chatto, 2012), 39.

70. Kushner, *Erotic Exchanges*, 48, 67, 156–57.

71. AGN, Mexico, Criminal, Vol. 89, "Contra María Manuela Castrejón por tener un prostíbulo," 3.

72. Ibid.,Castrejón 48.

73. Germeten, *Violent Delights*, 144–65.

74. AGN, Mexico, Criminal, Vol. 89, "Contra María Manuela Castrejón por tener un prostíbulo," 36–37.

75. Ibid.,Castrejón 7–8.

76. Statements regarding physical beauty rarely appear in archival documents in Spanish America, even when the individual's appearance directly related to the issue under discussion, such as recording a debatable race label, searching for or classifying a slave or criminal, or documenting someone's approved travel to the Indies. Joanne Rappaport, *The Disappearing Mestizo: Configuring Difference in the Colonial New Kingdom of Granada* (Durham, NC: Duke University Press, 2014), 171–85, 198–202.

77. AGN, Mexico, Criminal, Vol. 89, "Contra María Manuela Castrejón por tener un prostíbulo," 21–22.

78. Ibid.,Castrejón 21–22. María Hilaría and Clara specified that González Castrejón had tried to lure them into working for her with luxurious clothes like those worn by her daughter Francisca.

79. Ibid.,Castrejón 19.

80. Ibid.,Castrejón 25.

81. Ibid.,Castrejón 39. The daughter explained that the fact that they did not hide or move after receiving the warning proved they were innocent.

82. AGN, Mexico, Criminales 84, Exp. 14, "Prueba dada . . .," 213–14; and AGN, Mexico, Criminal, Vol. 89, "Contra María Manuela Castrejón por tener un prostíbulo," 15.

83. AGN, Mexico, Criminales 84, Exp. 14, "Prueba dada . . .," 209–10.

84. Ibid., 211.

85. Ibid., 212–14.

86. Ibid., 219, 226, 232. González Castrejón's fifteen-year-old daughter Francisca was judged as guilty of prostitution, a rare example of this specific charge. The judge decreed that she had to remain in an honorable house for a short time, but she fled with her belongings quite soon after the sentencing. The court mentioned putting her in her father's care, but he apparently did not satisfy requirements for respectable supervision. AGN, Mexico, Criminal, Vol. 89, "Contra María Manuela Castrejón por tener un prostíbulo," 55–57.

CHAPTER 7

1. AGN, Mexico, Civil 9, Caja 2316, 1801–1802, Exps. 11 and 12, "Denuncia que hace doña María Dolores Rodríguez contra su hermana dona Bartola Rodríguez," 1–124, quote from 41 and 45. The pagination continues through both *expedientes*. I give all of the credit to Linda Arnold for finding this case for me due to her meticulous AGN cataloguing efforts, without which this case would have remained invisible to historians.

2. Ibid., 1–2. Although the authorities put full faith in Rodríguez's denunciation of her older sister, a few complications arose. First, Vivar's husband was Don Ermengildo de Alcocer, a squadron corporal based in the viceregal seat *(cabo del regimiento del comercio)*. This meant that the alcalde forwarded Rodríguez's complaint to the military court, overseen by the Sergeant Major/Lieutenant Colonel Don Manuel Hermoso. Second, the sisters, on numerous occasions, entertained four friars in their home brothel. Due to their protected legal status, the documents do not reveal the friars' names or question them. Last, the ubiquity of the military almost prevented Rodríguez's alleged deflowerer from testifying. His father, an administrator in the royal gunpowder factory, tried to prevent the questioning, but the court mocked his "prideful" claims and denied his request. All of these factors highlight how the colonial courts could function to shelter certain elite men from involvement in potentially scandalous litigation.

3. Ibid., 54–57. The adjudicating military court questioned dozens of witnesses, but the most definitive evidence against Vivar came from the original denunciation by Rodríguez and the testimony of her young nephew, who lived with his aunts, as quoted above. The witnesses, drawn from businesses nearby, including a vinatería, a peanut shop, and a shoemaking workshop, either knew that friars and other men frequently visited or, in the case of the indigenous shoemakers, said that they were too busy to pay any attention to the neighborhood. Exp. 12 goes over the names of the *"personas reservadas,"* i.e., the friars, 119–24.

4. Of course, as noted since chapter 1, alcahuetas and rufianes received the ire of most authority figures from the king on down to the archbishop of Mexico, so they were ripe for further condemnation. My interpretation of the evidence in this chapter is inspired by the idea that the "archive becomes legible as such through its facilitation of systems and practices that press sexuality and gender into some form of signification (usually language)." See Daniel Marshall, Kevin P. Murphy, and Zeb Tortorici, "Queering Archives: Historical Unravelings," *Radical History Review* 120 (2014): 1–11, quote on 4.

5. Generalizing women as nothing more than economic pawns is the hallmark of older work on "prostitution." See Sue Gronewold, *Beautiful Merchandise: Prostitution in China, 1860–1936* (New York: Haworth Press, 1985), 3.

6. See Tortorici, "Contra natura," 155–60, 267, on the typical court-performance formulations of coercion and passivity and their ambiguity.

7. Voekel, *Alone before God,* 2–3, suggests that the late viceregal era initiated a trend of focusing on individualism as opposed to corporate (or perhaps family) cooperation.

8. Certain kinds of questions elicit results that the investigators expect, confirming their prejudices. See recent examples in Bill McCarthy, Cecilia Benoit, and Mikael Jansson, "Sex Work: A Comparative Study," *Archives of Sexual Behavior* vol. 43, 7 (2014): 1–7 (balanced); and the far more judgmental Mh Kong, "Material Girls: Sexual Perceptions of Korean Teenage Girls Who Have Experienced 'Compensated Dates,'" *Asian Journal of Women's Studies* 9, no. 2 (2003): 67–94. Although Perry does much more than her title suggests, see "Deviant Insiders," 138–41.

9. Several studies highlight the familial nature of sex work. Prieur discusses how young men take up transgender and gay prostitution to benefit their family's budget and even reintegrate themselves within the domestic context. Some families view these actions with humor and protectiveness. See Prieur, *Mema's House,* 53, 75, 96; White, *Comforts of Home,* 12–15, 20, 35, 38–39, 49–50,114–15. For example, in colonial Nairobi, the most aggressive, loud, public streetwalkers, known as *watembizi,* were viewed as the most dutiful daughters among other urban sex workers because they came to the city to make money as quickly as possible for their rural families. As fortunes based on land and livestock became precarious due in part to British colonial rule, African families found that their daughters could raise more fast money and help their families effectively with the cash they made by prostitution. Marriage, in contrast, took their profitable labor away from their natal families, but sex work helped these families keep their land and livestock. Similar to migrant women in twenty-first–century Spain, these African daughters did not worry about their wealth or reputation in the city but concerned themselves with fulfilling their duties in their home villages. Tambe praises White for her effective "unsettling" of the divide between "intimate family relations and commercial sexual relations." See "Brothels as Families," 220, 234; Laura Oso Casas, "Money, Sex, Love, and the Family: Economic and Affective Strategies of Latin American Sex Workers in Spain," *Journal of Ethnic and Migration Studies* 36, 1 (2010): 47–54. The women discussed completely avoided "pimps," clearly understanding that they needed to keep all of their money for their own goals. Sentiment could not tempt them to waste money on men; duty bound them to save it for their families. In more recent decades, Latin American women have traveled to Spain, seeking the quickest possible method for earning thousands of euros either to send home or to fund their families' immigration. Both African and Latin American migrant sex workers, as heads of household and breadwinners for their distant families, avoided entangling relationships or wasting any of their capital where they worked and quickly returned home to carry out their family obligations. While operating within traditional family hierarchies, these women also made effective economic and personal choices to benefit those who mattered most in their lives. While these examples extend into far-flung regions and modern times, more recent sex work as a family economic-survival strategy helps clarify the motivations of parents and the experiences of children in early-nineteenth-century New Spain. Pandering one's children could actually help hold the family together in the most difficult conditions of poverty and war, despite the challenge it posed to traditional gender and parental roles. Hunter, "Materiality of Everyday Sex," 112, 116.

10. Ashwini Tambe, "Brothels as Families: Reflections on the History of Bombay's 1 Kothas," *International Feminist Journal of Politics* vol. 8, 2 (2006): 222.

11. As a result of the divergent sexual histories within marriages, both wives and husbands sought sexual liaisons outside the marital bed. Germeten, *Violent Delights,* 34; and for further discussion of love, marriage, and adultery, see chapters 2, 3, 5, 10, 11, and conclusion.

12. Hunter, "Materiality of Everyday Sex," 108.

13. Tambe, "Brothels as Families," notes how "rescue" efforts that ignored the family did not work, resulting in women returning to the influence of those who had placed them in the brothel or pandered them.

14. Ibid., 221, 223. Tambe's article suggests a middle path between feminist theory that disconnects brothels from family ties and sex radical feminism that portrays sex work as "disembodied individualism": liberating or challenging female passivity. See 220–24, 234.

15. This is in line with the effectiveness of *mala vida* claims for divorce, the idea that women had church approval to receive an ecclesiastical divorce from men who did not provide for them. Richard Boyer, "Women, la Mala Vida, and the Politics of Marriage," 252–86.

16. AGN, Mexico, Indiferente Virreinal, Caja-Exp.: 3399-030, Criminal, 1799, "Causa criminal seguida contra Juana Munguia y María Rafaela Navarro, por el crimen de Lenonas."

17. Ibid., 3–4.

18. Ibid., 11–12.

19. Ibid., 4.

20. Ibid., 5.

21. The surviving documentation does not record Don Pedro's view on his visits or his intentions. The lieutenant avoided giving an official statement, although the soldier Guerrero did suggest that many of the resident military men knew of and mocked Munguia's machinations.

22. "Contra Juana Munguia," 7–8.

23. Ibid., 6.

24. Ibid., 15–16.

25. No evidence that I have found in my research for this book displays men as having an intense, provable erotic interest in women far below their social status—an interesting contradiction to Victorian fetishizing of working-class women. See Anne McClintock, *Imperial Leather: Race, Gender, and Sexuality in the Colonial Conquest* (New York: Routledge, 1995), 75–84.

26. AGN, Mexico, Criminal, Caja 28B, Exp. 112, "Adulterio, prostitución e incitación a la prostitución," 1798.

27. Ibid., 1–2.

28. Ibid., 3–6.

29. Ibid., 8.

30. AHM, Morelia, Justicia, Caja 184, Exp. 34, 1792, "Manuel Gaspar Ramírez indio del barrio de San Pedro de esta ciudad contra María Gertrudis Romualdo y su madre Guadalupe Carrasco por la vida escándalos que lleva con consentimiento de la madre y por haber agredido Romualda a su hijo, ante juez el señor alcalde de 2° voto," 1–12.

31. Ibid., 5, 7, 10.

32. Ibid., 6.

33. AGN, Mexico, Indiferente Virreinal, Caja-Exp.: 1425-024, 1814, "Expediente criminal contra el soldado Domingo Ximénez por mantener un lupanar, en donde prostituía a su mujer y a su hija política," 1–99. Within the case, the court said Don Domingo was accused of lenocinio, 38.

34. This case proves again, as stated by Gauderman in her discussion of adultery and spousal abuse, that most individuals in this society (including men) understood what was legal and illegal. In the latter case, women could take their complaints to court with valid hopes for judicial retribution. Abuse of women was not "male prerogative" but "illegal acts." *Women's Lives,* 58.

35. "Contra Domingo Ximénez," 1–2.

36. "Introduction," in *Prostitution in Eighteenth-Century Culture,* 11.

37. "Contra Domingo Ximénez," 3.

38. Ibid., 4–5.

39. Ibid., 5.

40. Sverre Molland, "The Trafficking of Scarce Elite Commodities: Social Change and Commodification of Virginity along the Mekong," *Asia Pacific Journal of Anthropology* 12, 2 (2011): 132–33, explains that perceived scarcity, symbolic cultural value, and its presumed binary quality increase the value of virginity, although he argues against a defined, preexisting market for all examples of sold virginity. For another example of allegedly deceptive virginity in Mexico City, see Penyak, "Criminal Sexuality," 69.

41. "Contra Domingo Ximénez," 87, 93.

42. Sex work can fund a sibling's education. See Prieur, *Mema's House,* 51.

43. "Contra Domingo Ximénez," 56.

44. Ibid., 7.

45. Ibid., 7–8.

46. Modern sex workers also express disgust with their families when they perceive that they have wasted the hard-earned money on gambling. This can be the motivation to quit working in a filial context and turn to self-enriching, independent strategies. See Yu Ding and Petula Sik Ying Ho, "Sex Work in China's Pearl River Delta," 51–52.

47. "Contra Domingo Ximénez," 10–11.

48. Ibid., 39–40.

49. Ibid.

50. Clearly stated consent was required for both spouses in the marriage ceremony, otherwise one of them had effective grounds for an annulment. Seed, *To Love, Honor, and Obey,* 32–35, 89.

51. "Contra Domingo Ximénez," 40–41.

52. The mother confirmed this version—that they had lied about Doña María de Jesus's virginity. Ibid., 23. But then Doña María Sanchez said that Don Joaquín was the deflowerer, which doesn't make sense in terms of her accusations of rape on the part of Don Domingo. While the rape seems real, this proves that the mother operated in a confusing world of lies and deceptions.

53. Ibid., 21–23.

54. Ibid., 14–15, 27.

55. Ibid., 13.

56. Ibid., 29–30.

57. Ibid., 56–57.

58. Ibid., 16–17.

59. Ibid., 26–27.

60. Ibid., 84–85.

61. Ibid., 32.

62. Ibid., 31–34.

63. Ibid., 24–25.

64. Ibid., 24–26.

65. Ibid., 26–27.

66. Ibid., 83.

67. Ibid., 96–97.

68. Ibid., 3.

69. Ibid., 14.

70. Molland, "The Trafficking of Scarce Elite Commodities," 139.

71. "Contra Domingo Ximénez," 76–78.

72. Ibid., 43–44.

73. Ibid., Petition from Don Domingo dated October 4, 1814, inserted between pages 24 and 25.

74. Ibid., 51–55.

75. William H. Hinrichs, *The Invention of the Sequel: Expanding Prose Fiction in Early Modern Spain* (Woodbridge, Ontario: Tamesis, 2011), 42–43.

76. Germeten, *Violent Delights*, 19–30; and Allyson Poska, *Women and Authority in Early Modern Spain: The Peasants of Galicia* (New York: Oxford University Press, 2005). For the idea of monetized virginity, see Molland, "The Trafficking of Scarce Elite Commodities," 134–35.

77. Kushner, *Erotic Exchanges*, 76–77, 88. Allegedly, one Mexican mother held a raffle for her daughter's virginity in late-nineteenth-century Mexico. See Bliss, *Compromised Positions*, 49.

78. In Thailand, sex-work scholarship has highlighted the value of familial reciprocity as a more powerful factor in holding families together than concerns about sexual transgression. Molland, "The Trafficking of Scarce Elite Commodities," 137–40.

79. Heather Montgomery, "Child Prostitution as Filial Duty?: The Morality of Child-Rearing in a Slum Community in Thailand," *Journal of Moral Education* vol. 43, 2 (2014): 169–70.

80. Montgomery, "Child Prostitution as Filial Duty," 173–78; Margorie A. Muecke, "Mothers Sold Food, Daughter Sells Her Body: The Cultural Continuity of Prostitution," *Social Science & Medicine* vol. 35, 7 (1992): 891, 897. Outsiders, who understand childrearing from a privileged, Western perspective, not surprisingly view underage sex work, when done as a family economic-survival strategy, as an egregious act of coerced rape and abuse and, of course, as a serious crime. But these acts occur in a particular context that differs radically from our own. No discussion of the agency of sex workers should be thought to diminish the suffering of underage rape victims by men who visit their countries as sex tourists, but one still needs to contextualize these occupations within the values of their societies. Children involved in sex work, in their interviews with researchers, certainly express disgust for how they supplement their families' incomes. But within some contexts,

children and young people who provide for their families in this way assert that they are fulfilling their roles as good, loyal offspring. Sex workers help their parents rebuild their homes and verbalize their pride in these responsible acts, while deriding siblings who do not send back money as "bad children," even if those family members have far more prestigious jobs. Sex workers can also decide to funnel their money into educating a younger sibling in preparation for another career. Their income can even fund religious institutions.

81. Stoler, *Along the Archival Grain*, 252; Marshall, Murphy, and Tortorici, "Queering Archives: Historical Unravelings," 1, 5.

CONCLUSION

1. Federico Gamboa, *Santa: A Novel of Mexico City*, ed. and trans. John Charles Chasteen (Chapel Hill: University of North Carolina Press, 2010), 148, 152.

2. For explorations of this term and its significance, as well as a call for more historicity in sex-worker studies, see Ronald Weitzer, "New Directions on Research in Prostitution," *Crime, Law & Social Change* 43. 4 (2005): 211–35.

3. Kelleher, *Measure of a Woman*, 107.

4. Poska, *Women and Authority in Early Modern Spain*, 75–110, explores how financial goals affected the sexual and judicial actions of peasant women in Spain.

5. Jean Louis Guereña, "Médicos y Prostitución: Un Proyecto de Reglamentación de la Prostitución en 1809: La Exposición de Antonio Cibat, 1771–1811," *Medicina e Historia* vol. 71 (1998): 14–16.

6. Jean Louis Guereña, "Prostitution and the Origins of the Governmental Regulatory System in Nineteenth-Century Spain: The Plans of the Trienio Liberal, 1820–1823," *Journal of the History of Sexuality* vol. 17, 2 (2008): 217–19, 222–23, 229. Despite these general health complaints for soldiers who visited prostitutes, by 1808, Guereña notes, condoms had definitely appeared in Spain.

7. Ibid., 216; Vasquez García and Moreno Mengíbar, *Poder y Prostitución en Sevilla*, Tomo II, 35.

8. Harsin, *Policing Prostitution*, 6, 80–87, 128, 312; Alain Corbin, "Commercial Sexuality in Nineteenth-Century France: A System of Images and Regulations," in *The Making of the Modern Body: Sexuality and Society in the Nineteenth Century*, ed. Catherine Gallagher and Thomas Laqueur (Los Angeles and Berkeley: University of California Press, 1987), 209–19.

9. See Nacif Mina, *La Policía*. On nineteenth-century prostitution in Spanish America, see José Rodolfo Anaya Larios, *Apuntes para la Historia de la Prostitución in Querétaro: un acercamiento histórico-literario* (Querétaro, Mexico: Universidad Autónoma de Querétaro, Facultad de Filosofía, 2010); Álvaro Góngora Escobedo, *La prostitución en Santiago, 1813–1931: Visión de las elites* (Santiago de Chile: Editorial Universitaria, 1994); and Aida Martínez Carreño, "De la moral pública a la vida privada, 1820–1920," in *Placer, dinero, y pecado*, ed. Martínez and Rodríguez, 129–49.

10. Bliss, *Compromised Positions*, 2–3, 27–32, 46.

11. Bliss's *Compromised Positions* stresses the difficulties of creating a Revolutionary approach to sex work within a male-dominant society. She notes that listening to reformers biases a scholar's angle but believes that there is some "real" voice to find (20), while acknowledging that all texts fit within a political conversation (1–7). But when it comes to

the scandalous tales of Porfirian excess, she remains seduced by politically motivated exposés. This continues to seduce readers into believing exactly what the late-nineteenth- and early-twentieth-century journalists, scientists, and reformers want us to believe about men, women, and sex (24–81). See Sloan, *Runaway Daughters*, 34–35, 109–10, 112, 120–22 for an acknowledgment of the fictional nature of these tales.

12. Guy, *Sex and Danger*, 28, 38–50, 133.

13. Levine, *Prostitution, Race, and Politics*, 70.

14. Dabhoiwala, *The Origins of Sex*, 74, 122; Catherine Lee, *Policing Prostitution, 1856–1886: Deviance, Surveillance and Morality* (London: Pickering & Chatto, 2013), 41, 110, 114.

15. Judith Walkowitz, *Prostitution and Victorian Society: Women, Class, and the State* (Cambridge[UK?]: Cambridge University Press, 1982); and Judith Walkowitz, *City of Dreadful Delight: Narratives of Sexual Danger in Late Victorian London* (Chicago: University of Chicago Press, 1992), 213–14.

16. Levine, *Prostitution, Race, and Politics*, 145–75.

17. A vision perfected in Theodore Dreiser, *Sister Carrie* (New York: Doubleday, 1900). We might like to think that we have complicated our attitudes toward women over time, but the idea of the "fallen" woman remains at the heart of "rescuing" sex workers.

> The view of prostitutes as pathological deviants and victims of feeblemindedness held by social workers in the 1950s continues to influence much of contemporary social work efforts with this population today. . . . Many of the beliefs and values that shaped early social work practice with fallen women continue to inform contemporary social work practice with women in the sex industry.

Stephanie Wahab, "'For Their Own Good?': Sex Work, Social Control and Social Workers: A Historical Perspective," *Journal of Sociology and Social Welfare* vol. XXIX, no. 4 (December 2002): 39–57, quote on 54. See also Laura S. Abrams and Laura Curran, "Wayward Girls and Virtuous Women: Social Workers and Female Juvenile Delinquency in the Progressive Era," *AFFILIA* vol. 15, no. 1 (Spring 2000): 49–64. This article emphasizes how social work perpetuated the criminalization of women for their sexuality:

> By advocating for the legal protection of girls, the social reformers ended up punishing them for deviating from white, middle-class standards of appropriate female behavior. . . . In the context of the child-saving movement, the social reformers helped to implement harsh forms of social control over working-class girls' transgressions of conventional gender expectations (59).

18. An enormous historiography deals with transactional sex in the United States, summed up in Gilfoyle, "Prostitution in the Archives." For the combined effects of zoning and racism, see Tong, *Unsubmissive Women*, 111–18; Blair, *I've Got to Make My Livin'*, 146; Barbara Antoniazzi, *The Wayward Woman: Progressivism, Prostitution and Performance in the United States, 1888–1917* (Madison, WI: Fairleigh Dickinson University Press, 2014), 106. For the results of zoning in Colorado, see Nicholas Ryan Gunvaldson, "Crimson Streets and Violent Bodies: Identity, Physicality, and the Twilight of Colorado's Vice Districts" (MA thesis, Colorado State University, 2015).

19. White, *Comforts of Home*, 5. Some settings, such as Tokugawa, Japan, appear to support the denial of agency: "Amy Stanley's sobering reassessment of Tokugawa history offers

a perspective on commercialization from the standpoint of women who became commodities, even as they were demonized for supposedly acting as free agents." See Sommer, "Foreword," in Amy Stanley, *Selling Women: Prostitution, Markets, and the Household in Early Modern Japan* (Berkeley: University of California Press, 2012), xvi. The idea of sexual stigma, of course, had very different implications in Japan, so it is still possible to complicate this history, as Stanley does in her book.

20. Regina G. Kunzel, *Fallen Women, Problem Girls: Unmarried Mothers and the Professionalization of Social Work, 1890–1945* (New Haven, CT: Yale University Press, 1993), 19–23, quote on 21. See also Levine, *Prostitution, Race, and Politics*, 240–50.

21. Bliss, *Compromised Positions*, 201–5.

22. Katsulis, *Sex Work and the City*, xi, 3, 12–15, 82. Prieur, *Mema's House*, also presents a complex tale of more recent sex work in Mexico.

23. Adanna Mgbako, *To Live Freely in This World*, 24. For in-depth studies of recent migration and sex work, see Laura Maria Agustín, *Sex at the Margins: Migration, Labour Markets, and the Rescue Industry* (New York: Palgrave Macmillan, 2007); and Denise Brennan, *What's Love Got To Do with It?: Transnational Desires and Sex Tourism in the Dominican Republic* (Durham, NC: Duke University Press, 2004).

24. Donna Guy, *Sex and Danger in Buenos Aires: Prostitution, Family, and Nation in Argentina* (Lincoln: University of Nebraska Press, 1991), 7, 73. Guy explains the various races, religions, and nationalities that became villains in the "white slavery" scare. Eastern European Jews received the most censure as procurers and procuresses.

25. Benson Tong, *Unsubmissive Women: Chinese Prostitutes in Nineteenth-Century San Francisco* (Norman: University of Oklahoma Press, 1994), 197.

26. White, *Comforts of Home*, 11, 18.

27. Adanna Mgbako, *To Live Freely in This World*, 29–32. The leading scholar on nineteenth- and twentieth-century global prostitution states, "In many areas of the world, prostitution . . . has provided women with a better living than many of the other employment options open to them." Philippa Levine, *Prostitution, Race, and Politics: Policing Venereal Disease in the British Empire* (New York: Routledge, 2003), 177. Levine's book stresses that British imperialists, with sweeping racism, denied the agency and humanity of only certain nonwhite prostitutes. A late-twentieth-century sociologist noted that antiprostitution laws have "criminalized . . . [youths'] survival strategies." Meda Chesney-Lind, *The Female Offender: Girls, Women, and Crime* (Thousand Oaks, CA: Sage Publications, 1997), 28. Chesney-Lind also provides an overview of how U.S. courts continued to criminalize girls by targeting their sexual behavior as crimes against "morality" well into the 1970s. See 60–68.

28. Adanna Mgbako, *To Live Freely in this World*, 30.

29. Levine, *Prostitution, Race, and Politics*, 220–22.

30. On the "sex wars" of the 1980s and 1990s, see Melinda Chateauvert, *Sex Workers Unite: A History of the Movement from Stonewall to Slutwalk* (Boston: Beacon, 2014); Lisa Duggan and Nan D. Hunter, *Sex Wars: Sexual Dissent and Political Culture* (New York: Routledge, 1995). Regarding historians' "restless discipline of context," see Kenneth Mills, William B. Taylor, and Sandra Lauderdale Graham, *Colonial Latin America: A Documentary History* (Lanham, MD, and Boulder, CO: Scholarly Resources, 2002), xxii, citing E. P. Thompson.

31. Gira Grant, *Playing the Whore*, 19.

BIBLIOGRAPHY

ARCHIVES

Archivo General de Indias, Seville, Spain

Archivo General de la Nación, Mexico City, Mexico

SECONDARY SOURCES

Abrams, Laura S., and Laura Curran. "Wayward Girls and Virtuous Women: Social Workers and Female Juvenile Delinquency in the Progressive Era." *Affilia* vol. 15, 1 (2000): 49–64.

Acosta Patiño, Rafael. *Criminología de la Prostitución: Realidad Actual.* Madrid: Universal Grafica, 1979.

Adler, Jeffrey S. "Streetwalkers, Degraded Outcasts, and Good-for-Nothing Huzzies: Women and the Dangerous Class in Antebellum St. Louis." *Journal of Social History* vol. 25, 4 (1992): 737–55.

Agustín, Laura María. *Sex at the Margins: Migration, Labour Markets, and the Rescue Industry.* New York: Palgrave Macmillan, 2007.

Álvarez Lleras, Antonio. *El Virrey Solís: Drama Histórico en Cuatro Actos, Divididos en Nueve Cuadros.* Bogotá: Editorial Minerva, 1947.

Amar y Borbón, Josefa. *Discurso Sobre la Educación Física y Moral de las Mujeres.* Edited by María Victoria López-Cordón. Madrid: Catedra, 1994.

Anaya Larios, José Rodolfo. *Apuntes para la Historia de la Prostitución en Querétaro: Un Acercamiento Histórico-Literario.* Querétaro, México: Universidad Autónoma de Querétaro, Facultad de Filosofía, 2010.

Angerman, Arina. *Current Issues in Women's History.* London: Routledge, 1989.

Antoniazzi, Barbara. *The Wayward Woman: Progressivism, Prostitution, and Performance in the United States, 1888–1917.* Madison, WI: Fairleigh Dickinson University Press, 2014.

Archer, Christon I. *The Army in Bourbon Mexico, 1760–1810*. Albuquerque: University of New Mexico Press, 1977.

Ariza Barrios, Ramón H. *Prostitución y Delito (Estudio Sociológico Jurídico y de la Posible Incorporación de esta Doctrina en la Legislación Colombiana)*. Cartagena: Imprenta Departamental Servicio Comercial, 1968.

Armstrong, Nancy, and Leonard Tennenhouse. *The Ideology of Conduct: Essays on Literature and the History of Sexuality*. New York: Methuen, 1987.

Arondekar, Anjali. *For the Record: On Sexuality and the Colonial Archive in India*. Durham, NC: Duke University Press, 2009.

Arrizabalaga, Jon, John Henderson, and Roger French. *The Great Pox: The French Disease in Renaissance Europe*. New Haven, CT: Yale University Press, 1997.

Arrom, Silvia Marina. "Cambios en la Condición Jurídica de la Mujer Mexicana en el Siglo XIX." In *Memoria del II Congreso de Historia del Derecho Mexicano, 1980*, edited by José Luis Soberanes Fernández, 493–518. Mexico City: Universidad Nacional Autónoma de México, 1981.

———. *Containing the Poor: The Mexico City Poor House, 1774–1871*. Durham, NC: Duke University Press, 2000.

———. *The Women of Mexico City, 1790–1857*. Stanford, CA: Stanford University Press, 1985.

Asenjo González, María. "Las Mujeres en el Medio Urbano a Fines de la Edad Media: El Caso de Segovia." In *Las Mujeres en las Ciudades Medievales, Actas III, Seminario de Estudios de la Mujer*, 109–24. Madrid: Universidad Autónoma de Madrid, 1984.

Atondo Rodríguez, Ana María. *El Amor Venal y la Condición Femenina en el México Colonial*. Mexico City: Instituto Nacional de Antropología e Historia, 1992.

———. "La Prostitución Femenina en la Ciudad de México: El Alcahuete y la Mancebía Pública (1521–1621)." PhD diss., Escuela Nacional de Antropología e Historia, México, 1982.

Ayala, Sergio Rivera. "Dance of the People: The Chuchumbé." In *Colonial Lives: Documents on Latin American History, 1550–1850*, edited by Richard Boyer and Geoffrey Spurling, 178–84. New York: Oxford University Press, 2000.

Bacelar, Jefferson Afonso. *A Família da Prostituta*. São Paulo: Editora Atica, 1982.

Barahona, Renato. "Courtship, Seduction, and Abandonment in Early Modern Spain, The Example of Vizcaya, 1500–1600." In *Sex and Love in Golden Age Spain*, edited by Alain Saint-Saëns, 43–55. New Orleans: University Press of the South, 1996.

———. *Sex Crimes, Honour, and the Law in Early Modern Spain: Vizcaya, 1528–1735*. Toronto: University of Toronto Press, 2003.

Barbeito, Isabel. *Cárceles y Mujeres en el Siglo XVII*. Madrid: Castalia Instituto de la Mujer, Biblioteca de Escritoras 21, 1991.

Barker-Benfield, G. J. *The Culture of Sensibility: Sex and Society in Eighteenth-Century Britain*. Chicago: University of Chicago Press, 1992.

Baserman, Lujo. *The Oldest Profession: A History of Prostitution*. New York: Stein and Day, 1967.

Bass, Laura, and Amanda Wunder. "The Veiled Ladies of the Early Modern Spanish World: Seduction and Scandal in Seville, Madrid, and Lima." *Hispanic Review* vol. 77, 1 (2009): 97–144.

Bazán Díaz, Iñaki. *Delincuencia y Criminalidad en el País Vasco en la Transición de la Edad Media a la Moderna*. Vitoria Gasteiz, Spain: Eusko Jaularitzaren Argitalpen Zerbitzu Nagusia, 1995.

———. "El Estupro: Sexualidad Delictiva en la Baja Edad Media y Primera Edad Moderna." In *Matrimonio y Sexualidad: Normas, Prácticas, y Transgresiones en la Edad Media y Principios de la Epoca Moderna*, edited by Martine Charageat, 13–46. Madrid: Casa de Velázquez, 2003.

Bazán Díaz, Iñaki, Francisco Vázquez García, Andrés Moreno Mengíbar, and Catherine Bremond. "La Prostitution au Pays Basque Entre XIVe et XVIIe Siècles." *Annales. Histoire, Sciences Sociales* vol. 55, 6 (2000): 1283–302.

Beck, R. "Iceberg Slim." *Pimp: The Story of My Life*. United States: Cash Money Content, 2011.

Becker, Daniel Charles. "'There Is No Harm in a Boy Talking to a Girl': The Control of Sexuality and Marriage in Early Modern Navarre and Guipúzcoa." PhD diss.,University of Maryland, 1997.

Behar, Ruth. "Sex, Sin, Witchcraft, and the Devil in Late-Colonial Mexico." *American Ethnologist* vol. 14 (1987): 35–55.

Behrend-Martinez, Edward. "Making Sense of the History of Sex and Gender in Early Modern Spain." *History Compass* vol. 7, 5 (2009): 1303–16.

———. "'Taming Don Juan': Limiting Masculine Sexuality in Counter-Reformation Spain." *Gender and History* vol. 24, 2 (2012): 333–52.

———. Behrend-Martinez, Edward. *Unfit for Marriage: Impotent Spouses on Trial in the Basque Region of Spain, 1650–1750*. Reno: University of Nevada Press, 2007.

Bellomo, Manilo. *The Common Legal Past of Europe, 1000–1800*. Washington, D.C.: Catholic University of America Press, 1995.

Bennett, Herman L. *Colonial Blackness: A History of Afro-Mexico*. Bloomington: Indiana University Press, 2009.

Bennett, Judith M., and Amy M. Froide. *Singlewomen in the European Past, 1250–1800*. Philadelphia: University of Pennsylvania Press, 1999.

Bernstein, Elizabeth. *Temporarily Yours: Intimacy, Authenticity, and the Commerce of Sex*. Chicago: Chicago University Press, 2007.

Bingham, Colin. *The Affairs of Women: A Modern Miscellany*. Sydney: Currawong Publishing Co., 1969.

Birocco, Carlos María. "La Primera Casa de Recogimiento de Huérfanas de Buenos Aires: el Beaterio de Pedro de Vera y Aragón (1692–1702)." In *La Política Social Antes de la Política Social: Caridad, Beneficencia, y Política Social en Buenos Aires, Siglos XVII a XX*, edited by José Luis Moreno, 21–46. Buenos Aires: Prometeo Libros, 2000.

Black, Chad Thomas. *The Limits of Gender Domination: Women, the Law and Political Crisis in Quito, 1765–1830*. Albuquerque: University of New Mexico Press, 2010.

Blair, Cynthia M. *I've Got to Make My Livin': Black Women's Sex Work in Turn-of-the-Century Chicago*. Chicago: University of Chicago Press, 2010.

Bliss, Katherine. *Compromised Positions: Prostitution, Revolution, and Social Reform in Mexico City, 1918–1940*. University Park: Penn State University Press, 2001.

Borja Gómez, Jaime Humberto, et al. *Inquisición, Muerte y Sexualidad en la Nueva Granada*. Santa Fe de Bogotá: Editorial Ariel—Ceja, 1995.

Boyer, Richard E. *Lives of the Bigamists: Marriage, Family, and Community in Colonial Mexico*. Albuquerque: University of New Mexico Press, 1995.

———. "Women, *La Mala Vida*, and the Politics of Marriage." In *Sexuality and Marriage in Colonial Latin America*, edited by Asunción Lavrin, 252–86. Lincoln: University of Nebraska Press, 1989.

Boyer, Richard E., and Geoffrey Spurling, eds. *Colonial Lives: Documents on Latin American History, 1550–1850.* New York: Oxford University Press, 2000.

Boyle, Margaret E. *Unruly Women: Performance, Penitence, and Punishment in Early Modern Spain.* Toronto: University of Toronto Press, 2014.

Brennan, Denise. *What's Love Got to Do with It?: Transnational Desires and Sex Tourism in the Dominican Republic.* Durham, NC: Duke University Press, 2004.

Bromley, Juan. "La Ciudad de Lima en el Año 1630." *Revista Histórica* vol. 24 (1959): 268–317.

Bronfen, Elisabeth. *Over Her Dead Body: Death, Femininity, and the Aesthetic.* New York: Routledge, 1992.

Brundage, James A. "Concubinage and Marriage in Medieval Canon Law." In *Sexual Practices and the Medieval Church,* edited by Vern L. Bullough and James A. Brundage, 118–28. Buffalo: Prometheus Books, 1982.

———. *Law, Sex, and Society in Medieval Europe.* Chicago: University of Chicago Press, 1987.

———. "Prostitution in the Medieval Canon Law." *Signs* vol. 1, 4 (1976): 825–45.

Bryder, Linda. "Sex, Race, and Colonialism: An Historiographical Review." *The International History Review* vol. 20, 4 (1998): 806–22.

Bullough, Vern L., and Bonnie Bullough. *Women and Prostitution: A Social History.* Buffalo: Prometheus Books, 1987.

Bullough, Vern L., and James A. Brundage. *Handbook of Medieval Sexuality.* New York: Garland Press, 1996.

———. *Sexual Practices in the Medieval Church.* Buffalo: Prometheus Books, 1982.

Burchill, Julie. *Damaged Gods: Cults and Heroes Reappraised.* London: Century, 1986.

Burkholder, Mark A. *Spaniards in the Colonial Empire: Creoles vs. Peninsulars?* Malden, MA: John Wiley & Sons, 2013.

Burns, Kathryn. *Into the Archive: Writing and Power in Colonial Peru.* Durham, NC: Duke University Press, 2010.

Calderón, Emilio. *Usos y Costumbres Sexuales de los Reyes de España.* Madrid: Cirene, 1991.

Calderón de la Barca, Fanny. *Life in Mexico during a Residence of Two Years in That Country.* Boston: Charles C. Little and James Brown, 1843.

Cámara de Comercio de Bogotá. *La Prostitución en el Centro de Bogotá: Censo de Establecimientos y Personas: Análisis Socioeconómico.* Bogotá: Cámara de Comercio de Bogotá, 1991.

———. *La Prostitución en el Sector Chapinero de Santafé: Censo de Establecimientos y Personas: Análisis Socioeconómico.* Bogotá: Cámara de Comercio de Bogotá, 1992.

Capel Martínez, Rosa María. "La Prostitución en España: Notas para un Estudio Socio-Historico." In *Mujer y Sociedad en España (1700–1975),* edited by Rosa María Capel Martínez, 265–98. Madrid: Dirección General de Juventud y Promoción Socio-Cultural, 1982.

Capp, Bernard. "The Double Standard Revisited: Plebeian Women and Male Sexual Reputation in Early Modern England." *Past and Present* vol. 162 (1999): 70–100.

———. *When Gossips Meet: Women, Family, and Neighbourhood in Early Modern England.* Oxford: Oxford University Press, 2003.

Carboneres, Manuel. *Picaronas y Alcahuetes o la Mancebía de Valencia: Apuntes Para La Historia de Prostitución Desde Principios del Siglo XIV Hasta Antes de la Abolición de los Fueros.* Valencia: Impresor de El Mercantil, 1876; reprint, Valencia: El Mercantil, 1978.

Castañeda García, Carmen. "Fuentes Para la Historia de la Mujer en los Archivos de Guadalajara." *Boletín del Archivo Histórico de Jalisco* vol. 6, 2 (1982): 14–18.

———. *Violación, Estupro, y Sexualidad: Nueva Galicia, 1790–1821.* Guadalajara: Editorial Hexágono, 1989.

Chateauvert, Melinda. *Sex Workers Unite: A History of the Movement from Stonewall to Slutwalk.* Boston: Beacon Press, 2013.

Chesney-Lind, Meda. *The Female Offender: Girls, Women, and Crime.* Thousand Oaks, CA: Sage Publications, 1997.

Chuhue Huamán, Richard. "Plebe, Prostitución, y Conducta Sexual en Lima del Siglo XVIII; Apuntes Sobre la Sexualidad en Lima Borbónica." In *Historia de Lima: XVII Coloquio de Historia de Lima, 2010,* edited by Miguel Maticorena Estrada, 127–51. Lima: Centro Cultural de San Marcos, 2010.

Claassen, Sandra, and Fanny Polanía Molina. *Tráfico de Mujeres en Colombia: Diagnóstico, Análisis, y Propuestas.* Bogotá: Fundación Esperanza, 1998.

Clark, Anna. "Whores and Gossips: Sexual Reputation in London, 1770–1825." In *Current Issues in Women's History,* edited by Arina Angerman, 231–48. London: Routledge, 1989.

Clark, Barrett. *European Theories of the Drama, an Anthology of Dramatic Theory and Criticism from Aristotle to the Present Day, In a Series of Selected Texts, With Commentaries, Biographies, and Bibliographies.* Cincinnati: Stewart & Kidd Company, 1918.

Cohn, Samuel K., Jr. *Women in the Streets: Essays on Sex and Power in Renaissance Italy.* Baltimore: Johns Hopkins University Press, 1996.

Collantes de Terán Sánchez, Antonio. "Actitudas Ante la Marginación Social: Malhechores y Rufianes en Sevilla." In *Actas del Coloquio de Historia Medieval Andaluza: La Sociedad Medieval Andaluza: Grupos No Privilegiados,* 293–302. Jaén: Diputación Provincial de Jaén, 1984.

Conner, Susan P. "Politics, Prostitution, and the Pox in Revolutionary Paris, 1789–1799." *Journal of Social History* vol. 22, 4 (1989): 713–34.

———. "Public Virtue and Public Women: Prostitution in Revolutionary Paris, 1793–1794." *Eighteenth-Century Studies* vol. 28, 2 (1994): 221–40.

Coolidge, Grace E. "'A Vile and Abject Woman': Noble Mistresses, Legal Power, and the Family in Early Modern Spain." *Journal of Family History* vol. 32, 3 (2007): 195–214.

Corbin, Alain. "Commercial Sexuality in Nineteenth-Century France: A System of Images and Regulations." In *The Making of the Modern Body: Sexuality and Society in the Nineteenth-Century,* edited by Catherine Gallagher and Thomas Laqueur, 209–19. Berkeley: University of California Press, 1987.

Córdoba de la Llave, Ricardo. "Adulterio, Sexo, y Violencia en la Castilla Medieval." *Espacio, Tiempo, y Forma* serie IV, 7 (1994): 153–84.

———. "Las Relaciones Extraconyugales en la Sociedad Castellana Bajomedieval." *Anuario de Estudios Medievales* vol. 16 (1986): 571–620.

———. "Violencia y Adulterio en la Andalucía Bajomedieval." In *Actas del Coloquio de Historia Medieval Andaluza: La Sociedad Medieval Andaluza: Grupos no Privilegiados,* 263–78. Jaén: Diputación Provincial de Jaén, 1984.

Córdoba de la Llave, Ricardo, and Iñaki Bazán Díaz. *Mujer, Marginación, y Violencia: Entre la Edad Media y los Tiempos Modernos.* Córdoba: Universidad de Córdoba, 2006.

Córdoba Ochoa, Luis Miguel. *De la Quietud a la Felicidad: La Villa de Medellín y los Procuradores del Cabildo entre 1675–1785.* Santafé de Bogotá: Instituto Colombia de Cultura Hispánica, 1998.

Cornwall, Andrea. "Gendered Identities and Gender Ambiguity among *Travestis* in Salvador, Brazil." In *Dislocating Masculinity: Comparative Ethnographies,* edited by Andrea Cornwall and Nancy Lindisfarne, 111–32. London: Routledge, 1994.

Cornwall, Andrea, and Nancy Lindisfarne. *Dislocating Masculinity: Comparative Ethnographies.* London: Routledge, 1994.

Crawford, Charlotte. "The Position of Women in a Basque Fishing Community." In *Anglo-American Contributions to Basque Studies: Essays in Honor of Jon Bilbao,* edited by William A. Douglass et al., 145–52. Grand Junction, CO: Desert Research Institute Publications on the Social Sciences, 1977.

Cruickshank, Dan. *London's Sinful Secret: The Bawdy History and Very Public Passions of London's Georgian Age.* New York: St. Martin's Press, 2010.

Cruz, Sor Juana Inez de la. *A Sor Juana Anthology.* Translated by Alan S. Trueblood. Cambridge, MA: Harvard University Press, 1988.

Curcio-Nagy, Linda A. "Josefa Ordoñez: The Scandalous Adventures of a Colonial Courtesan." In *The Human Tradition in Mexico,* edited by J. M. Pilcher, 5–22. Wilmington, DE: SR Books, 2003.

Cussett, Catherine. *Libertinage and Modernity.* New Haven, CT: Yale University Press, 1998.

Dabhoiwala, Faramerz. *The Origins of Sex: A History of the First Sexual Revolution.* New York: Oxford University Press, 2012.

Dandelet, Thomas James. *Spanish Rome, 1500–1700.* New Haven, CT: Yale University Press, 2001.

Dangler, Jean. *Mediating Fictions: Literature, Women Healers, and the Go-Between in Medieval and Early Modern Iberia.* Lewisburg, PA: Bucknell University Press, 2001.

Davidson, Roger, and Lesley A. Hall. *Sex, Sin, and Suffering: Venereal Disease and European Society since 1870.* London: Routledge, 2001.

Davis, Natalie Zemon. *Fiction in the Archives: Pardon Tales and Their Tellers in Sixteenth-Century France.* Stanford, CA: Stanford University Press, 1987.

Deans-Smith, Susan. *Bureaucrats, Planters, and Workers: The Making of the Tobacco Monopoly in Bourbon Mexico.* Austin: University of Texas Press, 1992.

Deleito y Piñuela, José. *La Mala Vida en la España de Felipe IV.* Madrid: Espasa-Cape, 1967.

Delicado, Francisco. *Portrait of Lozana: The Lusty Andalusian Woman.* Translated by Bruno M. Damiani. Potomac, MD: Scripta Humanistica, 1987.

DeWaard, Jeanne Elders. "The Crime of Womanhood: Ambivalent Intersections of Sentiment and Law in Nineteenth-Century American Culture." PhD diss., University of Miami, 2003.

Dillard, Heath. *Daughters of the Reconquest: Women in Castilian Town Society, 1100–1300.* New York: Cambridge University Press, 1984.

Ding, Yu, and Petula Sik Yink Ho. "Sex Work in China's Pearl River Delta: Accumulating Sexual Capital as a Life-Advancement Strategy." *Sexualities* vol. 26, 1 (2013): 43–60.

Dominguez, Jorge I. "International War and Government Modernization: The Military—A Case Study." In *Rank and Privilege: The Military and Society in Latin America,* edited by Linda Alexander Rodríguez, 1–10. Wilmington, DE: Scholarly Resources, 1994.

Donnelly, John Patrick. *Ignatius Loyola: Founder of the Jesuits.* New York: Longman, 2004.

Dopico Black, Georgina. *Perfect Wives, Other Women: Adultery and Inquisition in Early Modern Spain.* Durham, NC: Duke University Press, 2001.

———. "Public Bodies, Private Parts: The Virgins and Magdalens of Magdalena de San Geronimo." *Journal of Spanish Cultural Studies* vol. 2, 1 (2001): 81–96.

Dreiser, Theodore. *Sister Carrie.* New York: Doubleday, 1900.

Dudash, Tawnya. "Peepshow Feminism." In *Whores and Other Feminists,* edited by Jill Nagle, 98–118. New York: Routledge, 1997.

Duggan, Lisa, and Nan D. Hunter. *Sex Wars: Sexual Dissent and Political Culture.* New York: Routledge, 1995.

Dyer, Abigail. "Heresy and Dishonor: Sexual Crimes before the Courts of Early Modern Spain." PhD diss., Columbia University, 2000.

———. "Seduction by Promise of Marriage: Law, Sex, and Culture in Seventeenth-Century Spain." *The Sixteenth Century Journal* vol. 34, 2 (2003): 439–55.

Elbl, Ivana. "'Men without Wives': Sexual Arrangements in the Early Portuguese Expansion in West Africa." In *Desire and Discipline: Sex and Sexuality in the Premodern West,* edited by Jacqueline Murray and Konrad Eisenbicher, 61–86. Toronto: University of Toronto Press, 1996.

Eliot, Syr Thomas. *The Dictionary of Syr Thomas Eliot Knyght.* London: Thomas Bertheleti, 1538.

Estow, Clara. "Iberia and North Africa: A Comparative View of Religious and Sexual Discrimination in a Medieval Plural Society." In *The Medieval Mediterranean: Cross-Cultural Contacts,* edited by Marilyn Joyce Segal Chiat and Kathryn Reyerson, 81–95. St. Cloud: North Star Press of St. Cloud, 1988.

Evans, Hilary. *Harlots, Whores, and Hookers: A History of Prostitution.* New York: Taplinger Publishing Co., 1979.

Fairchilds, Cissie. "Female Sexual Attitudes and the Rise of Illegitimacy: A Case Study." *The Journal of Interdisciplinary History* vol. 8, 4 (1978): 627–67.

Farge, Arlette. *The Allure of the Archives.* Translated by Thomas Scott-Railton. New Haven, CT: Yale University Press, 2013.

Feldman, Martha, and Bonnie Gordon. *The Courtesan's Arts: Cross-Cultural Perspectives.* New York: Oxford University Press, 2006.

Fenster, Thelma, and Daniel Lord Smail. *Fama: The Politics of Talk and Reputation in Medieval Europe.* Ithaca, NY: Cornell University Press, 2003.

Ferguson, Margaret, Maureen Quilligan, and Nancy J. Vickers. *Rewriting the Renaissance: The Discourses of Sexual Difference in Early Modern Europe.* Chicago: University of Chicago Press, 1986.

Fernandez, André. "The Repression of Sexual Behavior by the Aragonese Inquisition between 1560 and 1700." *Journal of the History of Sexuality* vol. 7, 4 (1997): 469–501.

Few, Martha. *Women Who Live Evil Lives: Gender, Religion, and the Politics of Power in Colonial Guatemala.* Austin: University of Texas Press, 2002.

Fishbein, Leslie. "From Sodom to Salvation: The Image of New York City in Films about Fallen Women, 1899–1934." *New York History* vol. 70, 2 (1989): 171–90.

Foucault, Michel. *The Birth of the Clinic.* Translated by A. M. Sheridan Smith. New York: Pantheon Books, 1973.

————. *The History of Sexuality. Vol. 1, An Introduction.* Translated by Robert Hurley. New York: Vintage Books, 1978.

————. *The History of Sexuality. Vol. 2, The Use of Pleasure.* Translated by Robert Hurley. New York: Vintage Books, 1985.

————. *The History of Sexuality. Vol. 3, The Care of the Self.* Translated by Robert Hurley. New York: Vintage Books, 1986.

Franco, Jean. *Plotting Women: Gender and Representation in Mexico.* New York: Columbia University Press, 1989.

Freytag, Gustav, and Elias J. MacEwan. *Freytag's Technique of the Drama, An Exposition of Dramatic Composition and Art.* Chicago: S. C. Griggs & Co., 1895.

Furtado, Júnia Ferreira. *Chica da Silva: A Brazilian Slave of the Eighteenth Century.* Cambridge, UK: Cambridge University Press, 2009.

Gacto Fernández, Enrique. "La Filiación Ilegitima en la Historia del Derecho Español," *Anuario de Historia del Derecho Español* vol. 41 (1971): 899–944.

Galí í Boadella, Montserrat. *Historias del Bello Sexo: La Introducción del Romanticismo en México.* Mexico City: Universidad Nacional Autónoma de México, 2002.

Gallagher, Catherine, and Thomas Laqueur, eds. *The Making of the Modern Body: Sexuality and Society in the Nineteenth-Century.* Berkeley: University of California Press, 1987.

Gamboa, Federico. *Santa: A Novel of Mexico City.* Translated by John Charles Chasteen. Chapel Hill: University of North Carolina Press, 2010.

García, Juan Andreo, and Alberto Gullón Abao. "Vida y Muerte de la Mulata: Crónica Ilustrada de la Prostitución en Cuba del XIX." *Anuario de Estudios Americanos* vol. 4, 1 (1997): 135–57.

García Herrero, María del Carmen. "El Mundo de la Prostitución en las Ciudades Bajomedievales." *Cuadernos del Centro de Estudios Medievales y Renacentistas* vol. 4 (1996): 67–100.

————. *Las Mujeres en Zaragoza en el Siglo XV,* 2 vols. Zaragoza: Ayuntamiento de Zaragoza, 1990.

Gauderman, Kimberly. *Women's Lives in Colonial Quito: Gender, Law, and Economy in Spanish America.* Austin: University of Texas Press, 2003.

Germeten, Nicole von. *Violent Delights, Violent Ends: Sex, Race, and Honor in Colonial Cartagena de Indias.* Albuquerque: University of New Mexico Press, 2013.

Gilfoyle, Timothy J. "Prostitutes in the Archives: Problems and Possibilities in Documenting the History of Sexuality." *American Archivist* vol. 57, 3 (1994): 514–27.

Glasco, Sharon Bailey. "A City in Disarray: Public Health, City Planning, and the Politics of Power in Late Colonial Mexico City." PhD diss., University of Arizona, 2002.

————. *Constructing Mexico City: Colonial Conflicts over Culture, Space, and Authority.* New York: Palgrave MacMillan, 2010.

Góngora Escobedo, Álvaro. *La Prostitución en Santiago, 1813–1931: Visión de las Elites.* Santiago de Chile: Editorial Universitaria, 1994.

González Mínguez, César, Iñaki Bazán Díaz, and Iñaki Reguera. *Marginación y Exclusión Social en el País Vasco.* Bilbao, Spain: Universidad del País Vasco, 1999.

Grant, Melissa Gira. *Playing the Whore: The Work of Sex Work.* New York: Verso Books, 2014.

Greenblat, Stephen. *Renaissance Self-Fashioning: From More to Shakespeare.* Chicago: University of Chicago Press, 2005.

Greenow, Linda L. *Family, Household, and Home: A Micro-geographic Analysis of Cartagena (New Granada) in 1777*. Syracuse, NY: Syracuse University, Department of Geography, 1976.

Greer, Germaine. *The Female Eunuch*. New York: McGraw-Hill, 1971.

Groes-Green, Christian. "'To Put Men in a Bottle': Eroticism, Kinship, Female Power, and Transactional Sex in Maputo, Mozambique." *American Ethnologist* vol. 40, 1 (2013): 102–17.

Gronewold, Sue. *Beautiful Merchandise: Prostitution in China, 1860–1936*. New York: Haworth Press, 1982.

Grosz, Elizabeth. *Volatile Bodies: Toward a Corporeal Feminism*. Bloomington and Indianapolis: University of Indiana Press, 1994.

Güemes, Francisco. *Algunas Consideraciones Sobre la Prostitución Pública en México*. Mexico City: Oficina Tipográfica de la Secretaría de Fomento, 1888.

Guereña, Jean Louis. "Médicos y Prostitución: Un Proyecto de Reglamentación de la Prostitución en 1809: La 'Exposición' de Antonio Cibat, 1771–1811." *Medicina e Historia* vol. 71 (1998): 5–28.

———. "Prostitution and the Origins of the Governmental Regulatory System in Nineteenth-Century Spain: The Plans of the Trienio Liberal, 1820–1823." *Journal of the History of Sexuality* vol. 17, 2 (2008): 216–34.

Guerra, Francisco. *El Hospital en Hispanoamérica y Filipinas, 1492–1898*. Madrid: Ministerio de Sanidad y Consumo, 1994.

Guibovich del Caprio, Lorgio A. *Protección de la Familia en el Estado Incaico y la Prostitución en la Colonia*. Lima: Universidad Nacional Federico Villareal, Oficina Central de Investigación, 2009.

Gullón Abao, Alberto José. "La Prostitución Reglada en La Habana de Fines del Siglo XIX." In *"Mal Menor": Políticas y Representaciones de la Prostitución (Siglos XVI–XIX)*, edited by Francisco Vázquez García, 183–205. Cádiz: Universidad de Cádiz, 1998.

Gunvaldson, Nicholas Ryan. "Crimson Streets and Violent Bodies: Identity, Physicality, and the Twilight of Colorado's Vice District." MA thesis, Colorado State University, 2015.

Gutiérrez, Ramón A. *When Jesus Came, the Corn Mothers Went Away: Marriage, Sexuality, and Power in New Mexico, 1500–1846*. Stanford, CA: Stanford University Press, 1991.

Gutmann, Matthew C. *The Meanings of Macho: Being a Man in Mexico City*. Berkeley: University of California Press, 2007.

Guy, Donna. "Prostitution and Female Criminality in Buenos Aires, 1875–1937." In *The Problem of Order in Changing Societies: Essays on Crime and Policing in Argentina and Uruguay*, edited by Lyman L. Johnson, 89–115. Albuquerque: University of New Mexico Press, 1990.

———. *Sex and Danger in Buenos Aires: Prostitution, Family, and Nation in Argentina*. Lincoln: University of Nebraska Press, 1991.

Haidt, Rebecca. "The Wife, the Maid, and the Woman in the Street." In *Eve's Enlightenment: Women's Experience in Spain and Spanish America, 1726–1839*, edited by Catherine M. Jaffe and Elizabeth F. Lewis, 115–27. Baton Rouge: Louisiana State University Press, 2009.

Haidt, Rebecca, et al. *Women, Work, and Clothing in Eighteenth Century Spain*. Oxford, UK: Voltaire Foundation, 2011.

Hakim, Catherine. *Erotic Capital: The Power of Attraction in the Boardroom and the Bedroom*. New York: Basic Books, 2011.

Haliczer, Steven. "Sexuality and Repression in Counter-Reformation Spain." In *Sex and Love in Golden Age Spain*, edited by Alain Saint-Saëns, 81–94. New Orleans: University Press of the South, 1996.

Hamman, Amy C. "'Eyeing Alameda Park': Topographies of Culture, Class, and Cleanliness in Bourbon Mexico City, 1700–1800." PhD diss., University of Arizona, 2015.

Hamnett, Brian R. *The Mexican Bureaucracy before the Bourbon Reforms, 1700–1770: A Study in the Limitations of Absolutism*. Glasgow: Institute of Latin American Studies, 1979.

Harding, Susan. "Women and Words in a Spanish Village." In *Toward an Anthropology of Women*, edited by Rayna R. Reiter, 283–308. New York: Monthly Review Press, 1973.

Harper, Kyle. *From Shame to Sin: The Christian Transformation of Sexual Morality in Late Antiquity*. Cambridge, MA: Harvard University Press, 2013.

Harsin, Jill. *Policing Prostitution in Nineteenth-Century Paris*. Princeton, NJ: Princeton University Press, 1985.

Hart, Angie. "Missing Masculinity? Prostitutes' Clients in Alicante, Spain." In *Dislocating Masculinity: Comparative Ethnographies*, edited by Andrea Cornwall and Nancy Lindisfarne, 48–65. London: Routledge, 1994.

Haslip, Joan. *Madame Du Barry: The Wages of Beauty*. New York: Grove Weidenfeld, 1992.

Haslip-Viera, Gabriel. *Crime and Punishment in Late Colonial Mexico City, 1692–1810*. Albuquerque: University of New Mexico Press, 1999.

Haviland, John Beard. *Gossip, Reputation, and Knowledge in Zinacantán*. Chicago: University of Chicago Press, 1977.

Hazard, Paul. *European Thought in the Eighteenth Century, From Montesquieu to Lessing*. London: Hollis & Carter, 1954.

———. *La Pensée Européenne au XVIIe Siècle de Montesquieu à Lessing*. Paris: Boivin, 1946.

Hinrichs, William H. *The Invention of the Sequel: Expanding Prose Fiction in Early Modern Spain*. Woodbridge, UK: Tamesis, 2011.

Howell, Philip. *Geographies of Regulation: Policing Prostitution in Nineteenth Century Britain and the Empire*. New York: Cambridge University Press, 2009.

Hsu, Carmen Yu-Chih. "Courtesans in the Literature of the Spanish Golden Age." PhD diss., University of Michigan, 2002.

Hume, Martin A. S. *The Court of Philip IV: Spain in Decadence*. New York: Putnam's Sons, 1907.

Hunter, Mark. *Love in the Time of AIDS: Inequality, Gender, and Rights in South Africa*. Bloomington: Indiana University Press, 2010.

———. "The Materiality of Everyday Sex: Thinking Beyond Prostitution." *African Studies* vol. 61, 1 (2002): 99–120.

Hyam, Ronald. *Empire and Sexuality: The British Experience*. Manchester, UK: Manchester University Press, 1990.

Izcara Palacios, Simón Pedro. *Mujer y Cambio de Valores en el Madrid del Siglo XVIII*. Ciudad Victoria, Mexico: Universidad Nacional Autónoma de Tamaulipas, 2004.

Jaffe, Catherine M., and Elizabeth Franklin Lewis. *Eve's Enlightenment: Women's Experience in Spain and Spanish America, 1726–1839*. Baton Rouge: Louisiana State University Press, 2009.

Janer, Florencio, ed. *Obras de Don Francisco de Quevedo Villegas,* 3 vols. Madrid: M. Rivadeneyra, 1877.

Jaramillo de Zuleta, Pilar. *"Las Arrepentidas."* In *Placer, Dinero, y Pecado: Historia de la Prostitución en Colombia,* edited by Aída Martínez and Pablo Rodríguez, 91–128. Bogotá: Aguilar, 2002.

Jiménez Monteserín, Miguel. *Sexo y Bien Común: Notas Para la Historia de la Prostitución en España.* Cuenca, Spain: Instituto Juan de Valdés, 1994.

Johnson, Lyman L., and Sonya Lipsett-Rivera, eds. *The Faces of Honor, Sex, Shame, and Violence in Colonial Latin America.* Albuquerque: University of New Mexico Press, 1998.

Johnson, Walter. "On Agency." *Journal of Social History* 37, 1 (2003): 113–24.

Jones, E. D. "The Medieval Leyrwite: A Historical Note on Female Fornication." *The English Historical Review* vol. 107, 425 (1992): 945–53.

Karras, Ruth Mazo. *Common Women: Prostitution and Sexuality in Medieval England.* New York: Oxford University Press, 1996.

———. "Holy Harlots: Prostitute Saints in Medieval Legend." *Journal of the History of Sexuality* vol. 1, 1 (1990): 3–32.

———. "Prostitution and the Question of Sexual Identity in Medieval Europe." *Journal of Women's History* vol. 11, 3 (1999): 159–77.

———. "Sex and the Single Woman." In *Singlewomen in the European Past, 1250–1800,* edited by Judith M. Bennett and Amy M. Froide, 127–45. Philadelphia: University of Pennsylvania Press, 1999.

———. *Sexuality in Medieval Europe: Doing unto Others.* New York: Routledge, 2005.

———. "The Regulation of Brothels in Later Medieval England." *Signs* vol. 14, 2 (1989): 399–433.

———. "Women's Labors: Reproduction and Sex Work in Medieval Europe." *Journal of Women's History* vol. 15, 4 (2004): 153–58.

Katsulis, Yasmina. *Sex Work and the City: The Social Geography of Health in Tijuana, Mexico.* Austin: University of Texas Press, 2008.

Katzew, Ilona. *Casta Painting: Images of Race in Eighteenth-Century Mexico.* New Haven, CT: Yale University Press, 2004.

Kelleher, Marie A. "Like Man and Wife: Clerics' Concubines in the Diocese of Barcelona." *Journal of Medieval History* vol. 28, 4 (2002): 349–60.

———. *The Measure of a Woman: Law and Female Identity in the Crown of Aragon.* Philadelphia: University of Pennsylvania Press, 2010.

Kong, Mee-Hae. "Material Girls: Sexual Perceptions of Korean Teenage Girls Who Have Experienced 'Compensated Dates.'" *Asian Journal of Women's Studies* vol. 9, 2 (2003): 67–94.

Korns, Bonnie. "The Life of Micaela Villegas, La Perricholi and Her Influence on the Social Life of Her Time, With Special Reference to Spanish Colonial Lima." MA thesis, Claremont College, 1947.

Kuehn, Thomas. "Daughters, Mothers, Wives, and Widows: Women as Legal Persons." In *Time, Space, and Women's Lives in Early Modern Europe,* edited by Anne Shutte et al., 97–115. Kirksville, MO: Truman State University Press, 2001.

Kunzel, Regina G. *Fallen Women, Problem Girls: Unmarried Mothers and the Professionalization of Social Work, 1890–1945.* New Haven, CT: Yale University Press, 1993.

Kushner, Nina. *Erotic Exchanges: The World of Elite Prostitution in Eighteenth-Century Paris.* Ithaca, NY: Cornell University Press, 2013.

Kutinski, Vera M. *Sugar's Secrets: Race and the Erotics of Cuban Nationalism.* Charlottesville: University of Virginia Press, 1993.

Kuznesof, Elizabeth A. "Sexual Politics, Race, and Bastard-Bearing in Nineteenth-Century Brazil: A Question of Culture or Power?" *Journal of Family History* vol. 16, 3 (1991): 241–60.

Lacarra, María Eugenia. "El Fenómeno de la Prostitución y sus Conexiones con 'La Celestina.'" In *Historias y Ficciones: Coloquio Sobre la Literatura del Siglo XV: Actas del Coloquio Internacional Organizado por el Departamento de Filología Española de la Universidad de Valencia, Celebrado en Valencia los días 29, 30, y 31 de Octubre de 1990,* edited by Rafael Beltrán Llavador, José Luis Canet Vallés, et al., 267–78 Valencia: Universitat de Valencia, 1992.

———. "La Evolución de la Prostitución en la Castilla del Siglo XV y la Mancebía de Salamanca en Tiempos de Fernando de Rojas." In *Fernando de Rojas and Celestina: Approaching the Fifth Centenary: Proceedings of an International Conference in Commemoration of the 450th Anniversary of Fernando de Rojas, 21–24 of November, 1991,* edited by Ivy A. Corfis and Joseph Thomas Snow, 33–78. Madison, WI: Hispanic Seminary for Medieval Studies, 1993.

Lanz, Eukene Lacarra. "Changing Boundaries of Licit and Illicit Unions: Concubinage and Prostitution." In *Marriage and Sexuality in Medieval and Early Modern Iberia,* edited by Eukene Lacarra Lanz, 158–94. New York: Routledge, 2002.

———. *Estudios Históricos Sobre la Mujer Medieval.* Málaga: Diputación Provincial de Málaga, 1990.

———. "Legal and Clandestine Prostitution in Medieval Spain." *Bulletin of Hispanic Studies* vol. 79, 3 (2002): 265–85.

———, ed. *Marriage and Sexuality in Medieval and Early Modern Iberia.* New York: Routledge, 2002.

Lavrin, Asunción. "In Search of the Colonial Woman in Mexico: The Seventeenth and Eighteenth Centuries." In *Latin American Women: Historical Perspectives,* edited by Asunción Lavrin, 23–59. Westport, CT: Greenwood Press, 1978.

———, ed. *Latin American Women: Historical Perspectives.* Westport, CT: Greenwood Press, 1978.

———. "'Lo Femenino': Women in Colonial Historical Sources." In *Coded Encounters: Writing, Gender, and Ethnicity in Colonial Latin America,* edited by Francisco Javier Cevallos-Candau, Jeffrey A. Cole, Nina M. Scott, and Nicomedes Suárez-Araúz, 153–76. Amherst: University of Massachusetts Press, 1994.

———, ed. *Sexuality and Marriage in Colonial Latin America.* Lincoln: University of Nebraska Press, 1989.

———. "Sexuality in Colonial Mexico: A Church Dilemma." In *Sexuality and Marriage in Colonial Latin America,* edited by Asunción Lavrin, 47–95. Lincoln: University of Nebraska Press, 1992.

Lawrence, Paul, Francis Dodsworth, and Robert M. Morris. "Introduction." In *The Making of the Modern Police, 1780–1914,* vol. 1, edited by Francis Dodsworth, 1–40. London: Pickering & Chatto, 2014.

Leal, Juli, and J. Inés Rodríguez Gómez. *Carlo Goldoni: Una Vida Para el Teatro: Coloquio Internacional, Bicentenario Carlo Goldoni.* Valencia: Universitat de Valencia, 1996.

Lee, Catherine. *Policing Prostitution, 1856–1886: Deviance, Surveillance, and Morality.* London: Pickering & Chatto, 2013.

Leigh, Carol. "Inventing Sex Work." In *Whores and Other Feminists,* edited by Jill Nagle, 223–31. New York: Routledge, 1997.

Levine, Philippa. *Prostitution, Race, and Politics: Policing Venereal Disease in the British Empire.* New York: Routledge, 2003.

———. "Venereal Disease, Prostitution, and the Politics of Empire: The Case of British India." *Journal of the History of Sexuality* vol. 4, 4 (1994): 579–602.

Lewis, Ann M. "Classifying the Prostitute in Eighteenth-Century France." In *Prostitution and Eighteenth-Century Culture: Sex, Commerce, and Morality,* edited by Ann M. Lewis and Markman Ellis, 17–32. London: Pickering & Chatto, 2012.

Lewis, Ann M., and Markman Ellis, eds. *Prostitution and Eighteenth-Century Culture: Sex, Commerce, and Morality.* London: Pickering & Chatto, 2012.

Lindsey, Treva B., and Jessica Marie Johnson. "Searching for Climax: Black Erotic Lives in Slavery and Freedom." *Meridians: Feminism, Race, and Transnationalism* vol. 12, 2 (2014): 169–95.

Lipsett-Rivera, Sonya. "A Slap in the Face of Honor: Social Transgression and Women in Late-Colonial Mexico." In *The Faces of Honor, Sex, Shame, and Violence in Colonial Latin America,* edited by Lyman L. Johnson and Sonya Lipsett Rivera, 179–200. Albuquerque: University of New Mexico Press, 1998.

———. *Gender and the Negotiation of Daily Life in Mexico, 1750–1856.* Lincoln: University of Nebraska Press, 2012.

López Alonso, Carmen. "Mujer Medieval y Pobreza." In *La Condición de la Mujer en la Edad Media: Actas del Coloquio Celebrado en la Casa de Velázquez, del 5 al 7 de Noviembre de 1984,* edited by Yves-René Fonquerne and Alfonso Esteban, 261–72. Madrid: Casa de Velázquez, 1986.

López Beltrán, María Teresa. *La Prostitución en el Reino de Granada a Finales de la Edad Media.* Málaga: Diputación Provincial de Málaga, 2003.

———. *La Prostitución en el Reino de Granada en Época de los Reyes Católicos: El Caso de Málaga, 1487–1516.* Málaga: Diputación Provincial de Málaga, 1985.

López-Cordón Cortezo, María Victoria. "Women in Society in Eighteenth Century Spain, Models of Sociability." In *Eve's Enlightenment: Women's Experience in Spain and Spanish America, 1726–1839,* edited by Catherine M. Jaffe and Elizabeth F. Lewis, 103–14. Baton Rouge: Louisiana State University Press, 2009.

López Terrada, María Luz. "El Tratamiento de la Sífilis en un Hospital Renacentista: La Sala del Mal de Siment del Hospital General de Valencia." *Asclepio* vol. 41, 2 (1989): 19--50.

Lorenzo Cardoso, Pedro L. "Los Malos Tratos a las Mujeres en Castilla en el Siglo XVII." *Brocar: Cuadernos de Investigación Histórica* vol. 15 (1989): 119–36.

Lotte Van de Pol, Liz Waters. *The Burgher and the Whore: Prostitution in Early Modern Amsterdam.* Oxford: Oxford University Press, 2011.

Lozano Amendares, Teresa. *La Criminalidad en la Ciudad de México, 1800–1821.* Mexico City: Universidad Nacional Autónoma de México, 1987.

Lux Martelo, Martha Elisa. *Las Mujeres de Cartagena de Indias en el Siglo XVII: Lo que Hacían, Les Hacían y No Hacían, y las Curas que Les Prescribían.* Bogotá: Universidad de los Andes, 2006.

Lyman, Stanford M. *The Seven Deadly Sins: Society and Evil.* Dix Hills, NY: General Hall, 1989.

Lyons, Clare A. *Sex among the Rabble: An Intimate History of Gender and Power in the Age of Revolution, Philadelphia, 1730–1830.* Chapel Hill: University of North Carolina Press, 2006.

Macpherson, Ian, and Angus McKay, eds. *Love, Religion, and Politics in Fifteenth-Century Spain.* Leiden, Netherlands: Brill, 1998.

Mannarelli, María Emma. *Hechiceras, Beatas, y Expósitas: Mujeres y Poder Inquisitorial en Lima.* Lima: Ediciones del Congreso del Perú, 1998.

———. *Pecados Públicos: La Ilegitimidad en Lima, Siglo XVII.* Lima: Ediciones Flora Tristán, 1993.

———. *Private Passions and Public Sins: Men and Women in Seventeenth Century Lima.* Translated by Sidney Evans and Meredith D. Dodge. Albuquerque: University of New Mexico Press, 2007.

Manning, Jo. *My Lady Scandalous: The Amazing Life and Outrageous Times of Grace Dalrymple Elliot, Royal Courtesan.* New York: Simon and Schuster, 2005.

Marín, Manuela. "Marriage and Sexuality in Al-Andalus." In *Marriage and Sexuality in Medieval and Early Modern Iberia,* edited by Eukene Lacarra Lanz, 3–20. New York: Routledge, 2002.

Marsden, Jane I. *Fatal Desire: Women, Sexuality, and the English Stage, 1660–1720.* Ithaca, NY: Cornell University Press, 2006.

Marshall, Daniel, Kevin P. Murphy, and Zeb Tortorici. "Queering Archives: Historical Unravelings." *Radical History Review* 120 (2014): 1–11.

Martin, Luis. *Daughters of the Conquistadores: Women in the Viceroyalty of Peru.* Albuquerque: University of New Mexico Press, 1983.

Martínez, Aida. "De la Moral Publica a la Vida Privada, 1820–1920." In *Placer, Dinero, y Pecado: Historia de la Prostitución en Colombia,* edited by Aida Martínez and Pablo Rodríguez, 129–49. Bogotá: Aguilar, 2002.

Martínez, Aída, and Pablo Rodríguez. *Placer, Dinero, y Pecado: Historia de la Prostitución en Colombia.* Bogotá: Aguilar, 2002.

Martínez Alcubilla, Marcelo. *Códigos Antiguos de España: Colección Completa de Todos los Códigos de España, Desde el Fuero Juzgo Hasta la Novísima Recopilación, con un Glosario de las Principales Voces Anticuadas.* Madrid: J. López Comancho, Impresor, Administración, 1885.

Martínez Aler, Verena. *Marriage, Class, and Colour in Nineteenth-Century Cuba.* Ann Arbor: University of Michigan Press, 1989.

McAlister, Lyle N. "The Reorganization of the Army of New Spain: 1763–1766." *The Hispanic American Historical Review* vol. 33, 1 (1953): 1–32.

McCarthy, Bill, Cecilia Benoit, and Mikael Jansson. "Sex Work: A Comparative Study." *Archives of Sexual Behavior* vol. 43, 7 (2014): 1379–90.

McClintock, Anne. *Imperial Leather: Race, Gender, and Sexuality in the Colonial Conquest.* New York: Routledge, 1995.

McCormack, Brian. "Conjugal Violence, Sex, Sin, and Murder in the Mission Communities of Alta, California." *Journal of the History of Sexuality* vol. 16, 3 (2007): 391–415.

McDermott, M. Joan, and Sarah Blackstone. "White Slavery Plays of the 1910s: Fear of Victimization and the Social Control of Sexuality." *Theatre History Studies* vol. 16 (1996): 141–56.

McKay, Angus. "Women on the Margins." In *Love, Religion, and Politics in Fifteenth-Century Spain,* edited by Ian Macpherson and Angus McKay, 28–42. Leiden, Netherlands: Brill, 1998.

McKendrick, Melveena. *Women and Society in the Spanish Drama of the Golden Age: A Study of the "Mujer Varonil."* London: Cambridge University Press, 1974.

McKnight, Kathryn Joy. "'En Su Tierra Lo Aprendió': An African Curandero's Defense Before the Cartagena Inquisition." *Colonial Latin American Review* vol. 12, 1 (2003): 63–84.

McManamon, John M. *The Texts and Contexts of Ignatius Loyola's Autobiography.* New York: Fordham University Press, 2013.

Mehl, Eva Maria. "Mexican Recruits and Vagrants in Late Eighteenth-Century Philippines: Empire, Social Order, and Bourbon Reforms in the Spanish Pacific World." *The Hispanic American Historical Review* vol. 94, 4 (2014): 547–79.

Meijide Pardo, María Luisa. "Mendicidad, Vagancia, y Prostitución en la España del Siglo XVIII: La Casa Galera y Los Departamentos de Corrección de Mujeres." PhD diss., Universidad Complutense de Madrid, 1992.

Meisel Roca, Adolfo, and María Aguilera Díaz. "Cartagena de Indias en 1777: Un Análisis Demográfico." *Boletín Cultural y Bibliográfico* vol. 34, 45 (1997): 21–57.

Menjot, Denis. "Prostitutas y Rufianes en las Ciudades Castellanas a Fines de la Edad Media." *Temas Medievales* vol. 4 (1994): 189–204.

Merians, Linda E., ed. *The Secret Malady: Venereal Disease in Eighteenth-Century Britain and France.* Lexington: University Press of Kentucky, 1996.

México Dividida en Quarteles Mayores y Menores: Nombres de sus Calles: los de sus Jueces y Alcaldes, el de los Sujetos nombrados por el Superior Gobierno para Plantear su Nueva Policía en el Año de 1811. Mexico City: Manuel Antonio Valdez, 1811.

Mgbako, Chi Adanna. *To Live Freely in This World: Sex Worker Activism in Africa.* New York: New York University Press, 2016.

Michael, Ian. "Celestina and the Great Pox." *Bulletin of Hispanic Studies* vol. 78, 1 (2001): 103–38.

Milner, Christina, and Richard Milner. *Black Players: The Secret World of Black Pimps.* Boston: Little Brown, 1972.

Mills, Kenneth, William B. Taylor, and Sandra Lauderdale Graham, eds. *Colonial Latin America: A Documentary History.* Wilmington, DE: Scholarly Resources, 2002.

Mina, Jorge Nacif. *La Policía en la Historia de la Ciudad de México, 1524–1928.* Mexico City: Departamento del Distrito Federal, Secretaria General de Desarrollo Social, Dirección General de Acción Social, Cívica, Cultural, y Turística, 1986.

Miramón, Alberto. *El Secreto del Virrey Fraile.* Bogotá: Liberia Siglo XX, 1944.

Molina Molina, Ángel-Luis. *Mujeres Públicas, Mujeres Secretas: La Prostitución y su Mundo, Siglos XIII–XVII.* Murcia, Spain: Editorial KR, 1998.

Molland, Sverre. "The Trafficking of Scarce Elite Commodities: Social Change and Commodification of Virginity along the Mekong." *Asia Pacific Journal of Anthropology* vol. 12, 2 (2011): 129–45.

Montgomery, Heather. "Child Prostitution as Filial Duty? The Morality of Child-Rearing in a Slum Community in Thailand." *Journal of Moral Education* vol. 43, 2 (2014): 169–82.

Moreno, José Luis. "La Casa de Niños Expósitos de Buenos Aires, Conflictos Institucionales, Condiciones de Vida y Mortalidad de los Infantes, 1779–1823." In *La Política Social Antes de la Política Social: Caridad, Beneficencia, y Política Social en Buenos Aires, Siglos XVII a XX*, edited by José Luis Moreno, 91–128. Buenos Aires: Prometeo Libros, 2000.

———. *La Política Social Antes de la Política Social: Caridad, Beneficencia, y Política Social en Buenos Aires, Siglos XVII a XX*. Buenos Aires: Prometeo Libros, 2000.

Moreno Mengíbar, Andrés J. "El Crepúsculo de las Mancebías: El Caso de Sevilla." In *"Mal Menor": Políticas y Representaciones de la Prostitución (Siglos XVI–XIX)*, edited by Francisco Vázquez García, 45–98. Cádiz: Universidad de Cádiz, 1998.

Moreno Mengíbar, Andrés J., and Francisco Vázquez García. "Poderes y Prostitución en España (Siglos XIV–XVII): El Caso de Sevilla." *Críticon* vol. 69 (1997): 33–49.

Muecke, Margorie A. "Mothers Sold Food, Daughter Sells Her Body: The Cultural Continuity of Prostitution." *Social Science and Medicine* vol. 35, 7 (1992): 891–901.

Muir, Edward, and Guido Ruggiero. *Sex and Gender in Historical Perspective*. Baltimore: Johns Hopkins University Press, 1990.

Murray, Jacqueline, and Konrad Eisenbicher. *Desire and Discipline: Sex and Sexuality in the Premodern West*. Toronto: University of Toronto Press, 1996.

Nagle, Jill, ed. *Whores and Other Feminists*. New York: Routledge, 1997.

Narbona Vizcaíno, Rafael. *Pueblo, Poder, y Sexo: Valencia Medieval (1306–1420)*. Valencia: Diputación de Valencia, 1992.

Nesvig, Martin Austin. *Ideology and the Inquisition: The World of the Censors in Early Mexico*. New Haven, CT: Yale University Press, 2009.

Noonan, John T. *Contraception: A History of Its Treatment by the Catholic Theologians and Canonists*. Cambridge, MA: Harvard University Press, 1966.

Norberg, Kathryn. "From Courtesan to Prostitute: Mercenary Sex and Venereal Disease, 1730–1802." In *The Secret Malady: Venereal Disease in Eighteenth-Century Britain and France*, edited by Linda E. Merians, 34–50. Lexington: University Press of Kentucky, 1996.

———. "Goddesses of Taste: Courtesans and Their Furniture in Late-Eighteenth-Century Paris." In *Furnishing the Eighteenth Century: What Furniture Can Tell Us about the European and American Past*, edited by Dena Goodman and Kathryn Norberg, 97–114. New York: Routledge, 2007.

———. "In Her Own Words: An Eighteenth-Century Madam Tells Her Story." In *Prostitution and Eighteenth-Century Culture: Sex, Commerce, and Morality*, edited by Ann Lewis, 33–45. London: Pickering & Chatto, 2012.

———. "Salon as Stage: Actress/Courtesans and Their Homes in Late Eighteenth-Century Paris." In *Architectural Space in Eighteenth-Century Europe: Constructing Identities and Interiors*, edited by Denise Amy Baxter and Meredith Martin, 105–28. Farnham, UK: Ashgate, 2010.

———. "The Body of the Prostitute: Medieval to Modern." In *The Routledge History of Sex and the Body, 1500 to the Present*, edited by Sarah Toulalan and Kate Fisher, 393–408. London: Routledge, 2013.

Nuñez Becerra, Fernanda. *La Prostitución y su Represión en la Ciudad de México, Siglo XIX: Prácticas y Representaciones*. Barcelona: Gedisa Editorial, 2002.

Ocampo López, Javier. *Leyendas Populares Colombianas*. Bogotá: Plaza & Janes, 1996.

Olsson, Lena. "'A First-Rate Whore': Prostitution and Empowerment in the Early Eighteenth Century." In *Prostitution and Eighteenth-Century Culture: Sex, Commerce, and Morality*, edited by Ann M. Lewis and Markman Ellis, 71–85. London: Pickering & Chatto, 2012.

Osaba, Esperanza. "La Actividad Reguladora de los Consejos y las Mujeres Consideradas Sospechosas: Un Empleo de Política de Control de las Costumbres." In *La Mujer en la Historia de Euskal Herria,*, edited by Miguel Ángel Barcenilla, 47–54. Bilbao: IPES, 1989.

Oso Casas, Laura. "Money, Sex, Love, and the Family: Economic and Affective Strategies of Latin American Sex Workers in Spain." *Journal of Ethnic & Migration Studies* vol. 36, 1 (2010): 47–65.

Otis, Leah Lydia. *Prostitution in Medieval Society: The History of an Urban Institution in Languedoc*. Chicago: University of Chicago Press, 2009.

Padilla Gonzalez, Jesus, and José Manuel Escobar Camacho. "La Mancebía de Córdoba en la Baja Edad Media." In *Actas del III Coloquio de Historia Medieval Andaluza: La Sociedad Medieval Andaluza: Grupos no Privilegiados*, 279–89. Jaén: Diputación Provincial de Jaén, 1984.

Palma, Ricardo. "Genialidades de 'la Perricholi.'" In *Tradiciones Peruanas Completas,* edited by Ricardo Palma, 299–307. Lima: PEISA, 1976.

Parker, Geoffrey. *The Army of Flanders and the Spanish Road, 1567–1659: The Logistics of Spanish Victory and Defeat in the Low Countries; Wars*. Cambridge, England: Cambridge University Press, 1972.

Pastor, Reyna. "Texto Para la Historia de las Mujeres en la Edad Media." In *Textos Para la Historia de las Mujeres en España*, edited by Ana María Aguado, R. M. Capel, et al., 125–224. Madrid: Cátedra, 1994.

Pedraja, René de la. "La Mujer Criolla y Mestiza en la Sociedad Colonial (1700–1830)." *Desarrollo y Sociedad* vol. 13 (1984): 199–229.

Pendleton, Eva. "Love for Sale: Queering Heterosexuality." In *Whores and Other Feminists*, edited by Jill Nagle, 73–82. New York: Routledge, 1997.

Penyak, Lee. "Criminal Sexuality in Central Mexico, 1750–1850." PhD diss., University of Connecticut, 1993.

Pérez García, Pablo. "Un Aspecto de la Delincuencia Común en la Valencia Pre-Agermanada: La 'Prostitución Clandestina' (1479–1518)." *Revista de Historia Moderna* vol. 10 (1991): 11–41.

Pérez Gómez, Antonio. *Retrato de La Lozana Andaluza*. Valencia: Tipografía Moderna, 1950.

Peris, Carmen. "La Prostitución Valenciana en la Segunda Mitad del Siglo XIV." *Revista de Historia Medieval* vol. 1 (1990): 179–99.

Peristiany, John G. *Honour and Shame: The Values of Mediterranean Society*. Chicago: University of Chicago Press, 1966.

Perry, Mary Elizabeth. "Deviant Insiders: Legalized Prostitutes and a Consciousness of Women in Early Modern Seville." *Comparative Studies in Society and History* vol. 27, 1 (1985): 138–58.

———. *Gender and Disorder in Early Modern Seville*. Princeton, NJ: Princeton University Press, 1990.

————. "'Lost Women' in Early Modern Seville: The Politics of Prostitution." *Feminist Studies* vol. 4, 1 (1978): 195–214.

Perry, Mary Elizabeth, and Ann J. Cruz, eds. *Cultural Encounters: The Impact of the Inquisition in Spain and the New World.* Berkeley: University of California Press, 1991.

Pevitt, Christine. *Madame Du Pompadour: Mistress of France.* New York: Grove Press, 2002.

Pheterson, Gail. "Not Repeating History." In *A Vindication of the Rights of Whores,* edited by Gail Pheterson, 3–31. Seattle: Seal Press, 1989.

————, ed. *A Vindication of the Rights of Whores.* Seattle: Seal Press, 1989.

Poska, Allyson M. "Elusive Virtue: Rethinking the Role of Female Chastity in Early Modern Spain." *Journal of Early Modern History* vol. 8, 1 (2004): 135–46.

————. *Women and Authority in Early Modern Spain: The Peasants of Galicia.* New York: Oxford University Press, 2005.

Powers, Karen Viera. *Women in the Crucible of Conquest: The Gendered Genesis of Spanish American Society, 1500–1600.* Albuquerque: University of New Mexico Press, 2005.

Prieur, Annick. *Mema's House, Mexico City: On Transvestites, Queens, and Machos.* Chicago: University of Chicago Press, 1998.

Puig, Angelina, and Nuria Tuset. "La Prostitución en Mallorca (Siglos XIV, XV, y XVI)." In *La Condición de la Mujer en la Edad Media: Actas del Coloquio Celebrado en la Casa de Velázquez, del 5 a 7 de Noviembre de 1984,* edited by Yves-René Fonquerne, Alfonso Esteban, et al., 273–88. Madrid: Casa de Velázquez, 1986.

Pullen, Kristen. *Actresses and Whores: On Stage and in Society.* Cambridge: Cambridge University Press, 2005.

Quiroz Sandoval, Ana Patricia. "El Sacerdote, el Alcalde, y el Testigo: Tres Formas de Juzgar el Fenómeno de la Prostitución Femenina en la Ciudad de México (1777–1818)." Thesis, Universidad Nacional Autónoma de México, 2007.

Ramos Vásquez, Isabel. "La Represión de la Prostitución en la Castilla del Siglo XVII." *Historia. Instituciones. Documentos* vol. 32 (2005): 263–86.

Rappaport, Joanne. *The Disappearing Mestizo: Configuring Difference in the Colonial New Kingdom of Granada.* Durham, NC: Duke University Press, 2014.

Reddy, William. *The Making of Romantic Love: Longing and Sexuality in Europe, South Asia, and Japan, 900–1200 CE.* Chicago: University of Chicago Press, 2012.

Reed, Stacy. "All Stripped Off." In *Whores and Other Feminists,* edited by Jill Nagle, 179–88. New York: Routledge, 1997.

Rey de Castilla, Alfonso "El Sabio." *Las Siete Partidas: Selección.* Barcelona: Linkgua, 2010.

Reynolds, Elaine A. *Before the Bobbies: The Night Watch and Police Reform in Metropolitan London, 1720–1830.* Stanford, CA: Stanford University Press, 1998.

Rial García, Serrana M. *Las Mujeres en la Economía Urbana del Antiguo Régimen: Santiago Durante el Siglo XVIII.* Sada, Acoruña, Spain: Ediciós de Casto, 1995.

Rodríguez, Jaime E. "The Transition from Colony to Nation: New Spain, 1820–1821." In *Mexico in the Age of Democratic Revolutions, 1750–1850,* edited by Jaime E. Rodríguez, 97–132. Boulder, CO: Lynne Rienner Publishers, 1994.

Rodríguez, Linda Alexander, ed. *Rank and Privilege: The Military and Society in Latin America.* Oxford: Scholarly Resources, 1994.

Rodríguez, Pablo. "Las Mancebías Españolas." In *Placer, Dinero, y Pecado: Historia de la Prostitución en Colombia*, edited by Aída Martínez and Pablo Rodríguez, 39–65. Bogotá: Aguilar, 2002.

———. "Servidumbre Sexual: La Prostitución en los Siglos XV–XVIII." In *Placer, Dinero, y Pecado: Historia de la Prostitución en Colombia*, edited by Aída Martínez and Pablo Rodríguez, 67–88. Bogotá: Aguilar, 2002.

Rojas, Fernando de. *Celestina*. Edited by Roberto Gonzalez Echevarreía; translated by Margaret Sayers Peden. New Haven, CT: Yale University Press, 2009.

Roper, Lyndal. *Oedipus and the Devil: Witchcraft, Sexuality, and Religion in Early Modern Europe*. London: Routledge, 1994.

Rosenthal, Laura J., ed. *Nightwalkers: Prostitute Narratives from the Eighteenth Century*. Peterborough, Ontario: Broadview Press, 2008.

Rossiaud, Jacques. "Prostitution, Youth, and Society in Towns of South Eastern France in the Fifteenth Century." In *Deviants and the Abandoned in French Society: Selections from the Annales, Économies, Sociétés, Civilisations,* Volume IV, edited by Robert Forster and Orest Ranum, translated by Elborg Forster, 1–46. Baltimore: Johns Hopkins University Press, 1978.

Rouhi, Leyla. *Mediation and Love: A Study of the Medieval Go-Between in Key Romance and Near Eastern Texts*. Boston: Brill Publishers, 1999.

Rubin, Gayle. "The Traffic of Women: Notes on the Political Economy of Sex." In *Toward an Anthropology of Women,* edited by Rayna Reiter, 157–210. New York: Monthly Review Press, 1975.

Ruiz, Juan. *The Book of Good Love.* Translated by Rigo Migani and Mario Di Cesare. Albany: State University of New York Press, 1970.

Saint-Saëns, Alain. "It Is Not a Sin!: Making Love According to the Spaniards in Early Modern Spain." In *Sex and Love in Golden Age Spain,* edited by Alain Saint-Saëns, 11–26. New Orleans: University Press of the South, 1996.

———. *Religion, Body, and Gender in Early Modern Spain*. San Francisco: Mellen Research University Press, 1991.

———, ed. *Sex and Love in Golden Age Spain*. New Orleans: University Press of the South, 1996.

Salas, Elizabeth. *Soldaderas in the Mexican Military: Myth and History*. Austin: University of Texas Press, 1990.

Sánchez-Arcilla Bernal, José María. "La Administración de Justicia Inferior en la Ciudad de México a Finales de la Época Colonial. I. La Punición de la Embriaguez en los Libros de Reos." *Cuadernos de Historia del Derecho* vol. 7 (2000): 309–453.

———. "La Delincuencia Femenina en México a Fines del Siglo XVIII." *Cuadernos de Historia del Derecho* vol. 20 (2013): 89–154.

Sánchez Ortega, María Helena. "Sorcery and Eroticism in Love Magic." In *Cultural Encounters: The Impact of the Inquisition in Spain and the New World,* edited by Mary Elizabeth Perry and Ann J. Cruz, 58–92. Berkeley: University of California Press, 1991.

Sánchez Uriarte, María del Carmen. "El Hospital de San Lázaro de la Ciudad de México y los Leprosos Novohispanos Durante la Segunda Mitad del Siglo XVIII." *Estudios de Historia Novohispana* vol. 42, 34 (2010): 81–113.

Scardaville, Michael Charles. "Alcohol Abuse and Tavern Reform in Late Colonial Mexico City." *The Hispanic American Historical Review* vol. 60, 4 (1980): 643–71.

———. "Crime and the Urban Poor: Mexico City in the Late Colonial Period." PhD diss., University of Florida, 1977.

———. "Justice by Paperwork: A Day in the Life of a Court Scribe in Bourbon Mexico City." *Journal of Social History* vol. 36, 4 (2003): 979–1007.

Schwartz, Stuart B. *All Can Be Saved: Religious Tolerance and Salvation in the Iberian Atlantic World*. New Haven, CT: Yale University Press, 2008.

Scott, George Ryley. *A History of Prostitution from Antiquity to the Present Day*. New York: AMS Press, 1976.

Scott, Samuel Parsons, ed. and trans. *Las Siete Partidas*. Chicago: Commerce Clearing House, Inc., 1931.

Seed, Patricia. *To Love, Honor, and Obey in Colonial Mexico: Conflicts Over Marriage Choice, 1574–1821*. Stanford, CA: Stanford University Press, 1998.

Seijas, Tatiana. *Asian Slaves in Colonial Mexico: From Chinos to Indians*. New York: Cambridge University Press, 2014.

Sempere y Guarinos, Juan. *Historia del Luxo y de las Leyes Suntuarias de España*, 2 vols. Madrid: Atlas, 1973.

Sepúlveda Niño, Saturnino. *La Prostitución en Colombia: Una Quiebra de la Estructuras Sociales*. Bogotá: Editorial Andes, 1970.

Sevilla, Amparo. "Historia Social de los Salones de Baile." In *Los Espacios Públicos de la Ciudad, Siglos XVIII y XIX*, edited by Carlos Aguirre Anaya, Marcela Dávalos, María Amparo Ros Torres, et al., 150–64. Mexico City: Instituto de Cultura de la Ciudad de México, 2002.

Sheehy, Gail. *Hustling: Prostitution in Our Wide-Open Society*. New York: Delacorte Press, 1973.

Sherwood, Joan. *Poverty in Eighteenth Century Spain: The Women and Children of the "Inclusa."* Toronto: University of Toronto Press, 1988.

Shutte, Anne. *Time, Space, and Women's Lives in Early Modern Europe*. Kirksville, MO: Truman State University Press, 2001.

Sienna, Kevin. *Sins of the Flesh: Responding to Sexual Disease in Early Modern Europe*. Toronto: Centre for Reformation and Renaissance Studies, 2005.

Simposio de Historia de las Mentalidades. *Familia y Sexualidad en Nueva España: Familia, Matrimonio, y Sexualidad en Nueva España*. Mexico City: Fondo de Cultura Económica, 1982.

Sloan, Kathryn A. *Runaway Daughters: Seduction, Elopement, and Honor in Nineteenth-Century Mexico*. Albuquerque: University of New Mexico Press, 2008.

———. *Women's Roles in Latin America and the Caribbean*. Santa Barbara, CA: Greenwood Press, 2011.

Soares, Luis Carlos. *Prostitution in Nineteenth-Century Rio de Janeiro*. London: University of London, Institution of Latin American Studies, 1988.

Socolow, Susan. *The Women of Colonial Latin America*. Cambridge, UK: Cambridge University Press, 2000.

———. "Women and Crime: Buenos Aires, 1757–1797." *Journal of Latin American Studies* vol. 12, 1 (1980): 39–54.

Splendiani, Anna María, José Enrique Sánchez Bohórquez, and Emma Cecilia Luque de Salazar. *Cincuenta Años de Inquisición en el Tribunal de Cartagena de Indias, 1610–1660.* Santa Fe de Bogotá: Centro Editorial Javeriano, 1997.

Sprinkle, Annie. "Feminism: Crunch Point." In *A Vindication of the Rights of Whores,* edited by Gail Pheterson, 144–72. Seattle: Seal Press, 1989.

———. "We've Come a Long Way and We're Exhausted." In *Whores and Other Feminists,* edited by Jill Nagle, 66–71. New York: Routledge, 1997.

Stallybrass, Peter. "Patriarchal Territories: The Body Enclosed." In *Rewriting the Renaissance: The Discourses of Sexual Difference in Early Modern Europe,* edited by Margaret W. Ferguson, Maureen Quilligan, and Nancy Vickers, 123–43. Chicago: University of Chicago Press, 1986.

Stanley, Amy. *Selling Women: Prostitution, Markets, and the Household in Early Modern Japan.* Berkeley: University of California Press, 2012.

Steedman, Carolyn. *Dust: The Archive and Cultural History.* New Brunswick, NJ: Rutgers University Press, 2001.

Stevenson, Haroldo Calvo, and Adolfo Meisel Roca, eds. *Cartagena de Indias en el Siglo XVII.* Cartagena: Banco de la República, 2007.

Stolcke, Verena. *Marriage, Class, and Colour in Nineteenth-Century Cuba: A Study of Racial Attitudes and Sexual Values in a Slave Society.* New York: Cambridge University Press, 1974.

Stoler, Laura Ann. *Along the Archival Grain: Epistemic Anxieties and Colonial Common Sense.* Princeton, NJ: Princeton University Press, 2009.

Storey, Tessa. *Carnal Commerce in Counter-Reformation Rome.* Cambridge, UK: Cambridge University Press, 2008.

Suarez, Agueda Gómez, and Silvia Pérez Freire. "Prostitución en Galicia: Clientes e Imaginarios Femeninos." *Revista Estudios Feministas* vol. 18, 1 (2010): 121–40.

Tambe, Ashwini. "Brothels as Families: Reflections on the History of Bombay's 1 Kothas." *International Feminist Journal of Politics* vol. 8, 2 (2006): 219–42.

Taylor, Scott K. *Honor and Violence in Golden Age Spain.* New Haven, CT: Yale University Press, 2008.

Taylor, William B. *Drinking, Homicide, and Rebellion in Colonial Mexican Villages.* Stanford, CA: Stanford University Press, 1979.

Tomas y Valiente, Francisco. *El Derecho Penal de la Monarquía Absoluta, Siglos XVI–XVII–XVIII.* Madrid: Editorial Techos, 1969.

Tong, Benson. *Unsubmissive Women: Chinese Prostitutes in Nineteenth-Century San Francisco.* Norman: University of Oklahoma Press, 1994.

Torres Hernández, Ana Laura. "Pecado, Recogimiento, y Conversión: Un Proyecto Contra la Prostitución Femenina en la Ciudad de México del Siglo XVII." *Boletín de Monumentos Históricos* vol. 29 (2013): 52–71.

Tortorici, Zeb. "Contra Natura: Sin, Crime, and 'Unnatural' Sexuality in Colonial Mexico, 1530–1821." PhD diss., University of California, Los Angeles, 2010.

———. "'Heran Todos Putos': Sodomitical Subcultures and Disordered Desire in Early Colonial Mexico." *Ethnohistory* vol. 54, 1 (2007): 35–67.

———, ed. *Sexuality and the Unnatural in Colonial Latin America.* Berkeley and Los Angeles: University of California Press, 2016.

Toulalan, Sarah, and Kate Fisher, eds. *The Routledge History of Sex and the Body, 1500 to the Present*. London: Routledge, 2013.

Toxqui Garay, María Aureu. "'El Recreo de los Amigos': Mexico City's Pulquerías during the Liberal Republic, 1856–1911." PhD diss., University of Arizona, 2008.

Trexler, Richard C. *Sex and Conquest: Gendered Violence, Political Order and the European Conquest of the Americas*. Ithaca, NY: Cornell University Press, 1995.

Twinam, Ann. "Honor, Sexuality, and Illegitimacy in Colonial Spanish America." In *Sexuality and Marriage in Colonial Latin America*, edited by Asunción Lavrin, 118–55. Lincoln: University of Nebraska Press, 1992.

———. *Public Lives, Private Secrets: Gender, Honor, Sexuality, and Illegitimacy in Colonial Spanish America*. Stanford, CA: Stanford University Press, 1999.

———. *Purchasing Whiteness: Pardos, Mulattos, and the Quest for Social Mobility in the Spanish Indies*. Stanford, CA: Stanford University Press, 2015.

Universidad Autónoma de Madrid, Seminario de Estudios de la Mujer. *Las Mujeres Medievales y su Ámbito jurídico: Actas de las II Jornadas de Investigación Interdisciplinaria*. Madrid: Servicio de Publicaciones de la Universidad Autónoma de Madrid, 1983.

Uribe Urán, Victor. *Fatal Love: Spousal Killers, Law, and Punishment in the Late Colonial Spanish Atlantic*. Stanford, CA: Stanford University Press, 2016.

Valle-Arizpe, Artemio de. *La Güera Rodríguez*. Mexico City: M. Porrúa, 1960.

Van Deusen, Nancy E. *Between the Sacred and the Worldly: The Institutional and Cultural Practice of Recogimiento in Colonial Lima*. Stanford, CA: Stanford University Press, 2001.

Van Young, Eric. *The Other Rebellion: Popular Violence, Ideology, and the Mexican Struggle for Independence, 1810–1821*. Stanford, CA: Stanford University Press, 2001.

Vázquez García, Francisco. "Historia de la Prostitución: Problemas Metodológicos y Niveles del Fenómeno, Fuentes y Modelos de Análisis." In *"Mal Menor": Políticas y Representaciones de la Prostitución (Siglos XVI–XIX)*, edited by Francisco Vázquez García, 47–99. Cádiz: Universidad de Cádiz, 1998.

———, ed. *"Mal Menor": Políticas y Representaciones de la Prostitución (Siglos XVI–XIX)*. Cádiz: Universidad de Cádiz, 1998.

Vázquez García, Francisco, and Andrés Moreno Mengíbar. *Poder y Prostitución en Sevilla, Siglos XIV al XX: La Edad Moderna*. Sevilla: Universidad de Sevilla, 1998.

Vázquez Mantecón, María del Carmen. *Los Días de Josepha Ordóñez*. Mexico City: Universidad Nacional Autónoma de México, 2005.

Vega, Juan José. "La Prostitución en el Perú: Un Producto de la Conquista Española." In *Mestizaje, Cultura Afectiva, e Identidad Criolla en los Siglos XVI–XIX*, edited by Sara Beatriz Guardia. Lima: Centro de Estudios de la Mujer en la Historia de América Latina, 2004. Found at http://www.cemhal.org/publicaciones1c.html.

Vila Villar, Enriqueta. *Aspectos Sociales en América Colonial: de Extranjeros, Contrabando, y Esclavos*. Bogotá: Instituto Caro y Cuervo, 2001.

Viqueria Albán, Juan Pedro. *Propriety and Permissiveness in Bourbon Mexico*. Translated by Sonya Lipsett-Rivera and Sergio Rivera Ayala. Wilmington, DE: Scholarly Resources: 1999.

Vizcaíno, Rafael Narbona. *Pueblo, Poder, y Sexo: Valencia Medieval (1306–1420)*. Valencia: Diputación de Valencia, 1992.

Vizuete Mendoza, J. Carlos. "Mancebía y Casas de Recogidas en Toledo en el Siglo de Oro." In *Ensayos Humanísticos: Homenaje al Profesor Luis Lorente Toledo*, edited by Rafael

Villena Espinosa and Luis Lorente Toledo, 489–504. Cuenca, Ecuador: Universidad de Castilla, La Mancha, 1997.

Voekel, Pamela. "Peeing on the Palace: Bodily Resistance to Bourbon Reforms in Mexico City." *Journal of Historical Sociology* vol. 5, 2 (1992): 183–208.

Wahab, Stephanie. "'For Their Own Good?': Sex Work, Social Control, and Social Workers, A Historical Perspective." *Journal of Sociology and Social Welfare* vol. 29, 4 (2002): 39–57.

Walker, Charles F. *Shaky Colonialism: The 1746 Earthquake-Tsunami in Lima, Peru, and Its Long Aftermath*. Durham, NC: Duke University Press, 2008.

Walkowitz, Judith R. *City of Dreadful Delight: Narratives of Sexual Danger in Late-Victorian London*. Chicago: University of Chicago Press, 1992.

———. *Prostitution and Victorian Society: Women, Class, and the State*. Cambridge, UK: Cambridge University Press, 1980.

Weisner-Hanks, Merry E. *Christianity and Sexuality in the Early Modern World: Regulating Desire, Reforming Practice*. London: Routledge, 2000.

———. *Women and Gender in Early Modern Europe*. 2nd Edition. Cambridge, UK: Cambridge University Press, 2000.

Weitzberg, Keren. "The Unaccountable Census: Colonial Enumeration and Its Implications for the Somali People of Kenya." *The Journal of African History* vol. 56, 03 (2015): 409–28.

Weitzer, Ronald. "New Directions in Research on Prostitution." *Crime, Law, and Social Change* vol. 43, 4 (2005): 211–35.

White, Luise. *The Comforts of Home: Prostitution in Colonial Nairobi*. Chicago: University of Chicago Press, 1990.

Wynn, Thomas. "Prostitutes and Erotic Performances in Eighteenth-Century Paris." In *Prostitution and Eighteenth-Century Culture: Sex, Commerce, and Morality*, edited by Ann Lewis, 87–98. London: Pickering & Chatto, 2012.

Yánez Romero, José Arturo. *Policía Mexicana: Cultura Política, (In) Seguridad, y Orden Público en el Gobierno del Distrito Federal, 1821–1876*. Mexico City: Universidad Nacional Autónoma Metropolitana, 1999.

Zafra, Enriqueta. "La Prostituta y la Prostitución en 'Don Quijote': Modelos de 'Mujeres Libres.'" *The Bulletin of Hispanic Studies* vol. 86, 5 (2009): 625–40.

———. *Prostituidas por el Texto: Discurso Prostibulario en la Picaresca Femenina*. West Lafayette, IN: Purdue University Press, 2009.

Zahariades, Zabrina Zee. "The Great Social Evil: Images of Fallen Women and Prostitutes in American Literature from 1872 to 1952." MA thesis, California State University, Northridge, 2012.

INDEX